Classical *and* Contemporary Sociology:

Theory and Issues

Mike O'Donnell

Hodder & Stoughton

A MEMBER OF THE HODDER HEADLINE GROUP

Acknowledgments

For the reproduction of copyright material, the publishers would like to thank the following:

From *The Rules of sociological Method* by Emile Durkheim, translated by Sarah A. Solovay and John H. Mueller; edited by George E.G. Catlin. Copyright 1938 by George E.G. Catlin; copyright renewed 1966 by Sarah A. Solovay, John H. Mueller, George E.G. Catlin, reprinted by permission of The Free Press, A Division of Simon and Schuster, Inc; from *Outsiders: Studies in the Sociology of Deviance* by Howard S. Becker. Copyright 1963 by The Free Press; copyright renewed 1991 by Howard S. Becker. Reprinted by permission of The Free Press, a Division of Simon and Schuster, Inc. *Theories of the Information Society* by F. Webster; *Sociology Beyond Societies: Mobilities for the Twenty-First Century* by J. Urry, 'Different Youthful Objectives' by A. McRobbie from *The Post-Colonial Question: Common Skies, Divided Horizons* (ed) I. Chambers, and L. Curtis, *Globalisation* by Malcom Waters, *Gender Transformations* By S. Walby, *A Lesson for us All: The Making of the National Curriculum* by D. Graham and D. Tytler reprinted with permission by Gower Publishing; *The Third Way: The Renewal of Social Democracy* by A. Giddens, *Social Theory: A Historical Introduction* by A. Callinicos, *What is Globalisation?* By Ulrich Beck, *The Transformations of Intimacy: Sexuality, Love, and Eroticism in Modern Societies* by A. Giddens, *Masculinities* by W.R. Connell, 'The Question of Cultural Identity' by Stuart Hall from *Modernity and its Futures* (ed) S. Hall and T. McGrew, *Unthinking Social Science: The Limits of Nineteenth Century Paradigms* by I. Wallerstein, reprinted with permission by The Polity Press; 'Social Movements and Global Capitalism' from *The Cultures of Globalization* (ed) Jameson and Miyoshi reproduced with permission by Duke University Press; extract from 'the Work of Representation' by Stuart Hall from *Representation: Cultural Representations and Signifying Practices* (ed) S. Hall and *Understanding Social Theory* by Derek Layder reproduced with permission by Sage Publications; *Selected Works* by Lenin reproduced with permission by Lawrence and Wishart; 'Fordism and Post-Fordism' by R. Murray in *New Times and the Changing Face of Politics in the 1990s* (ed) S. Hall, and Martin Jacques reprinted with permission by Lawrence and Wishart; 'Confessions of a Curriculum Man' by Professor Jack Wrigley from *Life and Death of the Schools Council* (ed) Plaskow, M., reprinted with permission by The Falmer Press; 'Women online' article by Lisa Ramrayka; *Resistance Through Rituals: Youth Subcultures in Post War Britain* (ed) S. Hall and T. Jefferson, reprinted with permission by Hutchinson; Extract from *The Whole Woman* by Germaine Greer reprinted with permission by Transworld Publishers, copyright Germaine Greer; 'Erving goffman; by R. Williams in *Key Sociological Thinkers* (ed) R. Stones, *Policing The Crisis* (ed) S. Hall et al, *A Contemporary Critique of Historical Materialism* by A. Giddens reprinted with permission by Palgrave; *The Power of Identity* by M. Castells, *The Rise of the Network Society* by M. Castells, *From Post-Industrial to Post-Modern Society: New Theories of the Contemporary World* by K. Kumar, reprinted with permission by Blackwell Publishers; *Modern Social Theory* by Derek Layder, reprinted with permission by UCL Press; 'Subcultures or Neo-Tribes? Rethinking the Relationship between Youth, Style and Musical Taste' from *Sociology* no. 33 (3) reprinted with permission by Cambridge University Press; articles from 8/72000, 4/12/2000, 9/9/200; 'The collapse of the Cultural ...' by Fredric Jameson; article by John Hannington reprinted with permission by *The Guardian*. *The Manifesto of the Communist Party* by Karl Marx reproduced with permission by Foreign Languages Press; extracts from *The Penguin Dictionary of Sociology* reproduced with permission by Penguin Books.

For the reproduction of photgraphic material, the publishers would like to thank the following: figure 1.1 Hulton Getty; fig 1.3 Topham Picturepoint; fig 1.4 Corbis; fig 2.1 Hulton Getty; fig 3.3 Photofusion; fig 4.1 Corbis; fig 4.2 Corbis; fig 5.1 Topham Picturepoint; fig 8.1 Photofusion.

Illustrations (fig 2.2/5.2) by Ian Heard

Every effort has been made to trace the copyright holders of material reproduced in this book. Any rights omitted from the acknowledgments here or in the text will be added for subsequent printings following notice to the publisher.

Orders: please contact Bookpoint Ltd, 78 Milton Park, Abingdon, Oxon OX14 4TD. Telephone: (44) 01235 400454. Lines are open from 9.00–6.00, Monday to Saturday, with a 24 hour message answering service. Email address: orders@bookpoint.co.uk.

British Library Cataloguing in Publication Data

A catalogue record for this title is available from The British Library

ISBN 0 340 69722 9

2 001 003 097

First published 2001
Impression number   10 9 8 7 6 5 4 3 2 1
Year   2005 2004 2003 2002 2001

Copyright © 2000 Mike O'Donnell

Typeset by Fakenham Photosetting Ltd
Printed in Great Britain for Hodder & Stoughton Educational, a division of Hodder Headline Plc, 338 Euston Road, London NW1 3BH by Martins the Printers Ltd., Spittal, Berwick upon Tweed

Contents

Introduction

The original purpose of this book was to provide a shorter introduction to sociology than that offered by the many "bumper" texts now available. In particular, the intention was to introduce newer theories and topics in some depth. The introductory purpose of this book still stands but as an overview of the focal concerns of the discipline rather than as yet another trawl through its many topics. There is a unity to sociology that is in real danger of being lost as apparently endless new topics and theories get added to the subject.

I have sought to impart a sense of the unity of sociology by presenting the subject partly in terms of its core dualisms. Drawing on other authors I have defined these as: individual/society; action/structure; social integration/system integration; micro/macro; modernity/capitalism-socialism. If that looks to be a forbidding list, in practice it has proved relatively straightforward to handle. Further, because the approach is a fresh one, for me at least, it has proved satisfying and enjoyable. This does not mean that I now renounce the larger texts. Far from it. As someone who remembers (just) the days when all we had was "Cotgrove" and "Sargent" in their first editions, I would hardly do that. The quality and scope of many (and there are many!) of today's core texts is excellent. This book is intended to complement, not compete with, these textbooks. It is meant to add something extra to what an advanced student, already introduced to the subject, might already have. For undergraduates, it could serve as an initial introduction to the subject.

The approach I have adopted has produced something of a bonus. The tension between those sociological approaches which stress individuality and agency and those which emphasize structure has been fascinating to explore and, I hope, to read about. However, I have not allowed this book to become "too theoretical". Theory is grounded by being applied to areas such as globalisation, the new social movements, identity and social structure. I also employ the principle that sociological theory can best be understood, reflexively, in the historical context in which it is constructed and influenced by and is often intended to illuminate.

My thanks to Luke Hacker, Chris Loades, and Stephen Baker of Hodder and to Dori Chetty for her help and encouragement. I would like to dedicate this book to my uncle and aunt, Robert and Joyce Gregson and to my sister, Professor Anne Graham and her clan.

Mike O'Donnell, Preston, 2000.

Chapter 1

Sociology, Modernity and Capitalism

> **Key Concepts**:
> consciousness, determinism, dialectic, dualisms, ideology,
> conservative/liberal/radical, positivism, pluralist, reified,
> voluntarism.

Introduction

There are five purposes to this chapter. First, is to relate sociology to the context in which it emerged and which the work of the founders of sociology tried to understand. The founders of sociology were fascinated by their time, and their theories were partly attempts to explain what was happening to themselves and others. In doing so, they undoubtedly produced theoretical models which are useful in explaining societies in general.

Second, this chapter seeks to indicate the main types of theoretical and methodological approaches adopted by the founders of the discipline. Some tended to see sociology as a science after the model of the natural sciences whereas others tended to locate sociology closer to the humanities and concentrate on understanding the meanings of social actors. Since the beginnings of the subject, sociologists have used one or other or, perhaps more usually, various combinations of both models. In general, the founders of sociology took a broad approach to social science, using historical, economic and philosophical theory and methods as they considered appropriate.

Third, this chapter explores the main core *dualisms* or contrasting focal concerns around which sociology revolves. The starting point of sociology is the dualism of *individual/society* and in particular the relationship between the two. The point of sociology is not to define in any final way what the relationship of the two poles of this or other dualisms might be – such relationships vary with people and circumstances. Rather, the dualisms act as foci for sociological enquiry – although this does not prevent fierce debate about their significance and relative importance. The dualisms provide a thematic unity and underlying organising principle for this book.

Fourth, this chapter attempts to note how ideological values – mainly conservative, liberal, Marxist and other radical values – influence the work of most, if not all sociologists. This is perhaps surprising given the widespread aspiration to develop sociology as an unbiased, objective discipline! Nevertheless, it is a feature that steadily unfolds in the following account.

The fifth purpose of this chapter is the sum of the previous four. It is to produce a brief account of the development and main concerns of sociology in historical context. This chapter presents sociologists and their work as vitally involved in rather than as somehow detached from the concerns of other people. The aims here are closely related and they will be discussed and presented more in terms of these relationships rather than in separate sections. First, then, what was it about the nineteenth century that inspired the birth of sociology?

The Historical Context in Which Sociology Developed

Sociology was founded during a time of revolutionary change – and it shows. The nineteenth century was one of massive upheaval in every sphere of society: industrial, social – particularly class relations, political, military, and cultural. No doubt the origins of the industrial and agricultural revolutions can be traced well beyond the nineteenth century, but the speed and scale of change accelerated to such an extent during this epoch, that by the end of it Britain was clearly a fundamentally different kind of society than it had been in the eighteenth century. From being a predominantly agricultural and largely feudal society, Britain had become a predominantly industrial capitalist one and with this came other major changes. Other European countries, notably Germany, Holland, Belgium and France and the United States were also developing in the same direction. By the early twentieth century Germany and the United States had overtaken Britain in industrial production and had the potential to challenge Britain's premier economic and political position in the world. However, at the turn of the century, Britain still appeared to be the dominant world power, mainly because of its naval strength and Empire. Rapid urbanisation was a major consequence of the industrial revolution. By the late nineteenth century, great manufacturing towns in the North and Midlands and in Scotland and Wales had grown to dwarf such medieval cities as Canterbury, Edinburgh, Aberystwyth and even Norwich, once England's second city. In addition to substantial migration from the countryside to urban areas to find work, there was an increase in the birth rate particularly in urban areas.

Inevitably, such fundamental economic and demographic change was reflected in the political and cultural spheres. Shifts in the relative power and in the culture of the country's social groups occurred. The great estates of feudal England – the aristocracy, the church – and also the peasantry – entered a period of long-term, if uneven, decline. The industrial, commercial and financial middle classes or bourgeoisie as well as the leading independent professions increased in size and power. There was a significant amount of intermarriage between the aristocracy and the newly wealthy as well as business investment by more entrepreneurially minded aristocrats. The peasantry shrank rapidly in numbers as less labour intensive forms of agriculture were developed. Their decline was comparable in its huge scale to the more recent decline of the manual working class in the second half of the twentieth century. Many peasants who had smallholdings lost them as the enclosure movement increasingly turned arable land into pasture. In the absence of any alternative, many peasants simply migrated to industrial areas and became wage-labourers. Others had more positive hopes of achieving a better life in the burgeoning towns and cities rather as some urban migrants do in today's developing societies. The quality of the working and living conditions of the British industrial working class became a central area of concern and struggle throughout the nineteenth century and twentieth centuries. It was not until the latter part of the twentieth century when, partly due to changes in class structure, the focus of social policy and reform shifted away from the welfare of the industrial working class to those 'excluded' from paid work.

The Struggle for Political Power and Rights

The rise and decline of social groups in the nineteenth century was reflected in political struggle. At the beginning of the century Britain was far from being a democracy although the government was answerable to parliament which was elected by a small minority of the population, exclusively male and overwhelmingly upper or upper middle class. Among the privileged, it was thought that the right to vote was a function of having a substantial property stake in the country and certainly not a matter of individual right. Progressive extensions of the franchise throughout the nineteenth century and even into the twentieth tended to reflect this linking of voting and property rights. The Reform Act of 1832 extended the franchise mainly to more members of the middle class and it was not until 1884 that substantial numbers of working class males obtained the vote. Universal suffrage for men over 21 was achieved with the Representation of the People Act of 1918. The Act also extended the vote to women for the first time. However, only women over 30 were allowed to vote. It was not until 1929 that women obtained the vote on the same basis as men. This gendered political inequality reflected a deep social inequality between men and women. For instance, women were not allowed to own property in their own right until the Married Women's Property Act of 1883. Given that the debate about extending the franchise was partly expressed in terms of property rights, it is not surprising that the arguments of the women's suffrage movement were for so long ignored by men who controlled their wives' property. It must be said that the founders of sociology were in most respects 'men of their time' in matters of gender relations and none is noted for having a strong commitment to gender equality. The impact of feminism on sociology was to come later.

The political rights achieved by working class people and by women and the social improvements gained in working, family and community life involved long and intense struggle. In Britain, lawful persuasion and protest were the means used by most of the activists most of the time in pursuit of their causes. However, sometimes the rights of protest and freedom of expression were severely curtailed and some feminists and socialists were prepared to act outside the limits of the law in pursuit of their causes. In their eyes it was those who controlled society that were in the wrong. One tactic adopted was that of non-violent civil disobedience, for example, the disruption of parliamentary proceedings by suffragettes. Some conflicts between radicals and the forces of the status quo involve violence and even death. Even so, there was rather less violent confrontation and revolutionary activity in Britain than in some other European countries. 1848 was a year of protest and revolutionary activity across Western Europe with which Marx himself was actively involved. The issue of how to pursue change remains just as relevant in the contemporary world. A more recent radical social movement, the struggle for civil and political rights by black people in the United States, adopted a variety of different strategies. Martin Luther King, inspired by the Indian pacifist Mahatma Ghandi, developed a strategy of non-violent civil disobedience to pressurise for change. Later, some black activists claimed that violent means were justified in pursuit of their cause. Malcolm X, a prominent member of the black religious-political group, the Nation of Islam, asserted that racial equality must be achieved 'by any means necessary'.

Cultural and Ideological Change

Changes in the economic and social structure of Britain and Western Europe during the nineteenth century were complemented by cultural changes on a comparable scale. Culture here refers to the people's way of life, particularly their everyday customs and habits, including their leisure habits. German sociologist, Ferdinand Tönnies (1855–1936), and French sociologist, Emile Durkheim (1858–1917), particularly concentrated on the changes involved in the shift from a predominantly rural to a more urban way of life in the newly industrialising countries. They were especially concerned that the decline of traditional values and relationships might threaten social order. In contrast, the radical Karl Marx (1818–1883) welcomed the apparent break-up of the old order and was optimistic that eventually it would be replaced by a freer and more equal society. From the beginning, sociology was characterised by conservative and radical strands as well as by a liberal strand.

Marx focused on class culture as the most important area of cultural life, particularly the cultures of the working class or proleteriat and capitalist class or bourgeoisie, which he argued, had become the most powerful class. Marx considered that the central struggle of capitalist society was between the proleteriat and the bourgeoisie. At the heart of this struggle was the battle of ideas or the battle for *ideological* dominance. He saw religion as a conservative force which acted as an opium of the people, dulling their awareness of exploitation and suffering. He also argued that the bourgeoisie sought to influence the culture of the working class through the press to persuade them to accept and conform to capitalist society despite its great inequalities and poverty. He believed that the mainly capitalist owned press tried to get working class people to be involved in and excited about the expansion of the British empire, partly to distract them from their own miseries as well as to persuade some to join the armed forces. He regarded imperialism and nationalism – a powerful force in Europe in the nineteenth and twentieth centuries – as reactionary ideologies. Although Marx considered that nationalist movements had the potential to weaken feudal privilege, he regarded them as bourgeois in ideology and was concerned that they would hamper the development of socialism in Western capitalist societies. However, he also considered that the working class had the potential to develop an independent Enlightment and revolutionary culture which would help them to envisage what a more equal and freer society – in Marx's view a socialist society – might be like. He thought this would happen as they began to understand and organise against their 'exploitation' in the workplace and against their degradation in the urban slums. He saw the radical press, trade unions and socialist political groups and parties as part of the process of promoting revolutionary consciousness or awareness and action.

The Intellectual Context in which Sociology Developed: Its Theories and Methods

This section briefly discusses four intellectual movements, each of which had enormous influence on the development of sociology. These are the Enlightenment, the conservative reaction to the Enlightenment, the romantic movement which was also partly formed in response to the Enlightenment, and evolutionism. Although the movements are presented separately here, each occurs within the influence of the Enlightenment even where they react against it. In so far as the Enlightenment inspired the other three, it can be regarded as the seminal movement which led to the development of the discipline of sociology.

1) The Enlightenment: Sociology as Part of the Enlightenment

The eighteenth century is often referred to as the 'age of reason'. This is because during the later half of that century there was an outpouring of philosophical and social theory across Western Europe and the United States based on rational thought and scientific analysis. It is this outpouring that is referred to as the Enlightenment. Among the leading contributors to the Enlightenment were the Scottish philosopher D. Hume; the German philosopher I. Kant; the French dramatist and social commentator, Voltaire; and the American polymath and President, Thomas Jefferson. The Enlightenment has had a major if not a dominant influence on the intellectual life of the Western hemisphere throughout the nineteenth century and remains a central though sharply debated frame of reference at the dawn of a new millennium. Although by no means all the intellectuals associated with the Enlightenment supported the American and French revolutions, the Enlightenment came to be widely linked with a broad spectrum of liberal and revolutionary thought and movements. As well as reason, the principles of freedom (particularly of thought and expression) and individual rights were widely espoused by Enlightenment thinkers. These conflicted with the claims of traditional privilege, authority and 'knowledge' and as a result many Enlightenment intellectuals were viewed as dangerous to social order and several spent time in prison.

The power of the Enlightenment is not difficult to explain. It is the power of reason. Philosophers such as Hume sought to apply rigorous logic to the analysis and interpretation of phenomena. The scientific method was seen as embodying rational principles, including those of cause and effect

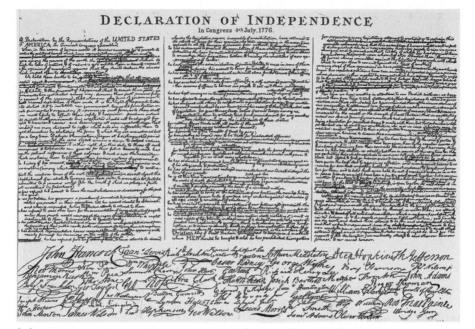

Figure 1.1 A Commitment to Human Rights was a central feature of the Enlightenment.

and the systematic use of evidence in proof. Although some of the intellectuals of the Enlightenment were anti-religious, not all of them were. Importantly, however, their approach to explanation was simply not a religious one but was based on secular reason. Some did conclude that religion served to confuse the masses and lead them to accept their lot in society. Voltaire, like Marx later, thought along these lines. Deism was one position which attempted to reconcile religion and science by arguing that God was, above all the God of Reason, the rational creator of the universe. Broadly, this was the view adopted by Thomas Jefferson as it had been by the great scientist, Isaac Newton, before him (1642–1727).

The period of the Enlightenment was characterised by a widespread belief in progress. Again this is not difficult to explain. Scientific discovery and experiment, the practical application of science to industrial production and civil engineering, the improved standard of living of the upper and middle classes, all gave rise to a feeling that things were getting better and would go on getting better. To the extent that the 'masses' were involved in the French and American revolutions, and the push for democratic change and social improvement in Britain, they, too, caught a whiff of the pervasive optimism and a sense that the future might bring improvements in their lot. It has recently become common to criticise as naive the belief in progress characteristic of the Enlightenment, but even at the time there were dissenting voices. Notable among these was the English political philosopher, Burke, whose work is discussed below. The Enlightenment was a time of intellectual ferment, one aspect of which was the diversity of views expressed.

Responses to the Enlightenment among the founders of sociology were mixed but none could avoid being influenced by it. They lived and worked within an intellectual climate in which the application of rational and scientific analysis had already brought about great achievements and consequently had immense prestige and authority. They hoped to acquire a comparable status for systematic social analysis and in doing so addressed most if not all the fundamental issues of social science. The founders of sociology had various views on other key values and assumptions of the Enlightenment. They did not all embrace a belief in human progress nor in individual rights against tradition. There are strong conservative as well as liberal and radical strands in classical sociology.

2) The Conservative Reaction to the Enlightenment: Auguste Comte

Of the many intellectual opponents of the ideas of the Enlightenment, Edmund Burke (1729–97) was perhaps the most influential. In his 'Reflections on the Revolution in France'(1790), Burke reasserted the wisdom of tradition against meddling reason. He argued that established authority was necessary to ensure social order and institutional continuity. He believed that hierarchy and inequality were inevitable and he was deeply anti-individualistic in his social and political philosophy. He favoured the restoration of the monarchy and the old order in France.

It is perhaps no coincidence that it was in France, the seedbed of revolutionary ideas, that a tradition of sociology developed which expressed a profound concern for social order. Henri Saint-Simon (1769–1825) and his student, Auguste Comte (1798–1857), were arguably the joint founders of sociology. They disagreed with Enlightenment thought in two respects. First, they came to believe that the Enlightenment had failed sufficiently to address the problem of social order. Comte described individualism as 'the disease of the Western world' and felt it was threatening social order (Nisbet in Bottomore and Nisbet,1979:92). He made the issue of social order and cohesion central to his model of society and this gave it a strongly conservative bias. Comte saw society as a complex and dynamic structure of interdependent parts which required basic order or harmony if it were to function effectively. He referred to the study of social structure as *social statics* and to that of change as *social dynamics* – a dualism that has had great and continuing influence in sociological theory. Neither Comte nor Saint-Simon wished to restore the old regime – but both seriously entertained the idea that sociology itself might inspire a new secular 'religion' based on respect for certain social principles, including that of social order. Somewhat absurdly, in his later years, Comte imagined that he might be a 'Pope' of a new sociological 'religion' which might establish the principles of social life. This otherwise bizarre episode is useful in that it illustrates the enormous faith and optimism that many intellectuals of the period had in science and social science. Comte believed that sociology could become the queen of the sciences as it dealt with the highest form of life – human life – and could unify all science.

The second conservative element in the work of Saint-Simon and Comte pertains to the nature of their theory and method. They described their approach to social analysis as *'positivist'*, and they regarded it as genuinely and definitively scientific in contrast to what they saw as the abstract, philosophical, and non-empirical form of reasoning characteristic of the Enlightenment 'philosophes'. Briefly, positivism meant that social explanation should be based on the laws of cause and effect and that theoretical explanations require empirical proof. Comte argued that sociology should systematically study the links between different structures or institutions of society – including the causes of stability and order (necessary for the conduct of social life) and change. Comte's confidence in the superiority of his social scientific methodology is reflected in his historical and sociological model. He argued that society had evolved through three stages, in each one of which a particular system of social explanation predominated: theological, metaphysical (rational-philosophical); and positivist. He associated the second phase with the Enlightenment and argued that the positivist period, characterised by positivist explanations based on factual evidence, was superseding it.

In fact, although many Enlightenment intellectuals did tend to think and write in a rather abstract and general way, few were opposed to the empirical approach. Comte's concern to distinguish his own work from that of the philosophers partly reflects his wish to be seen as the initiator of a new approach to knowledge and as the founder of a new discipline, sociology. In practice, Comte has had a great influence on French sociology and, via Durkheim, on American Functionalism, but traditions of sociological enquiry just as influential as positivism have developed. One of these is symbolic interactionism, which gives more emphasis to meaning than to social causation.

It may seem paradoxical to describe positivism as conservative. Comte certainly thought of himself as in the van of social analysis, and the extent to which he was genuinely innovatory is indicated by the fact that it was he who invented the term 'sociology'. Despite his criticism of Enlightenment intellectuals, in fact most of them shared with him a belief that science would provide a basis for human progress. However, it can be cogently argued that the precise theoretical approach prescribed by positivism complements the conservative bias of Comte's concern with social order. Positivism treats human beings as objects of study within the organ of society rather than as actors who themselves meaningfully make society. Comte's anti-individualism and illiberalism is inherent to his methodology and it is in that sense it is termed conservative here. Significantly, a conservative concern with social order and an approach to method which regarded individual action as irrelevant to sociological study was taken up by the greatest of French sociologists, Emile Durkheim. Prioritisation of the social over the individual and of structure over agency characterised much French social science long after Durkheim and the intellectual origins of this emphasis are to be found in Comte. This at times extreme emphasis in the Comtean/Durkheimian tradition of French sociology has given it, if not always an anti-humanist character, at least a somewhat *deterministic* one in which human beings have seemed moved by events rather than initiators of them.

3) The Romantic Movement: Tönnies and Simmel

Romanticism is based on the view or feeling that emotions are what is most importantly and characteristically human, and that too much emphasis on reason and science can smother and even destroy them, turning human beings into little more than extensions of machines. Romanticism is often thought of as conservative or reactionary, in that it sometimes involves an appeal to tradition against social engineering and planned change (which are associated with socialism and liberal social democracy). However, there is an equally strong radical romanticism of the left. The latter takes the form of a radical commitment to basic human rights, including equality, life, liberty and the pursuit of happiness and tends to be as critical of traditional vested interests as it is of newer ones. Romanticism of the left has been much stronger in the United States than in Britain where left-wing thought has been virtually synonymous with socialism. As Staughton Lynd has shown in his *The Intellectual Origins of American Radicalism* (1969), in the United States anarchism, pacifism, populism and progressivism as well as other movements have sustained a much more radical commitment to the ideals of the American revolution than has the liberal centre. In particular, 'the pursuit of happiness' has been pursued with notable commitment by the bohemian or cultural left, notably the Beats and the Hippies, and now, arguably by 'New Agers' – albeit with a leavening of environmental seriousness.

The relationship of the romantic movement to the Enlightenment is paradoxical. On the one hand, the romantic movement can be seen as a reassertion of the importance of emotion, feeling, and the aesthetic in the face of the enlightenment emphasis on reason and science. Romanticism also focuses on the personal and subjective rather than social factors 'external' to the individual. On the other hand, romanticism can be regarded as part of the Enlightenment itself in that the latter can be thought of, not simply as a movement based on reason, but as an interplay or dialogue between reason and emotion (see Kumar, 1995). In some cases these two concerns were expressed by a single thinker. Thus, Rousseau (1712–1728) developed if he did not introduce the social scientific concept of socialisation (the process by which an individual comes to participate in a culture), but he also enthused about the natural qualities of the unspoiled 'noble savage'. Comte himself after establishing a reputation as an uncompromising empiricist, became very interested in the study of emotions in his later life. His attempt to establish a sort of sociological religion was in part an inept effort to combine reason and emotion within one framework.

Among the most familiar non-sociological examples of romanticism was the work of the English romantic poets including Wordsworth, Coleridge and Shelley. They expressed an unease about the effects of industrialisation – the 'dark, satanic mills' in Blake's famous phrase – comparable to similar reservations expressed in much sociological writing of a slightly later period. A theme that frequently occurs both in romantic poetry and in sociology is a concern that modernisation has involved a dehumanisation of social life, not only at work, but in terms of a 'loss of community'. It was a pet project of Wordsworth to establish a genuine community in a rural setting – an aim he to some extent achieved when he repaired to the Lake District with a number of fellow poets, having earlier failed to get started on a similar project near the Susquehanna river in the United States.

Among the sociologists already mentioned here, several express strong sentiments of romantic nostalgia. Simmel was notably concerned about the apparent depersonalisation of social life brought about by modernity and particularly by the rush of urban life. Ferdinand Tönnies' 'Community and Association'(1887) is the classic conservative romantic lament for what he perceived as the loss of community and the rise to dominance of competitive individualism in modern society. In contrast, Marx's later writings including 'Capital' represented the culmination of what he saw as his scientific analysis of capitalist society. He rejected nostalgia for the past as futile and considered that although it was not possible to reverse capitalism, it was possible to move beyond it in the form of communism. However, although the mature Marx was indisputably in the rationalist rather than the romantic tradition, he was motivated by a concern for human suffering and loss of potential. This is most evident in his earlier writings, particularly those on *alienation*. Although these writings are correctly described as humanist rather than romantic, they were emotionally and morally inspired (despite the abstruse quality of much of his writings, Marx was capable of quite moving prose-poetry). In *Economic and Philosophical Manuscripts* (1844) he developed the concept of alienation to describe the way that work under capitalism removed the product of workers' labour from them and isolated them from each other. Marx saw this as a terrible waste of human potential and creativity. The year after the publication of the later volume, Marx's close colleague Engels published *The Condition of the Working Class in England* (1845), a passionate exposé of urban degradation and poverty in early Victorian England. Like Marx, Engels was a socialist rather than a romantic radical but both clearly felt moral outrage and compassion at the poverty and misery of the English proletariat.

As will become obvious, it is especially in the writings of Max Weber that the struggle to balance the rational and the emotional, the social and the personal, is particularly obvious and poignant. Here, the point that can be taken from Weber is that these two aspects are best regarded not so much as opposites but as equally unavoidable elements in human experience which, nevertheless, often co-exist in some degree of tension.

4) Evolutionism

Comte's 'law of three stages' – the theological, metaphysical and positivist or scientific industrial – is based on the analysis that society develops in a progressive way i.e., *progress occurs*. He attributed the instability of Europe of his time to the interrupted transition from the second to the third of these stages. Despite his criticism of the philosophes, therefore, Comte was as much in the thrall of the idea of progress as they were. Comte himself initiated a strand of evolutionary assumption within sociology which included the controversial notion that sociology itself was the science that could bring to culmination the work of other sciences through synthesising their findings.

Karl Marx dedicated the first volume of *Capital* to Charles Darwin, the founder of evolutionary theory. As this indicates, Darwin's evolutionary mode of thinking had an enormous influence on Marx. It also illustrates the immense prestige in which natural science was held in the mid nineteenth century and the preoccupation of many sociologists with achieving scientific rigour in developing their new subject and so gain for it the status of a scientific discipline. Just as Darwin saw a direction and logic to the development of biological life, so Marx saw a pattern in human history and society. For Darwin, the mechanism which explains biological evolution is natural selection by which those organisms which happen to be most suitable for survival in a given environment are naturally selected to survive. For Marx, the mechanism of historical and social change was class conflict. Marx presented a model of historical evolution which involved transitions from primitive communist societies through various forms of class societies to a developed form of communism (see page 14). These transitions involved revolution at the point at which the old order was no longer able to sustain itself, so paradoxically but not illogically Marx's evolutionism involved revolution.

If Marx thought he had discovered some scientific law of history in the above model, he is open to the criticism of misapplying the approach of natural science to human society. However, the Marxist theory which most conveys that implication was, in fact, developed by Engels rather than Marx. This is the theory of the *dialectical* materialism. The concept was widely used by Marx but it was most rigorously and some would say, rigidly developed by Engels. In the context of historical change it refers to how, in Engels's view, the emergence of a dominant social class (thesis) causes another class to develop in opposition to it (antithesis) with the result that change occurs producing a new set of social relationships (synthesis). The same basic process is repeated until the final synthesis – communist society – is produced. Both Marx and Engels considered this to be a material process rather than one driven by ideas. The important issue of how useful or not the dialectical method is need not be discussed here. The point is to appreciate the extent to which this aspect of his thinking reflected their determination to develop sociology in what they saw as scientifically acceptable terms and within an evolutionary framework.

Ian Craib has suggested that to a greater or lesser extent Marx, Durkheim, Weber and Simmel all adopted an evolutionary view of social development (1997:21). He explains this statement by observing that all of them 'work with some idea of social evolution from some primitive state to some more complex and presumably civilized state' (21). While this is true, it is also the case that Weber and Simmel gave more emphasis than Marx and Durkheim to individual choice, meaning and experience in the process of social action and change.

Why Sociology – *Then*: Classical Sociology

Classical sociology can be partly understood as a series of attempts to explain the vast changes described so far in this chapter, including the character of the new type of society that was developing. The main contributors to what is known as classical sociology were Marx, Durkheim and Max Weber (1864–1920). Many would also consider George Simmel (1858–1918) to have made as comparable a contribution to sociology as this celebrated trio albeit of a slightly different kind. All four of these sociologists published what are arguably their major works between 1867 and 1905 – a period of less than forty years and one in which the changes referred to above had become obvious but were still rapidly developing. Marx published the first volume of *Capital* in 1867 in which he put forward his analysis of some of the key weaknesses, or more precisely what he thought of as *contradictions* of the capitalist system – contradictions which he believed the organised working class could exploit to destroy capitalism. Durkheim's main work on the structure of industrial society was *The Division of Labour* and this was published in 1893. Durkheim was primarily concerned with understanding the different bases of *social solidarity* in traditional and in modern societies i.e., how societies 'hang together'. An important aspect of this was his interest in social order, law and justice and the changing principles on which these are based. This focus is not surprising given the social turmoil in the Europe of Durkheim's youth.

Max Weber published his main book on culture – *The Protestant Ethic and the Spirit of Capitalism* – in 1905 although his major work on social structure, *Economy and Society*, was only published posthumously in 1922. Weber is a pre-eminent theorist of modern industrial society. This latter description is crucial and points to the fundamental difference between Weber and Marx. Whereas Marx considered that the precise description of the period under discussion to be '*the capitalist epoch*', Weber thought in terms of *modern industrial society* or simply modern society. The difference is that Weber thought that the main features of the emerging, new society were the product of rational thinking, science, technology and bureaucracy whereas Marx thought they were the product of the capitalist economic system – the way it organised the production, distribution and exchange of economic goods and services. This difference led them to view the new epoch in importantly different ways. Whereas Marx envisaged socialism and communism as the next stages in historical development and as fundamentally different from capitalism, Weber considered that, as both modern capitalist and modern socialist societies were bureaucratically organised, they shared a number of central characteristics – although there were important differences between them as well. The debate between Marx and Weber on this, as on other matters, has been a focal concern around which the discipline has developed and is one of the dualisms around which this book is organised.

George Simmel's *The Metropolis and Mental Life* was published in 1893. Like Durkheim, Simmel was concerned with the shift from rural, agricultural to urban, industrial society. However, whereas Durkheim sought to explain and present these changes by use of large-scale or structural concepts, Simmel focused more on changes in the everyday lives of ordinary people. He argued that urbanisation and the development of a money economy had transformed the quality of human life. He found that the sheer number of interactions and exchanges, particularly of a monetary/commercial kind made by city dwellers had increased the intensity and impersonality of life. Simmel saw society as a web of individual interactions and sought to capture a sense of authentic human experience in his work.

The work of the above four sociologists is of such quality and scope that they are widely regarded as having produced a 'classical' core of sociological thought. This body of work raises key questions about society and social change and offers a range of concepts and theoretical models which, not only illuminate their own and previous societies, but which remain indispensable to the understanding of our own time. However, it is important to realise that the classic sociologists did not provide answers to all the questions they raised – they produced no sociological 'canon' – indeed, it is stimulating that on some matters they sharply disagreed with each other. The founders of sociology were not the only people trying to make sense of and interpret the tumultuous developments of the time. Two British-born sociologists, Herbert Spencer (1820–1895) and Leonard Hobhouse (1864–1949) achieved bigger contemporary reputations than have been sustained since. Spencer, in particular, strongly reflected the influence of Darwin and evolutionary thought in his own model of social evolution. From the wider point of view, the writings of first generation feminists such as Harriet Martineau (1802–76) and anti-racist black scholars such as, American, W.E.B. du Bois (1868–1963) provided impressive social commentary and analysis. Like Marx, their theoretical work supported their practical politics.

The Central Themes of Sociology: The Sociological Dualisms

Classical Sociology

According to Charles Wright Mills, 'classic' or classical sociology addresses key questions about society. He went on to say:

> These questions are generally of wide scope: they concern total societies, their trans-formations, and the varieties of men and women that inhabit them. (1961:1)

In other words, classical sociology was concerned with big questions involving society as a whole, particularly social change, and the different people that live in them. Mills went on to say that the classic sociologists attempted to build models of societies in order to understand better how they worked and how people experienced them. These models were dynamic in the sense that the classic sociologists tried to analyse how the main parts or institutional systems of society related to each other. For instance, Marx closely examined the relationship between the economy and social class and between social class and politics and so on. Marx's model of society is particularly well known and relatively straightforward to describe in outline, but both Weber and Durkheim also produced clear working frameworks of society or of particular aspects or institutional areas of society.

Mills suggested that the achievement of the classical sociologists lay in the various insights their conceptual models afforded about society rather than their 'correctness'. Obviously, they sought to describe and explain society as precisely as possible but Mills seems to imply that their work is best approached non-dogmatically and with the realistic expectation of learning *something* rather than everything about society. Mills certainly believed that the study of sociological clas-sics – indeed, simply adopting the sociological perspective – could help people to understand and even cope with their lives better. In a famous phrase, he argued that sociology can enable us to see the links between 'personal troubles and public issues'. He argued that individuals can gain 'orientation' if they are able to see that problems they experience such as poverty or unemployment may be caused by factors outside themselves. Rather than blame themselves needlessly, Mills suggested that people should seek to understand their situation in social con-text and to empower themselves by attempting to change what they find oppressive. Of course, sociology itself is not about changing society but it can certainly be useful to those who want to do so.

Mills gives an excellent idea of the scope of classical sociological theory, but it is necessary to be more detailed about its central theoretical concerns. Ian Craib suggests four pairs of concepts which 'provide an organising framework for social theory' in general, not only that of the founders of sociology (1997:7). He refers to these pairs of concepts as dualisms because each pair addresses two-sides of a given key issue of social theory. The four dualisms which are explained below are individual/society, action/structure, social integration/social system, and modernity/capitalism-socialism. Derek Layder (1994) has adopted a similar list of dualisms in presenting the common concerns of social theory. Significantly, he adds the dualism of micro/macro which raises issues of methodology in relation to theory. These five dualisms require some definition.

1. Individual/society:

Every human being is born into an existing society however that society is defined. A recurrent concern of sociology and specifically social theory is the relationship of the individual to society and, in particular, as Craib suggests, which takes priority. Analysis of the relationship of the individual to society long predates the development of sociology. For instance, it was a major theme in the writings of Thomas Hobbes (1588–1679) and John Locke (1632–1702). Their focus was on the respective claims of the individual and society and, in particular, the extent to which the state – as the dominant power in society – can limit individual freedoms in order to facilitate social order. The debate about the relationship between individual human rights and the power of the state is scarcely less intense at the turn of the second millennium than it was in their time. Although the relationship between individual rights, on the one hand, and government and law on the other is primarily an issue of political philosophy, the principles, motivations and conflicts involved are central to the study of sociology. Recently, issues of human rights have come to have a prominent place in sociology.

2. Action/Structure:

The action/structure dualism is closely related to the individual/society but includes group or collective action as well as individual. The relationship between action and social structure defines the nature of social process itself. Explaining what people do in particular social circumstances is pretty much what sociology is about: action/structure. Because the concept of structure implies that society is made up of inter-connected parts, it enables sociologists to 'get a grip' on the 'big concept' of society. Derek Layder usefully provides a working definition of social structure as 'the social relationships which provide the social context or conditions under which people act' (5). These relationships include the familial, communal, economic, and cultural and political – and all are shaped by formal and informal rules or structures and continuously reshaped by action. The focus of sociological analysis is often on the extent to which individual action is 'chosen' and 'free' (*voluntarism*) or constrained or even caused by social factors (*determinism*) or, as most would see it, some combination of the two. Layder prefers to use the dualism of agency/structure rather than action/structure – using the term agency primarily to mean 'the ability of human beings to make a difference in the world' (5). Action can be collective – such as military action – as well as individual – and both are equally areas of sociological analysis. Marx, in particular emphasised the importance of the collective action of social classes. Indeed, it was one of Marx's contributions to social science that he systematically theorised human beings as members of collectivities as well as individuals and in so doing moved debate about structure and agency onto a more social plane of analysis.

3. Social integration/system integration:

Social integration, as defined by Craib, is 'about what it is that relates actors or individuals within society' (7). What mainly relates individuals is shared norms and values and in the absence of this there may be an increased possibility of social conflict. Individual socialisation – through the family, education system and other agencies -is the main way in which people are integrated into society. The effectiveness of socialisation can be partly gauged by the extent to which individuals accept the values and norms of their own society as entirely 'natural' and imagine, so often wrongly, that these are universal. Another means of achieving social integration is through the exercise of social control such as through the legal system or peer group approval/disapproval although these processes may well be contested and involve conflict. Different classes, religious, ethnic and other groups invariably possess some norms and values different from and sometimes in disagreement with each other. The degree of tolerance in a society influences the extent to which such cultural differences bring about conflict.

Whereas social integration is concerned with integrating people into society, in contrast, system integration is about how the various parts of society – its institutions and systems – are integrated.

Thus, Marx examined how the law and justice system related to economic power and interests (his analysis was that the law tended to be used to justify or legitimise the interests of the dominant class). In our own time, we are constantly hearing of the importance of an effective education system to the efficient functioning of the economic system.

4. Micro/Macro:

Whereas the above three dualisms focus primarily on the relationship between human action and social context, that of the micro-macro, in the words of Layder, 'is rather more concerned with the level and scale of analysis and the research focus' (5). Thus, a somewhat different range of concepts and methods would be required for research into couple relationships (micro) than into the correlation between class origins and social mobility (macro). As a broad generalisation, it is true to say that the exploration of individual action and meaning is best suited to micro level research and the study of structural and systems issues best suited to macro level research. Thus, particular theoretical issues are associated with particular, complementary research methods and the micro-macro dualism usefully indicates this link. In general, the founders of sociology were more concerned with macro sociological issues – particularly relating to social change and structure – whereas postmodernists have focused more on personal experience and identity albeit often within a global perspective.

5. Modernity/capitalism-socialism

The four dualisms presented above are so fundamental that they are relevant to the study of any type of human society and the study of it. They indicate universal dimensions of social life. This is not true of the modernity/capitalism-socialism dualism. There have, of course, been many societies which were neither modern nor capitalist or socialist and, in the Amazon basin and elsewhere, there still are some. The modernity/capitalism-socialism dualism applies only to how the classical and more recent sociologists have categorised and interpreted the contemporary epoch. The central and classic disagreement was between Marx and Weber. Weber regarded the term modernity as the best description of the new epoch brought about by the changes discussed above. Marx regarded the term capitalism as the best description of this epoch and he argued that the next epoch would be a socialist/communist one. In contrast, Weber regarded socialism as it occurred in Russia as a modernising force. For him, the term modern society could equally describe capitalist and socialist societies. He considered that the basic character of modern societies was the result of industrialisation which, in turn, had produced the proliferation of bureaucracy, extensive urbanisation and other features of modern life. Weber certainly regarded the spread of capitalism as immensely important but his disagreement with Marx on this matter is crucial and one of the major defining differences in their sociological approaches. Their disagreement has implications for the way we view our own period – are we still in a capitalist epoch as more orthodox Marxism would suggest (and does, therefore, the prospect of socialism still await?) or is our time best described as late modernity or even postmodernity? Or, finally, can the two approaches be constructively reconciled?

The Classical Foundations: Contested Interpretations of the Dualisms

The dualisms described above can be illustrated by examining the work of the classical sociologists in relation to concrete aspects of society. Thus, issues pertaining to individuality/society and action/structure frequently arise and can be well illustrated in the context of the topic of stratification – the division of societies into hierarchical strata. Marx and Weber both produced frameworks to explain how societies are stratified and how systems of stratification come to be changed. On the basis of that discussion, their debate about the dualism of modernity/capitalism–socialism can be better explored. The dualism of social integration/system integration is a recurrent theme in the work of all the classical sociologists but is perhaps most central to Durkheim's work which is discussed in relation to the topics of social solidarity and social order. That dualism will there-fore be the main focus of the section on Durkheim.

Marx and Weber's Models of Society: Stratification and the Dualisms

The scope of this chapter does not allow for an extensive discussion and comparison of the work of Marx and Weber. However, their debate on stratification focuses on a core area of society and has been highly influential in shaping modern sociology. Their two models of stratification have fundamentally different starting points. Whereas Marx considered that class stratification is the most important type of stratification, Weber considered that status groups (defined by social pres-tige/respect not necessarily based on material possessions) and party (a form of political stratifica-tion – explained below) can be, and in some societies are, more important than class stratification. The discussion of stratification leads on to a consideration of cultural issues. Marx's analysis will be presented first, followed by Weber's and then the two will be compared on the basis of the dualisms listed above.

1) Marx on Stratification

Marx argued that all societies, other than communist ones, are class divided societies and are strat-ified into two main antagonistic classes: the class that owns the means of production and the class that works the means of production. The only two exceptions to this were early 'primitive com-munist' societies in which property was held in common and the mature communist society that Marx expected to succeed capitalism following a transitional phase of socialism. In the feudal period, the class that owned the means of production was the feudal aristocracy and gentry and the class that worked them was the serfs. The independent peasantry and the business middle class or bourgeoisie were minor classes but it was the emergence to power of the latter that brought about the new epoch of capitalism. In the capitalist period, the two antagonistic classes were the capitalist class or bourgeoisie and the working class or proletariat. It was the struggle between these two classes that Marx believed would result in the birth of a new epoch, socialism/communism.

The following is an outline of Marx's model of historical stages and it clearly reflects the evolu-tionary thinking characteristic of his time:

Primitive Communism	Classless Society
Asiatic Mode of Production	
Ancient Form of Society	Class Societies
Feudalism	
Capitalism	
Communism	Classless Society

Marx's view of political power was that it closely reflected class stratification. He stated that the dominant economic class in any period was also the dominant class politically. In the feudal period the landed aristocracy and gentry was the ruling class and in the capitalist period the bourgeoisie was the ruling class. However, although the dominant class held power, Marx emphasised that subordinate classes could organise in groups and parties to change things – his model of stratifica-tion and of history was highly dynamic.

Marx considered that status was overwhelmingly the product of wealth and the power that comes from wealth. Thus, the feudal aristocracy might claim the sanction of religion and tradition for their position in society but, according to Marx, it actually depended on their economic dominance. He regarded such claims as ideological or false justification which, if believed, would be taken to *legitimise* their position. Once another class became economically dominant, it would eventually become politically dominant – as had happened in the case of the bourgeoisie – and its social status would rise accordingly. Marx tended to regard traditional symbols of status associated with the medieval church and nobility as outmoded and likely to decline.

Within Marx's model of society, other types of stratification, including race/ethnicity and gender are always related to class context and identity. It is debatable whether nationality is most usefully considered as a form of stratification, but Marx viewed it as a conservative and even reactionary form of identity as he did race and ethnic identification. According to Marx, the capitalist class in imperialist countries adopted ideologies of nationalism and racial superiority partly to justify exploiting other societies and to unify their own class-divided societies. By propagandising in this way, they hoped to direct the awareness of working class people away from their own exploitation and give them a sense of relative status. Marx regarded such nationalist and racist ideologies when held by working class people as examples of 'false consciousness' because they did not represent their 'true', long-term interests. Marx regarded national and racist divisions among working class people as destructive to their interests as a class. He may not have invented the phrase 'workers of the world unite' – but he certainly thought that they should do so.

It was Engels rather than Marx who wrote the most influential early Marxist analysis on the family and gender: *Origins of the Family, Private Property and the State* (1884). Engels explained the subordination of women in terms of the development of institutions of private property and monogamy which helped to lay a basis for the development of capitalism. He argued that historically men's greater involvement in hunting and trading and lesser involvement in childcare and domestic matters had enabled them to accumulate and control more personal private property than women. They sought to secure this through establishing their sons as inheritors – in many societies, the eldest son. Although it seems that Engels's historical account of the rise of patriarchy is factually imprecise, it has provided a rough starting point for much Marxist-Feminist analysis. It is an analysis which has the seeds of gender equality because it implies that childcare is a matter of public as well as family responsibility and that women should be enabled to seek employment outside the home on the same basis as men. Within the Marxist tradition, class is the primary and defining identity and gender, like ethnicity, is secondary.

Marx on Class Culture, Consciousness and Action: The Base and Superstructure

Marx's analysis of culture and consciousness, like his analysis of stratification, is dominated by class. Class structure itself is determined by relations to the means of production. Together, the economy and structure of stratification make-up what Marx referred to as the *base*. The rest of society – the political system and everything covered by the term culture (education, religion, art, particular 'ways of life' etc.) are termed the *superstructure*. In Marx's formulation of it, the base is dominant over the superstructure. In other words, people's relations to the means of production structures their culture. Logically, it would seem to follow that in capitalist society, the bourgeoisie would have a bourgeoisie culture and the working class a working class one. Thankfully, Marx's model is not as crude as this although this is the general direction of his analysis in that he envisaged that ultimately the two main classes – the capitalist and working classes in capitalist society – would become aware (conscious) of their different values and material interests and as a result come into direct conflict. However, two factors complicate the development of such an outcome.

First, is the fact that the dominant class has more power than the subordinate class to impose and diffuse its cultural values. Thus, in capitalist society, the bourgeoisie is able to use its control over the means of communication to disseminate its *ideology* (bourgeoisie class-interested values and beliefs) to the subordinate class, in this case the working class. The opportunity of the working class to 'see through' the dominant ideology depended on its developing its own alternative ideology reflecting its genuine class interest. Such developments were more likely to occur at times of weakness in capitalism. Such weaknesses could occur due to what Marx believed were *contradictions* in capitalism such as the declining rate of profit due to competition between capitalists. Second, as was discussed above, other factors such as racism and nationalism can interfere with members of the working class achieving a true consciousness of their own class interest which Marx saw as socialist/communist. The following passage is quite lengthy but it illustrates all the above points and is an excellent example of Marx's mode of thought:

> In the social production which men carry on they enter into definite relations that are indispensable and independent of their will; these relations of production correspond to a definite stage of development of their material powers of production. The sum total of these relations of production constitutes the economic structure of society – the real foundation, on which rise legal and political superstructures and to which correspond definite forms of social consciousness. The mode of production in material life determines the general character of the social, political, and spiritual processes of life. It is not the consciousness of men that determines their existence, but, on the contrary, their existence determines their consciousness. At a certain stage of their development, the material forces of production in a society come in conflict with the existing relations of production (i.e., with class relations – my brackets), or – what is but a legal expression of the same thing – with the property relations within which they had been at work before. From forms of development of the forces of production, these relations turn into fetters. Then comes the period of social revolution. With the changes of the economic foundation, the entire immense superstructure is more or less transformed.
>
> (Marx, '*A Contribution to the Critique of Political Economy*' extracted in Mills, 1967:44)

Marx argued that it is classes that are the agents of historical change, not individuals. He made an important distinction between class 'in' itself and class 'for' itself, which provides a useful perspective for understanding the more dynamic aspects of his approach to culture, consciousness and politics. Class 'in' itself is economic class in the sense of an individual's relationship to the means of production and a class 'for' itself is one whose membership is aware or conscious of its 'objective position' and expresses this consciousness politically and culturally. Marx considered that factors existed for and against the proletariat becoming conscious of its objective position. The proletariat's collective experience of exploitation in the factories and urban areas were factors which Marx expected to raise its consciousness. Such consciousness of the need for change might find expression in revolutionary political propaganda and artistic activity although the proletariat of Marx's time had little opportunity for the latter. From Marx's point of view, the development and spread of socialist and communist ideology among the working class would have represented an expression of a 'true' consciousness of their interests and needs. Despite the potential for revolutionary consciousness and action among the proletariat, Marx saw formidable obstacles to its development. Mainly this was because it is in the interests of the bourgeoisie to stop the proletariat from achieving such consciousness and action and to continue exploiting it. According to Marx's observation, the bourgeoisie was prepared to use ideological means – the press and religion – to create a 'false' consciousness and conformity among the proletariat and to use force if that failed.

Marx tended to dismiss 'individualism' as a characteristic associated with the capitalist or bourgeois class. In contrast to Weber (see pp. 21–22), Marx saw the origin of bourgeois individualism in the nature of the capitalist economy. The self-interested pursuit of profit and wealth defined bourgeois individualism. He saw political liberalism and artistic 'freedom' in capitalist society broadly as extensions of bourgeois individualism. He envisaged that the working class, reflecting the material conditions of its experience in exploited labour, would develop a more collective, ultimately a socialist, consciousness. Marx's analysis made him critical of the Enlightenment's celebration of individual potential and rights which, again, he saw as bourgeois ideology and as of little use to the majority of people. This issue is taken up in the context of 'identity' in Chapter 4.

There is a tension in Marx's model of society around the extent to which people can affect and change society and the extent to which they are formed by it. On balance, Marx's model weighs firmly on the side of society rather than the individual and by extension on the side of structure rather than agency. The agency that was crucial to his model of change was not the individual as such but working class people collectively. In contrast to the humanistic concern Marx showed for working people in his earlier writings, it is arguable that in his later work, the proletariat becomes almost *reified* into a phenomenon of social structure. Other aspects of Marx's thought that strongly weigh the balance towards social structure are his use of the dialectic, with its rather mechanical implications for historical change and his base/superstructure model which emphasises the influence of the former over the latter. Even granted that Marx's theory was about collectivities – mainly classes – rather than individuals, there is a strong element of determinism in how he envisaged classes collectively thought and acted. However, whether Marx is seen as a determinist is ultimately a matter of individual judgement about the overall emphasis of his thought. The making of such a judgement should be made easier by comparing Marx's thought to that of the liberal, Max Weber.

2) Weber on Stratification

Weber regarded the various types of stratification as aspects of the way power is hierarchically distributed in society. In other words, some individuals and groups have more power than others. According to Weber, there are three main sources of power. In Weber's words:

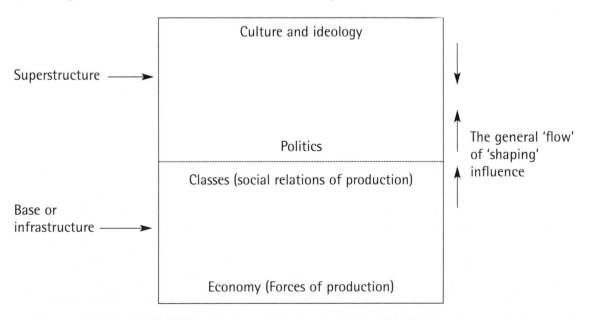

Figure 1.2 Marx's Model of Society

> Classes, status groups and parties are phenomena of the distribution of power within a community
>
> (Quoted in Gerth and Mills, 1970:181)

The term pluralist which literally means 'several' applies to Weber in various ways, including in the context of stratification where he observes several (three) distinct types of stratification rather than one dominant type. Weber regarded class as a highly important type of stratification but not necessarily as more important than status and party. In his view, class had become much more important during the industrial age when social change meant that more individuals changed their social situation than in feudal or caste societies. He considered that in the later period society was primarily differentiated and stratified by a hierarchy of status (see below). He therefore did not agree with Marx's model of historical stages based on the dominance of successive classes. Rather, Weber distinguished between traditional societies stratified mainly on the basis of status and modern societies stratified mainly on the basis of class. Weber's definition of class is significantly different from Marx's. He stated that class situation is:

> the typical chance for a supply of goods, external living conditions, and personal life experiences, in so far as this chance is determined by the amount and kind of power, or lack of such, to dispose of goods or skills for the sake of income in a given economic order. The term 'class' refers to any group of people that is found in the same class situation. (*Ibid.*, 181).

Thus defined, class is fundamentally an economic category. It describes the assets or lack of assets – goods and property, experience and skills – an individual can bring to the market for the purpose of earning an income. Publishing some 50 years after Marx, Weber gave more emphasis to the groups of clerks, bureaucrats and professionals which were growing rapidly around the turn of the century and beyond. His model of class was much more finely graded than was that of Marx who had anticipated an increasing polarisation between the bourgeoisie and proletariat and a decline of other classes.

A slightly different way of expressing Weber's definition of class and one he often used was a group of people who shared the same or very similar 'life-chances'. A major aspect of 'life-chances' is the chances of social mobility up or down the class hierarchy. Weber argued that, in general, the rate of social mobility was greater in modern than in traditional societies. The study of social mobility has become a central part of Weberian stratification theory.

Weber distinguished between class and status situation as follows:

> In contrast to the purely economically determined 'class situation' we wish to designate as 'status situation' every typical component of the life of men that is determined by a specific, positive or negative, social estimation of *honour* (*Ibid.*,185).

Status can derive from any quality shared by a given group which others hold in esteem. Thus, people of aristocratic birth may derive status from their nobility and certain religious functionaries from their holy office. In feudal society, the law provided a framework for stratifying the main estates – nobility, church and peasantry – according to differential status. In caste societies such as India, it was religion that underpinned status stratification. Weber recognised that in modern societies status is often closely linked to class. He observed that while the newly rich may initially have difficulty gaining access to the higher social echelons, eventually, they usually do. Thus, in our own time, we have seen some of the rock and roll rebels of the 1960s, such as Elton John and Paul McCartney, honoured as knights. Nevertheless, modern Weberians by no means consider that status has 'collapsed' into class. Age groups – particularly youth – and racially and ethnically stratified groups have been commonly theorised as types of status groups by Weberians (see Berger and Berger,1976:chapter 11).

Weber makes a crucial distinction between class and status in respect of 'community'. He states that '(i) in contrast to classes, status groups are normally communities'(186). By communities, Weber means a group which shares a common sense of identity and co-operates in common action. Weber considered it fairly obvious that people in a similar work situation would sometimes find they shared common interests and would organise accordingly but he did not consider that this necessarily led to the development of strong class-based communities or what Marx termed the creation of 'a class for itself'. Rather, Weber considered that groups which consciously formed themselves around a common interest, cause or situation, such as religious or leisure groups were more likely to become communities. Status groups were usually of this kind.

While Weber agreed that members of particular classes often develop a sense of community he specifically rejected any implication in Marx that those who are members of class-based communities enjoy a superior or 'truer' form of consciousness and identity than do those individuals who feel and think differently. The following quotation from Weber could hardly be more explicit:

> Above all, this fact (that members of classes often act together to protect their interests – my brackets) must not lead to the kind of pseudo-scientific operation with the concepts of 'class' and 'class interests' so frequently found these days, and which has found its most classic expression in the statement of a talented author (whom we can assume to be Marx!), that the individual may be in error concerning his interests but that class is infallible' about its interests (my brackets) (*Ibid.*, 184–85).

Setting aside Weber's obvious disagreement with Marx, he does seem to have clearly understood Marx's position both on the 'scientific' nature of Marxist theory and on the relative irrelevance of the individual and individual consciousness to the process of historical change. It is worth quoting further from Marx's 'A Contribution to the Critique of Political Economy' to illustrate both points:

> In considering such transformations the distinction should always be made between the material transformations of the economic conditions of production, which can be determined with the precision of natural science and the ... ideological forms in which men become conscious of this conflict and fight it out. Just as our opinion of an individual is not based on what he thinks of himself, so we cannot judge of such a period of transformation by its own consciousness; on the contrary, this consciousness must rather be explained from the contradictions of material life.

> (Marx in Mills, *op. cit*: 43)

As will be further illustrated below, Weber did not prioritise material conditions over either individual consciousness nor cultural values (which he considered ultimately had their origin in the thought and interaction of individuals).

Here, the fundamental difference between Weber and Marx is apparent. Whereas Marx's model of history – and the future – was based on the primacy of collective class action, Weber's was not. For Weber, individual consciousness and meaning were to be understood primarily at the level of the individual and not on the basis of a superior 'true' consciousness and meaning. Quite simply, Weber did not think that class consciousness and class communal action had the decisive importance which Marx attached to it. On the contrary, individuals might well think and act in ways that did not conform to their class situation and as far as Weber was concerned that might simply reflect their individual choice rather than 'false' consciousness. Weber's pessimism about modernity lay in his concern not about class oppression but about the swamping of the individual by bureaucratic rationality. For Weber, what defines the modern period is its rational-scientific, industrial, bureaucratic character rather than the class conflict generated by capitalism. If Weber was right, then Marx, of course, was wrong – and vice-versa.

All stratification involves the unequal division of power but according to Weber 'parties live in the house of power'(193–95). By parties Weber means much more than formal political parties and pressure groups. The term also covers the organised factions and groups that come together in any organisation or institution to control or influence decision making. Parties sometimes exist as the political wing of classes or status groups – where they develop one. Thus, parties have been founded to represent the interests of the working class and, similarly, religious groups are often represented by parties and pressure groups. Whatever the basis of its electoral support now, the British Labour Party was founded to represent the working class and several parties in Northern Ireland have very strong religious bases of support. However, Weber observed that the same party may represent more than one class or status group and in this respect as in others his analysis is pluralistic (based on the perception that in modern society, a number and variety of groups are typically involved in a given process – in this case the struggle for power). In contrast, Marx's analysis in this context as in others tends to polarise the classes.

Weber on Culture, Consciousness and Action

Starting with Marx's concept of class, it is possible to build up a complete description of his model of society, including his analysis of culture and consciousness. Quite obviously, this is not the case with Weber. Even including a study of the concepts of status and party along with class only goes some way to describing how he saw society. Even here, a significant part of what Weber is trying to show is that class, status and political groups partly and unpredictably overlap. His pluralistic model of stratification was meant to illustrate that social differentiation and division is not a clear cut matter easily fitted into an all-explanatory model of society. Weber did not intend to create a model of society which was as integrated as or had the explanatory power of Marx's model because he did not believe such a model was possible. Weber considered Marx's model to be misleading because social action and its outcomes involve a degree of unpredictable choice and consequence which cannot be presented in the over-systematic way attempted by Marx. He rejected the view that the cultural and political areas of society are tightly structured by the economic and argued

Figure 1.3   Weber wrote within the German tradition of meaningful social action.

that the links between them were much looser and freer (or more autonomous) than Marx stipulated. Weber and Marx's crucial disagreement on culture is explored below.

Weber aimed to create a sociology based on the understanding of individual meaning within the context of social interaction. To the extent that the study of meaning is a cultural issue his sociology had a strong cultural orientation. A brief description of Weber's ideal type model of social action will make it clear how varied he considered human motivation to be.

Weber's Model of Social Action

Instrumentally rational action (action geared to 'the attainment of the actors own rationally pursued and calculated ends')

Value-rational action (action 'determined by the conscious belief in the value for its own sake of some ethical, aesthetic, religious or other form of behaviour, independently of its prospect for success')

Affectual action ('determined by actors' specific affects and feeling states)

Traditional action (determined by ingrained habituation)

In Weber's view, each individual is capable of all the above types of action and various combinations of them and this helped to create great cultural variety. Given such a varied input into human culture, it is not surprising that Weber considered it impossible to establish laws on which predictions about social functioning and change could be made. Nevertheless, Weber did consider that the historical and comparative study of societies allowed certain *generalisations* to be made. For instance, he argued that in status stratified societies, such as feudal and caste societies, traditional action predominated whereas in modern, more class stratified societies, instrumental rational action predominated. He argued that the organisation typical of modern society is a bureaucracy and this embodies the principle of instrumental rational action. For him, bureaucracy, not class conflict was the defining feature of modern society. Although he considered that the capitalist corporation was the prototype of a modern bureaucracy, he also stressed the extreme bureaucratic character of early communist party organisation and the bureaucratic structure of the communist state. Weber was often eloquent about the constraining and dehumanising effects of what he referred to as 'the iron cage' of bureaucracy and the culture of calculation and conformity it produced.

Weber did not consider that culture reflected material interests, particularly class interests, to the same close degree that Marx did. He certainly accepted that individuals and groups, including classes, tend to adopt ideas – what Marx would call ideologies – which justified their situation and behaviour. Thus, he could see the rational appeal of socialism to many working class people. However, the purpose of perhaps his best known work, *The Protestant Ethic and the Spirit of Capitalism* (1905), was to show that ideas and values can arise independently of material interests and even influence the development of material interests. The specific case study he made was the relationship between Calvinism and capitalism. He concluded that neither 'caused' the other although Calvinist ideas were highly compatible with capitalism or, as Weber put it, had an 'elective affinity' with capitalism.

The following quotation from Weber is more easily understood in context but it is worth giving here because it is an unambiguous statement of his view that values – in this case religious values can influence the way a society is organised or to use Weber's term, 'rationalised':

> (R)eligion, its doctrine, also have an autonomy: for instance, the Indian doctrine of Kharma, the Calvinist belief in predestination, the Lutheran justification through faith,

and the Catholic doctrine of sacrament ... have under certain conditions had far-reaching results for the fashioning of a practical way of life.

These comments presuppose that the nature of the desired sacred values has been strongly influenced by the nature of the external interest-situation and the corresponding way of life of the ruling strata and thus by the social stratification itself. But the reverse holds true: wherever the direction of the whole way of life has been methodically rationalized, it has been profoundly determined by the ultimate values towards which the rationalisation has been directed. These values and positions were thus *religiously* determined.

(Quoted in Gerth and Mills: 286).

In slightly simpler terms, what Weber is saying is that people may pursue goals by rational means that are not themselves based on materialistic motives but on particular values (i.e., value-rational action) including religious faith. For instance, a monastery is generally a highly organised institution – and it is organised in pursuit of religious values. In his key work on values – *The Protestant Ethic and the Spirit of Capitalism* – Weber argues, as the title suggests, that Protestant values have affected the organisation and development of capitalism. In particular, the Calvinist view that salvation could be made manifest by good works but that riches should not be used for self indulgence encouraged the hard work and capital accumulation and reinvestment that were characteristics of capitalism in Western Europe in the sixteenth and seventeenth century. Of course, capitalism has changed since, both in its 'spirit' and organisation – generally in the direction of a more purely materialist ethic. Weber's central point then – and perhaps the most important one in his whole work – is that values and ideas can and do make a difference in the material world.

Marx and Weber and the Dualisms

It is illuminating to set the thinking of Marx and Weber against the template of the five dualisms presented above. However, such is the scope and complexity of their thinking that such an exercise is unlikely to give more than a rough and ready notion of where they stood. It will be helpful to repeat the list of five dualisms in summary form:

The Core Sociological Dualisms

Individual	Society
Agency (Action)	Structure
Social Integration	System Integration
Micro	Macro
Modern Society	Capitalist Socialist Society

This section will initially discuss the first two of the dualisms – which are so closely related that they can be dealt with together. Weber's model of society gives more emphasis to the role of the individual, including the individual as agent, than does that of Marx. That said, Weber does not quite deliver on the following statement in which he declares his intention to construct a sociology based on individual meanings:

(S)ociology considers the individual and his action as the basic unit, as its 'atom' ... In this approach, the individual is also the upper limit and sole carrier of meaningful conduct ... In general, for sociology such concepts as 'state', 'feudalism', and the like, designate certain categories of human interaction. Hence it is the task of sociology to reduce these concepts to 'understandable action', that is, without exception to the actions of participating individual men.

(Quoted in Gerth and Mills: 55).

In practice, Weber generalised about social action without being able to do justice to each individual 'without exception'. He was interested in widely shared *types* of action and their social implications. Nevertheless he made meaningful social action the core of his sociological approach. Even when he stresses the constraints of social structure as in his analysis of bureaucracy, he emphasises both that structures are themselves the product of action, and that they have effects on individuals. Thus, he explained bureaucracy as the expression of *instrumental rational* action and continually pointed out that bureaucracy controls and constricts individual conduct in sometimes dehumanising ways. It was only after Weber's death that certain approaches to sociology, mainly in the United States, made the detailed examination of individual inter/action the core of their focus (see pp. 47–54).

It would be unfair to say that Marx's model of society and historical change ignores the individual but what is central for him is the impact of the social relations of production on collective class consciousness and action. Marx simply would not have written the above quotation from Weber anymore than Weber would have written the following one from Marx:

In the social production which men carry on they enter into definite relations that are indispensable and independent of their will ... It is not the consciousness of men that determines their being, but, on the contrary, their social being determines their consciousness.

(Marx in Mills, *op. cit.*: 43).

In Marx's view, the agency for historical change is social class not the individual or even individuals other than as members of social classes. He anticipated that the agency for change from capitalist to socialist society would be the working class. In contrast, Weber argued that it is impossible to predict how various individuals and groups will act and create the future. On the other hand, much of Weber's sociological work focuses on collective action – albeit of status groups and parties as well as classes – and he was well aware not only that people frequently act in groups but that they need to do so in order to be effective. Perhaps the key theoretical difference between Weber and Marx is the relative emphasis they give to, respectively, individual and class action. In turn, their very different emphasis in this respect has had a definitive influence on liberal and Marxist thought – the two major competing socio-political philosophies of the twentieth century.

How individuals are integrated into society (social integration) and how institutions are integrated into society (system integration) will be dealt with more fully below. Here it is enough just to indicate the thrust of Marx and Weber's work. Marx considered that the dominant class in a given society attempts to socialise subordinate classes into accepting its beliefs or ideology by control of the means of public communication – including religion, education and the media. How 'tight' this control needed to be could change with circumstances. Marx argued that the dominant or ruling class could be challenged – ultimately with success – if the subordinate and exploited class correctly interpreted its situation and effectively organised to change it. As described above, Marx took a similar view in relation to the institutional integration of society. As Figure 1.2 page 17 indicates, when the dominant class is in effective control, the institutional structures of a society tend to work smoothly in its interests but the built-in conflict of class-based societies meant that there is always potential for challenge and change.

Weber's sociology of social action did not mean that he considered individuals to be entirely free agents able to disregard the constraints and demands of society (social integration). Despite his consistent concern for individual freedom, he also emphasised that societies require authority – which when effective ensures an adequate degree of conformity from its members. He distinguished between traditional authority characteristic of traditional societies and legal-rational authority, characteristic of modern societies, as well as authority derived from personal charisma. Weber did not address the issue of systems integration – the way the various institutions of society work or do not work together – in as direct a way as did Marx or Durkheim. His pluralist view of strati-fication and power in liberal democratic societies was complemented by a pluralist analysis of economic and political systems. He thought that modern societies were best served by the free market and by political democracy although he also saw a role for political leadership and inter-vention. On balance, he feared an excess of systems integration either through bureaucratic or per-sonal tyranny rather than too little. The abiding impression from reading Weber is of someone primarily motivated by a concern that individual human beings should not be depersonalised by rational systems – and in this respect he is broadly in accord with the younger Marx's thinking on alienation.

Marx and Weber's clash on the relationship of the individual to society is of monumental import-ance. In ways that will become clear, this issue remains of central importance today, not least in global context. In his commitment to understanding individual consciousness and meaning, Weber spoke for the mainstream tradition of the liberal Enlightenment. Marx reflected this tradition in terms of his belief in rationality and progress but in introducing and prioritising a collectivist element into historical and social analysis, he launched a hugely influential challenge to liberal thought and to liberal capitalist societies. This conflict of ideas and social organisation became the defining feature of the twentieth century save for the distorting and grotesque influence of Fascism.

The micro/macro dualism can be dealt with briefly here. The main theoretical and methodologi-cal approach adopted by both Marx and Weber was the historical/comparative one. As Mills noted, both were concerned with whole societies and in the development of societies. Within this framework, Weber made more frequent reference to the micro level of individual meaning than Marx and, in fact, also carried out a number of seldom referred to small-scale social surveys, mostly about workers' feelings and about their working conditions. However, the widespread develop-ment of small-scale research by sociologists occurred after their time, particularly as universities adopted the new discipline.

Capitalist or Modern Society?

We now turn to consider the fifth dualism, Marx and Weber's clash on whether the period under discussion is best described as capitalist or modern. Marx's analysis was, that with the rapid devel-opment of financial, commercial and industrial capitalism in the nineteenth century a new epoch – the capitalist epoch – had begun which would last until the coming of the next epoch – com-munism. Weber's analysis was that other factors as well as capitalism define the character of what he referred to as modernity. These are rational thought, science and bureaucratic organisation. Who was right? Alas, the answer cannot be as simple as the question! However, particularly in the light of developments since their deaths, it is possible to offer assessments on some aspects of this great debate. Historically, Weber seems right that science, rational thinking and bureaucracy had origins distinct from capitalism and that their growth greatly contributes to the character of moder-nity. However, from a Marxist point of view, it is arguable that capitalism itself has become the dominant force in the funding and direction of science and rational thinking and that capitalist cor-porations are a major expression of bureaucracy, the other being what some Marxists refer to as 'the capitalist state' (Weber found the socialist state even more bureaucratic). Such is the global dominance of capitalism at the millennium, that the prime characteristics of modernity are capitalist. So, although emphasis in interpretation will vary depending on what aspect is seen as predominant, it is quite logical to refer to modern capitalist or, capitalist modern society.

Marx and Weber both contribute uniquely to our understanding of modern capitalist society but on one crucial theoretical matter Weber can be declared, if not in the right over Marx, at least as much more clear. Weber understood that the social sciences cannot predict the future whereas Marx's model of social science was much closer to that of natural science and some of his statements clearly aspire to predict. To get the best out of Marx's thinking and to reveal his impressive array of concepts and theory, it is necessary to strip out its awed imitation of natural science and pretensions to prediction. Marx illuminated much about capitalist society but created problems for himself and his followers in trying to crack 'the code' of history.

Durkheim and the Dualisms

There is no doubt that in terms of the first two dualisms, Durkheim's emphasis is on society and structure rather than the individual and action. This does not mean that he considered individuals incapable of meaningful action but simply that such action is not the concern of sociology.

Figure 1.4 Durkheim greatly contributed to the emphasis of French sociology on the powerful effect of social structure.

Durkheim considered that the subject matter of sociology was the influence or effect of social factors or 'social facts' as he referred to them on individuals and groups. Complementary to his focus on the societal and structural level, he was interested both in social and systems integration. For him the related issue of social order was of primary sociological concern.

Throughout his writings, Durkheim sought to develop a science of society. Like his compatriot, Comte before him, he believed that it is possible to uncover certain laws of society which influence the behaviour of individuals whether they know it or not. He separated off sociology from psychology and confined the former to the study of the effects of the social on groups and individuals and excluded issues of personal meaning. This approach shaped his understanding of the relationships between the core dualisms.

Durkheim: Social Integration/System Integration

The prime focus of Durkheim's work was on integration, the study of which also required him to consider the relationship of the individual to society. Durkheim argued that all societies are characterised by a *collective conscience*. The collective conscience refers to shared values, norms, ideas and beliefs in a given society. In traditional societies religion is the basis of the collective conscience and in more complex societies individualism, as, for instance, expressed in the philosophy of the Enlightenment, is the basis of the collective conscience. It was always a concern of Durkheim that an individualistic collective conscience or shared ethic had a tendency to promote egoistic and therefore socially disintegrative behaviour. He saw excessive rates of crime and deviance as evidence of development in this direction. However, it is arguable that the modern 'religion' or ideology of humanism, has provided a powerful, if less formalised, new basis of social morality for many.

Durkheim's first major work was *The Division of Labour in Society* (1893). In it, he contrasted the basis of social solidarity in traditional and more complex, mainly modern, societies. Solidarity or social unity is dependent on the type and degree of social integration. *Mechanical solidarity* is characteristic of traditional societies and is based on shared morality founded on belief in magic or religion. Thus, social integration is achieved by everyone being socialised into one community. As Craib succinctly puts it – in societies characterised by mechanical solidarity 'system integration is social integration' (84). Durkheim's work, *The Elementary Forms of Religious Life* (1912) sought to show how *collective representations and rituals* reinforced collective conscience in traditional societies and therefore also social solidarity and integration. Setting the matter of religious truth aside, he argued that from a social point of view religious worship is the worship of society itself.

Whereas Marx's interest in solidarity centred on issues of conflict and exploitation, Durkheim saw the complex division of labour in modern society as a means of integrating the social system, or, as he put it, as a basis of *organic solidarity*. This was because the high level of job specialisation in modern societies creates an equally high level of mutual dependence – people are integrated because the system requires them to be. Despite his argument that organic solidarity provided a new basis of integration, Durkheim was concerned that the decline of a shared moral basis in modern societies would weaken social solidarity. He considered that one function of the modern education system is to strengthen common morality but he also recognised that the opportunities which it offers to individuals might also free them from traditional social constraints.

Durkheim's analysis of the law and justice in *The Division of Labour in Society* parallels his contrast between mechanical and organic society. Mechanical societies were characterised by what he termed *retributive* justice and organic societies by *restitutive* justice. The former type of justice is based on retribution on those who have offended against shared morality. In organic societies, however, the basis of justice tends to shift from the moral to the contractual. Thus, restitutive justice restores to the aggrieved party that which is contractually theirs. The system of justice in societies characterised by organic solidarity increasingly reflects the need to resolve the many practical issues which emerge from inter-dependence rather than the settling of matters in terms of moral 'right and wrong'. Many laws reflect organisational and bureaucratic necessity rather than morality and the increase in civil suits also reflects people's need to settle practical conflicts of interest. However, there remains an effective consensus in relation to many major criminal offences whether based on religious or human morality. As Durkheim anticipated, in the case of law and justice, modern individualism has led to much resort to the law in pursuit of perceived rights and grievances.

Durkheim: Individual/Society and the Scope of Sociology

As the previous paragraphs illustrate, Durkheim considered that there is distinct collective or social level of operation and experience which cannot be reduced to nor understood simply as the aggregate of the free actions of individuals. For him, society is more than the sum total of the actions of its individual members – rather it is collectively embodied in norms, values and other constraining entities which have a real and in many cases quantifiable effect on people. In addition to religion, another example of a collective or social phenomenon is the law. He argued that formally codified law played a growing part in establishing social solidarity in modern societies, although as discussed above in modern societies the law itself reflects more individualistic values and norms. The following quotation from Durkheim's 'Rules' is quite uncompromising in its assertion of the external (to the individual) nature of social facts and of their power to 'coerce'. He begins by indicating the immense scope and effects of social facts before giving a definition of social facts:

> But in reality there is in every society a certain group of phenomena which may be differentiated from those studied by other social sciences. When I fulfil my obligations as brother, husband or citizen, when I execute my contracts, I perform duties which are defined, externally to myself and my acts, in law and in custom. Even if they conform to my own sentiments and I feel their reality subjectively, such reality is still objective, for I did not create them ...
>
> Here then, is a category of facts with very distinctive characteristics: it consists of ways of acting, thinking, and feeling external to the individual , and endowed with a power of coercion, by reason of which they control him.
>
> (Durkheim: *The Rules of Sociological Method*:1,4)

Given that he believed society to exist and that it affects individual behaviour, Durkheim was determined to develop and set out effective means of studying it. His *Rules of Sociological Method* (1895) stipulates that sociologists must 'treat social facts as if they were things'. It is necessary to treat social facts in this way so that they can be more easily defined, isolated and their effects measured. He insisted that a given social fact can only be explained in terms of reference to other social facts – i.e., the social must be explained in terms of the social. This point will become clearer by referring to Durkheim's famous practical demonstration of his rules of method in his celebrated study of suicide.

Durkheim argued that the rate of suicide in a society is a social fact which can be explained in terms of other social facts. On the basis of a wide international comparative study of suicide statistics, he explained variations in the suicide rate between and within societies in terms of the degree of social integration of those societies. This was true of all four types of suicide that Durkheim indicated: anomic, egoistic, altruistic, and fatalistic. As the *Penguin Dictionary of*

Sociology (1994) succinctly puts it, anomic and egoistic suicide 'were most commonly found in modern societies where, as *The Division of Labour in Society* had previously shown, traditional forms of social regulation and integration like the *conscience collective* of mechanical solidarity had declined'. Anomic suicide is more likely to occur when the collective norms and values of a society are relatively weak in their capacity to integrate individuals. Durkheim illustrated this explanation by observing that suicide tended to increase during periods of rapid economic change, whether recession or expansion. Durkheim exemplified egoistic suicide with reference to the higher rate of suicide in Protestant than in Catholic societies which he considered reflected their greater individualism and corresponding lesser degree of social interaction. Altruistic and fatalistic suicide are more typical of traditional socieites. Altruistic suicide occurs when an individual is so identified with the social collectivity that s/he sacrifices his or her individual life for it. Hari-kari is often given as an example of the latter. Fatalistic suicide occurs when a person kills him or herself because society is perceived as offering no hope. In the case of all these types of suicide, it is either too little or too much social integration that explains the level of the suicide rate.

Durkheim, Marx and Weber

1) Theory and Method

There is an impressive consistency in Durkheim's model of society and in his method of studying it. In part, this consistency is achieved by 'bracketing off' issues of individuality to be studied by other disciplines, in particular by psychology. In his attitude to the role of the individual in society, Durkeim is closer to Marx than to Weber. This is partly because both Durkheim and Marx see sociology as a discipline primarily concerned with seeking explanations at the social rather than the individual level. Not surprisingly, therefore, their sociological models seem to depict individuals as very much in the power of social forces. The term positivism has been widely used to describe this approach although it is not a term one finds much in the writings of either man. However, both Marx and Durkheim's approach to causation, especially the latter's, is comparable to that of Comte, the founder of positivism. Comte famously stated that the purposes of sociology are to know, in order to predict, in order to control and in some of his writings Marx, too, seems to harbour a similar view of the subject. Such aspirations have proved absurdly ambitious. Even if it were possible to know so much about the present that the future could be predicted and controlled, it is doubtful whether such a state of affairs would be desirable. In particular, who would do the controlling? Pope Auguste Comte? However, while sociology cannot establish the laws of social functioning – because there aren't any – it can make informed generalisations and establish trends and probabilities. So sociologists are useful in research and planning. Studying the influence of social facts or factors on action has become a central task of sociology and a substantial methodology involving historical and comparative research, social surveys and the use of statistics has built up around it. Since the time of Comte, Marx and Durkheim, most sociologists have reduced their expectations about how precise social science can expect to be in relation to establishing causation and particularly in making predictions.

In contrast, Weber tried to build in an analysis of the experience and effects of individual values and action into his sociological model. He attempted to bridge the gap between individual and collective action by stipulating certain types of action into which individual action would fall. By this device he sought to generalise about social action – the Protestant ethic was an example of value-rational action – while also doing justice to individual action.

Whether or not Weber was wholly successful in this attempt, it is partly on the basis of his approach to individual and social action that his reputation as the great liberal sociologist rests.

2) Capitalist or Modern Society?

The fundamental views held by the founders of sociology deeply affected their work. Marx is clearly a sociologist of revolution and much of his work is about the inequality and exploitation of capitalist society and the conditions of social change, including the emergence of a collective agent of change. Weber was pre-eminently the sociologist of modernity for whom instrumental rationality, particularly in the form of bureaucracy was what characterised the new period. He was also the sociologist of liberalism and pluralism and rejected what he saw as the over-simplified and deterministic aspects of Marx's model. Durkheim's sociology is also based on a fundamental dichotomy between the traditional and the modern. Although Durkheim recognised and to some extent welcomed the growing individualism of modern society, there is a theme of profound social conservatism throughout his work. He was deeply concerned at the disorder and dis-integration brought about by the forces of modernity.

Whereas Weber's critique of modernity focused on instrumental rationality particularly as manifested by the iron cage of bureaucracy, Durkheim was more discomfited by the egoism which he found rampant in modern society. He understood that the ultimate logic of the pursuit of self-interest unconstrained and unguided by common law and morality would be social chaos. Like his predecessor, Saint-Simon, he toyed from time to time with suggestions about how a greater degree of social integration and cohesion might be achieved. One of his ideas was the founding of employer/worker communal organisations. Durkheim was a modernist in that he could see potential for progress in capitalist, industrial society but he believed that revolution was no short cut and that improvement could be most securely achieved cumulatively and therefore gradually. Although not illiberal, he was more conservative in his thinking than Weber. In particular, he ruled out as irrelevant on methodological grounds the latter's driving concern with individual meaning. In his focus on the collective aspects of social life and in his commitment to studying them along the lines suggested by the model of natural science model Durkheim has something in common with Marx. However, whereas Marx saw conflict as fundamental to capitalist society, Durkheim regarded order as a pre-requisite of civilised social life. This latter concern was taken up by the American Functionalist, Talcott Parsons, who was the dominant sociologist of the middle third of the twentieth century.

Conclusion

Marx, Weber and Durkheim were men of their time whose work retains substantial relevance – in many fundamentals if not in all detail – beyond their time. They achieved the creation of sociological models and concepts which have had enormous explanatory power throughout the modern period and retain much usefulness even in late modernity. Coming first, they had the opportunity to paint the big picture. However, they were not prophets and at the turn of the millennium, major attempts are being made to add fundamentally to their analyses and, where it seems necessary, to depart from them. Perhaps the deepest continuity between their work and contemporary social theory is less in inherited theory and more in the continuing attempt by sociologists to address the profound issues raised by the dualisms discussed recurrently in this chapter. Reviewing their work as various dialogues with the perennial dualisms – most importantly that of individual/society – makes it clear that no final 'answer' is possible or desirable as to how these core social processes inter-relate because societies themselves differ not only comparatively, but also individually over time. Nevertheless, if some are now trying seriously go beyond the legacies of Marx, Weber and Durkheim, the story of sociology throughout most of the twentieth century has been one of building on or, at worst, arguing about their work. It is to some of the main theoretical developments that occurred within fifty years of their deaths and within the long shadow of their influence – what for simplicity I refer to as 'the second wave of theory' – that I now turn.

SUMMARY

1. THE FOUNDING OF SOCIOLOGY: SOCIAL CONTEXT

Sociology was founded in Europe at a time of great economic, social and political change and developed largely as an attempt to understand and explain these changes. Prominent issues included industrialisation; urbanisation; the development of the capitalist and working classes; poverty, inequality and exploitation in Europe and the European empires; the struggle of working class people and later women for labour and political rights; and the maintaining of social order and stability during a period of profound and rapid change.

2. THE FOUNDING OF SOCIOLOGY: INTELLECTUAL CONTEXT

The intellectual and cultural climate which paralleled the above changes was the Enlightenment. Sociology itself greatly – though often critically – reflected the core ideas of the Enlightenment including a belief in:

◆ reason

◆ science

◆ humanism

◆ individual rights (in Marx's case the collective rights of the working class)

◆ progress

3. THE POLITICS OF THE FOUNDERS

Inevitably, the classic sociologists had different perspectives on these changes and this greatly affected their interpretations and the models of society they constructed. Marx was a revolutionary socialist and class conflict is at the heart of his model. Weber was a liberal and his model emphasises individual meaning and the conflict and negotiation of status and political groups as well as classes. Durkheim believed in individual rights but as a sociologist his primary focus was on social integration – a classically conservative priority.

4. CORE SOCIOLOGICAL DUALISMS

Although the classic sociologists presented different interpretations of society and social change to a greater or lesser extent, they addressed the same core dualisms or pairs of contrasting concepts. Their debates around these dualisms provide the central theoretical focus around which this book is written. These dualisms are:

◆ individual/society

◆ action (agency)/structure

◆ social integration/system integration

◆ micro/macro

◆ modernity/socialist society – capitalist society

The great intellectual clash between Marx and Weber stretches across these and other issues, and their work perhaps offers more insight into the character of our epoch than any other body of writing.

Chapter 2

The Second Wave of Sociological Theory (1914–1960)

> **Key Concepts**:
> humanism, labelling, populism, pragmatism, self, self-referential, social action/social system, stereotype

Introduction

In their different ways, the founders of sociology mixed hope and concern in their attitude to modern industrial society. Marx was dead long before the Bolshevik revolution of 1917 and although both Weber and Durkheim lived for a few years after the 1914-18 war, most of their works had already been published. Between the first and second world wars, substantial development in sociological theory occurred and in turn this reflected the reality of historical events. One tradition of Marxist thought was developed in the heat of action – by Lenin, Trotsky and others. A second tradition of Marxist thought, critical theory, often at odds with the first, was developed by a group of German academics who founded what came to be known as the Frankfurt school.

Otherwise, the centre of dynamism in the development of the discipline passed from Europe to the United States. There, two major theoretical models emerged – functionalism and symbolic interactionism – although it is arguable that the latter is more a series of related concepts rather than a fully developed model. Talcott Parsons, the most influential functionalist sought to integrate the work of Durkheim and Weber into a single model of society. George Herbert Mead was the main figure in the earlier development of symbolic interactionism. Although interactionism is the sociological theory most indigenous to the United States, Mead's concern with subjectivity and meaning echoes that of Max Weber. One other sociologist appears substantially in this chapter, Charles Wright Mills. Mills was something of a one-off, and typically, it is not clear where best to put him. An American, he owed more to European traditions of sociological thought, particularly to Marx and Weber, than to those of his own country. Nevertheless, he was a great synthesizer and there are clear strains of American *pragmatism* and *populism* in his work, not to mention a tough individualism of style that has no obvious parallel in Europe. Chronologically, his work comes towards the later part of the period covered in this chapter and I have given him the last word.

Marxism between the Wars

It is commonly observed that there are two legacies left by Marx reflecting two distinct and arguably incompatible strands in his work. First, is an almost mechanistic view of historical change which reflects an application of natural science thinking to social analysis. In this model, socialist revolution is presented as 'inevitable' due to the 'contradictions' of capitalist society. The other strand in Marx's thought is sometimes referred to as humanistic. It reflects a concern about human exploitation, alienation and loss of potential under capitalism. It is therefore a theory of liberation. However, in this interpretation of Marx the exploited are seen as liberators of themselves rather than as a sort of collective robot churning out pre-programmed historical change. For the proletariat to liberate itself it must become conscious of its position and exploitation in the capitalist system and organise to bring about change. Broadly speaking, the Bolsheviks and their successors adopted the first strand in the Marxist tradition and the Frankfurt school the second. In fact, the thinking of the Frankfurt school was partly a response to the perceived failures of the Bolshevik revolution and early Soviet society.

The Bolshevik Legacy: Marxist Leninism

This section will give an account of Bolshevism in terms both of individual freedom/democracy and equality. As we have seen, the concept of individual freedom was not one Marx saw as relevant in the transformation to socialism. What Marx did emphasise was equality of access to material and cultural resources – albeit 'after the revolution'. First, then, is the issue of individual freedom.

Neither the circumstances in which the Bolshevik revolution occurred nor the course it took conformed to Marx's own theory of revolution. According to his analysis, socialist revolution would occur in relatively mature capitalist society weakened by its own contradictions whereas, in fact, early twentieth century Russia was among the most feudal and industrially least developed of European societies. Further, because the Russian proletariat was small and limited in its power, it played quite a limited part in the development of the revolution which was largely the work of a small and committed group of revolutionary activist-intellectuals who exploited widespread social chaos and discontent caused by the war. However, by 1917 Marxism was the dominant international revolutionary ideology and had been adopted by Lenin, the leading Bolshevik.

Figure 2.1   Marxist-Leninism: Lenin imposed an authoritarian version of Marxism on the Soviet Union which was developed into fullscale totalitarianism under Stalin.

If the Bolshevik revolution itself did not conform to Marx's expectations of a proletarian revolution, he similarly cannot be held responsible for the extreme centralisation of power in the party and state under the Bolsheviks which reached its height under Stalin. Nevertheless, it is not difficult to find an incipient authoritarianism in Marx's work, not least, in his notion of 'the dictatorship of the proletariat' which he anticipated would pave the way to communism. Dictatorship is by definition both undemocratic and anti-democratic. It is a tragic gap in Marx's work that he did not devote a comparable amount of time to developing a theory of socialist democracy as he did to attacking liberal democracy. As a result of this omission, those who tried to put his ideas into practice did not have much to go on in this crucial area. Historically – and almost by definition – dictatorship is exercised by a single person or by a small group and never by a large class, particularly one with little experience in exercising power. The dictatorship that Russia actually got conformed to the more usual historical pattern of the rule of the many by the few.

Further, there is an implicit authoritarianism in Marx's schematic attempt to predict – perhaps prophesy would be a more accurate description – what would be 'the next stage' in history. Pretension to such knowledge is in itself authoritarian because it closes down, and in the extreme excludes rational and democratic debate about how to create the future. It is a short step from refusing to tolerate the expression of others' opinions to persecuting them. These are telling criticisms of Marx and they have a relevance not only to what others did in his name but to his theoretical model itself. Ironically, despite his powerful critique of the ideologically repressive role of religion, Marx himself adopted a quasi-religious approach to communism. Like millenarians who 'know' the date of the end of the world, Marx seemed to claim that he 'knew', if not precisely when capitalism would end, that it would certainly do so. It is the quasi-religious, utopian and prophetic element in Marx that a number of critics, including some ex-communists, satirize in such judgements of Marxism as 'the God that failed'.

Whether partly because Marx's theory was undemocratic or not, the major Marxist regimes of the twentieth century have been undemocratic and sometimes totalitarian. One of Lenin's more controversial contributions to the development of Marxist thought, was, then, to promote the role of activist-intellectuals and the vanguard party in leading the proletariat or, as it more often turned out, peasant masses in fostering the revolution (*What is to be Done*: 1905). Mao, Fidel Castro and others have put forward and practised a similar approach. It would be naive and unrealistic to criticise these revolutionaries for opposing with force undemocratic and often brutal regimes or for maintaining military discipline in the insecure days following revolution. The serious and damaging criticism of these revolutionary leaders is that the majority in whose name revolution had been undertaken were never themselves allowed to control democratically and therefore shape the new societies. Lack of democratic freedom and 'ownership' by the majority of their societies is one of the main reasons for the faltering of communism worldwide in the 1980s. There were experiments and initiatives in economic and even limited ones in political democracy in so-called communist societies prior to the collapse of the Soviet Union in 1989. However, as Milovan Djilas noted in *The New Class (1957)* the development of centralised state bureaucracies, including agencies of surveillance and control, was more typical of these societies. Whatever the flaws in Marx's own work, this presumably cannot have been what he intended.

The Soviet Union and Marxist regimes in general have a better record on the issue of equality than individual liberty and democracy. The Soviet Union developed an excellent public education system which enabled its people to be educated to a standard comparable to that achieved in the wealthier Western countries. Until the later part of the twentieth century it was able to compete with the United States in the area of technological development and application. Successive regimes pursued massive house building programmes to the obvious benefit of the people. China and Cuba have achieved comprehensive public health systems of real quality. These achievements appear not to have been sufficient to win the whole-hearted popular backing for these regimes. There are many reasons for this, including the spectacular economic success of the capitalist West and the equally taunting appeal of its greater political and cultural freedom. However, something of the ideal of socialist equality was achieved.

Lenin: 'The Final Stage of Capitalism'.

Lenin's essay, *Imperialism, the Highest Stage of Capitalism* (1916) made a substantial contribution to Marxist theory and continues to have some relevance in our own time. Lenin argued that capitalist imperialism developed as the rate of profit came under pressure in Western economies and companies went further afield in search of markets. In the latter part of the nineteenth century, the emphasis had been on extracting raw materials cheaply and in developing new international markets for manufactured products. In the early part of the twentieth century, a new form of imperialism had developed – *finance imperialism*. Finance imperialism was based on the investment of Western capital in poorer countries for the purposes of cheap labour and achieving a flow of income from profits. According to Lenin, finance imperialism was at the centre of the development of a new stage in capitalism – monopoly capitalism. He considered that the larger banks financed and largely controlled the development of world capitalism and that control and profitability was enhanced through the process of monopoly. Lenin thought that finance capitalism would be the final stage of capitalism. Like Marx he was confident that the contradictions of capitalism would ensure its downfall and pave the way to international socialist revolution:

> The extent to which monopolist capital has intensified all the contradictions of capitalism is well known. It is sufficient to mention the high cost of living and the oppression of the cartels. The intensification of contradictions constitutes the most powerful driving force in history, which began from the time of the definite victory of world finance capital.
>
> (Lenin, 'Selected Works' in Mills, 1967: 201)

With the benefit of hindsight, it is beginning to seem a little intellectually weak to imagine that the 'contradictions' of capitalism will conveniently conspire to engineer the downfall of the system. Nor, almost 100 years later, does Lenin seem right about capitalism being in its 'final phase'. To that extent, the Marxist claim to have developed a 'scientific' method of socio-historical analysis may seem weakened. Weber, of course, referred to Marxism as 'pseudo-science'. Be that as it may, it remains the case that the extreme inequalities created by what Lenin called 'monopoly capitalism' but which we now refer to as global capitalism are one of the pressing issues of the contemporary world. If world socialism is not the answer to the problems generated by world capitalism, a reasonable question remains – 'what is'?

Lenin: Freedom and Equality

Like Marx, Lenin's thought reflects the events and developments of his time. Even more so in Lenin's case, because he himself was at the heart of some of the key events of the period. Although Lenin ensured that a major experiment reflecting some sort of Marxism took place, it is arguable that he also sowed the seeds that would eventually cause the majority of people of Eastern Europe to turn away from Marxism. In the end, the powerful, centralised Communist state crumbled under the nationalistic and democratic aspirations of the peoples of Eastern Europe. China remains the last of the large-scale experiments in communism and the signs there are that economic liberalisation may not sit easily with political and cultural control and repression.

The most formidable criticism of both Marx and Lenin is that they failed adequately to conceptualise and, in the latter case, to deliver individual freedom. They saw individual liberty as either 'bourgeois freedom', which they dismissed, or as something which would develop in the collective context of a fully communist society – once this was attained. In fact, the relationship between equality and freedom is highly complex and contradictory. It is obvious that a regime of total equality would greatly restrict freedom because the huge individual differences between people would have to be controlled to prevent them producing inequality. Similarly, a regime of total freedom would produce massive inequalities – the unchecked expression of individual differences would ensure this. Neither equality nor freedom can exist as an 'absolute' or 'totality' without reducing or damaging the other. Another way of putting this is to say that as absolutes, these 'first principles' are contradictory. This, incidentally, is as much a criticism of regimes based exclusively or almost exclusively on free market principles as on wholly egalitarian ones – as a result, any society must seek some sort of balance or compromise between the two – of which there are many. Here is not the place to pursue the philosophics of this issue but it is a reasonable proposition to suggest that Marx and Lenin might have made a more measured, less politically rhetorical attempt to do so.

The Frankfurt School: Critical Theory

The Frankfurt school was a group of social scientists who came together at the Institute of Social Research at Frankfurt between the late 1920s and mid-1930s. Among its most influential members were Theodor Adorno, Max Horkheimer and Herbert Marcuse. Under the threat of Nazi persecution, leading members of the school emigrated to the United States in 1935 and re-established the institute at Columbia University, New York. The influence of the school continued through the work of some of its more prominent individuals after the Second World War. Marcuse, who died in 1979, became something of a guru to the American New Left during the 1960s. Hans Gerth became an important link figure between the Frankfurt school and the radical American sociologist, Charles Wright Mills (see pp. 54–58). Gerth and Mills worked together in Wisconsin and co-translated and edited *From Max Weber* (1948), a selection of the latter's key writings. Thereafter, Mills went to Columbia University where the influence of the Frankfurt school on his work continued to be apparent. The much younger Jurgen Habermas brought the influence of the Frankfurt School into the latter part of the twentieth century. Habermas is an original thinker in his own right and ranks among the great sociologists. His work is analysed in a later chapter in the context of his defence of Enlightenment ideals against the postmodern onslaught.

By the early 1930s, it was obvious to leading members of the Institute at Frankfurt that progress towards socialism was not proceeding smoothly. Already, political and bureaucratic repression in the Soviet Union had dimmed hopes of socialist liberation there and the Soviet example reduced support at the Institute for the official German communist party. In Germany, Fascism seemed to be winning its battle with the Left. The amount of popular support for Hitler and the Nazis among the lower middle and even working class was a cause of deep disillusionment among many left-wing intellectuals. Not only was the working class not emerging as the agency of historical change, large numbers of working people were becoming dangerously reactionary and a significant minority were inclining towards Fascism.

It became the central concern of the school to explain this crisis of socialism and particularly the apathy or hostility of many members of the working class to it. They found their answer in the area of cultural analysis and especially in the relationship between consciousness, ideology and the media. They argued that 'the masses' – i.e., many of the working and middle classes – were being seduced by the capitalist media into accepting the values of consumerism. Materialistic values expressed in the media, especially through advertising, were persuading people that fulfilment lay in commodity consumption rather than, as Marx had argued, in free, and non-alienated productive (creative) activity. If this analysis of capitalism has now become quite commonplace, this is partly due to the influence of the Frankfurt School. Much of the cultural analysis of the Left of the later part of the twentieth century, including some postmodernist writing, re-works themes raised and explored by the Frankfurt School. Along with their contemporary, the Italian Marxist, Gramsci, they shifted Marxist theory in the direction of cultural and ideological analysis and somewhat away from supposed contradictions in the economic infrastructure.

A second and related area of analysis developed by the Frankfurt School was the role of reason in social life. Perhaps because the topic seems somewhat abstract, their work in this area has been less widely diffused although it has been extremely influential among some radical intellectuals of the Left. They argued that in capitalist society reason had become the instrument of capitalist acquisitiveness or, simply, greed. Increasingly reason, including scientific thought, was used, not in the pursuit of high personal or public ideals but to make money or to gain control or both. Ironically, this analysis was closer to Weber than to Marx. Weber had argued that *instrumental rationality* embodied in bureaucracy had become the dominant type and expression of reason in modernity. There is no need to rehearse here the extent of Weber's concern and foreboding at this development. While the Frankfurt School argued that rationality was becoming subject to the pursuit of self-interest under capitalism, Weber linked instrumental rationality to modern bureaucratic structures in general, and particularly to their tendency to produce conformity. Nevertheless, the theme is basically the same and it has been constantly echoed throughout the twentieth century – arguably to little effect.

In his *Dialectic of Enlightenment* (1947), written with Max Horkheimer, Adorno (1903–69) was highly critical of Enlightenment reason, virtually identifying it with instrumental reason – a position Habermas was radically to revise later. Equally controversially, he was sweepingly dismissive of the scientific method – in this case rather narrowly identifying it with positivism. Arguably, it is his more constructive works which were his best. His last book, 'Aesthetic Theory' argued that in an age of instrumental rationality, art still provided a means for the subjective expression of critical and dissenting opinion. His liking for jazz and avant-garde classical music was partly based on their quality to disrupt the expected and predictable, including, by implication, these characteristics in capitalist society.

Adorno also believed that disciplined philosophical thought could provide a means for criticising the system. In particular, he developed an approach termed 'negative dialectics' which he believed could be used to go beyond simple criticism to the articulation of alternatives.

There is some debate about whether Adorno, despite his criticism of the Enlightenment, believed that informed consciousness provides a possible means to emancipation from the consumer capitalism as is perhaps implied in his commitment to philosophy. Against this is the view he developed from Freud, that social forces – such as consumerism – can stimulate and manipulate unconscious desires that can overwhelm conscious thought and judgement. It has also been suggested that he foreshadowed the French structuralists with his notion of 'non-identity' which posited that the surface level of identity is often socially imposed and that the 'materiality' of a given object is a more fundamental touchstone of identity. Adorno was a highly influential thinker but all the directions of his influence are not easily reconciled. He is clearly a substantial figure in his own right.

As far as social science was concerned the Frankfurt School rejected an approach based on 'a science seeking social laws' which they equated with positivism in favour of *critical reason* which they saw as 'intrinsically connected with the ideas of freedom' (Marcuse, quoted in Bottomore and

Nisbet *eds.*,1979:133). In order to make the observations they considered morally and humanly necessary, and to forward the cause of human liberation, they adopted a critical rationality. Thus, their approach became known as *critical theory*.

Adorno and Horkheimer's *Dialectic of Enlightenment*(1947), written in the United States, signalled many of the themes which members of the Frankfurt School were to address. Centrally, they contended that the Enlightenment project of human progress and liberation had become flawed because of the way it was being pursued. They argued that belief in the beneficial effects of technology and the material progress had marginalised the search for a better quality of human relations and cultural life. They were deeply pessimistic about modern 'mass' culture as it was developing in Western capitalist societies. Instead of uncritical acceptance of the prevailing direction of social development they advocated not merely critical theoretical analysis of the capitalist system but a reflexive self-awareness of the impact of the system.

Freud and the Frankfurt School: Enter the Psychoanalytic Perspective

Freud ranks alongside Marx and Darwin as one of the main seminal influences on twentieth century thought and he was no less controversial than either of them. Whatever one's opinion of Freud, there is no denying his impact, not only on social science and social theory, but on the way many people think about and interpret their everyday lives, including their relationships.

Freud's thought has entered sociology and social theory through several routes. Since the 1960s, Freud has figured in much feminist theory. Despite turning to him for conceptual framework and insight, feminists have often been sharply critical of Freud mainly because of his perceived chauvinism on matters of gender and sexuality. Freud has also had considerable influence on postmodernism. Through his interpretation of the meaning of dreams, Freud illustrated that the language of the unconscious is mainly visual and symbolic rather than verbal and literal. Poststructuralists and postmodernists have used the work of Freud and others to argue that much human behaviour can be explained in terms of the influence of structured codes (such as certain visuals used in advertisements).

In respect to the Frankfurt School, it is Freud's mapping of the psyche and his psycho-social theory or meta-psychology that was most influential. In the latter context, it is Freud's attempt to analyse the relationship between instinctual drives and social structure and control in *Civilisation and its Discontents* (first published in 1930) rather than his more specifically psychoanalytic writings that is the key text. Although no school named Freudian-Marxism was ever established – perhaps because the Frankfurt School was not dogmatic enough to fix such a label – their working together of Freudian and Marxist thought literally gave a new depth to social science – an awareness of the structure, processes and effects of the unconscious. What the Frankfurt School added was a fuller and more detailed understanding of the interaction between the individual and society. This went beyond Weber's typology of action to embrace how instincts, emotions, imagination and even fantasy inter-relate with culture.

The following outline of Freud's theory of the mind is necessarily brief and over-simplified. Freud's basic map of the psyche consisted of the id, ego and superego overlaid by the pleasure and reality principles. The id is the seat of the instincts – aggression and sexuality – which are 'civilised', respectively, into competitiveness and love through socialisation. Also located in the id is the unconscious part of the psyche, and its language is that of fantasy and dream – although these do relate back to the real world of everyday experience. That part of the id concerned with sexuality is governed predominantly by what Freud referred to as the pleasure principle, which describes the tendency of the id to seek instinctual gratification or, in more neutral biological terms, to seek energy release on some desired object. That part of the id concerned with aggression-competition is governed by the reality principle in that it is directed and disciplined by socially organised work. Freud considered that in order for society to function efficiently, both individual aggression and also pleasure-seeking, particularly sexual gratification, require to be controlled by the reality principle i.e., directed by society in an orderly way for the purpose of production/reproduction. Freud described the ego as the centre of the rational self – that part of the psyche that relates and filters the internal world of the psyche to the social world. The ego operates in tandem with the super-ego which is the framework of moral and normative guidance inculcated by a particular culture i.e., the superego internalises the particular content of the reality principle of a given society (thus, the values and norms of a Muslim society will differ from that of a secular capitalist one). Although not original in all its aspects, Freud's mapping of the psyche provides a framework for understanding and interpreting how individuals and groups relate psycho-dynamically to society. Even had Freud not further developed his basic theory of the mind, his would have been a substantial achievement but, in fact, throughout his long life he generated an array of social-psychological concepts and interpretations which others still struggle to employ or reject and in a few cases significantly to extend. Among two thinkers who notably extended Freud's ideas were two members of the Frankfurt School, Herbert Marcuse and Jurgen Habermas. Marcuse's work is presented below partly because it illustrates particularly strongly the influence of Freud. Habermas is presented later and in a still wider context as befits his status as a leading theorist of modernity.

Herbert Marcuse: Pleasure, Reality and Liberation

One of the boldest and most original interpreters of Freud was Herbert Marcuse (1898–1979)). In his period as a political refugee in the United States, he continued his reflections on repressive and liberating reason. His two works *Eros and Civilisation* (1955) and *One Dimensional Man* (1964) represent one of the most ambitious attempts by any of the Frankfurt School to integrate Freud and Marx.

In the early post second world war period, he began to argue that Western societies, particularly the United States, had achieved an adequate material basis to sustain a culturally and sexually liberated society. However, the opportunity to create and enjoy such a society had not been grasped because capitalist society was locked into a form of the reality principle which was repressive and manipulative. As Marcuse bluntly put it : 'Reason has conquered the world in the image of repression'(1954: 60). Repression had occurred not by force but by the creation of 'false needs' by capitalism. This requires explanation.

Along with Freud, Marcuse considered that all societies needed to direct sufficient energy of their members towards work (survival): the reality principle. Ensuring this requires a necessary degree of social control and repression of individual activity but beyond this members of a society could and, in Marcuse's view, should be free to pursue their own activity, including pleasurable activity. Marcuse argued that in capitalist societies far more repression of wage-workers was occurring than was necessary – *surplus repression* – because of the desire of capitalists to make as much profit as possible. Surplus repression, as Marcuse saw it, involved not only sexual repression – although this was the core repression – but also repression of emotional, artistic and intellectual potential which in Freud's model are partly forms of sublimated sexual energy (i.e., sexual energy transformed into in other activities). Marcuse and other members of the Frankfurt School were particularly concerned that mass culture under capitalism was manipulated in order to make people consume and conform. Instead of developing more of their human potential as was now possible, the creation of 'false needs' was producing a society of 'happy robots'. It was trivialising people's emotional sensitivities and undermining their creative potential. These arguments extended Marx's theory of alienation from the area of production to consumption. Thus, by his use of Freud, Marcuse attempted to give greater psychological depth and detail to Marx's theory of alienation and *commodity fetishism*.

Whereas Marx saw a way out of exploitation and repression for the working class, Marcuse was much more pessimistic. Marx was aware of the power of the dominant ideology to create 'false consciousness' among the proletariat and to confuse its members about their 'true' interests. Marcuse had concluded that false consciousness among the proletariat had become endemic and longterm if not permanent. The proletariat had been sealed into the capitalist system by consumerism and, as far as Marcuse could see there was little prospect of it breaking out. Marcuse had even less belief in the revolutionary potential of the growing numbers of white collar employees in the capitalist labour force than that of industrial workers. Departing sharply from Marx but consistent with most other thinkers of the Frankfurt School, he substituted the concept of 'mass society' for class analysis. The 'mass' or 'masses' were the majority of employees in capitalist society whom he considered to have been integrated into the capitalist system. Marcuse's view of the quality of 'mass culture' under postwar capitalism was highly critical. He regarded much media output as superficial and the obsession with consumerism at the core of the capitalist lifestyle as destructive of human value and potential. He coined the term *repressive desublimation* to describe the emotional and cultural character of this lifestyle. Freud used the term sublimation to describe what he regarded as the normal process by which raw instinctual energy – erotic but also aggressive – is transformed into creative and 'civilised' activity in the form of, among others, artistic and intellectual work. For Freud, sublimation is essential to civilised activity, including creative activity of the highest order. Marcuse's deeply pessimistic view was that sublimation in capitalist society had become so centred on commodity consumption and vacuous entertainment that it was not genuine sublimation at all. Rather, the quality of the leisure and cultural life of 'the masses' in mid-twentieth century capitalist society was so poor that it was better described by the terms 'desublimated' – and 'repressive desublimation'. As far as Marcuse was concerned, the creative potential of human nature was being undermined not only through alienating work but increasingly through capitalist consumerism – which was directing and shaping activity in a way that pacified while at the same time generating profits.

Despite the pessimism of *Eros and Civilisation* and *One Dimensional Man*, like all members of the Frankfurt School, Marcuse developed ideas about what a more liberated and culture and society might be like. It is arguably in this area that his thinking – never less than controversial – is at its most radical and, for some, shocking. Marcuse argued that whereas in the past economic necessity had meant that societies had been structured on the repressive work/survival values of the reality principle, the massive increase in productivity brought about by technology had greatly reduced the necessary amount of human labour. In this historical situation, Marcuse believed it had become rational to envisage a new reality principle based predominantly on the values of the pleasure principle rather than those of the 'old', work-based reality principle. Work would continue but – aside from what was necessary – it would become the free play of human activity. His distinction between necessary work and the *performance principle* is relevant here. Some societies, including capitalist ones, 'perform' more work than is necessary. Rather than driving on irrationally in this way, Marcuse suggests a more considered way of expending energy – including pleasurably. Marcuse conceded that this was utopian but he contended that utopianism had now become realistic because it was underpinned by material sufficiency, indeed surplus. What was lacking for the attainment of utopia, was the consciousness of its possibility and the imagination to bring it about. He came almost to regard it as his mission to keep this kind of 'realistic' utopian thinking alive at a time when culture had become 'one dimensional'.

As it turned out, Marcuse was unduly pessimistic. His writings and ideas became among the most popular points of reference for the young countercultural radicals of the 1960s. His thinking on sexuality resonated strongly with the sexual permissiveness and experimentation of the time. In particular, his reassertion of Freud's concepts of polymorphous sexuality – i.e., the sexuality of the whole body in infancy, potentially reclaimable in adulthood – and of universal early bi-sexuality provided a framework against which to interpret the burgeoning sexual revolution. For many young radicals, it was less the precise, often difficult, detail of Marcuse's work that mattered than his symbolic status as a guru-intellectual who appeared to endorse their politics and lifestyle. In his relatively late piece – *An Essay on Liberation* (1969), Marcuse went some way towards recognising radical students and intellectuals, if not as a new agency of social change, then as the dynamic group generating change. He had long since ceased to believe in the revolutionary potential of the working class.

Both Freud and Marcuse were well aware that the central place they gave sex and sexuality in their psycho-social models was likely to cause great offence and outrage. Driven partly by such reaction, Freud retreated from some of his more controversial findings and generally adopted a fairly conservative attitude to sexual control. In contrast, Marcuse was enthusiastic in his belief in sexual and human liberation. There is, then, no ducking the centrality of sex in the Freudian tradition. That said, it is equally important to stress that their analysis of sex and sexuality is only part of both their general social theories. There is a sense in which both consider sexual energy as symbolic of creative energy in general. Both were aware that creativity involves rational engagement as well as instinctual and emotional motivation. For Marcuse liberation certainly meant a restructuring of society – he called it 'socialism' – to provide greater opportunity, resources and freedom across the full range of human activity, not just the sexual.

It is not easy to find a balance in the work of so radical and uncompromising a figure as Marcuse but there is, nevertheless, a rational balance to be found there.

Functionalism

Whereas Marxism is based on the analysis that conflict reflecting differential class interests is the key social process, functionalism is based on the analysis that social order and consensus among its members is necessary if a society is to function effectively. Of course, Marxists appreciate that class divided societies can experience periods of order, and functionalists that social disorder occurs. Nevertheless, if conflict and consensus/order are two sides of the process of interaction and change, these two models are very different in the emphasis they make. In the case of Marxism, the political commitment to change through conflict is explicit and obvious even though Marx also claimed scientific status for his work. Functionalists do not generally claim so explicit a political commitment and the extent to which functionalism can be considered socially conservative in its implications is a matter of interpretation and judgement. What is clear, however, is that the model is premised on the assumption that societies require equilibrium and order effectively to function.

Many functionalists deeply resented the 'accusation' that their thinking was conservative. Most saw themselves as liberals in the sense that they were supporters of liberal democracy. For many of their Marxist critics and other radicals critical of what some referred to as the American military-industrial complex, this was conservative enough!

Talcott Parsons

The American sociologist Talcott Parsons (1902–79), established the framework of functionalism in impressive detail and on a grand scale. Other than Habermas, he is the most recent sociologist to attempt a comprehensive model of society comparable to that of the subject's founders. Parsons addressed directly the issues raised by the core sociological dualisms most notably in his *The Structure of Social Action* (1937) and *The Social System* (1951). He considered that his theory encompassed both individual action/meaning and systems/structure dimensions. He also substantially addressed the matters of both social and systems integration. His aim was to integrate the action theory of Weber's sociology and the collective perspective of Durkheim. His tendency to ignore Marx partly accounts for the de-emphasis of class conflict in Parsons' model although, as will become obvious, this is also partly a consequence of the properties of the model itself.

Parsons' sociological theory went through three broad stages of development. Although these stages involved changes of emphasis they built upon each other. These were the action framework; the systems or structural functional framework; and the exchange framework. However, it is the middle phase which had the greatest influence and on which his reputation rests.

The Theory of Social Action

The action framework can be fairly briefly dealt with. Parsons' *Structure of Social Action* is more voluntarist in tone than his later work but still gives substantial emphasis to the social constraints on actors. According to Parsons, social actors can be individual or collective and are capable of striving to achieve goals which reflect subjective meaning. Actors have different personality orientations which will influence their social opportunities. Social norms provide a means for achieving and choosing goals. However, action does not take place within a vacuum but within a situational context or environment comprised of physical, social and cultural elements. Crucially for the whole character of Parsons' theory, he states that human actions always exhibit the properties of the social system. His key concept of *unit act* embodies both individual and social elements.

Parsons' central concern with the issue of social order is stated in the *Structure of Social Action*. For him, the problem is how the pursuit of individual goals is reconcilable with the general achievement of social order. His answer follows Durkheim in that he argues that individuals internalise social values, norms and behaviour patterns and in so doing act in a way that reflects and reproduces social order. Whereas the work of the symbolic interactionists examined below concentrates mainly on theorising social action, the balance of Parsons' work, especially his later work, is about the social system.

Figure 2.2   Parsons was one of the last 'grand' or 'total' theorists.

In his middle period, Parsons examines how actions are 'congealed' or channelled into socially functional systems. The evaluation of Parsons' theory given later is based mainly on how he executed this major theoretical task. However, in order to establish how Parsons conceived the integration of action and the social system, an outline of the latter must be given.

The Social System and Sub-systems: Structural Functionalism

Parsons argued that social systems, like biological systems, must meet four functional *prerequisites* if they are to achieve longterm survival. These are : *adaptation; goal attainment, integration, and latency or pattern maintenance* . What Parsons means by these terms is given immediately below and then the way they are met by the social system is broadly described.

Adaptation refers to the need of a system to adapt to its environment;

Goal Attainment refers to the need for a system to harness resources in order to achieve its objectives and the satisfaction or gratification that it brings;

Integration refers to the need for a system to coordinate its various parts and sub-systems and deal with disorganisation and deviance;

Latency or Pattern maintenance refers to the need for a system to maintain a state of equilibrium (in the case of the human body this involves maintaining a constant temperature and a regular heartbeat).

The four prerequisites are sometimes referred to by the acronym AGIL.

Four subsystems respectively meet the four functional prerequisites of the general system action. The pairings are as follows:

Economy	Adaptation
The Polity (Political System)	Goal Attainment
Societal Community	Integration
Cultural (Socialisation)	Pattern Maintenance

The economy is the key social sub-system concerned with material survival (which in Marx's model is largely covered by his analysis of labour, production and markets). The polity functions to enable the goals of society to be established and decided upon. The function of the societal community is to ensure that the institutions of society work together reasonably effectively. This is a function of social control and coordination and is based on the enforcement/observation of rules whether these are consensual or imposed. In more functionally differentiated societies, there exists a complex of institutions, including the police and judicial system, which execute this function. Socialisation refers here to the cultural values and societal norms into which individuals are inculcated. This process enables individuals to conform to the general patterns of behaviour in a given society. Families, the education system and the media are major agents of socialisation.

Parsons argues that the social system like biological systems seek to survive, and that this requires a degree of order. Survival requires the maintenance of *equilibrium*. If the four subsystems are functioning effectively, social equilibrium will be maintained. The role of the cultural subsystem is particularly important in contributing to equilibrium because it socialises individuals into the values, norms and behaviours of a given society. Parsons considers that such *consensus* is necessary for the efficient functioning of society. This prioritisation of social consensus over conflict has led Marxists and other radical sociologists to argue that Parsons' model has a built-in conservative bias.

Parsons described three systems of action which congeal or organise actions of individuals: the personality system; the social system; and the cultural system. The personality system is the product of socialisation by which individuals are oriented to gratification in socially prescribed ways. The social system is the product of the creation of norms, values and roles through interaction over time and which structure present action. The cultural system is the framework of beliefs which influence action. In this formulation of systems of action the systems tend to dominate if not determine action – even the individual personality is presented as being constructed from the outside. However, in so far as society is characterised by a variety of acceptable values, beliefs, norms and roles, individuals are presented with a range of potential choices.

An informed assessment of Parsons' work in terms of the dualisms cannot be made without commenting on his typology of pattern variables. As Ian Craib points out, the pattern variables bring together two concerns in his work: 'the voluntaristic theory of action, concerned with individual choices, and systems theory'(1992:45). The main pairs of pattern variables refer both to choices of the social actor and also to the general characteristics of particular social systems. The main pairs of pattern variables are:

Particularism-universalism: A social actor may treat an individual, group or object as unique or as one of a general class – e.g., 'my' local M P / politicians. From a social systems point of view, Parsons argued that the evolution from traditional to modern societies is characterised by the development in the public sphere of universal rules governing social roles and a decline in appointments based on birth, privilege and favouritism (i.e., particularistic criteria).

Affective-affective neutrality: A social actor may become involved with another or others at the level of emotion and feeling or maintain a non-emotional, instrumental relationship – e.g., a lover/ a customer.

Quality-performance: A social actor may value an object or a person intrinsically i.e., for their own sake, or for the use they can be put to e.g., the difference between buying a work of art because of its perceived artistic value or simply as an investment.

Diffuseness-specificity: A social actor may become involved in a broad relationship or one with a specific purpose e.g., a relationship with close friends/ a relationship with a shopkeeper or a bus-conductor.

Parsons sees an historical tendency for the second in all the above pairings to emerge more prominently. They are all characteristics of character/actions and institutions in modernity whereas the first of all the pairings tend to be more predominant in traditional societies. As is usual with Parsons, aspects which define individual behaviour are also features of society or a particular social institution and vice-versa. Thus, because modern societies generate a greater range of specific roles – especially in the workplace – individuals in modern societies are likely to experience a wider range of roles both in relation to others and through performing more roles themselves than was typical in traditional societies. What some critics object to in Parsons' systems approach is the implication they take that it is the functional adaptation/evolution of systems rather than social actors that is the main emphasis.

The Exchange Framework

In this period of his work, Parsons retained the basic assumptions of his systems approach and concentrated on how the subsystems functioned together to form the total social system. The exchange between the systems can be material or symbolic. Thus, the family as an integrating institution provides labour for the economy and receives wages. The exchange between the family and the polity involves mainly loyalty/leadership and compliance/decisions. He further described a series of mainly symbolic exchanges throughout the social system. During this period, Parsons also did a lot of work illustrating the relationship of different functional systems and different pattern variables. Parsons drew on cybernetics which involves the concept of system self-adjustment which some saw as a further shift to an impersonal and 'objectifying' approach to social analysis.

Comment on Parsons' Work

In evaluating Parsons' sociological theory, it is helpful to begin with Guy Rocher's key observation that Parsons' model is mainly descriptive rather than explanatory – although it is obvious that this was not Parsons' intention (1974). To the extent that Parsons' work appears descriptive it is because he presents the 'functionings' of society almost as a mechanic might present those of a motorcar. However, Rocher's insight opens the way to the familiar criticism that Parsons' model lacks human dynamism and direction. Sociology is concerned not merely with describing the structure and functions of systems and institutions but also with *why* people act in particular ways, and Parsons' approach fails to do the latter. This point is extended below. What accounts for the apparently dehumanised quality of Parsons' model, given his stated intention to make meaningful action the foundation and starting point of his theory and given that he does, in fact, incorporate into his model concepts which seem to meet this intention (e.g., action, meaning, choice)?

First, even taken simply at the level of theory – setting aside issues of its application to the real world – Parsons' model emphasises the influence of society on social actors rather than the power and scope of actors to influence society. This is despite his explicit and often stated intention to produce a theory that integrates both sides of the action/structure dualism. A major reason for this is that the inspiration for the model lies in the natural sciences, particularly biology, in which human agency generally enters only marginally into the explanatory process. What Parsons takes from natural scientific theoretical approaches is, above all, the concept of system. This is not surprising because non-human species do behave overwhelmingly in instinctually programmed systematic ways (whereas many would contend that, to a greater or lesser extent, human beings act consciously). Just as the body can be divided into various subsystems, so, according to Parsons, can society be divided into four subsystems which meet basic human social needs. So far and descriptively, Parsons is right but the crucial difference between biological systems and human social systems is that whereas the former operate mainly through unconscious, automatic processes, societies are to a much greater extent run consciously and, because debate over decisions occurs, less predictably. It is highly significant that two main concepts that Parsons borrows from biology are those of 'equilibrium'(or 'homeostasis') and 'adaptation'. He transfers the concept that biological systems have mechanisms and processes to maintain a stable state or equilibrium to society. These two concepts address respectively issues of order and change and reveal the extent of the influence of evolutionary biological theory on Parsons' social systems model. The social system is assumed generally to seek orderly equilibrium so that 'it' can function effectively. Change occurs and the system evolves because of the need of one part to adapt functionally to changes in other parts – say, family size/structure changing in relation to the demands of the industrial economy. Thus, by his choice and particular use of a predominantly natural science model on which to base his analysis of society, Parsons produces a rather mechanistic, or rather, biologistic theory of society.

A second point which explains the allegedly dehumanised quality of Parsons' theory is that the empirical reference is used to support the abstract theories rather than giving rise to them. Even his specific applications of his theoretical postulations towards the later part of his career had an 'added on' quality. Parsons' theoretical approach and assumptions can be clarified further by contrasting it with that adopted by sociologists who have more effectively incorporated the concept of individual/group motivation and interaction into their theoretical approaches. The relative success of, for instance, Max Weber and Charles Wright Mills in achieving accounts of social life based on human action is partly founded on their extensive use of historical/comparative material i.e., theory and empirical data have a complementary and equal relationship. Mills himself made this criticism with admirable succinctness:

> The basic cause of grand theory is the initial choice of a level of thinking so general that its practitioners cannot logically get down to observation. They never, as grand theorists, get down from the higher generalities to problems in their historical and structural contexts ...

> (1959: 33)

The crucial point of difference is that an approach which focuses primarily on the actions of groups and individuals is distinguished by its concentration on what people do and why they do it, rather than the supposed functioning of systems. As will be discussed later, this different starting point results in the production of a different kind of sociology: the one being an analysis of action in particular structural contexts and the other being an analysis of systems. Weber approached sociology predominantly in the former way as did Mills himself. Because the emphasis of Weber and Mills is on people unpredictably making history within social constraints, both of them use a mass of empirical data of an historical and/or comparative kind to illustrate agency and diversity, whereas Parsons uses such material to illustrate how he thinks systems function. Thus, for Mills power is a resource individuals and groups struggle for and often use self-interestedly whereas Parsons concentrates on the necessary use of power in running society i.e. on the functional and, he seems to think, largely neutral and consensual use of power.

Weber and Mills considered society to be made up of and by groups whose members interact with one another in a vast variety of ways but roughly along the spectrum of cooperation-competition-conflict. Marx particularly focused on class groupings and the conflict between them, although, like Parsons, he often reduces action to a function of his grand scheme. Weber brought ethnic and other forms of status groups more into the sociological account. Sociologists influenced by feminism have radically altered how women are perceived within sociology. It is the relations between groups – classes, ethnic, gender or whatever – which make up the substance of this approach to sociology. The only way satisfactorily to practise this sociological approach is in a comparative and, especially, in an historical way. The only way to know what individuals and groups do and why they do it is to study their actions and – with appropriate scepticism – their pronouncements. History provides the factual detail necessary to test and illustrate sociological theory and, in addition to providing factual data, comparative study provides insight into how and why societies and their members differ or resemble each other. Parsons is right that the functional imperatives he points to are universal because they meet fundamental human needs but beyond that important fact, the ways societies meet or do not meet these needs varies enormously. Social variety is largely a product of human action. It is the action side of the action/structure dualism that Parsons is weakest on.

It is arguable that there is nothing in Parson's functionalist sociology that prevents the study of the interaction of groups in historical and comparative context. After all, he seeks and seems to claim that his social systems theory can accommodate all other relevant sociological theory. Parsons does not substantiate this claim. In practice he develops his model overwhelmingly towards the functioning of systems rather than the actions of individuals and groups. This does not at all mean that his work is of no use to other sociologists. He is hardly alone in failing to integrate the two sides of the core sociological dualisms! Parsons' analysis of the structural/systems side generated or clarified a stream of concepts which remain current in sociology and which it is difficult even for 'non-Parsonites' not to use. Nevertheless, Anthony Giddens, one of Parsons' foremost critics specifically disavows the use of sociological concepts such as function or adaptation which seem to endow social structure with a will of its own. In particular, Giddens opposes social theory that rest on assumptions of systems evolution rather than the actions of people (see pp. 141–2 – for further discussion of this point).

In any case, merely to make occasional use of some of Parson's many concepts is far short of what he intended. For those who adopt a functionalist model, he achieved much more than that and some would put him in the first rank of sociological theorists. He did succeed in establishing a framework of sociological theory – commonly known as functionalism – which others have built on, including George Murdock and Robert Merton. However, it sustains the argument made above that Parsons emphasises systems rather than action and that it is also the former aspect that these two and other functionalists have chosen to develop. Murdock analysed 'the family' in exclusively functionalist terms – arguing that the nuclear family is universal and that only it can satisfactorily meet all the functions of sex, reproduction, education (socialisation) and economics. Many sociologists have criticised this account of 'the family'. In particular, a number of feminists have argued that the single-parent family can adequately meet the needs indicated by Murdock, particularly if assisted by other adults or the state, and that the single-parent family should not be regarded as either a dysfunctional or as a deviant family form. Rather than present the nuclear family as the norm and other family forms as 'deviant, many contemporary sociologists contend that 'families' are characterised by a 'plurality' of forms.

Robert Merton's influential model of conformity and non-conformity (a broader term than deviance) is also heavily oriented towards the systems/structural rather than to subjective action/meaning. He conceives of nonconformity in terms of deviation from the values or means (i.e., of achieving goals) of mainstream society. Nonconformity occurs in four main types: innovation, ritualism, retreatism and rebellion (see Table 2.1)

In principle, such a typology does not preclude an account of why, subjectively, individuals are so categorised but in practice, such accounts are seldom offered. Indeed, it is part of Parsons' model that individual action and interaction are oriented towards social norms and values to the point where they are not considered in terms of their subjective meanings. As has frequently been argued, Parsons presents an *oversocialised* view of the social actor to the point where s/he scarcely seems to act with any autonomy at all. This emphasis is carried over into the work of Merton on nonconformity and into his standard book on social problems written with Robert Nisbet, *Contemporary Social Problems* (1976). Again, in the latter book, individual behaviour is seen primarily in terms of how functional or dysfunctional it is from the point of view of how the social

TABLE 2.1 MERTON: CONFORMITY AND NON-CONFORMITY

	Culture goals	Institutionalised means
1 Conformity	+	+
2 Innovation	+	−
3 Ritualism	−	+
4 Retreatism	−	−
5 Rebellion*	±	±

This fifth alternative is on a plane clearly different for that of the others. It represents a transitional response which seeks to institutionalise new procedure orientated toward revamped culture goals shared by members of the society. It thus involves efforts to change the existing structure rather than to perform accommodative actions within this structure, and introduces additional problems with which we are not at the moment concerned.

(Source: Taken from Peter Worlsey, ed., Modern Sociology, 1978:619)

system works rather than in terms of and motives and meanings of social actors. It was the symbolic interactionist, Howard Becker, who was the first to reverse this order of priority in respect to 'deviance' and 'social problems'.

I will not review here the various more recent attempts to revive and reconceptualise functionalism some of which have been highly ambitious and well received. Perhaps the real issue in assessing Parsons is whether, in fact, he did veer sharply towards presenting society as a system which he thought could be analysed in a neutral scientific way. Mills thought he did and criticised him for it and, in turn, presented a radically different approach to sociology based on the tradition of the humanities.

Symbolic Interactionism

Symbolic interactionism is concerned with how society is constructed through the meaningful interaction of individuals. It represents a more sustained attempt than Weber's to understand society in terms of individual action and interaction. Whereas Weber generalised social action into four broad types which he then used mainly to facilitate structural analysis, symbolic interactionists typically give much closer attention to the details of subjective and immediate inter-subjective level of experience in both their theoretical and empirical work. As might be expected, therefore, much symbolic interactionist research occurs at the micro or middle level. For instance, it is the individual and group experience of, drug taking (Becker,1963; Young, 1970), the strategies for coping with institutional domination and control of the 'mad' or imprisoned (Goffman, 1961; Taylor and Cohen, 1976), which indicate the typical level of interactionist analysis. Society is not described in terms of systems or structures 'external' to individuals which 'act upon' them although there is an explicit consideration of the social structural dimension in Mead's work. The collective side of social existence is also recognised in the concept of 'shared meanings'. In their focus on the symbolic and the inter-subjective construction of society rather than on social systems and structures, symbolic interactionists are sometimes compared to postmodernists. However, there are many substantial differences between the two approaches, notably, the greater emphasis of interactionists on consciousness and the power of agency. The fundamental intellectual thrusts of the two approaches are, in fact, antagonistic, symbolic interactionism being relatively voluntaristic and postmodernism, despite conceptual contortions to the contrary, relatively deterministic.

George Mead and Herbert Blumer

George Herbert Mead (1863–1931) was the founder of symbolic interactionism although it was his close colleague Herbert Blumer who actually coined the term 'symbolic interactionism' and assembled and edited Mead's, *Mind, Self and Society*(1934) after the latter's death. According to Mead, 'it is the self that makes the distinctively human society possible' (quoted, Oxford Dictionary of Sociology:589). Although Mead thought of himself as a social psychologist, his three concepts of the I, Me and Generalised Other stipulate a strong social influence in individual development (although not as strong as that insisted on by Durkheim). The self develops in a dynamic relationship with society (others). The 'I' is the creative, acting ego: the 'Me' is the socialised self comprised of the organised attitude of others, such as parents. Mead describes two stages through which the self develops: the 'play' stage and the 'game'stage. Both aspects of the self are engaged in these stages. The play stage is characterised by the trying out of various social roles – often these performed by 'significant others' such as mother or father. In the game stage, the individual is able to conceptualise beyond specific roles to the values and norms of the whole society or Generalised Other. Crucially, however, the individual does not necessarily internalise wider social morality in an unquestioning way but has the capacity to evaluate and accept or reject them. In other words, the developed or mature self has consciousness and the capacity to make moral (and other) judgements and choices.

Mead observed that the main medium through which social interaction and communication takes place is language and symbols: thus, Symbolic Interactionism. Language is the chief means through which people construct and communicate meanings. Meaningful thought and communication is intimately related to purposeful practical activity and so the continuous construction and reconstruction of society is itself meaningful. Mead saw society as a web of meaningful symbolic communication and purposeful action rather than as a set of structures or systems external to the individual. In arguing that society is a symbolic construction, Mead foreshadowed the poststructuralists and postmodernists although he gave much greater emphasis than many of them to the capacity of people to construct and interpret their own meanings as opposed to merely internalise dominant ones. However, it was later interactionists such as Erving Goffman and Howard Becker who explored more empirically the extent to which individuals and groups can and do disagree about or negotiate the meaning and significance of many actions and symbols (see below).

Mead's view that people can use words and symbols to convey their own meanings has been described above and demonstrates that he believed that consciously directed individual action is central to social process. He considered that the *Self is conscious of itself and others* and this is also related to language. The ability to name objects, feelings and ideas enables individuals not only to talk with others but also to conduct internal dialogues with themselves. These internal dialogues are virtually synonymous with thinking and, in so far as they assume the capacity to consider between alternatives, also imply the capacity to choose which is central to human agency. *Self-referentiality* is related to self-consciousness and is the capacity to think and act with one's own priorities and feelings in mind. This is another concept which is very similar to one currently in widespread use, reflexivity, which is especially favoured by Anthony Giddens.

Mead's analysis of the capacities of the Mind and Self made a lasting and crucial contribution to the tradition of sociological theory that emphasises individuality and agency. However, he appreciated that most people do not radically change society. Generally, the greater the capacities of the mind, the greater the potential of the individual or Self to affect society. Mead was particularly concerned to refute the influential social behaviourism of J. B. Watson which explained human behaviour in terms of external stimulus.

Blumer made several distinctive contributions to the development of symbolic interactionism. He both further developed the concept of the self and the interactive dimensions of symbolic interactionism. However, he did not acknowledge a social structural dimension. First, Blumer further developed the concept of self-referentiality and self-interaction explicitly to include the concept of choice. This was explained in term of the self's capacity to think through alternative courses of action rather than in terms of external options. Thus, a student may think through the various consequences of taking or not taking a given course. Centrally for symbolic interactionism and all relative voluntaristic approaches to social theory, such self interactions are regarded as 'real' rather than as either the consequences of external stimulus or as illusionary. A related and comparably important conceptualisation was that objects acquire meanings as a result of the actions actors take to them. Thus, the world football cup may be symbolic of great achievement to the winners but a source of money to someone who steals it. This relationship between meaning/act/object has been substantially adopted by Giddens in his structuration theory (see pp. 142–5).

Second, Blumer fleshed out the concept of interaction. He introduced the concept of *joint action* which are the acts of a number of individuals which produce organisation and in some cases routinised actions characteristic of *an* organisation. The totality of joint acts form society. This was no more than an embryo attempt to deal with the issue of individuality/society and agency/structure from an interactionist point of view. However, Blumer simply sees joint acts as being comprised of individually meaningful acts with organisational consequences and does not raise the structural dimension. Two problems are obvious. First, the sense that many have of society and organisations being a constraint on individuality and autonomy is not addressed (though later interactionists did deal with this issue – see below) Second, the inheritance of many past interactions codified into laws and rules which constrain those in the present was not dealt with.

Blumer's use of the concept of *shared interpretation* further clarified the organisational aspect of social interaction. By interpreting actions in the same way actors are able to progress action. For instance, a shared view of what the colours of traffic lights mean helps both drivers and pedestrians to know what to do on the roads. He emphasises that re-interpretation occurs continuously and that it needs to be communicated for the purposes of continued smoothly routinised interaction.

Put in extreme form, the difference between sociologists who emphasise agency and those who emphasise structure are that the former explain human conduct in terms of the reasons and motives of actors and the latter in terms of external causes. It will be obvious that symbolic interactionists incline to the former point of view. However, if it is fair to suggest that Parsons has an 'over-socialised' view of human beings, it is less fair to suggest that interactionists have an 'under-socialised' one. The individual can only develop a 'full' self through the acquisition of language and symbolic literacy and so through exposure to the meanings of others: it is only in the social context of symbolic interaction that the limited autonomy of the individual is possible.

Erving Goffman and Howard Becker

It would be impossible here to cover even the main contributions of two such substantial social theorists as Erving Goffman (1922–82) and Howard Becker (1928–). What it is possible to show from their work is the extent to which they built the concept of power into symbolic interactionist theory. The purpose of doing this is to demonstrate that although there is not a developed structural dimension to symbolic interactionism, even broadly conceived, it does provide substantial analysis of the use of power, particularly symbolic power, at the small and middle range.

Whereas Becker has spent many years at Chicago University, the former academic base of Mead and Blumer, Goffman lived and worked in California. However, they were contemporaries and both showed signs of imbibing the radical ethos of the 1960s when each produced some of his best work. Unlike European radicals whose social perspective is generally focused on material and cultural inequality both of them were far more concerned with how some individuals or groups use power in relation to others. Beyond this, there were many differences between Goffman and Becker. Goffman did not want to be identified with any particular theory and was, in fact, quite eclectic in his use of theoretical sources. On the other hand, Becker employed and developed a series of concepts which were organically connected to earlier symbolic interactionism.

Both Goffman and Becker developed a fuller social dimension to symbolic interaction, not as some British sociologists were later to attempt by linking interactionist theory to structural concepts such as class and racial stratification, but by taking account of – if not always fully analysing – institutional power. In particular, both Goffman and Becker consider the power of institutional officials, such as doctors and police, to define certain others as, in various ways, deviant and so requiring treatment or correction. However, in looking particularly at how interactionists treat the wider sources of power, it is important not to lose sight of the fact that it is the small and middle range of interaction that primarily interests them. In this respect, it is worth recalling Goffman's definition of social interaction as 'environments in which two or more individuals are physically in one another's presence' (1983:4). Although the bulk of Goffman's own work is concerned with interaction so defined, many interactionists, including Becker, reach far beyond. Nevertheless, interactionism has never produced or, perhaps sought to produce, a fully developed analysis of the macro level of social structure.

Goffman's first published book, *The Presentation of Self in Everyday Life* (1959), was close to Mead in describing the self as conscious, knowledgeable and as capable of directing his or her action within a given social context. His use of the dramaturgical metaphor to explore the possibilities of self-presentation in micro social contexts produced an analysis of the self that was skilled almost to the point of being calculating! Goffman's analysis of the self as composed of 'character' and 'performer' which can come together in 'the self as performed character' integrates agency and the social (quoted Williams, 1998: 155). Although Goffman emphasises the capacity of the individual to act or perform (agency), the influence of the social on the self is prominent in his early work. First, character is formed in relation to significant others. Second, individuals act or perform in relation to significant others. Third, and relatedly, Goffman stresses the extent to which individuals take heed of social rules, rituals and conventions. The influence of Durkheim is almost as apparent in the work of Goffman as that of Mead.

Goffman's second book, *Asylums* (1961), as its title suggests, deals with interaction within a very specific institutional context, that of a mental hospital. Robin Williams suggests that Goffman introduces a second version of the self in this work which incorporates the version just given but adds the formative impact on the self of organisational arrangements. It may be that this emphasis is the result of the fact that here Goffman is analysing a particularly oppressive type of institution, indeed, a 'total institution'. In any case, perhaps the most memorable feature of the book in relation to the self is the variety of responses to institutional totalitarianism. At the heart of this work is Goffman's description and categorisation of five possible *modes of adaptation* adopted by inmates in the face of 'the mortification of self' which he sees as systematically occurring in asylums (and other 'total' institutions such as prisons). The modes of adaptation are as follows:

Situational withdrawal	ignoring, as far as possible, the surrounding environment
Intransigent line	refusal to cooperate
Colonization	accepting the institution as home, becoming institutionalised
Conversion	accepting the staff's definition of reality
Playing it cool	getting by and hoping to get out with the minimum of trouble

Goffman's analysis substantially illustrates the resourcefulness of self – very much in the Meadian tradition – but he does so by relating the self to an institutional context, in this case a total institution. In a chilling phrase in which he refers to the possible 'destruction of self' through institutional oppression, he makes it quite clear that self assertion does not necessarily have a positive outcome (49). Goffman does not reduce institutional oppression to the individual actions of various staff although it is their actions that mediate institutional rules and values. He gives an almost Durkheimian presentation of the objectivity of social constraints. The processes of *mortification* carried out on inmates by staff reflect institutional procedures established at a level above the latter's individual authority and will. Even in his early work, therefore, Goffman is envisaging that interaction can be shaped and constrained by power and rules established outside of the immediate context of interaction. Robin Williams argues that Goffman develops a 'third version' of the self incorporating both performance and social determination but it is highly arguable that both elements characterise Goffman's concept of the self from the beginning (see p. 53 for further discussion of this point).

As Derek Layder notes, Goffman does not merely recognise by implication the institutional level of power and decision making (1997: 11–12), he explicitly refers to the 'institutional order' as well as the 'interaction order' and in Layder's view 'his work must be viewed as an attempt to trace the ligatures (connections) that bind institutional constraints and resources with those that are specific to the interaction order itself' (11–12). This slightly overstates the case in that Goffman analysed the level of interaction in much greater detail than the institutional level but, as is clear from 'Asylums', he did recognise that interaction is influenced by institutional constraints.

Howard Becker's approach to institutional constraints is similar to that of Goffman's: he recognises it and refers to it and its effects but is far more concerned to analyse interaction than the origins of institutional power, or how the latter relates to the more fundamental sources of power and stratification in society. This is apparent in his influential work on deviance and social problems. His definitions of deviance and social problems are classically interactionist in that they are both defined in culturally relative terms i.e., what is considered deviant in a given society reflects what has emerged as the dominant view – from which there may be dissent and opposition. Becker has done more than anyone to popularise the concept of labelling and 'labelling theory'. Here are his definitions of deviance (and the deviant) and social problems, respectively:

> The deviant is one to whom the label has been successfully applied. Deviant behaviour is behaviour that people so label.
>
> (1963:8)
>
> Social problems are what people think they are . . .
>
> (1966:2)

It becomes clear in Becker's examination of specific cases that power plays a major role in the successful labelling of particular behaviours as deviant or as social problems. Power is involved both in getting a particular behaviour defined as deviant or problematic and, perhaps more obviously, in enforcing the rule or law that institutionalises 'correct' behaviour. The process of defining a behaviour as deviant may involve genuine public debate although Becker recognises that one or other party to it may have more access to the media and more influence on the decision making process. Becker – himself a jazz musician of high skills – illustrates how the greater power of one group over another can enable the former to get its version of the rules enacted in relation to the passing of Marijuana Tax Act of 1937 which was 'designed to stamp out the use of the drug'(135). In this case, the Federal Bureau of Investigation (FBI) manipulated the media and public opinion to get the Act passed. Among other things, the FBI wanted to replace the work and jobs it had lost after the raising of the prohibition on alcohol consumption. Becker contrasts the power and organisation of the FBI with the lack of both of marijuana smokers. Becker comments:

> Marijuana smokers, powerless, unorganized, and lacking publicly legitimate grounds for attack, sent no representatives to the (congressional) hearings and their point of view found no place in the record . . . The enterprise of the Bureau had produced a new rule, whose subsequent enforcement would create a new class of outsiders – marijuana users
>
> (1963:145)

Once a rule is institutionalised, it is the job of relevant officials and agencies to enforce it. It is only when a behaviour is officially labelled as deviant that public or social deviance occurs. Here, Becker echoes a distinction made by Lemert, who first used the concept of labelling, between primary and secondary deviance. Primary deviance is an act which infringes a given rule and secondary deviance occurs if and when an act and its perpetrator are publicly labelled as deviant. In focusing so much on rule enforcers – police, hospital nurses, judges, teachers, figure prominently in interactionist works – Becker, Lemert and other interactionists are dealing with power at the micro level. However, they are aware that the deeper sources of power lie elsewhere in the structures and processes of government, the media and opinion makers and in the system of stratification although the latter was not their favoured terrain of analysis.

In general, interactionists have been greatly interested in how certain individuals become defined as deviant rather than others. They explain this partly by the tendency of law enforcement officials to employ *stereotypes* by which certain characteristics, such as age or 'race' are associated with other, deviant characteristics. Here links are made between the macro and micro levels. Thus, according to Cicourel, there was a tendency among some police officers whom he researched to see the typical criminal as young, male, working class and black (1976). No doubt the officers in question found such constructions as functional in terms of predicting who they thought was likely to commit crime. Crucially, however, such stereotypes direct police-officers towards certain groups and away from others in their law enforcing activities and can, therefore, become *self-fulfilling*. The social consequences of this can be very considerable. Often targeted groups feel a sense of harassment and injustice and resent the negative public image created of them. Further, as Cicourel points out, the statistical data that such stereotyping builds up is often perceived as an 'objective' picture of 'reality' when, in fact, they are constructed and reflect, a particular point of view.

Comment on Symbolic Interactionism. Ethnomethodology

Symbolic interactionism makes a huge contribution to sociological theory and research at its major level of relevance, the 'interaction order'. Interactionists have generated a large range of concepts which have greatly facilitated the analysis of face to face interaction. Equally importantly, although less often referred to, Mead and Blumer defined the capacities of the mind (as it develops in social context) in a way that has provided the basis of a relatively voluntarist approach to social analysis.

To illustrate the first point: simply to list some of the main concepts which interactionists are partly or wholly responsible for introducing into sociology is to appreciate the extent and nature of their achievement (see glossary for definitions):

○ Self
○ Significant/Generalised Other
○ Interaction
○ Symbol
○ Inter-subjectivity
○ Meaning
○ Labelling
○ Negotiation
○ Stereotype
○ Self-fulfilling Prophesy
○ Stigma
○ Deviant Career
○ Moral Panic
○ Moral Entrepreneur
○ Signification Spiral
○ Amplification
○ Social Construction of Reality

The above list could be greatly extended. However, the point to take from it is that interactionism has fleshed out a framework of conceptual analysis that provides a tool-kit for analysing the subjective and inter-subjective in society. The work of Becker and later, Stanley Cohen in Britain, goes further in extending analysis of symbolic communication beyond the face to face to the modern mass media. Whereas the terminology of functionalism has not entered the language of everyday life to any significant extent, that of interactionism has. Perhaps, after all, the approach that is about the meanings of people is found by people to be the more meaningful!

Given the deterministic strands in both the Marxist and functionalist traditions, an approach that explores society in terms of subjective and inter-subjective meaning and action can be seen as resetting the balance. It is obvious which way interactionists incline in the debate about the respective relevance of the individual and society and agency and structure. The stress that interactionists put on the individual undoubtedly reflects the place of individualism within American culture whereas Marxism reflects the collective ethic of European socialism. Indeed, individualism is perhaps the core American value. However, the fact that interactionism mirrors a fundamental American value does not mean that it is a conservative perspective even within the American context. It is highly arguable that individualism is itself a radical value when juxtaposed to the demands and constraints of society. In the American context, much radicalism takes the form of criticising institutional power in terms of the limits it can put on and sometimes damage it can do to individuals. This is precisely what Goffman does in *Asylums* and Becker in *Outsiders*.

While it is true that interactionists do not provide a developed analysis of social structure, particularly social class, or adequately theorise how interaction both creates and is constrained by structure, they recognise that inequalities of power are pervasive and shape interaction. In this respect, interactionists treat power in a somewhat similar way to poststructuralists such as Foucault. Both approaches conceptualise agency, ideas/beliefs and structure as related aspects of a wider field of definition/action (interactionism) or discourse (poststructuralism) rather than as separate entities. Both approaches have also been accused of romanticising 'the under-dog'. Where interactionism and poststructuralism differ, and differ profoundly, is on their view of the human subject. For the former, the human subject is central to society and social theory whereas for the latter s/he is the construction or object of discourse (see p. 123).

Recently, a number of interactionists have gone further in conceptualising what others refer to as social structure by defining the results of actions of the past as potential constraints on the actions of contemporary actors. As yet this approach has not generated significant macro-level analysis. It seems more likely and consistent with the interactionist emphasis on meaningful action that when they wish to address macro issues they do so by means of historical narrative and analysis as Becker did in relation to the banning of marijuana.

It is also a fair criticism of symbolic interactionism that it does not provide or even attempt a theorisation of the relationship between the emotional side of the individual and society. Freud and also Durkheim argued that the socialisation and control of instincts and emotions is necessary for social order. Further, emotions can provide powerful motives – sometimes more so than conscious reasoning. Mead's references to Freud are few and tend to be brief. Both the Frankfurt School and, later, structuralism and poststructuralism put forward powerful arguments that it is primarily through the social shaping of emotions that human beings acquire identity. Symbolic interactionism is compatible with a more voluntaristic view of emotions, in which the self might be envisaged as more the agent of expression than the object of social forces.

After stimulating much controversial debate in the 1970s, ethnomethodology 'has now settled into an accepted but minority preoccupation' (ODS: 203). Although it has distinct origins from symbolic interactionism, it is mentioned here because both approaches stress the central role of social actors in constructing society. However, whereas symbolic interactionism has a range of concepts which deal with the macro level of power and coercion, ethnomethodology is committed to discovering the 'commonsense meanings' of individual subjects. Its conceptual vocabulary is devoted to this level of analysis and lacks a social frame of reference.

Charles Wright Mills: An American Radical Sociologist

Mills is arguably the only radical American sociologist of the left of indisputably international stature. Certainly he is the most influential and original to fit this description in the post second world war period. Mills' distinctive contribution reflects the integration of a variety of intellectual influences, European and American. He drew freely from both Weber and Marx, fitting the former's elites/mass framework over a more detailed partly Marxist influenced class analysis. As has already been mentioned, Mills was familiar with and influenced by the Frankfurt School – without ever working predominantly within their tradition of philosophical and social theory. Yet, in effect, Mills arrived at his own brand of critical theory through a different route. His own graduate research had been a study of the American pragmatic tradition in philosophical and social thought. The leading pragmatists such as John Dewey and William James insisted on the need to apply philosophical ideas to practical circumstances and Mills himself strongly adopted this approach. He frequently articulated this practical commitment in terms of building a 'public sociology' which addressed major social issues in a way that enabled individuals to make better sense of their lives and act in a more informed way. As he put it, sociology should enable people to make the link between 'public issues' and 'personal troubles'.

Mills' great theme, and one that runs throughout his work, was power – its unequal distribution and the often self or class interested use of it. For Mills power is predominantly about who has it and what they do with it:

> 'Power', as the term is now generally used in social science has to do with whatever decisions men (and women – my brackets) make about the arrangement under which they live, and about the events which make up the history of their period . . . (i)n so far as such decisions are made(and in so far as they could be but are not) the problem of who is involved in making them (or not making them) is the basic problem of power
>
> (1959: 4).

Nothing, could be further from this action and interest-group based approach to power than Parsons' functional concept of the political system or, for that matter, Foucault's concept of power in discourse in which people seem moved by some hidden hand (see pp. 120–4). As Mills defines power, there is a basis for picking out 'winners' and 'losers' and for understanding their actions. Or, to put it another way, as Mills describes it, individuals and groups can be held responsible for the use they make of power. Mills willingness to do this partly accounts for the distinctive moral tone of his writings.

In a relatively short life, Mills was nevertheless able to write a trilogy of books which together make-up an extensive critical analysis of United States society in the immediate postwar period. The three works were *The New Men of Power: America's Labor Leaders*(1949); *White Collar: the American Middle Class*(1951); and *The Power Elite*(1956). Only the gist of Mills' analysis need be given here. In *The New Men of Power* he argued that the top leadership of the trade unions in America was now comfortably integrated into the capitalist system. Far from being anti-capitalist, top union leaders were now part of its system of regulation – delivering discipline and productivity in the workplace, in return for satisfactory settlements on wages and conditions for the workforce. Personally well paid, the radicalism of these men did not extend beyond tough rhetoric and occasional industrial action for specific and limited economic goals. Mills was no more optimistic in the immediate radical potential of the working class as a whole. Like the Frankfurt School he saw little sign that the working class would fulfil the role of historic agency for change anticipated by Marx. Mills had drawn his own conclusion on this matter well before the argument had been fully engaged within British sociology. In effect, his analysis roughly fore-shadowed the theory of corporatism applied to several Western cities of the 1960s and 1970s in which government, industry and the unions collaborated to ensure generally harmonious industrial relations.

Mass Society: The Working and Middle Classes

To some extent Mills considered that the industrial working class had been misled and let down by its self-interested leadership and he was frustrated rather than angered by its members' apparent apathy towards radical change. He was far more ascerbic about the new white collar middle class whom, in a somewhat idealised picture, he contrasted with the older, independent, and publicly aware small business middle class. He saw the expanding white collar class as over-concerned with petty status pretensions as they strove to establish distinction between themselves and the manual working class. He saw the 'mass media' as a trivialising cultural force which drew both the working and white collar class into capitalist consumerist values and away from the consideration of more significant issues. The majority of Americans were in his view, drifting into a mass society, comfortable but characterless – 'cheerful robots' in one of his unkinder phrases. In language highly reminiscent of Max Weber and also evocative of the Frankfurt School's critique of rationality without principle, Mills decried the unimaginative conformity of petty bureaucrats:

> Great and rational organisations – in brief, bureaucracies – have indeed increased, but the substantive reason of the individual at large has not. Caught in the limited milieux of their everyday lives, ordinary men often cannot reason about great structures – rational and irrational – of which their milieux are subordinate parts. Accordingly they often carry out series of apparently rational actions without any idea of the ends they serve, and there is increasing suspicion that those at the top as well – like Tolstoy's generals – only pretend they know.
>
> (Mills in Horowitz edited, 1963:237–8).

Mills' point about the sometimes unthinking conformity of those at the lower levels in organisations is well made. In the twentieth century there have been many examples of unquestioning conformity in that most bureaucratic of all institutions, the military. Soldiers of many nations, often excusing themselves as 'just following orders', have been guilty of killing innocent civilians without any need to. If that can happen, we can be sure that many acts of damaging bureaucratic ritualism occur on a daily basis – acts which might be 'right' by the rules but wrong in terms of the needs of the person being administered. Of course, it is easy for Mills and other intellectuals to rail at 'mindless' bureaucratic conformity. However, it may be less lack of moral understanding than fear of the consequences of disobedience that provokes conformity from 'ordinary' people.

Mills not only criticised the conformity of the 'masses' but also offered a perceptive and early analysis of how whereas in industrial society people had sold their labour, in a service society, they sell themselves as well. He wrote of 'the personality market' in which an instant smile along with an instant personality might be the key to pleasing customers and to job success. This was a new kind of alienation in which people sold 'little pieces of themselves' rather than simply their labour skills.

The Power Elite and Opposition to it

Mills completed his analysis of American society with the influential *The Power Elite*. He argued that American society was run by three elites – the top of the military, big business and government – which together made up the power elite. Particular individuals moved between the three elites – General, later President Eisenhower was an obvious example – facilitating communication and coordination. Mills' willingness to draw on Weber as well as Marx is apparent in his view that during the period of the Cold War, it was the military rather than the business elite which was in the ascendant within the power elite although he stressed the common interests of the elites. These interests were largely served by government's endorsement of the demands of the *military-industrial complex* whose engine of wealth creation and international domination was armaments production. Mills argued that this model applied equally to Republican and Democratic governments whose leading members routinely networked within the power elite. In Mills' model, representative democracy functioned only at the middle level of power, such as decision-making on education and welfare policy, while decisive economic and political power was exercised by the power elite. Mills considered that compared to the vitality that had characterised it in the past, local democracy was moribund in the United States. Partly this was due to the increased centralisation of power and decision-making and partly to the growing domesticity and media-mesmorisation of the American people.

Overall, Mills' model is predominantly an elite/masses model rather than a class one. The elite/masses form or structure defines American society and overlays social classes that Mills regards as relatively weak in collective awareness and motivation to act. This is much less true of the upper class than of others whose interests would generally equate with those of the power elite. However, in this matter Mills is Weberian rather than Marxist. The power elite or ruling elite is defined not primarily in economic terms but on the different but complementary bases of military, political and economic power. Mills' consideration of the millions of poor Americans – typically from among the unemployed, the low-paid, the old and ethnic minorities – also resonated of Weber rather than Marx and foreshadowed the underclass debate of the mid 1990s. Whereas Marx was relatively uninterested in the sub or lumpenprolateriat, Mills commented extensively on its powerlessness and marginalisation. Although he had no blueprint for the revitalisation of the poor he did make a brief reference in *The Power Elite* to the poor in relation to 'the moral idea of a counter-elite'(14). In the early 1960s, one of the key strategies of the New Left was on participatory community politics and, in fact, concern with the poverty and powerlessness of the poor remained a central issue in American politics for a few years.

Like many of the Frankfurt School, Mills saw more radical potential among intellectuals and students than among the working class. Although he died in 1961, he is sometimes referred to as 'the big daddy of the American New Left'. In his determination to employ sociological imagination in addressing the main social issues of the epoch, Mills exemplified in his own practice the ideals of a public sociology which he had advocated. The strong empirical basis of his work gave it a relevance sometimes less apparent in the more abstract and philosophically grounded theory of the Frankfurt School. It is possible that had he lived, Mills could have given the authoritative guidance to the American New Left that it ultimately seemed to lack. Many leading liberal thinkers of about Mills' age such as Lipset, Bell and Shils saw the radical youth politics as in part a revolt against necessary authority and restraint – an unresolved collective Oedipal complex! If so, no effective father figure or 'big daddy' emerged from their ranks to supply mature direction. Nor did perhaps the best known figure from the Frankfurt School, Theodor Adorno, seem to want to have much truck with the young rebels. When in 1968, German students, frustrated at his lack of engagement in radical action, occupied his office, Adorno, called the police. It is difficult to imagine that Mills would have got himself into this situation!

Comment on Mills and the Frankfurt School

Mills was untypical of America and of American sociology in that he was a genuine radical of the left, but there is still something typically American about him. Partly, this is his big bustling individualism – taking on the world – and partly it is his determination that his work should 'make a difference' in the form of helping people to understand and so better deal with the circumstances that affect their lives. In this, he strongly reflected the spirit of American pragmatism and the more radical expressions of American democracy. Mills' radicalism was all the more distinctive because he was intellectually distanced from the broad tradition of European Marxism. In Europe, radicalism of the left came to be dominated by Marxism if not entirely equated with it. For a variety of reasons, this was not the case in the United States where radical ideas, if not full blown radical ideologies, have often been expressed through populism and quasi-anarchist movements and ideologies. There is little in his work to suggest that Mills was a socialist in the sense of favouring the nationalisation of industry – although he clearly favoured substantial wealth redistribution. What he did consistently argue for was the downward redistribution of power. In other words, he advocated the maximum feasible participation of people in decision making processes. The tradition of radical, populist democracy in the United States has not produced any social restructuring on the scale that socialism has in some European countries but it has been a recurrent factor in American politics, in sometimes rendering the powerful more responsible to the people.

Although Mills did not write specifically within the Marxist tradition, he arrived at a number of the same main conclusions as the Frankfurt School. The geographical and intellectual distance between Mills and the Frankfurt School was bridged by Mills' association with Hans Gerth with whom he exchanged ideas about Weber as well as Marx. Further, several members of the Frankfurt School spent long periods in the United States, including at Columbia University during the period when Mills was a Professor of Sociology there. Further, the logic of events, particularly the development of Soviet totalitarianism, suggested similar conclusions to them. The following is a list of analytical conclusions arrived at by both Mills and the Frankfurt School:

1 Communism as it had been enforced in the Soviet Union and, later, Eastern Europe, did not represent a model for imitation

2 The working class was no longer the sole nor necessarily the primary agency for change

3 A 'mass society' had developed in Western Europe and in the United States in which not only were the traditional working class incorporated into the system but also the growing white collar groups

4 Reflecting conclusion 3, culture and ideology were now even more central to sociology and should not be understood merely as reflections of productive relations but as partly autonomous. Cultural analysis was particularly important in relation to the development of political and social consciousness and conformity/non-conformity

5 Intellectuals, including the more critically aware members of the middle class, were considered as a more dynamic source of radicalism than the traditional working class. Mills indicated his support for the burgeoning student and intellectual led American New Left and Habermas has identified the new social movements as the most relevant and creative force for change.

These theoretical differences from Marx himself and more especially from Soviet Marxism are on such a large scale that they scarcely seem compatible with the description, Marxist. This is not a problem in the case of Mills who did not seek to describe himself under that label. In Europe, the influence of Marxism was much stronger, although many European Marxist intellectuals became ex-Marxists often in disillusioned reaction to developments in the Soviet Union or to Soviet imperialism, especially its conquests in Eastern Europe. What Marxism uniquely provided in Europe was an alternative theoretical and socio-political framework in which it became almost habitual for left of centre intellectuals to work within. This was only a problem when some intellectuals treated Marxism as a dogma and sought to generate a kind of secular orthodoxy with the whole regalia of high priests, heretics and mindless mantras. This happened in the Soviet Union and to some Soviet inspired sects elsewhere, but it did not happen to Mills nor to the Frankfurt School.

The content of the sociology of the Frankfurt School and of Mills matters far more than the label we attach to it. A name or label gives a focus for identity and for that reason is important. Whether 'Marxism' or 'socialism' are the best names to describe early third millenium sociology and politics of the left is open to debate. Time will tell. In a statement of extraordinary prescience, Mills sensed not only that the socialist and liberal traditions would struggle to carry the weight of new insight and theory but employed the term 'postmodern' to describe what he saw as an approaching new age:

> We are at the end of what is called the Modern Age. Just as Antiquity was followed by several centuries of Oriental ascendancy which westerners provincially call the Dark Ages, so now the Modern Age is being succeeded by the postmodern period...
>
> The ending of one period and the beginning of another is, to be sure, a matter of definition. But definitions, like everything social, are historically specific. And now our basic definitions of society and of self are being overtaken by new realities. I do not mean merely that we feel we are in an epochal kind of transition, I mean that too many of our explanations are derived from the great historical tradition from the Medieval to the Modern Age; and that they are generalised for use today, they become unweildy, irrelevant and not convincing. And I mean also that our major orientations – liberalism and socialism – have virtually collapsed as adequate explanations of the world and of ourselves.

> (Mills in Horowitz edited, 1963: 236)

Over 40 years ago, Mills was suggesting that liberalism and socialism as major orientations had become 'unweildy, irrelevant and not convincing'. Even today this reads as a bold and controversial statement. Liberalism was flawed in practice by its excesses in the global context and by the inequality it created and in theory by what Mills saw as its flacid attempts to promote consensus while failing adequately to confront social inequality and injustice. Socialism had become bloodied and discredited in much of its practice and sectarian in much of its thought. Mills, like the American New Left he helped to inspire was looking for a 'third way'. This phrase which was used widely in the New Left, had far more radical connotations than it came to have when employed by Tony Blair as he struggled to give focus to his government in the late 1990s. As we enter the new millenium, a revitalised left, capable of engaging powerfully and effectively with heaving global capitalism, is still struggling not only to organise and make an impact but adequately to define itself and its objectives.

Conclusion: Re-working the dualisms

Whereas there are certain measurable standards of progress in the natural sciences and technology, sociological theory often seems less cumulatively progressive, with one generation simply retravelling the circuits of previous ones. What I have referred to as the second wave of theorists certainly wished to progress social science and one way of getting some purchase on whether they did so is by looking at them in terms of the dualisms. As with the work of the founders of sociology, there is a tendency for sociologists working within the traditions discussed above to incline to one or other set of the dualisms although this is predictably less true of approaches which systematically seek to integrate both sets of dualisms. Symbolic Interactionism provides the strongest example of a consistent emphasis on one 'side' of the dualisms: the individual, agency, social integration (seen as interactive not socially determined) and micro level research.

Although the individual/society and agency/structure dualisms are very closely related, theoretically and methodologically it can be useful to distinguish between them along the lines indicated earlier. Within social science generally, particularly political science and classical economics, the individual is often juxtaposed to society in terms of the putative rights, on the one hand, and the requirements of social order, on the other. Related to the issue of human rights and preliminary to it is that of 'human nature'. It is obvious that the rights of humans must be related to what human beings are thought to be (although a valid position on this matter is that there is no 'essential' human nature and that each generation redefines human rights in terms of its own conceptions and circumstances).

The chapter began by discussing two traditions of Marxism: Marxist-Leninism forged in the heat of action and humanistic Marxism forged in the ivory tower. The considered verdict of history is that Marxism in its Bolshevik and Stalinist forms was brutally oppressive to the rights of human beings. This was partly because of the perceived need to suppress opposition from within and without a severely threatened regime, but also because the 'end' of a communist society was seen as justifying the 'means' of destroying those who opposed it. However, the fusion of Marx and Freud's thought in the work of the early Frankfurt School revived the concept of human liberation present in the writings of the younger Marx. What Marcuse primarily took from Freud was that people have an unfulfilled capacity for pleasure which capitalist society unnecessarily represses, manipulates and distorts for reasons of profit. Extravagant as Marcuse's concept of a liberated society is, it was to some extent mirrored in practice in the 1960s counterculture. The relatively unconstrained pleasure of the kind some pursued in the sixties counterculture does not figure in most thinkers' notion of human rights but in an age of increased wealth and leisure, pleasure as part of a right to self-expression and development is relevant to rights theory. After all, it is over 200 years since the American Declaration of Independence stated 'the pursuit of happiness' as one of the three basic human rights – the others being the right to 'life' and 'liberty'. In retaining Freud's analysis of the human psyche as in part structured by egoism and aggression as well as by more positive dispositions, Marcuse shows a realism appropriate to a century of unprecedented conflict and violence. Of the two major theories developed in the United States – Functionalism and Symbolic Interactionism – it is the latter which more substantially contributes to our understanding of the capacities of the mind and self and how individuals create society through meaningful action and interaction. If the Freudian tradition enhanced understanding of emotions within the social sciences, symbolic interactionism did the same for consciously directed action.

Of the two post-classical 'totalising' theorists, Parsons and Habermas (see Chapter 5), it is the latter who has achieved a more convincing account of how the dualisms inter-relate in late capitalist society. Despite his intentions otherwise, Parsons disproportionately emphasises the more social side of the dualisms. Habermas draws substantially but selectively from the main sociological traditions of symbolic interactionism, functionalism and Marxism. From Mead he derives his emphasis on language as the key medium of rational communication and on the human subject as rational and purposive. His presentation of what he termed the system world reflects Weber's analysis of bureaucracy and Parsons' social systems theory. From the Marxist tradition comes his reassertion of the capitalist nature of late modern society and his continuation of the Marxist commitment to the possibility of liberation from it. Although they overlapped, Habermas is not of Parsons generation. Mills was Parsons' great antagonist of the time. Mills by no means dismissed all aspects of

Parsons' work but like Giddens after him he found it both over–inflated and lacking in a genuine dimension of action. Mills was much more explicit in acknowledging the extent to which his radical values affected his sociological interpretations but for all his attempts at scientific objectivity, the liberal values of Parsons, or, as Mills saw it, his liberal–conservative values were just as obvious in his work.

SUMMARY

1. SOCIOLOGY AFTER THE FOUNDERS: Following the work of the founders of sociology, the subject continued to develop. In Europe Marxism was the main influence although Freud also had an impact. In the United States approaches developed which reflected American culture and values as well as, to a greater or lesser extent, the thought of Marx, Weber, and Durkheim.

2. MARXIST-LENINISM: CRITICAL THEORY: Two broad traditions of Marxism developed, both of them reflecting the Marxist commitment to political change as well as to social analysis. These were Marxist-Leninism and the critical theory of the Frankfurt School.

3. MARXIST-LENINISM: is associated with two major theoretical positions. First, that the Communist Party is in the vanguard of the revolution and must give leadership to the proletariat. Second, Lenin developed a theoretical analysis of monopoly capitalism in the age of capitalist imperialism.

4. CRITICAL THEORY: is associated with a number of theoretical arguments not all equally shared by members of the School. These include:
   ◆ that Marx's thinking and the development of Marxist thought must be pursued critically
   ◆ that the working class alone is unlikely to be an effective agency for change
   ◆ that consumerism promoted by the media has blunted the revolutionary potential of the proletariat and helped to produce a mass society
   ◆ (drawing on Freudian psychoanalysis) that capitalism manipulates and trivialises human emotions as well as thought and consciousness
   ◆ that the 'rationality' of Western capitalism is repressive as it harnesses people to alienated labour and prevents them from fulfilling their potential

5. TALCOTT PARSONS: the founder of Functionalism, attempted to combine the social action approach of Weber with the more structural emphasis of Durkheim although the detail and complexity of his systems theory was characteristically his own. Much of the debate about Parsons' work focuses on the extent to which he lost the human, voluntaristic element in his systems model as it developed.

6. SYMBOLIC INTERACTIONISM: is predominantly an interactionist rather than a structural theory of society. Blumer refused to theorise in structural terms at all but Goffman, by no means a 'pure' interactionist, analysed what he referred to as the 'institutional' as well as the 'interactional' order. Mead and Blumer described the capacity of social actors to think and communicate symbolically and later interactionists applied and extended their insights to empirical situations, particularly in relation to the social construction of deviance. Interactionism is cricitised for its relative lack of a macro/ structural dimension and for over-stressing the rational motivations of action at the expense of emotional ones.

7. CHARLES WRIGHT MILLS: was a radical who absorbed a variety of influences including aspects of Marx and Weber and American pragmatism and populism. He analysed the unequal distribution of power in American society and the frequently self/group interested way in which it is used. His theory of the power elite is a radical alternative to Marxist ruling class theory and remains of relevance in understanding the motivations and operation of elites in contemporary society. Reflecting

Weber, Mills argued that occupational bureaucratisation was generating mass conformity, and reflecting the Marxist Frankfurt School he was critical of media led consumerism. The scourge of functionalism and particularly Talcott Parsons, Mills was viewed by the latter as an extreme critic of democratic consensus. Mills' riposte was that he wanted genuinely participatory rather than manipulated democracy.

Chapter 3

Social Structure: 'Postindustrial/PostFordist Society' (The Third Wave of Theory or New Sociology)

> **Key Concepts**:
> deskilling, Fordism/postFordism excluded/included, information age/society, late modernity/postmodernity, objective/subjective class, postindustrial, racialise, underclass.

Introduction: The Historical Context of the New Sociology

First of all, what is 'the new sociology'? As used here, the phrase new sociology refers to a wide range of attempts to understand and interpret the changes covered by terms such as 'late modernity' or 'postmodernity'. The latter terms are discussed in greater detail below but both attempt to give a name to a cluster of key changes which have taken place in the post-second world war period although their origins can be traced back to earlier modernity. In their widest usage, these changes include developments in production and in patterns of consumption and related changes in the system of stratification, globalisation, the rise of the new social movements, including feminism and the black liberation movement, and the emergence of a range of related communication, media and cultural developments. Focusing on new or newly perceived areas of social development has pushed sociology in new directions and prompted new attempts at theoretical interpretation.

The description of what may be a new historical epoch requires many more concepts than simply a general descriptive term such as late modern or postmodern. The emphasis of this chapter is on social structure in the classic sense of the economy and system of stratification. In this context, the term postindustrial has been used to describe the shift from a predominantly industrial to a predominantly service economy and postFordism has been used to describe a proposed shift from the hierarchical and rigid types of organisation, particularly industrial, of the industrial age to 'flatter' and more flexible forms of organisation and production of the postindustrial period. Both these terms and the theories they indicate are to some extent controversial and will be treated here as such. Of the two, postindustrial society theory has much wider acceptance than postFordist theory. Nevertheless, what both concepts do is highlight areas of profound structural change. The next chapter and to a large extent the following two concentrate on the cultural changes of late modernity or postmodernity. The justification for separating the structural and the cultural in this way is partly the practical one of a necessary division of labour and focus. However, there is an important argument that the economic and cultural are becoming increasingly intertwined if not 'collapsing into' each other and this view is referred to several times in this book (pp. 180–1 and 207–8). For those who prefer their structural and cultural sociology together, the sections on class, 'race'/ethnicity, age and gender in this and in Chapter 5 could be read consecutively.

New historical periods or even 'sub-periods' do not happen frequently. Often, part of what causes them is a fundamental technological development or series of developments, particularly where these fundamentally affect the system of production and as a consequence that of social stratification. One such historical change occurred around the latter part of the eighteenth and earlier part of the nineteenth century. A series of applied inventions moved Britain from predominantly agricultural to predominantly industrial production and changed the class structure and culture of British society with it. Of course there were and still are continuities as well as breaks with previous periods, but that Britain had entered a new historical epoch by the late nineteenth century is not in dispute. Is the same true of the late twentieth century and the beginning of the twenty first? If so, what kind of period are we entering? Three characteristics of the proposed late modern or postmodern period need to be stated.

First, in the view of many social scientists, developments in information technology (hardware and software) allied to developments in communications (e.g., television and telephone) are the main forces behind contemporary historical change and in structuring the way the new society is stratified. In this respect the effect of the new technology is comparable to that of the new industrial technology in the nineteenth century remarked on by Marx. However, there is an important difference in what happened then and what is happening now. Then, as Marx rightly observed, it was material change – in the technology and whole scale of production – that led general social and cultural change. In late modern society , the effect of the new technology is as much on intellectual and cultural 'production' as on material production. This crucial difference is apparent in two respects, first, whereas the nineteenth century technological changes were massively and visibly material, the most powerful contemporary technology controlling production other than the human brain which it supports or even partly supplants – is software – physically tiny packets of knowledge or culture. Second, basic material products, though necessary, are now increasingly taken for granted in the rich world and it is cultural, mainly leisure, products that are characteristic of the new age. Of course, the precise distinction between what is a material and what is a cultural product is debatable, but few doubt that there has been a substantial 'shift to the cultural' as Fredric Jameson puts it (1998). Stuart Hall makes much the same point when he states that though sociology needs both the concepts of structure and culture, culture has moved 'to the fore' (1996, B.S.A. Conference). Increasingly, then, social life and public debate focuses on cultural rather than 'bread and butter' issues. The British now spend more on leisure than food. What is more, much of contemporary life is conducted symbolically, through the media.

Second, late modernity is a global period. By this is meant that the world or globe we experience operates in many important respects in a transnational or global way. Necessary to and partly causal of this is the growing infrastructure of global communication, including global channels of information and entertainment (technologically sometimes the same channel). The new technology is now essential to the functioning of the most powerful transnational business and financial institutions. Their wealth and power depends on their control of the means of communication. This control is not total nor uncontested but it is generally adequate to support their economic, financial and arguably, cultural dominance. The global scope of capitalism is not new but, as is elaborated below, its scale and character has changed as a result of the information and communications revolution.

Third, with the decline of the industrial age, there has been a corresponding decline in the size and influence of the traditional working class and the emergence of a number of other social groupings, notably youth, women and certain ethnic minorities, as well as a number of issue oriented movements and pressure groups such as the environmental movement and animal rights. To ask an odd but usefully leading question: 'Where did these groupings and movements come from?'. In capitalist-industrial society the kind of individuals who have formed these movements tended to be locked into the functioning of society to such an extent that they found it difficult to develop the collective awareness and organisation effectively to challenge the existing power structure. The society of which they were a part was dominated by, white, upper and middle class, usually older, males. In other words – although the judgement is inevitably retrospective and anachronistic – it was more or less racist, classist, gerontocratic and patriarchal. If this judgement does, indeed, seem ahistorical, it is at least supported by the fact that all the relatively powerless groups referred to here have embarked upon struggles for greater freedom and equality.

The first to do so was the working class – mainly male industrial workers (women were legally barred from working in factories and mines for most of the nineteenth century). In most Western capitalist countries the working class movement achieved the vote, the welfare state and better pay and working conditions for most workers. In the current phase of global information capitalism, all but the first of these can reasonably be regarded as more or less insecure. The emergence of non-class based social movements certainly does not mean that class issues are not still of compelling importance.

The above developments and movements have profoundly changed the structure of stratification in Britain and elsewhere. Class, patriarchy (including dominant modes of sexuality), racial stratification and age stratification have all been reshaped. In different times and places in the nineteen fifties and sixties, young people, women, black people, environmentalists and others increasingly began to question the basis of Western patriarchy, capitalism, racism, and age-related hierarchy. These structures of stratification have been radically changed and to some extent the social movements of liberation have increasingly shifted focus from oppression to identity and even cultural celebration. The relevant section in this chapter will concentrate mainly on structural issues in relation to these movements and matters of culture and identity will be analysed in later chapters (see, pp. 157–78). First, however, the technological basis and occupational and class structure of late modern society must be mapped out in more detail. Here, I will follow these issues through the literature as it appeared chronologically but adding some more recent references. This makes it easier to deal with the central process of globalisation separately and more fully in a later chapter as the immense impact of the new technology on global processes only became apparent to most theorists in the 1980s and 1990s and not to all of them even then.

Late Modern or Postmodern Society?

Before describing and interpreting contemporary society, an issue of terminology must be dealt with. There is some debate about whether contemporary society is best referred to as late modern or as postmodern. The former description is preferred by Anthony Giddens and the latter particularly by Jean-Francois Lyotard and Jean Baudrillard. The term late modern implies that contemporary global society is still predominantly modern in orientation. This indicates that more recent social developments although radical are currently best thought of as occurring within modernity. In contrast, postmodernists argue that a new condition – that of postmodernity – now exists which is distinctly different from that of modernity. Lyotard suggests that we have been living in a condition of postmodernity from the early 1960s.

Giddens suggests that modernity is characterised by the application of rational thinking to every area of life, cultural and material. The theoretical and applied achievements of science through technology are the most obvious monument to the march of modernity. In the realm of culture rational explanations have dominated over religious ones and quasi-scientific rather than more intuitive modes of literary and artistic criticism have been widely adopted. Giddens associates rational thinking with self-consciousness and what he terms reflexivity. Self-consciousness allows human beings constantly to evaluate and develop not only the external world but themselves both individually and in a collective, social sense. It is this process of critical 'self-scanning' that Giddens refers to as self-reflexivity. In Giddens' view, reflexivity has always been a feature of modernity but it has become significantly heightened in late modernity. Giddens sees heightened reflexivity as pervasive but he particularly comments on it in terms of the information revolution and in personal relationships. He also sees it in the growing awareness that modernity, far from being a steady march of progress, has both failed to solve some old problems – such as poverty – and brought along some newer ones such as the pollution of the global environment. Nevertheless, Giddens keeps faith with the characteristic belief of the Enlightenment that the application of reason, perhaps now more tempered with experience and humanity, can provide means for a progressive improvement in the human condition.

Whereas the concept of late modernity implies substantial continuity between the contemporary and the modern world, postmodernism in Lyotard's celebrated formulation of it stipulates a break or rupture between modernity and postmodernity. Lyotard claimed in *The Postmodern Condition* (1979), that the two myths or 'meta-narratives' that legitimated science, including social science, no longer carried widespread credibility. These are 'The Myth of Liberation' and 'The Myth of Truth'. The former had lost credibility as a result of the implication of science in the appalling inhumanity meted out in the name of those two ideologies of modern progress, Fascism and Soviet Communism. The latter had become incredible because certain leading philosophers of science, such as Thomas Kuhn, had persuasively argued that scientists themselves are not wholly objective but work within the boundaries of given theoretical assumptions or paradigms. It has further been argued, including recently by Zygmunt Bauman, that twentieth century history clearly demonstrates that reason and science can be applied in the cause of destruction as well as constructively – in that sense, against truth. Bauman particularly had in mind the bureaucracy and technology that enabled the Holocaust to be carried out with such clinical efficiency(1989). Thus, science is a guarantee of neither liberation nor truth. In itself it is morally neutral, what it achieves is dependent on the morality (and other qualities) of human beings.

Some twenty years before the publication of Lyotard's influential work, Daniel Bell had developed what was basically to become the postmodern thesis but in relation specifically to political meta-narratives or ideologies. In *The End of Ideology* (1960), Bell stated that Fascist and Communist ideas, indeed all 'utopian' ideologies were 'exhausted' – irretrievably discredited by the main attempts to put them into practice. The crucial difference between Lyotard and Bell was that, whereas for Lyotard liberalism as well as Fascism and Communism had become tainted with the failure of enlightenment idealism, Bell argued strongly that a pragmatic, problem-solving and non-ideological liberalism was the sole remaining viable basis of political practice in the West. In my view, Bell's thesis was empirically somewhat undermined by the often highly ideological radical revival of the 1960s but his case for a pragmatic liberalism remains powerful – not least because the consensus that Fascism and the Soviet model of Communism have failed is even greater now than in the early nineteen sixties. Fukuyama's *The End of History and the Last Man* (1992) basically repeats Bell's argument that the only safe and constructive political approach left is liberalism – out of the smoke of twentieth century destruction emerges the survivor, liberal man . . .

The key point conveyed by both the terms late modernity and postmodernity is that the high optimism about human progress and self-improvement that flows most recently from the Enlightenment and more remotely from the Renaissance/Reformation needs drastically to be revised. For theorists of late modernity, such as Giddens, the need for greater realism does not mean that the enlightenment project need be abandoned. The struggle to increase human prosperity and happiness may be more difficult than was anticipated and may never be fully achievable but some progress is still possible. Giddens himself is said to be the favourite sociologist of Tony Blair, leader of a would-be reformist Labour government!

Postmodernists begin from the premise that the current historical period is not best thought of as 'modern' and that, indeed, the discredited, utopian dreams of modernity had better be put aside (in this important respect they have arrived at the same conclusion as liberals). Such scepticism invites the question 'what, then, do postmodernists believe in of a positive kind'? Lyotard's own answer was unambiguous enough – and what it amounted to in terms of traditional philosophical and political beliefs was 'nothing'. When it was suggested that postmodernism is itself a metanarrative, Lyotard turned the suggestion on its head by stating, negatively, that it is the metanarrative to end all metanarratives. However, no social theory can thrive for long exclusively in the ashes of the supposed failure of others.

Two influential lines of social analysis have emerged from postmodernism. First is the view put forward by Lyotard and Jean Baudrillard that the contemporary world – in the absence of credible religous and political ideologies – has become superficial, concerned with style and image rather than substance and meaning. Unsurprisingly, this analysis has provoked the accusation that postmodernism is itself a superficial view of the contemporary world. Second, a prominent strand in postmodernism has been to emphasise individual and group difference and identity. This can be seen as a positive corollary to the critique of those universalising philosophies such as Communism which postmodernists see as homogenising individual difference. Celebration of pluralism has led some postmodernists to embrace tolerance and compromise typical of pragmatic liberalism. Thus, whereas his earlier work was clearly Marxist in inspiration, Stuart Hall's later writings have a more reformist liberal tone which seems partly to be the effect of a postmodern influence. To the extent that postmodernism has found a place within established political and social theory, it would seem to bear out Giddens' point that much postmodernism thought is not fundamentally new.

At the very least, the debate around the use of the terms late modern and postmodern focus on an important issue of emphasis i.e., whether the contemporary period is 'new' and distinctive in the sense that modernity itself was in comparison with the medieval epoch. Only time will see this question resolved. Here the term late modern will generally be preferred on the grounds that the hailing of a new epoch is far too important a matter to essai in the absence of utterly decisive evidence. Evidence of that kind may not exist but the arguments that radical change has been occurring and on a global scale continue to accumulate. The next section begins the detailed consideration of these arguments.

Late Modern Society: Structure, Information and Occupation

The remainder of this chapter attempts to develop the argument of many social commentators that society has undergone radical change during roughly the second half of the twentieth century. Change can be seen at every level from the global to the local and individual. The discussion in the previous section about what to call this new epoch gives no more than a general idea of its character. In order to gain a fuller understanding of late modern society it is necessary to make a more systematic sociological analysis of it. This is made somewhat more difficult because of the turmoil in sociological theory that has occurred in parallel with rapid social change and partly as a result of trying to understand it. However, carefully used, both established and more recent sociological theory offer the prospect of substantial understanding.

Perhaps what continues to be of most use from the founders of sociology is not the Marxist or liberal metanarratives as general theoretical paradigms but their shared concern with the relationship between structure and culture. There is no need here to rehearse in detail the many insights of Marx, Durkheim and Weber about this relationship but it is useful to reiterate their shared basic perspective. They each sought an understanding of society and social change in the analysis of the interplay of the material structure (mainly economic and occupation/class) and cultural practices and beliefs (including ideologies). Each is built distinctively within this framework but it is perhaps the framework itself which remains most useful in analysing our own historical period. The relationship between structure and culture is no less important in late modernity than it was a century ago although many aspects of that relationship have changed. The newness and even modishness of postmodernism and related theories has sometimes left the misleading impression that established sociological conceptualisation has suddenly been made redundant. The utopian elements in Marxism and liberalism may now seem 'incredible', but paradoxically accepting this may make it easier to see and apply the substantial concepts, theories and insights of the founders of sociology. As contemporary social theorists, Daniel Bell and Fredric Jameson demonstrate, the current 'post' theories can be powerfully and effectively linked with established social theory.

Krishan Kumar suggests that taken together the 'post' theories are highly complementary and even go some way to providing an integrated theory of the contemporary world. Kumar makes the following comment on the four 'post' theories – postindustrial society theory, post-Fordism, postmodernism and poststructuralism (the last two of which he treats as a single body of theory):

> (W)hat seems to me remarkable is how much of the present state of the world they manage to capture. We do live in a world saturated with information and communication. The nature of work and industrial organisation is truly changing with unnerving speed. Modern societies have indeed reached a point where even if they have not given up on modernity, many of its classic attitudes have become seriously questionable.
>
> (Kumar 1995:201)

It is helpful from the point of view of this chapter that postindustrial society theory and post-Fordist theory can be regarded as broadly structural and postmodernism/poststructuralism as broadly cultural. Important qualifications to this generalisation will be made in the course of this chapter but it provides a clear basis on which to present the following material.

Late Modernity: Structural Theory

Postindustrial/Information Society

In 1996 Manuel Castells published the first volume of his trilogy *The Information Age: Economy, Society and Culture*. This trilogy is widely recognised as a major – perhaps the major – social scientific analysis so far of contemporary global society. Further references will be made to this work latter. Here it is sufficient to note that Castells very amply acknowledges that Daniel Bell's 1973 publication *The Coming of Post-Industrial Society: A Venture in Social Forecasting* was itself an impressive attempt to analyse and understand some of the main longer term social consequences of the information revolution. By his own account, Bell's book is an analysis and forecast of structural change from the then existing circumstances:

> The thesis advanced in this book is that in the next thirty to fifty years from the time of writing we will see the emergence of what I have called 'the post-industrial society'. As I emphasise, this is primarily a change in the social structure ...
>
> (Bell 1973: x)

Bell goes on to make clear what he means by social structure and what are the main changes that are bringing about postindustrial society:

> Analytically, society can be divided into three parts: the social structure, the polity and the culture. The social structure comprises the economy, technology, and the occupational system ... The concept of the post-industrial society deals primarily with changes *in the social structure*, the way in which the economy is being transformed and the occupational system reworked, and with the new relations between theory and empiricism, particularly science and technology.
>
> (Bell 1973: 12,13).

Of the three 'parts' of society he refers to, it is the social structure that we are primarily concerned with here. The other two, polity and culture, are analysed in greater detail in later chapters. Bell specifies five dimensions or characteristics of the social structure of emerging postindustrial society. These are:

1. **Economic sector**: the change from a mainly goods-producing to a mainly service economy;

2. **Occupational Distribution**: the pre-eminence of the professional and the technical class;

3. **Axial principle**: the centrality of theoretical knowledge as the source of innovation and policy for the society;

4. **Future orientation**: the control of technology and technological assessment;

5. **Decision-making**: the creation of a new 'intellectual technology'.

It is now over a quarter of a century since Bell published his forecast of the impending arrival of postindustrial society and so it is coming up to the time when we can begin to assess how accurate he was. This is done below. Points 1 and 2 are closely related to each other as are points 3,4, and 5. For reasons that will be made clear later, the first two points will be more fully discussed here.

1. *Economic Sector: Postindustrial Society*

As Bell states, 'the first and simplest characteristic of a postindustrial society is that the majority of the labor force is no longer engaged in agriculture or manufacturing but in services'. In particular, Bell projected that there would be substantial expansion in the following areas: health, education, research and government. It is not surprising that Bell was correct in forecasting this shift because it was the direction in which most of the advanced economies were moving in at the time. However, at the time he was writing, only the United States had a service sector that accounted for more than half of total employment and more than half of the Gross National Product. In the 1990s, most European and several Asian countries, including Japan, were service societies.

Britain has become a service society to a particularly marked degree. By the mid-1990s, the value produced by Britain's financial service sector alone was greater than that of its manufacturing output. Whereas the value of manufacturing output had slipped to about twenty percent of GDP, that of financial services was over twenty percent of GDP and growing. The picture was similar in relation to exports, with Britain increasingly dependent for paying its way on the provision of financial, legal, educational and cultural services to the rest of the world. On the other hand, manufactured products used in Britain itself came increasingly from other parts of the world or from foreign owned factories in Britain. Higher quality manufactured products came typically from Germany, Japan and the United States and lower quality ones from emerging economies.

There is no doubt that Bell was right that a relative shift from predominantly industrial to a service economies was occurring in the more technologically advanced societies and that the shift would subsequently continue to develop (although the precise extent and form of this shift varied between societies). It is important to note that Bell is insistent that his post-industrial society thesis is not deterministic and on this point his case is convincing. He repeatedly points out that although a postindustrial economy shapes a postindustrial social structure, ideas and invention underlie economic and technological innovation. Following Bell, we next examine the typical occupational and class structure of postindustrial society and then the cultural and intellectual context that helped to produce it.

2. *Occupational Distribution: The Postindustrial Occupational Structure*

TABLE 3.1 SOCIO-ECONOMIC GROUPS: ENGLAND AND WALES, 1921–91 (ECONOMICALLY ACTIVE

SEG/Year	1921	1961	1991
Employers and managers	6.6	7.6	14.6
Self-employed professionals	0.5	0.5	0.9
Employed professionals	0.9	2.2	3.6
Technicians	2.9	5.8	12.5
Junior non-manual	11.8	20.2	20.0
Personal service	8.1	4.7	4.4
Manual supervisors	1.2	2.3	1.9
Skilled manual	30.8	23.7	12.7
Semi-skilled manual	15.3	15.0	10.7
Unskilled manual	8.3	7.8	5.4
Non-professional self-employed	5.1	3.1	6.3
Farmers and farm managers	1.7	1.4	0.7
Agricultural workers	4.3	1.8	0.7
*Other	2.3	3.8	5.6
Total	17,178,050	22,296,010	23,895,910

*Other – Armed forces, Government Training Scheme (1991) and not stated.
Source: OPCS, Population Census Reports
In T. Spybey ed., 'Britain in Europe' (London: Routledge, 1997): 115.

The large and decisive change in the occupational structure hailed by Bell was the rise of managerial, professional and technical employment and the decline of manual employment. Using comparative international statistics, Bell claimed that in the United States and Western Europe 'the most startling change' in the occupational structure had been 'the growth of professional and technical employment jobs that usually require some college education'(note, here 'college' includes all higher education). Bell also noted that by the late 1960s, the number of white collar employees outnumbered the number of blue-collar employees.

A glance at Table 3.1 at the beginning of this section, which uses much more contemporary data than Bell's, will show that the trends noted by him did indeed occur progressively and emphatically in England and Wales between 1921 and 1991 and that the speed of change accelerated in most occupational areas between 1961 and 1991. Between 1961 and 1991 there was a large increase in the two categories seen by Bell as particularly central to postindustrial society. Aggregated, the percentage of self-employed and employed professionals increased from 2.7 to 4.5 per cent of the total labour force and that of technicians from 5.8 to 12.5 of the total labour force. If we add the percentage of employers and managers in the labour force in 1991 – 14.6 – to that of technicians and professionals, it comes to over 30 per cent – more than the aggregated percentage of skilled, semi-skilled and unskilled manual workers for the same year. What is more, these trends have continued strongly in England and Wales throughout the 1990s.

As Table 3.2 shows, the occupational transition from industrial to service sector employment is not especially strong in Britain in comparison to other European countries. As the table indicates, Britain is closer to the mean in this trend rather than especially marked by it. It is significant that all the countries in the table which had a larger percentage of jobs in the service sector in 1990 than did Britain also had a higher standard of living while most of those with a smaller percentage had a lower standard of living. There is a clear correlation between the size of a country's service sector and its average standard of living.

TABLE 3.2   OCCUPATIONAL TRANSITION IN EUROPE: PROFESSIONAL, TECHNICAL AND RELATED WORKERS (% OF ECONOMICALLY ACTIVE POPULATION)

Country	1960	1990
Sweden	12.9	31.8
Finland	8.2	23.8
Denmark	7.8	22.9
Norway	8.0	22.3
Netherlands	9.2	22.0
France	9.1	18.0*
Britain	8.6	17.0*
W. Germany†	7.6	15.0
Ireland	7.1	14.3
Austria	6.8	14.2
Greece	3.4	11.7
Spain	4.1	9.6
Portugal	2.7	8.5

Source: Adapted from Sulkunen, 1992: 26

Note: *Authors' own estimate.

† The former West Germany

In Spybey, op. cit. :115.

Impressive though these statistical shifts in occupational categories are, it is the crucial role that professional and technical groups play in the running and development of society that is most significant. Among these groups, it is scientists (including social scientists) – the theoreticians and researchers of postindustrial society – and engineers – who apply knowledge practically – that he saw as most important. Since the publication of *The Coming of Post-Industrial Society*, Bell has increasingly emphasised that the production, processing, and application of *information* is the core dynamic of postindustrial society. In this respect, Bell is very close in his analysis to Manuel Castells who adopts the term 'the informational society' as his key descriptor of post-industrial society. Arguably, Castells' trilogy *The Information Age* (1996) supersedes the theoretical framework of Bell but if so, he does so by 'standing on a giant's shoulders'. The three key aspects of postindustrial society which address the issue of the role of theoretical knowledge will now be discussed.

3. *The Centrality of Theoretical Knowledge in Postindustrial Society*

4. *Future Orientation: The Control of Technology;*

5. *Decision Making: The Creation of a New 'Intellectual Technology'*

In a later publication than the one under detailed discussion here, Bell clearly stated what he considered to be the basis in information of postindustrial society and crucially distinguished the latter from industrial society:

> My basic premise has been that knowledge and information are becoming the axial resource and transforming agent of the post-industrial society .. just as the combination of energy, resources and machine technology were the transforming agencies of industrial society'
>
> (Quoted in Kumar, 1995: 9)

Bell includes a wide range of activities in 'the information economy'. In addition to educational research and much planning activity, he includes marketing and electro-communications. In fact, it is the conjunction of information and the new electro-communications technology which generates the transformation of one type of society to another. In terms of the quantity, quality and speed of transmission of information, a new age has emerged.

Although writing well before the widespread adoption of environmentalism, Bell showed a keen awareness of the need to control the potentially destructive effects of economic development reinvigorated by the application of information technology:

> A feeling has begun to spread in the country that corporate performance has made the country uglier, dirtier, trashier, more polluted, and more noxious. (1973:272)

However, the solutions Bell then put forward have little in common with the naturalism of the 1960s hippies or 1990s New Age movement. Rather, he argues that government intervention – legislation, inspection and planning – is required in order to exercise the necessary control and restraint on economic development. This approach reflected the pragmatic liberalism with which Bell has long been associated. Now, at the beginning of a new millennium, it seems that a more radical and far-reaching approach, global in scope, will be needed to deal with environmental pollution and disturbance.

Bell's key point, then, is that theoretical knowledge is the *axial* principle of the information age. In the information age, the role of information in the running of society has been elevated to a qualitively different level than was the case in previous societies. Of course the processing of information requires material technology – though the amounts become relatively smaller and smaller – but it is the information itself – knowledge building upon knowledge – that is axial to the information age. Bell adopts a definition of technology which itself stresses the intellectual (or software) rather than the material (or hardware) aspects. He states that technology 'is the use of scientific knowledge to specify ways of doing things in a reproducible manner'(1973:29). In the industrial age, the main technology of reproduction was machine technology. In the information age, the main technology of reproduction is information technology. This is a much more powerful means of production than machine technology alone. Bell states that: 'An intellectual technology is the substitution of algorithms (problem-solving rules) for intuitive judgements'(29). Various kinds of computer software can make calculations at a speed and level of complexity far beyond the capacity of the human brain. For instance, without the help of computer-based calculations the recent mapping of the human gene pool would not have been possible with all the implications this has for the screening and prevention of disease. Given the appropriate input or software package, high-powered computers are able to examine various possibilities and probabilities in relation to a given problem much more quickly than the human brain. Computers are also able to produce models and images of great precision – virtual reality – which are equally good at presenting something or somebody that does exist or might exist – according to given specifications.

Computers provide a vast mass of processed information that can help in planning both in the small-scale and large-scale context. Thus, they tend to accelerate change and give information societies a strong orientation to the future – Bell's fourth point (for a discussion of the impact of this phenomenon on generational relations, see pp. 97–8). Bell's fifth point emphasises that computerised information can play a major role in decision-making. Arguably, he at times over-stresses the extent to which political and policy decisions can be resolved 'technically'. To be meaningful such decisions must also be motivated and directed by values – an issue to which we return several times.

In Bell's view as in that of Castells', theoretical knowledge or processed information is central or axial to the formation of a new type of society. Bell initially termed this new society 'post-industrial society' and later 'the information society'. Castells terms it 'the informational society' and sometimes also refers to it as 'the network society', a term which stresses more the ease and extent of communication in late modernity. In general, the term information society will be used here as it is simple and explicit. The next section attempts to describe in greater detail how production is organised in the information society.

Bell's information society thesis has not gone uncriticised, although in my view the broad thrust of it looks more credible with the passage of time. In *Theories of The Information Society* (1995), Frank Webster finds Bell's thesis both too sweeping (and historically unspecific) and too deterministic. Webster accepts what he calls the 'informatisation' of life but rejects the concept of the information society. He sees the process by which more and more information is generated and put to social use as one 'that has been ongoing, arguably for several centuries but which certainly accelerated with the development of industrial capitalism .. and moved into overdrive in the later twentieth century as globalisation and the spread of transnational organisations especially have led to the incorporation of hitherto untouched realms ..' (217). So for Webster the contemporary period is less dramatically and qualitatively different than Bell (and the present author) believe. Further, Webster argues that the process of informatisation, considered in itself as a single or mono-causal factor, has changed much less than he believes Bell claims in his information society thesis. Webster insists that beliefs and values that are reflected in the contest and debate about why and how information is used are crucial to the kind of society that is created.

I agree with Webster's last point but so, too, I think would Bell. There is less distance between Bell and Webster than the latter believes on the importance of values and beliefs. In his introduction to *The Coming of Post-industrial Society,* Bell makes it clear that while changes in the occupational and social structure will be driven by the new technology he does 'not claim that these changes in social structure determine changes in the polity or the culture' (13). He also denies that his thesis is over-generalised, claiming only to be pointing out certain, admittedly very significant, tendencies. Where Bell and Webster do differ, at least in emphasis, is that whereas the former tends to take some form of capitalist market economy for granted in his analysis of information technology, the latter is more explicit in insisting that capitalism shapes the use of information technology just as it shapes much else.

Almost thirty years after Bell published his book, and six after Webster published his, we see changes occurring almost on a daily basis in which information technology is centrally involved if not the main causal factor. Old style factories have gone and, with the arrival of e-commerce, we are beginning to see what may well be a radical restructuring of the physical organisation of retailing. The revolutions in information and communications have changed much of the form if not necessarily the content of interpersonal relations. And so it will go on. Nevertheless, Webster is right that the capitalist system shapes the nature of all that has been discussed above. But Bell is right, too: capitalism or not, the information revolution itself has fundamental social consequences. We can all agree that these need to be consciously and wisely mediated on the basis of human values.

PostFordism and the Information (Postindustrial) Society

PostFordism is relevant here because, according to some authorities, it is the typical and preferred organisational form of late modern society. PostFordist organisational structure is substantially dependent on the information revolution discussed above and is said to require greater flexibility of labour as well as technology. To the extent that PostFordist structures affect the way the workforce is organised and recruited it is highly relevant to issues of power and control in the workplace and to class/stratification structure. These issues are traditionally of central concern to Marxists some of whom are highly critical of the postFordist thesis as little more than an elaborate justification by capitalists to lay off workers as it suits their investment strategies. Whatever the causes of postFordism, there is little doubt that it is an organisational approach that strongly tends to increase the power of capital-management. What follows initially provides definitions and explanations of Fordism/postFordism and moves on to debates about its extent and influence.

PostFordism is a more flexible form of organising and managing production than Fordism. Fordism refers to rigidly organised – typically assembly line – forms of production and hierarchical systems of management. The term has sometimes been extended to cover all large top-downward forms of organisation considered typical of industrial society, including vast central and local state bureaucracies. It has also been used to refer to the pattern of mass consumption common in industrial society. Fordism produced the same or a very limited range of a product – a Ford Popular, a can of Heinz beans, a packet of Kellogg's' cornflakes – for the masses. Expensive luxuries were for the rich few. Philip Cooke gives a useful summary indication of the wide scope of the term.

> Fordism was associated with large-scale, mass production methods as pioneered by Henry Ford in Detroit and extended even to the factory building of mass housing in the 1960s. 'Fordism' is short for the method of social, political and economic regulation which linked, by making interdependent, mass production and mass consumption.
>
> (1989:8–9)

The description of Fordism as a 'method of social, political and economic regulation' indicates the huge scope of the term. The idea of Fordism and post Fordism as 'regimes of regulation' is strongly associated with Bob Jessop (1994) and Lash and Urry (1987). The basic notion is that in Fordist period the state, business and the trade unions worked together to regulate the economy and welfare system. The mode of organisation was large-scale and bureaucratic – as in Fordist production. In the postFordist period or period of 'disorganised capitalism', as Lash and Urry put it, this arrangement breaks down as capital becomes dominant and operates relatively autonomously in a global context. Here, it is the postFordist theory in relation to production that will be evaluated. Its relevance to wider social and political matters will be discussed later.

Just as Fordism originally applied to production, so the early descriptions of postFordism focused on production and the organisation of the workforce. One of the earliest uses of the term was by Piore and Sabel in *The Second Industrial Divide*. They described a system of manufacturing in part of Northern Italy which was based on co-operative networking between firms and the flexible use of labour and technology within firms (1984). The term *flexible specialisation* was used to describe computerised production – which facilitated changes in product design – and also indicated the growing demand of consumers for more varied, niche products. Some of the debate around post-Fordism reflects the fact that the early descriptions of postFordism, including Piore and Sabel's, presented it as highly positive for employees as well as for capital-management. Employees were seen as experiencing 'job enrichment' and as having greater and more meaningful levels of participation in the production process – rather as is supposed to be the case in the Japanese model of production. Not surprisingly, this interpretation of postFordism was picked up by management 'gurus' and became an important feature in portraying capitalism as benign both in business schools and more widely in the press. Some more recent sociological accounts of postFordism, including those of Jessop and Lash and Urry, have argued that capital-management have been the clear primary beneficiaries of postFordism. Other sociologists, including some more traditional Marxists, have doubted whether the flexibility associated with postFordism is occurring more widely than in the past and have emphasised the enduring subordination of labour to capital in production relations even where variations in the organisation of production do occur(Pollert:1991).

Robin Murray provides a useful if somewhat idealised description of the term postFordism which illustrates how the term has come to be applied to *consumption* as well as production. It is given in Hall and Jacques' edited book *New Times: The Changing Face of Politics in the 1990s* (1989) which was a keynote text for the 'post' theories:

> We can see in this country a culture of post-Fordist capitalism emerging. Consumption has a new place. As for production the keyword is flexibility – of plant and machinery, as of products and labour. Emphasis shifts from scale to scope, and from cost to quality. Organisations are geared to respond to rather than regulate markets. They are seen as frameworks for learning as much as instruments of control. Their hierarchies are flatter and their structures more open. The guerrilla force takes over from the standing army'
>
> (1989:47)

Murray goes on to emphasise that postFordism allows for specialist or niche production/consumption whereas Fordism tends to be inflexibly geared to large-scale standardisation. What Murray failed to stress was the extent to which mass consumer markets persist in many product areas and that current production techniques are equally able to cater for mass middle or low-quality demand as well as niche consumption. Despite some postFordist tweaks of design, many lines in, for instance, T-shirts and trainers are predominantly mass-produced although usually not now in a labour intensive way.

John Atkinson's ideal type presentation of the 'flexible corporation' was published as long ago as 1985 but it remains very useful as a way of envisaging key elements of the postFordist firm and for that reason is reprinted here. Atkinson's model emphasises the functional flexibility of the skilled core labour force and the numerical flexibility of the peripheral labour force which shades off into various types of part-time and occasional labour. Atkinson's model is worth looking at in some detail and will be very useful later when the occupational and stratificational structure of late industrial society is discussed. But how typical in reality is the 'flexible firm' and the various satellite smaller firms and individuals that it uses? The McDonaldization thesis, discussed later, suggests that as far as larger, especially multinational, companies are concerned, the new flexibility occurs within familiarly hierarchical and still relatively bureaucratic structures of power and organisation (see pp. 198 and 208).

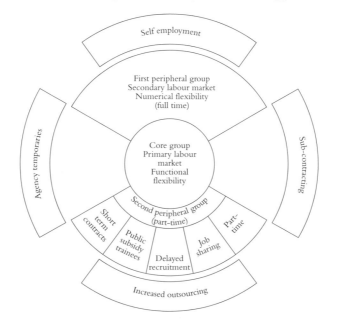

Figure 3.1   The flexible firm
Source: John Atkinson, 1985

Comment on Postfordist Theory

Three important debates about postFordism are:

- ❍ the extent to which it has occurred;
- ❍ the intentions behind postFordist strategies, including who benefits from them;
- ❍ the effects of postFordism.

Let us look at each of these points of dispute in turn, with a view not so much of resolving them in detail but of obtaining insight into how information society is run. The initial focus will be on the organisation of production and later on patterns of consumption.

Has a strong trend to postFordist organisational forms occurred? This question is so much one of empirical fact that it may seem odd that it has not yet been decisively resolved one way or the other. One problem is that the selective use of evidence for and against a proposed trend of this scale is easy and might give credence to either side of the argument. However, some things are virtually certain. First the new technology certainly allows for the changes in production, including replacing human labour with technology/machinery on a large scale. Second, the evidence is now overwhelming in many sectors of the biggest Western economies, especially the 'free-market, Anglo-Saxon' economies of the United States and Britain, postFordist techniques of production have indubitably been introduced whether one wishes to use the term 'postFordist' or some other to describe them. This has occurred not only in the manufacturing sector – such as the car industry – but also in the production of services, such as banking. New labour-saving, more flexible technology has been introduced across much of the economy and this has enabled more flexible use of the workforce, including some devolution of certain mainly routine functions to lower-level employees. The driving force behind these developments is the application of information technology rather than any postFordist grand plan. However, the term postFordist remains useful to the extent that the characteristics associated with it such as flexibility and decentralisation have become part of the politics and social policy as well as the economics of late modern societies.

We now turn to the second of the three questions posed above – why were postFordist forms of organising production introduced? The short answer to this question is that postFordism was introduced so that capitalists and managers could gain more control over the process of production and of the labour force. PostFordism required high level technology but it was not a neutral process because it was intended to strengthen capital and higher management and weaken labour. Although useful at a descriptive level, unless it is more fully theorised, the postFordist thesis fails to explain the nature and extent of recent changes in the contemporary capitalist economy – both British and global. The concept of postFordism describes what is happening in parts of the capitalist economy but it does not deal with motive and interests – who benefits from its introduction? – and so it fails to address the big picture. PostFordism is simply an organisational form and strategy and is insufficient in itself to explain the direction of the contemporary capitalist economy and society. Robin Murray indicates this when he refers to 'postFordist capitalism' rather than simply 'postFordism'. However, arguably the term postFordism is a red-herring and a better and increasingly used term is 'flexible capitalism'.

PostFordism theory does, indeed, have to be linked to a wider analysis of how capitalism again became globally hegemonic. As Paul Thompson points out (1993), given that the world economy is now overwhelmingly a capitalist one, to understand it requires a general theory of capitalism – not just a postFordist theory. This is neither a controversial nor an exclusively Marxist notion. Thompson adds the further uncontroversial observation that to understand capitalism at any given time, 'historically specific capitalist economies' must be analysed: in other words, a general theory must be informed by and responsive to the facts. Fortunately, there is a growing body of fact and theory available about contemporary capitalism.

Contemporary capitalism is not best summarily described as 'postFordist capitalism' because postFordist type organisational forms are only one aspect of its flexibility, albeit an important one. Contemporary capitalism is flexible in other ways. Indeed, as Anne Pollert has pointed out, capitalism is flexible enough to relocate around the world to make whatever 'efficiency gains' might be available. This includes using labour intensive methods of production (i.e., Fordism) in parts of the third world labour where the cost of labour is so low that the full-scale automation of production would cost more. Descriptions which capture the character of contemporary capitalism somewhat more fully than 'postFordism' are 'global capitalism' and 'information capitalism'. The term 'global capitalism' best describes the worldwide scope and dominance of capitalism but does not indicate the character of its new dynamic. Probably the term 'information capitalism' does this best because it is through highly flexible access to and use of information that contemporary capitalism achieves its current spectacular dominance. Various aspects of capitalism's flexibility are discussed in more detail in chapter 7.

The main effects of postFordism will by now be obvious. PostFordism, along with other strategies of control, played a part in strengthening capital and weakening labour. Some managerial theory has suggested that the devolution of certain administrative and minor decision making powers to lower levels in organisations is democratic and empowering (in the 1980s and early 1990s, a parallel was drawn with Japanese production techniques in these respects). In some cases these effects may have occurred but in others the workforce simply found itself with more to do – particularly if 'restructuring' or 're-engineering' (the jargon largely reflected managerial faddism) the organisation involved the redundancy of co-employees. Ironically, in Britain the 'public' sector, particularly education and the health service, was subject to particularly severe doses of such strategies with no obvious general enhancement of the experience of work and plenty of indications of increased stress among the workforce.

Social Structure in Late Modernity

The Stratification of Late Modern Society: Class, Gender, Race/Ethnicity and Age

This section concentrates on the 'hard' infrastructure of stratification rather than culture and consciousness. Stratification is the term used to describe the division of society into broad and unequal strata and occurs on the basis of class gender, race/ethnicity, and age. In this section the focus is on how groups defined by these terms relate to the division of labour, paid and domestic. This includes both Marxist analysis of relations to the means of production and Weberian analysis of market position. The structure of stratification always reflects changes in the technology of production and in the occupational structure. Classes grow and decline largely as the demand for their occupational skills ebbs and flows. The position in the division of labour of gender, ethnic and age groups also changes over time. As is discussed below, the demand for minority black labour and paid female labour and the removal of most younger teenagers from the labour market in the postThatcher period has not only radically affected the social positions of these groups but has also impacted on society in general. While social changes have been shaped by developments in the technology and organisation of paid and domestic work, they have also been caused by competition for money, power and status.

It will be obvious from the previous paragraph that class, gender, ethnic and age groups do not exist in separate compartments either as structural influences or as subjective identities. Most individuals have a routine self awareness which unifies all these aspects although they may be more conscious of one or other in any given social situation. The separate presentation below of these factors is a matter of convenience and, in any case, is only partial as issues of overlap and integration are considered. It will emerge that arguably the most important class development in postwar Britain and much of the Western world has been the impact of gender on class – the re-gendering of class.

Class

Figure 3.2 gives a composite summary of contemporary Marxist and Weberian views of class in modern Britain and also provides some basis for a wider discussion of class in the context of global capitalism. It is simply a working model and is not intended either to be definitive or to reflect equally the work of all contributors to this huge area.

Marxist	**Weberian**
Capitalist Class	(Capitalist Class)
Intermediate/Contradictory e.g., prof., managerial, admin..	Service Class prof., managerial, admin..
Working Class 1) Manual 2) Routine Non-manual	Intermediate Class(Lower White Collar) Working Class
Lumpenproleteriat	Underclass

Figure 3.2 Marxist and Weberian views of class summarised

Before making a more detailed analysis of changes in the British class structure, it is worth briefly addressing the global situation. Marx may have been mistaken about many things but his basic observation about the central role of capital and the power of capitalists in the economic context in the contemporary epoch is difficult to contest. He observed not only the dynamic role of national capitalist elites within their own country's economies but also the fast developing global dominance of Western capitalism. At the beginning of the new millennium, the world is even more capitalist than in Marx's time. Traditional economies have seldom survived the impact of capitalism intact and the major communist ones have either succumbed to or greatly compromised with capitalist principles. The extent to which capitalist economic power translates into political power and cultural control is discussed later.

Capitalism and the Capitalist Class

John Scott (1994) divides contemporary capitalists into three groups: entrepreneurial, internal and finance. Entrepreneurial capitalists are typically those who establish and build up their own businesses which they may or may not float on the stock exchange (i.e., make share ownership open to others). It is indicative of the independent and controlling character of these (mainly) men that they often have a love/hate relationship with the stock market – wanting to raise capital from share sales but sometimes resenting having to be answerable to and evaluated by others. Richard Branson of Virgin and Alan Sugar of Amstrad are examples of this type as, on a more global scale, is the media tycoon, Rupert Murdoch. Even when they do float their companies, major entrepreneurial capitalists sometimes maintain controlling shareholdings or, as in Murdoch's case, operate with share-blocs owned by family and friends.

Entrepreneurial capitalists are often at the centre of innovation and risk in contemporary capitalism but they are no longer the system's main centre of power and control. Nevertheless, the distribution of wealth in Britain has shown a steady rise in their fortunes relative to that of traditional landed wealth. In 1996, four of the top five wealthiest individuals were businessmen. The Duke of Westminster who occupied the number four slot had inherited major urban residential and commercial interests. Marriage of business and aristocracy has been one way of adding status to the former and wealth to the latter.

Internal capitalists are top career managers – for instance, those who sit on the Board of leading companies such as Glaxo-Welcome, British Telecom or Shell. It was suggested by Ralf Dahrendorf as long as forty years ago that 'managerial capitalism' was emerging as the typical and most powerful form of advanced capitalism (1959). It is vital to appreciate that the economic power of these top managers is institutional and systemic in nature rather than individual (although, of course, individual performances will vary in quality and effect). Their power is institutional in that they act on behalf of and are answerable to major capitalist companies i.e., they work for a collective or corporate entity rather than as individual entrepreneurs. Moreover, although individual managers will put the interest of 'their' company first, they routinely act in concert with managers from other companies. This is achieved largely through the mechanism of interlocking directorships by which managers sit on the Boards of other companies in order to provide advice and guidance. Apart from the legitimate functioning of interlocking directorates, the charge is sometimes made and has in some cases been proven that managers co-operate illegally, for instance, in price-fixing. Undoubtedly, Dahrendorf has been proven correct in that managerial or what might better be termed institutional capitalism has become the dominant form of industrial and commercial capitalism in the late twentieth century. It is the big corporations – many of them transnational – that dominate most national economies and the global economy.

Few career managers, even those with considerable shareholdings in their company, are quite as wealthy as the wealthiest entrepreneurial capitalists. The wealth built up by entrepreneurs such as the late Sir James Goldsmith and the Sainsbury family (in their case the work of several generations) is scarcely going to be matched by the rewards of paid employment even in these days of bonuses, share options and golden helloes and goodbyes. Interestingly, it is the salaried wealth of paid managers that has caught media attention and provoked public anger rather than the greater wealth of entrepreneurs. It was the salaried managers of public companies such as Cedric Brown of British Gas who were tagged as 'fat cats' rather than the much wealthier Branson or Murdoch. Two reasons can be suggested for this. First, all paid/salaried workers can be clearly perceived as a coherent reference group in that they all receive a wage or salary from some other individual or organisation. Thus, while one occupational group may not resent the principle of salary differentials, it may fiercely object if it receives a significantly lower percentage pay increase than another occupational group. This was what often happened in the 1990s, when top business managers received relatively much higher salary increases than many middle and lower paid occupational groups. As a result, inequality in Britain increased although apart from the poorest ten per cent, all groups became better off in absolute terms. A second possible reason for the apparent acceptance of entrepreneurial wealth compared to resentment of salaried wealth can be suggested – although there is less evidence for it. It may be that successful entrepreneurs are perceived as reaping the fair rewards of risk-taking and effort whereas those who get salary increases well beyond the national average are perceived as second-besting other ordinary people.

Scott suggests that financial or finance capitalism is perhaps the dominant form of capitalism in Britain. Financial capitalism refers to the financial operations of banks, pensions and insurance companies, in particular investment in and loans to industry and in currency and stock-market trading and speculation. As Scott points out, however, financial and managerial capitalism work

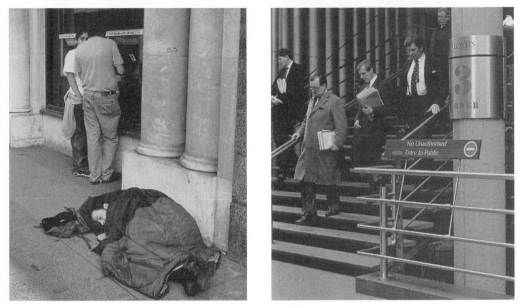

Figure 3.3 Relative inequality has increased under modern capitalism.

closely together and both are part of the structure of contemporary capitalism. Over fifty per cent of UK equities are owned by pension and insurance companies, which often have representation on the Boards of companies in which they have large investments (the profits from which they fund their pay-outs to policy holders). In other words these institutions own most of Britain's big companies. It hardly needs saying that if a company 'fails to perform', major institutional investors make their opinions felt.

The main investment banks are not the familiar high street banks such as Nat West or Barclays, although some of these have investment arms, but City based banks such as Morgan Stanley or Deutsche Bank. These are overwhelmingly American, Japanese and continental European owned, although they bring wealth, prestige and work to London. In recent years these banks have pursued currency and other forms of financial speculation as a means of making huge sums of money very quickly. However well informed, financial speculation, like most gambling, occurs in a variety of complicated forms but basically the aim is to buy cheap and sell expensive. In pursuit of profits in this way, in recent years speculators have precipitated the devaluation of the pound, and the collapse of currencies of Russia and several East Asian countries. Financial speculators tend to claim that they merely take advantage of or even clarify existing economic/financial conditions. However, by the late 1990s, not only many national governments but some influential financiers, including arch-speculator, George Soros, were firmly of the view that the world capitalist system urgently required to be reformed to curb the disruptive effects of massive speculation.

Inequality has always been an outcome of the capitalist system and under the operation of contemporary capitalism inequality has increased both between social groups within Britain and between countries globally. Given that capitalism involves the pursuit of profit in a competitive context, it inherently produces inequality but this does not explain the trend to greater inequality. Nor can the trend be explained simply in individual terms – the enterprise of some and the sloth of others – although the media may present it that way and under their influence, the public may see it that way. The deeper explanations are, respectively, structural, organisational and technological. Structurally, capital has become more powerful in relation to labour. The ability to switch production globally has been used to 'discipline' and in some cases reduce its rewards. As explained in the section on postFordism, information technology has been used to re-organise much of the workforce in a way that maximises capitalist-managerial control. Given the massive shift of labour out of the heavy industrial sector into the routine service sector this was not difficult to do.

The Service or Intermediate Class

The term 'service class' used by a number of Weberians and the term 'intermediate class' used by Marxist Harry Braverman refer to much the same occupational grouping – professional, managerial administrative and higher grade technical. Weberian, John Goldthorpe argues that this grouping has a specific class location largely based on its status, relatively high pay and superior work situation. Marxist, Harry Braverman employs the term 'intermediate' to indicate the buffer position occupied by many of this grouping in relation to capitalists and the majority of paid workers(1974). This role is obvious in terms of industrial managers but Braverman extends it to cover professional and semi-professional employees in the public services such as teachers and social workers whose role is to socialise individuals into conformity either through persuasion, coercion or financial inducement.

As was noted earlier in this chapter, the service class has grown rapidly in size since the second world war. Even at the beginning of the 1960s, Bell saw its emergence as the main development in the occupational structure of the period. Considered along with the parallel, and to some extent complementary decline of the manual working class, Bell is probably right. It is this class more than any other that has driven – and ridden – the information revolution. It has 'driven' it in the sense that it has used its technical, organisational and communication skills to provide the higher level services that characterise and to a great extent define late modern society. The expansion of financial, education and health services, the supply of 'high tech' skills on which these services increasingly depend, are all the work of this class. The service class also drives modern society in that it directs or interfaces with lower status non-manual and manual employees. The service class has 'ridden' the information revolution in that it has grown in size and generally prospered as a result of it. While it is true that the crucial technological inventions and applications that are the material foundation of modern society are the work of a gifted few, in a more routine sense the service class can be considered the architect of its own good fortune. The typically diligent and prudent attitudes of this class, particularly the commitment of many of its members to education and the achievement of financial security and home-ownership, have established it as a model of solid achievement to which many outside it aspire.

However, the security, power and influence of the service class is by no means entirely in its own hands. In this respect, the Marxist theorising of Braverman and Eric Olin Wright is perhaps most to the point. Apart from self-employed professionals, most of the service class are dependent for their income either on the state or commercial enterprise. They may have more authority and status and enjoy better rewards than most wage-workers, but they are wage-workers still. As Wright puts it, they are in an 'ambiguous' class position. Recession or technological/organisational change in an industry can and has resulted in members of the service class being made redundant or having their contracts renewed on less favourable terms. The better working conditions and benefits traditionally enjoyed by the service class and emphasised by Weberians are increasingly less likely to be secured by contracts for life. As older managers and professionals have moved out of or been moved out of their jobs, younger ones have been employed often on shorter term contracts and performance related pay/perks. For some service as well as manual employees' 'flexibility' at work can mean losing their job: one person's flexibility plans can be another's redundancy notice.

Despite being affected by the insecurities generated by contemporary capitalism, the increasing size and prosperity of the service class justifies the importance attached to it by Bell. Much of the management and planning, as well as some of the inventiveness of late modern society depends on its work. Further, as is discussed below, employees in education or the media members of the service class play a significant role in the formation of culture and opinion. Aristotle contended that the stability of a society depends on it having a substantial and prosperous middle class and it may well be that this argument partly explains the relative orderliness of the Western democracies in the postwar years. Nevertheless, substantial though the service class is, it is not in terms of decision-making the most powerful class. A minority of its members move on to the highest levels of power but as a class grouping the service class is at the intermediate level of power. Still less does it control the often unpredictable functioning of the capitalist system.

The Lower White Collar and Manual Working Class

It may seem odd to discuss these two class groupings together. The manual working class has had an especially prominent and controversial place in class theory whereas the lower white collar or lower middle class, though surveyed and analysed often enough, has not attracted the same lively attention. Whereas in Marxist theory, the manual working class has been described as having a potentially highly active and even heroic role, Weberians, who have given more attention to white collar employees, tend to portray a rather conformist, security-minded and bureaucratically flattened class – 'cheerful robots' in Marcuse's unflattering description.

The reasons for the importance attached to the manual working class in stratification theory are largely historical. First, is the empirical reality that the manual working class used to be overwhelmingly the biggest class. Shortly after the second world war, over 50% of the employed population was manual working class whereas the recent figure is about 20%. Other things being equal, the potential for decisive action of over 50% of the population – given effective leadership – must be a great deal more than for 20%. Second, Marx argued that the working class was the historical agency for change in capitalist society. It had an absolutely central position in his scheme of historical change. In so far as Marx was attempting prophesy here, then he was methodologically wrong (prophesy being no part of social science) and many would argue that empirically by the end of the twentieth century, the balance of the facts has gone against him. However, although Marxists may be thin on the ground among the general populace, there remain formidable intellectuals who, while making no claim to prophesy, work within the broad Marxist model of change. Third, the manual working class has had a major place in stratification theory – especially Marxist but also Weberian – because of the obvious issues of inequality, exploitation and social justice its class position provokes. Controversially, many observers consider that its situation has substantially improved in relation to these matters, and that as a consequence it commands less of their attention and concern.

The decline in the size and influence of the manual or traditional working class is a matter of fact. It is manifest in a myriad of ways. Millions of British working class people have simply been replaced by technology in the location of their core identity – in the process of production. As a consequence traditional working class occupational communities – mining, factory, docking – have virtually disappeared. This is true both culturally as well as physically. The highly distinctive, gender-segmented, localised and, in its own way excluding, way of life of the traditional working class, so affectionately and painstakingly described by Richard Hoggart, has gone(1957). Indeed, Hoggart himself observed the early signs of its demise, commenting tartly on the emergence of an Americanised British youth culture and the growth of the sex industry ('sex in shiny packages'i.e., 'dirty magazines'). Of course residues of traditional working class culture remain, if often in transmuted forms. One such manifestation is middle class 'new laddism' which has 'stolen' some of the 'rougher' and more macho aspects of the language and style of working class youth, not least, their identification with football.

Faced with the above developments, it might seem that the Marxist analysis of the working class has become almost irrelevant. However, Marxism at its best is a living tradition, not an orthodoxy carved in rock, and has been reworked to reflect historical developments. One of the most significant disagreements between Marxists and Weberians is over how to define the class position of routine non-manual workers such as office workers and sales personnel. Harry Braverman's *Labor and Monopoly Capital* (1974) remains one of the more comprehensive arguments that these employees should be classified as working class. He points out that their relationship to the means of production is that of wage-workers rather than owners. Although they are not directly involved in the material production of commodities, in a broader sense they play a part in facilitating the production and distribution of goods and services. The most original part of Braverman's argument is that, as a result of *deskilling*, routine non-manual workers (as well as some higher level non-manual workers) were being *proleterianised*. Braverman contended that new office technology and organisational methods were being introduced to control and standardise the office work just as industrial technology had been employed in relation to, typically, assembly line workers. As a result, the working situation of many routine non-manual workers was little, if any better than that of manual workers and, in addition, their pay was often worse.

Weberian class theorists use the term intermediate class grouping to refer to the grouping below that for which the Marxist Braverman reserves the term. Weberians invariably argue that the class situation of intermediate level employees – for example, routine non-manual, small proprietors, lower-grade technicians – is different and, in key respects, better than that of the manual working class. Among the first to make this analysis in the postwar era was David Lockwood who argued in *The Blackcoated Worker* that there are three aspects to class situation: market situation (e.g., wages, job security, promotion prospects) work situation (e.g., relations with managers, including the extent of autonomy), and status situation (the social prestige attached to a particualar job). While accepting that the wages of better paid manual workers often exceeded that of clerks – blackcoated workers – Lockwood argued that in all three aspects, the latter were generally in the better situation and were therefore in a different class position. Fundamentally, this position has been maintained by leading Weberians since the publication of Lockwood's book. Marshall *et al*'s *Social Class in Modern Britain* (1988) which appeared some thirty years after Lockwood's book, specifically rejected the deskilling and proleterianisation theses in relation to clerks. Only four percent of respondents stated that their jobs required less skill. Most respondents also did not perceive any decline in the autonomy they enjoyed in their work situation.

Although Marxists and Weberians differ about the class situation of clerical workers, there is a measure of agreement between them that the class situation of personal service workers – checkout operators, receptionists, shop assistants – is no better in terms of pay and conditions than that of the manual working class. It seems logical, therefore, to classify these employees as working class although this adjustment does not yet seem generally to have been implemented (thus, Marshall *et al*'s 1988 survey broadly endorses Goldthorpe's, 1972 class schema which classifies these occupations as intermediate).

Although it is logical to regard these occupations as working class in terms of levels of pay, conditions of work, and status, they bear little resemblance to traditional manual working class jobs. The latter were manned overwhelmingly by male, full-time, workers who were members of trade unions whereas the former are manned mainly by women, the majority of whom are not members of trade unions and who work on a part-time or temporary basis. There is no immediate basis for seeing this class grouping as inheritors of the Marxist mantle of the key agency of change.

The Lumpenproleteriat or Underclass (or, simply, 'The Excluded'?)

As the rather dismissive pre-fix 'lumpen' (lump) implies, what Marx termed the lumpenproleteriat was as peripheral to his theoretical schema as the proleteriat proper was central to it. Similarly, his undoubted concern with human exploitation and alienation was expressed much more in relation to the working class than to the economically marginalised. Ironically in this limited but significant context, Marx could be accused of being a touch elitist and of not really sympathising with society's biggest losers. The following quotation from Marx and Engels expresses both their view of the proleteriat as 'special' and of the lumpen as volatile and even degenerate:

> Of all the classes that stand face to face with the bourgeoisie today, the proleteriat alone is a really revolutionary class. The other decay and finally disappear in the face of modern industry; the proleteriat is its special and essential product.

> The 'dangerous class,' the social scum, that passively rotting mass thrown off by the lowest layers of old society, may, here and there, be swept into the movement of a proleterian revolution; its conditions of life, however, prepare it far more for the part of a bribed tool of reactionary intrigue.

> (Marx and Engels in Bottomore and Rubel, 1981:92)

Marx and Engels's attitude to the lumpenproleteriat seems to be shaped by the fact that the latter does not fit into their schematic analysis of historical development whereas the proleteriat is its dynamic driving force. They wrote long before the welfare state was envisaged as a partial solution to the poverty and discontent of the non-working poor.

The Weberian-inspired concept of the underclass is of more recent origin than that of lumpenproleteriat. It describes roughly the same groups as those indicated by the later term i.e., all those outside of regular employment and likely to be in poverty. However, there has been much more contemporary analysis of what the term underclass might imply and which groups might comprise it. The latter have variously been considered to be the longterm unemployed, irregularly or never employed youth, poor single parents, the poor and vulnerable elderly. Given the great diversity of the so-called underclass and their non-existent or irregular ties to work and the occupational system, Dahrendorf is surely correct to state that 'the underclass .. is not a class'(1992:57). Indeed, it is not. This leads to the question of what, then, is the underclass and what do its 'members' have in common. Clearly, they do not share a common work situation, still less a shared class consciousness. What they do share is the negative experience of *exclusion* from regular employment and resulting deprivation – even though these factors are suffered in very varying degrees. To be socially excluded or marginalised is a highly significant personal and social experience. It can imply low status and involve stigmatisation and this has certainly been the experience of some groups, such as poor single mothers, sometimes considered to be part of the underclass. To this extent, the underclass more resembles a caste or status group than a class, although it lacks the communal ties of status groups proper.

The more closely focused concept of black underclass draws on the concepts of both status/caste and class to explain the high level of exclusion of black people from better paid jobs. John Rex, in particular, has argued that racial discrimination and class disadvantage reinforce each other in respect to black immigrants into Britain (1986), although more latterly evidence has emerged that non-white ethnic communities as well as individuals can achieve upward mobility despite widespread discrimination. More recently, the right wing social scientist, Charles Murray, initially used the term black underclass to describe black single parents and their, according to his statistics, often delinquent male offsprings (1989). He described their way of life as a *culture of dependency* and advocated cutting back on and ultimately withdrawing their welfare payments. He suggested that in such circumstances, their children could be adopted by more thrifty adults. In a later publication, Murray linked his analysis of the black underclass with iq theory, implying that relatively lower average intelligence compared to other racial groups might explain their relatively lower social position (*The Bell Curve*: 1995). Many sociologists and other commentators felt that this was to racialise the concept and to flirt with social policies which were not merely discriminatory but which echoed fascism in their authoritarianism and racial overtones.

The black sociologist, William Julius Wilson, who had originally played a part in popularising the concept of the underclass stated that it had become too associated with negative implications and that he intended to stop using it (1987; 1991). In any case, the concept has drifted into relative disuse in the late nineteen nineties – doubtless because of the difficulty in giving it consistent and useful application and because of the stigma it has acquired.

The term 'excluded' is even less of a 'class' term than 'underclass' and in fairness is not intended to be. What is more likely is that it is intended by the Blair government to draw attention away from class-based and systemic analysis of poverty in contemporary Britain. What the government wants to focus on is not the extent to which (global) capitalism generates poverty but on ensuring that as many of the exluded as can work, do work. Those that cannot are offered, in principle at least, security. The continuing historically high numbers of people sleeping on the streets indicate the problems faced by this tidy solution.

Whatever their limitations, terms such as 'underclass' and 'excluded' do, at least, draw attention to those who are not sharing in the increasing affluence of the West. They represent the last unconquered frontier of welfare capitalism.

How Much Does Class Matter Now, Anyway?

Class is made up of two aspects which can be presented in a variety of ways. There is the material side of class which pertains to occupation and property and there is the cultural side which pertains to how people live and think. It is the strength of the link between the two that gives class its degree of potency and meaning as a basis of collective action. If members of the occupational working class do not share common values and goals, they are unlikely to act together in any substantial, sustained or effective way. Another way of expressing this distinction is through the terms objective and subjective class. Objective class membership is allocated on the basis of some predetermined criteria of classification, such as relations to the means of production or market situation or occupation and subjective class membership is that selected by the person or subject him or herself. Marx expressed the same distinction by use of the terms *class in itself* and *class for itself*. In his terms, a class in itself is defined by its relations to the means of production and class for itself by a collective awareness of class position and identity which Marxists tend to refer to as class consciousness. It is when many members of a class are aware of their position in the socio-economic system and can actively consider how to sustain or improve their position that Marx speaks of a high level of class consciousness. Finally, it makes little sense to talk of the decline of class in an objective sense in a capitalist society although it is to be expected that class structure will change and that the relative income and wealth of classes may also change. Class structure and inequality are inherent to capitalism – changes in the shape of class structure should not be confused with its disappearance.

There is no doubt that class in itself or objective class remains of immense importance in Britain and, arguably, is of major and growing importance in the global context. During the Thatcher–Major period, both wealth and income became more unequally distributed. The very rich became better-off in relation to all other groups and middle income earners became better-off in relation to the poor (the bottom 20% of income earners/welfare recipents). In other words, as might be predicted in a period of Conservative, radically pro-capitalist government, relative inequality increased although 90% per cent of the population saw some increase in their income.

The first effect of class inequality, then, is that it shapes the material circumstances of people's lives to the advantage of some and to the disadvantage of others. The differences in property owner-ship and purchasing power between the very rich and very poor can hardly be overemphasised and even the differences between the very poor and the merely better-off than average have fun-damental effects on their lifestyles, prospects and attitudes.

The differences between the lifestyles of the rich and the rest – but especially the poor – are the easiest to imagine and illustrate. Their lifestyles are the daily stuff of the news media, particularly the tabloids, but increasingly, too, of the broadsheets and magazines, whereas the conditions of the poor warrant occasional coverage – often of a sensationalist but transient 'shock, horror' variety. Ownership of six houses scattered round the world has 'better' news-value (i.e. is a better story) than ownership of none or of only an inadequate one. Even the limited wealth of a service class family may enable it to buy something as basic as better medical treatment and so better health than those who cannot afford to and have to suffer the pain of long waits. Of course, one of the great objective facts of class in the postindustrial Britain is the enormous growth in the numbers of people in the middle of the class hierarchy whose material condition has improved relative to that of their parents and grandparents and who do not wish to risk what they have gained. The 'new middle classes' have undoubtedly been a major cause of a shift in British politics towards the fostering and protection of their interests. Indeed, in the late 1990s the Labour Party was pre-emi-nently the party of the middle class if not that of the very rich and may well remain so. However, right-wing commentators who argue that the substantial, and to some extent increasing inequali-ties that characterise the British class system reflect the arrival of a meritocracy are as much the vic-tims of self-delusion as dogmatic Marxists who believe that the revolution of the proletariat is inevitable. Social inequality still reflects the luck of birth and the power of position as well as dif-ferences in individual merit.

It is precisely in the hampering of the rise of talent, on the one hand, and protecting privilege on the other that class inequality appears to have a further major effect. Put more technically, class position substantially affects life chances. This point has been strongly made by Weberian analysts of class and is worth pursuing in some detail. The Oxford Mobility Survey examined patterns of social mobility in Britain between 1949 and 1972 and a follow-up survey covered the period between 1972 and 1983. Prominent Weberians A. H. Halsey and John Goldthorpe were involved in the first and Goldthorpe again in the second. The findings of these surveys can be summarised as follows:

1. There has been a significant absolute (i.e. overall historical) and steady increase in upward social mobility due almost entirely to an increase in professional, administrative and mana-gerial positions and a decline in manual wage-earning positions;

2. These changes do not reflect any changes in relative mobility rates between the classes – as the service class has benefited from the expansion of service sector jobs roughly in the same proportion as the working class (i.e. its downward mobility decreased as upward mobility from the working and intermediate classes increased). The relative chances of a son of a serv-ice class father maintaining service class status against the son of a working class father obtain-ing it remain about 6:1. So, although there has been greater overall opportunity for upward mobility in absolute terms, equality of opportunity has not increased. Indeed, the follow-up survey covering the 1972 to 1983 period suggested that the recession in the latter part of that period had increased downward mobility among the working class, and it can be conjectured

that the same process may have occurred during the recessions of the early and late 1990s although there may also have been some 'shake-out' and resulting increased downward mobility from higher social classes.

3. The above trends enhanced the stability of the service class while the working class became somewhat less stable inter-generationally.

In the liberal tradition of Max Weber, Weberian class theorists point out that, given a roughly equal spread of intelligence across the classes, the relative inequality of access of working class compared to service class offspring to the service class indicates a continuing high degree of inequality of opportunity. This has persisted despite the expansion of the education system, including the steady rise in the minimum school leaving age. The question of what is to be done about this is, of course, a policy issue. What Weberian class theorists have done is present the issue sharply and lucidly. It is not a question which has quite the same import to Marxist sociologists who have generally argued that upward mobility from the working class weakens its solidarity (a point which Weberian research implicitly appears to support).

Both Marxists and Weberians have extensively examined the role of the education system in the reproduction and possible reduction of class inequalities and although their theoretical angle is somewhat different, there is considerable agreement on the ineffectiveness so far of education reform to increase equal opportunity between the classes. While there is no agreement on the relative effects of material and cultural disadvantages on educational attainment, there is general agreement that the former can have a significant effect, even if in exceptional cases they are overcome. Such problems, as not having a quiet room to work in, or enough money to buy educational materials can affect attainment even in the face of strong parental and child motivation. Marxists, in particular, have emphasised what Bourdieu refers to as the cultural capital of middle class children which he sees as 'fitting' better the norms values and operation of the middle class dominated education system than working class culture. The Weberian educationalist A.H. Halsey argues that cultural capital is more important at primary than secondary school level. Thus, at secondary school level a working class child of equal ability and attainment as a middle class child is more likely to be hampered in future progress by material than cultural factors. Whatever the precise reasons why, the middle class is able to use education to maintain its relative advantage over the working class. On the other hand, the several millions of sons and daughters of manual workers who have achieved upward mobility would in many cases have been unable to do so without the benefit of extended secondary and, in an increasing number of cases, higher education which became steadily more available in the postwar period. An important related argument not pursued here is that a more affluent and middle class society has shifted its interest from matters concerning production to consumption and lifestyle – thus further undermining the basis of class conflict (see pp. 179–80).

Objectively, class is very important in the above ways. But, subjectively, do people think it is important? This question has provoked lively and at times sharp debate. The answer seems to be a highly qualified 'yes'. In summary, the main qualification that individuals make about class is that it is only one (and not, in all cases) the most important, influence in their life. Thus, Fiona Devine argues that it cannot be assumed that people automatically give priority to one identity over another and that social context is crucial in shaping people's sense of and definitions of identity. Her own empirical work was in Luton where she carried out a series of in-depth interviews with thirty two working class couples on the subject of their lifestyles and social and political identities. While her sample is made-up entirely of working class people, it is quite likely that her wider conclusions are more generally applicable. It is best to quote from her own summary of her findings:

> .. (P)eople hold a variety of social identities which influence the way in which they see themselves, the ways in which they interact with other people, and their beliefs,

attitudes, hopes and plans, fears and misgivings. One of the most important of these social identities is a sense of place .. Moreover, it was found that other social identities, such as a regional or national identity, coexist with a high level of class awareness .. Class was clearly a salient social identity in the political domain although it did not always translate into votes. The main finding to emerge from the qualitative data is that a high level of class awareness can coexist with other significant social identities.

(Devine, 1992:249)

The importance of Devine's comments in relation to social groupings other than class can now be examined, initially in concrete terms of social structure and resources, power and status, and later in terms of their personal and cultural identities.

Gender (and the Division of Labour)

The division of labour in Western industrial societies developed along clearly demarcated lines of gender as well as class. Generally, women did the childcare, kept the home and did the shopping, while men sold their labour for money and did the more physical repair jobs around the house which did not require hiring a skilled worker. The capitalist and professional classes were made up almost exclusively of men – indeed, the major professions were excluded to women by law. The millions of women who did paid work had little option but to work in stereotypically female areas of employment, typically as domestics or servants or, for middle class women, in nursing and primary school teaching. These occupations were poorly paid and of relatively low status.

At the risk of being simplistic, it is possible to differentiate both a liberal and a socialist/Marxist stream of feminist thought and policy-orientation. A third orientation, radical feminism, will be dealt with later. The liberal feminist tradition sought and seeks to achieve for women the same rights and opportunities as are available to men. It does not seek to change the hierarchical structure of capitalist society itself. Given the unequal way the division of labour was gendered, it is not surprising that many early feminists saw fairer access to paid work as a major element, if not *the* major element in the road to greater freedom for women and gender equality. The right to vote was also seen as giving women crucial access to democratic power.

The more Marxist stream of feminism argues that capitalism is structured in a way that exploits both working class men and working class women but in so far as the latter are subject to patriarchy, as well as to capitalism, they are subject to a dual oppression. Thus, not only did women maintain the male capitalist labour force and bring up future ones for no reliable material reward, but they were expected to be subservient to their husbands in the domestic context. At marriage, a woman lost not only her 'maiden-name' but whatever property she had to her husband as well. Given, the near impossibility of divorce for most women, they were embedded in this situation for life. Engels argued that it is capitalism that is fundamentally responsible for the oppression of both the majority of males and females and with its abolition and the introduction of socialism, gender inequality would be removed along with class inequality (1884). In structural terms, then, Marxists see capitalism and patriarchy as *articulating* or interlocking closely but with the former as dominant.

In practice, as far as Western society is concerned what progress there has been made towards gender equality in the public sphere has been largely along liberal lines. However, the Scandinavian countries have adopted a more socialist approach, providing universal childcare facilities and maternity and paternity leave (the latter not transferable to female partners) on better terms than elsewhere. Nevertheless, even these societies are far from having abolished either class or gender inequality. In Britain, women only gradually won political rights, specifically, voting rights and the right to work on equal terms with men. A partial if largely temporary breakthrough came by dint of national necessity during the 1914–18 war, when women did much heavy work in civilian occupations previously reserved to men. It was briefly common for women to work in areas such as munitions production and as drivers of heavy goods vehicles. Partly, in recognition of their efforts, after the war, in 1918, the vote was extended to women over 30 years old but this was still not on an equal basis with men who could vote at 21. It was only in 1929 that the right of women to vote on an equal basis to men was finally recognised.

The progress of women towards achieving equality of access to work and equal opportunities within the work place has been a longer and more difficult matter than achieving the franchise on an equal basis with men and, despite legislation, has not yet been fully achieved . After the first world war the pre-war sexual division of labour was largely re-established. The recessionary 1920s were in any case not helpful to those women seeking paid work, although the expanding female stereotyped occupations of secretarial and sales continued to offer low-paid, low status jobs – mainly taken up by women before or after bringing up a family. To a large extent, the experience of women during and after the second world war repeated that of the first world war. During the war they demonstrated that they could competently do many of the jobs usually done by men and then largely returned to domestic work after the war.

The work of Sylvia Walby provides a perspective on patriarchy which gives an overview of its changing structures and the changing position of women within it (*Theorising Patriarchy*, 1990). A great strength of Walby's approach is that it provides a coherent and comprehensive theoretical framework which enables consideration of the approaches referred to above with reference to historical and contemporary empirical detail. Walby describes six inter-related patriarchal structures:

○ paid work
○ patriarchal relations within the household
○ patriarchal culture
○ sexuality
○ male violence towards women
○ the state

Reflecting the structural concerns of this chapter and bearing in mind that the structures are inter-related, I will concentrate here mainly on the first two and the last of them. Walby argues that the dominant form of patriarchy has shifted from predominantly *private* in the nineteenth century to predominantly *public* patriarchy in the twentieth. In the nineteenth century household production was the dominant structure and in the twentieth, employment. In private patriarchy men as individuals exploit women within the household. In public patriarchy women have access to the public as well as the private arenas but are generally subordinated and exploited within it. She argues that the state has played a substantial role in the shift from private to public patriarchy, mainly by passing legislation which facilitated it, whereas in the nineteenth century the state intervened little in private patriarchy. In the nineteenth century most women effectively had no choice but to engage in unpaid household production from which men benefited. She refers to this *mode of expropriation* as *individual* whereas the mode of patriarchal expropriation in employment as *collective*.

Despite the above major structural shifts, Walby is arguing that there has been a continuity in patriarchal power between the two periods. Simply, men have in general sought to maintain an advantage over women and to exploit them. She summarises the change in patriarchal strategy to achieve this as being *exclusionary* in the nineteenth century and *segregationist* in the twentieth. In the former period women were excluded from better paying working class and middle class occupations and

TABLE 3.3 PRIVATE AND PUBLIC FORMS OF PATRIARCHY

Form of Patriarchy	Private	Public
Dominant Structure	Household Production	Employment/State
Wider patriarchal structures	Employment	Household production
	State	Sexuality
	Sexuality	Violence
	Violence	Culture
	Culture	
Period	Nineteenth Century	Twentieth Century
Mode of Expropriation	Individual	Collective
Patriarchal strategy	Exclusionary	Segregationist

Source: Walby, 1990: 24.

in the twentieth century they have been largely segregated from the better paying jobs within particular employment sectors. Thus, women employed within the education service are segregated into secretarial work and primary school teaching (although they are increasingly now being employed at the secondary level). Table 3.3 summarises Walby's theoretical model.

In *Theorising Patriarchy*, Walby sees patriarchal power as shifting between the two above periods, and such progress towards gender equality as has been made by women as patchy and uncertain. An increase in women in employment has provided significant opportunities for some but the majority are in low-paid, part-time or temporary work. The book is more an account of continuing domination than an even emerging liberation. Her more recent *Gender Transformations* indicates developments in her approach (1997).

First, the tone of this work is more optimistic about the position of women, both in terms of employment and political power, although in both cases there is much qualification. In reviewing the position of women in the labour market between 1971 and 1981 Walby concludes:

> The reduction in forms of patriarchal closure against women in the decade 1971–81 dominates the period ...; women increased their access to all jobs and a disproportionate share of the best new jobs. It was the decade of the Equal Pay Act and Sex Discrimination Act, of women increasingly joining unions, of previous forms of patriarchal exclusion being undermined. It was a decade in which the wages gap between women and men started to narrow. So it was an unusual decade. The new rounds of industrial restructuring embody the newer forms of patriarchal relations of employment which are less exclusionary, allowing women greater access to employment.
>
> (Walby 1997:99)

The period to which the above comments apply is now twenty years ago and more. Nevertheless, most of the positive developments referred to have been maintained albeit still within a predominantly patriarchal framework. Walby also notes the particular progress in education and employment made by younger women and the corollary that older women are often particularly marginalised in both respects.

Second, by examining the changing position of women in specific labour markets, *Gender Transformations* arrives at the conclusion that none of the various theories seeking to explain the unequal position of women in employment best explains every case. She finds that empirical evidence from local labour markets fails to sustain the thesis that women are routinely used as a reserve army of labour; that women are being used as part of an international process of deskilling, often to replace more expensive men's labour; that the economy is developing in a way that expands sectors of the economy in which women employees are concentrated. She reasserts her position in relation to Marxist explanations that patriarchy as well as capitalism accounts for the gendering of labour markets and that the study of the latter needs to be made in specific historical and spatial contexts.

Finally, two important theoretical issues arise in *Gender Transformations*. First, Walby defends the relevance of structural approaches but argues that they should not be structuralist. By this she means that structural analysis should give due consideration to the institutionalised inequalities of power and resources rather than merely the operation of differing discourses i.e. 'viewpoints', 'ideologies'. Readers may well confirm the wisdom of this observation after having read the next chapter of this book. Second, in using the term 'gender' in the title of this book, Walby may be taken as implying that gender is the appropriate core concept for analysing the relations between men and women and that patriarchy is only one form of gender relations. This may seem self evident but in the wider context of gender theory it can be interpreted as highly significant. It indicates that patriarchy can be changed and that a different mode of gender relations is possible.

For reasons explained there, the concept of gender relations rather than patriarchy is the base concept adopted in the relevant section in the chapter on 'culture and identity'. Some readers may want to continue the gender theme by turning to that section now (pp. 166–73).

Ethnicity (and the Division of Labour)

The pattern of employment among Britain's minority ethnic and majority ethnic populations is as variable as it is interesting. The pattern is affected by class and gender as well as ethnic factors. Another factor relevant for consideration is racial discrimination. It is apparent that different ethnic groups are affected to different degrees and in different ways by the interplay of these factors.

The starting point for consideration must be the pattern of employment itself. Table 3.4 and Table 3.5 provide the required data (Modood *et al.*, 1997). The division between manual and non-manual work is quite close to 50:50 for white, Indian, African Asian men and is almost two thirds to one third in favour of non-manual work for Chinese men. A much higher proportion of Caribbean, Pakistani and Bangladeshi males are in manual work at about two thirds each.

TABLE 3.4   JOB LEVELS OF WOMEN IN WORK (BASE: FEMALE EMPLOYEES AND SELF-EMPLOYED)

					column percentages	
	White	**Caribbean**	**Indian**	**African Asian**	**Pakistani**	**Chinese**
Professional, managerial and employers	16(15)[1]	5(5)	11(7)	12(10)	12(6)	30(25)
Intermediate non-manual	21	28	14	14	29	23
union non-manual	33	36	33	49	23	23
Skilled manual and foreman	7(2)	4(2)	11(3)	7(3)	9(3)	13(–)
Semi-skilled manual	18	20	27	16	22	9
Unskilled manual	4	6	4	1	4	2
Armed forces/inadequately described/not stated	0	1	1	1	0	0
Non-manual	**70**	**69**	**58**	**75**	**64**	**76**
Manual	**29**	**30**	**42**	**24**	**35**	**24**
Weighted count	*734*	*452*	*275*	*196*	*60*	*120*
Unweighted count	*696*	*336*	*260*	*164*	*64*	*63*

[1] The figures in parentheses are exclusive of self-employed
From: Modood: 1997

TABLE 3.5 JOB LEVELS OF MEN (BASE: MALE EMPLOYEES AND SELF-EMPLOYED)

							column percentages
Socio economic group	White	Caribbean	Indian	African Asian	Pakistani	Bangladeshi	Chinese
Prof./managers/employers	30	14	25	30	19	18	46
Employers and managers (large establishments)	11	5	5	3	3	0	6
Employers and managers (small establishmens)	11	4	11	14	12	16	23
Professional workers	8	6	9	14	4	2	17
Intermediate and junior	18	19	20	24	13	19	17
Skilled manual and foreman	36	39	31	30	46	7	14
Semi-skilled manual	11	22	16	12	18	53	12
Unskilled manual	3	6	5	2	3	3	5
Armed forces or N/A	2	0	3	2	2	0	5
Non-manual	**48**	**33**	**45**	**54**	**32**	**37**	**63**
Manual	**50**	**67**	**52**	**44**	**67**	**63**	**31**
Weighted count	789	365	349	296	182	61	127
Unweighted count	713	258	356	264	258	112	71

From: Modood: 1997

The broad appearance of equality between white, Indian, African Asian and Chinese men needs to be sharply qualified. White men are much more likely than those of any other minority to be employers and managers of large establishments and to the extent that Chinese and Indians are employed in the professional managerial and employers category, this is due considerably to the contribution of self-employment. A separate source, The Labour Force Survey, showed that while the total percentage of self-employed white males and females was 12.5%, it was 25% for Chinese, 19% for Pakistanis and Bangladeshis, and 14% for Indians. In contrast, it was only 7% for minorities of African descent – mainly African Caribbeans (Social Trends, 1998:79). The quite large percentage of minority men other than Chinese and Bangladeshi in the skilled manual category is also partly explained by self-employment.

As has already been noted, employment is gendered to a remarkable extent, with males tending to be concentrated in different occupational strata (horizontal segregation) and in more senior positions in both the non-manual and manual sectors where they are in the same occupational areas as women (vertical segregation). However, there also appears to be quite a strong ethnic factor in the occupational pattern. In other words, within an overall pattern in which men clearly tend to have higher status jobs than women, men and women of the same ethnic group tend to be concentrated at similar occupational levels. Thus, 30% of Chinese women, 16% of white women and a somewhat smaller percentage of South Asians and African Asians are in the professional, managerial and employers category in which men of these ethnic groups also tend to be over-represented. Only one in twenty of Caribbean women are in this category and again this broadly reflects the similar position of Caribbean men. However, two points need to be made in qualification of the above observation. First, the most significant fact about the employment of women is that the majority are concentrated in intermediate or junior non-manual work and about another 20% in semi-skilled manual work. Whatever the cause of this concentration it presents itself primarily as a fact of gender rather than of class or ethnicity. Modood specifically suggests that the similar pattern of women's employment across ethnic groups, indicates that gender divisions in the labour market are more deeply rooted than ethnic ones (104). The second qualification to be made is that racial discrimination plays a role in the occupational distribution of ethnic groups, but as will be illustrated below, can affect them differently.

What explanations are offered for the above patterns of employment by ethnic groups ? The differences between ethnic groups are sufficiently striking to suggest that the combined factors of ethnic history/culture, class, gender and racial discrimination impact on different ethnic groups in different ways. On the other hand the employment experience of all these groups is mediated by a predominantly capitalist mixed economy and this is likely to flatten out differences (this point is explained below).

The history and experience each ethnic group brought with it to Britain provided its members with both potential resources and, conceivably, disadvantages. In occupational and educational terms, the Chinese are the most middle class group. Surprisingly, perhaps, they have the highest *per capita* income of any ethnic group in the country, including the majority one. Many are from Hong Kong which has a highly entrepreneurial culture. At the same time, many Chinese businesses have a strong family and communal base and so combine business orientation with collective support. A relatively high proportion of Indian immigrants into Britain during the 1950s and 1960s, were also middle class, particularly Hindus and Sikhs. Many were professionals, particularly in the medical profession, and others had experience in the public services. From this basis, British Indians have achieved a class profile not dissimilar from that of the white majority, with the notable exception that they have not significantly gained access to the very top positions in management, nor do they own large business establishments in the same proportion as white males. It may well be that the strength of the white, ex-public school, 'old boy' network plays a substantial part in hampering the achievement of full ethnic equality at the top level as it may also do for women. This factor may weaken as a relatively high proportion of young Indian males now attend private schools although it is likely that relatively fewer attend the small number of 'top' public schools which feed into Oxbribge and ultimately into the old boy network. In contrast to Indians, a much higher proportion of Pakistanis and Bangladeshis come from poor peasant backgrounds and have less proficiency in the English language.

The historical experience brought by Caribbeans to Britain was very different than that of the Chinese and Indians. A majority of men had been manual workers and that is the kind of work they were originally invited to Britain to do and by and large did – albeit in some cases at a less skilled level than they had been trained. The fact that the large majority of Caribbean males in employment still do manual work requires explanation. Part of the explanation is the relatively poor qualification profile of young Caribbean males but the larger part is probably the racial discrimination many experience in the employment market and the resulting understandable disillusionment some feel as a result. It is a remarkable fact that a majority of Caribbean males qualified at A level or above are in manual work. To be blunt, the main explanatory factor here appears to be racial discrimination. An element in the discrimination is the stereotyping of young Caribbean males as troublesome and uncooperative and even as stupid. Racial discrimination in employment has arguably been uniquely damaging to the longer term job prospects and life chances of African-Caribbeans. Although research shows similar levels of discrimination in the employment market against people of African and Asian descent, the latter tend to have more communal resources to cope with it. Whereas Indian, Chinese and Bangladeshi immigrants into Britain came with strong entrepreneurial traditions, African Caribbeans came as manual workers. They had less business experience as individuals or family networks and less institutional support in their communities – in the form of sympathetic banks or advisors – with which to embark upon the hazardous challenge of establishing a small business. Further, as Ward and Cross point out, it is precisely in the area of manual work where jobs have been lost on a large scale since the 1960s. Thus, African Caribbeans have been hit by the double disadvantage of racial discrimination and deindustrialisation.

In the light of the long experience of African Caribbeans of racial oppression, including discrimination in the contemporary employment market, it is not surprising that they have developed subcultures expressing degrees of resistance to white-dominated systems of power and authority and/or retreatism. These attitudes are understandable but the subcultural lifestyles with which they are sometimes associated can themselves become obstacles to employment in mainstream jobs (see Chapter 6 for a more detailed discussion of this point). On the other hand, the cultural experience of young black males generates marketable skills at least for a minority. For some, unemployment becomes creative leisure time and skills are developed which generate 'alternative' opportunities, for instance, in the music and sports industries. It is far too crude simply to regard achievement in these areas as a function of stereotyping. Just as Asian minorities have used their own cultural resources as a basis for remarkable entrepreneurial achievements, so have African Caribbeans in the area of music and entertainment. Both these minority ethnic groupings have responded to complex and often oppressive historical circumstances in various but often resourceful ways. They have *negotiated* solutions – of differing degrees of adequacy and effectiveness – sometimes even turning negative stereotyping to positive advantage. As Robert Merton pointed out as long ago as 1938, exclusion from the legitimate opportunity structure can be a stimulus to innovation. It is by now incontrovertible that British culture and society has been greatly enriched and diversified by the work of its minority ethnic groups – the achievements of which have often been wrought in oppressive and discriminatory circumstances. Discrimination is also a main reason for high rates of unemployment among Britain's minority ethnic groups which is discussed below.

There are some parallels and some differences in comparison with males in the way African-Caribbean women have operated and been treated in the employment market. On balance, the data seems to sustain the view expressed both by Sheila Allen (1987) and Modood that the occupational position of women is better explained by gender than by ethnicity. However, like African Caribbean males, African Caribbean females are under-represented at the highest levels in both non-manual and manual work. In both cases, discrimination and a lack of an ethnic tradition in business – a more frequent route to upward mobility of Asian ethnic groups – are likely explanatory factors. It is also the case that, despite relatively more African Caribbeans now having higher level qualifications, a higher percentage of African Caribbean females – 64% – are concentrated in the most typical areas of female employment, intermediate and junior non-manual, than are females of any other ethnic group. A similarly high percentage of African Caribbean males are concentrated in skilled or semi-skilled manual work (61). Even allowing for the historically high working class composition of the African Caribbean ethnic group, this pattern of employment further suggests that there is a blockage, probably in the form of discrimination, inhibiting the progress of more African Caribbeans into professional, managerial and employers group. Whether or not the next generation of African Caribbeans are more equally represented at the highest level may be regarded as an important test of the extent to which equal opportunity in employment is operating effectively.

The pattern of unemployment among the majority and minority ethnic groups is highly significant in indicating the comparative extent of poverty and inequality between them. In general, the pattern of unemployment is broadly similar for both sexes in each ethnic group but differs substantially between ethnic groups. The lowest rate of unemployment occurs for white males and females (and it occurs at roughly the same level for both). Indian males are some twenty percent more likely to be unemployed than white males and Indian women some thirty percent more likely to be unemployed than white females. African Caribbean males are almost twice as likely to be unemployed as white males and more likely to be so than African Caribbean females who are about 50 percent more likely to be unemployed than white females and males. Unemployment is by far the highest among the Pakistani/ Bangladeshi ethnic group, reaching an average of about 25 percent for males in periods of high unemployment and higher still for the relatively small number of women in these groups registered for work.

The pattern of inequality in unemployment is a mirror image of that of employment. Those ethnic groups which tend to be concentrated in lower paid and status occupations are most likely to be unemployed. The reasons for the similar distribution of advantage and disadvantage in employment and unemployment are similar and have been indicated above. There follows a discussion of more theoretical explanations of these patterns.

Theoretical Explanations of the Ethnic Pattern of Employment and Unemployment

This section discusses liberal, Marxist and Weberian interpretations of the position of Britain's black and Asian populations in the employment market. Liberal views are divided into assimilationist and pluralist. In the 1950s and 1960s, a broadly liberal view of the position and prospects of Britain's 'coloured', immigrant population was quite commonly expressed both among politicians and commentators and among the public. 'Liberal' is a wide term and covers a particularly broad spectrum of opinion in relation to ethnic relations. Many thought that minority ethnic groups would eventually achieve a more similar occupational profile to the majority population when they had 'adjusted' to 'British society' and dealt with particular issues emerging from immigration. The latter were perceived as differing between ethnic groups. Thus, members of South Asian groups were less likely to speak English than African-Caribbeans – a problem partly dealt with by making learning English as a second language widely available to adults as well as children. Some assumed that the new immigrants would be *assimilated* into the mainstream but a better informed view soon emerged that Britain had become and would almost certainly remain an ethnically *pluralist* society and that policy in relation to ethnic groups – so-called 'race relations' policy – would have to accomodate this reality. Thus, Ballard and Driver argued that the ethnic minorities 'will have to strike bargains with one another . . .' and that they 'have organised themselves as autonomous collectivities, and they are out to get the very best for themselves that they can' (Quoted in Mercer and Prescott, 1982:100). Arguably, this overstated the pluralist case but it recognises what has become obvious – that ethnicity remains a significant aspect of identity and basis of organisation and action. The employment statistics cited above do give some support for the view often expressed in the 1970s, that the progress of the minority ethnic groups would depend on their own internal cooperation and organisation and on a legislative framework which made discrimination illegal in the workplace and other major areas of public life. However, substantial inequalities persist.

Marxists see no reason in principle why members of a particular ethnic group should belong to any given social class. Classes may contain people of all or any ethnic group. For this reason perhaps, Marxists have been able readily to accept that the middle class in Britain contains a small but generally increasing number of people of Asian, and, to a lesser extent, African Caribbean origin. However, classes may be *fractionalised* by ethnicity in so far as the latter becomes a divisive factor between members of the same class (Miles, 1989). Historically, Marxists have attributed such fractionalisation to capitalist business strategy sometimes supported by government and to the racist ideology of sections of the capitalist owned media. Both Castles and Kosack (1973) and later Miles (1990) have argued that the policy of encouraging immigration into both postwar Britain and Germany in the 1950s not only helped to meet the immediate demand for labour in these countries but also facilitated the creation of a 'reserve army of labour'. This served to undermine the strong position of white labour and give capitalists the kind of 'flexible' labour market they preferred. The unions countered this by recruiting for membership among the new immigrants but were often much less ready to promote them within the union structure or even press for ethnically fair and equal practices in the workplace. Again, the upward mobility of significant numbers of minority ethnic people is no more inconsistent with Marxist than with liberal analysis. The difference is that liberals see such mobility as an indicator of progress whereas Marxists are critical of the deeper class inequalities which remain and may be little affected by individual upward mobility whatever the ethnic identity of the individual concerned.

Marxist influenced commentators (as well as others) on the high increase in asylum seekers to Britain since the late 1990s, have observed that ethnic/racial discrimination is not simply a 'colour' issue. They also point out that, despite the panic response to this increase, Britain and other Western European countries need a steady and substantial flow of immigrants in order to replenish their ageing labour forces. The two countries which send by far the largest number of immigrants to Britain are the United States and Australia – though it would be impossible to guess this from the (racist) way the immigration debate is often conducted in Britain (see Table 3.6).

Most, if not all, commentators acknowledge that racial discrimination has played a significant role in the pattern of occupational distribution of members of non-white minority ethnic groups. In any case, four surveys carried out by the Policy Studies Institute, published between 1977 and 1996, clearly show that discrimination against Asians and African-Caribbeans in the employment market is substantial. The first survey, conducted by Smith, showed that when a number of whites, Asians and Africans sent letters of application for a white-collar job which were identical in all respects except in the name of the applicant, the members of the minority groups were 30% less likely to be invited for interview. More recent evidence suggests that the level of discrimination has not decreased but that whereas in the earlier period more prejudiced attitudes were somewhat more likely to be expressed against African Caribbeans than Asians, in the mid-1990s the opposite is the case (cited in Modood, 1997:352).

Weberian, John Rex regards racial discrimination as the distinctive feature which accounts for the generally greater occupational disadvantage experienced by non-white ethnic minorites than by whites (1986). He fully acknowledges that many whites and non-whites experience class disadvantage but only non-whites are substantially affected by racial discrimination in employment. This observation is central to his theory of a black underclass. In similar terms to exponents of postFordist theory, he argues that a dual labour market operates, characterised by a primary and a secondary sector. More recently, Rex has acknowledged that Britain's non-white minorities are distributed more widely in the class structure than at the time of his earlier studies, but makes the point that discrimination causes disadvantage at every level. In this sense there remains a caste like aspect to the British class system.

While there is enough upward social mobility among Britain's non-white minority ethnic groups to suggest that the term black underclass is inappropriate, the position of black youth is particu-

TABLE 3.6   UK IMMIGRANTS INTO BRITAIN

Country of Origin	Nos in 000s
United States	42.5
Australia	26.5
India	16.1
South Africa	13.0
New Zealand	12.1
Japan	10.4
Pakistan	9.6
Canada	8.3
Philippines	7.5
Poland	5.4

Source: OECD, 1997

larly disadvantaged and requires specific discussion. In the wake of Charles Murray's controversial publications on the subject, Michelle Conolly and her co-researchers surveyed a representative cross-section of black youth in Liverpool (1991). Her approach was more structurally informed than Murray's. In general, she found that black youth was in a structurally worse position than white youth. Black youth were twice as likely to be unemployed (52%) as white youth and over twice as unlikely to be in full-time work. These facts indicated a substantial and unique level of social exclusion. However, the study did not conclude that black youth constituted an underclass because a large majority retained conventional job aspirations. Nevertheless, the potential for the development of a culture of disillusion, alienation and resistance existed.

The above explanations of the pattern of ethnic employment and unemployment have a substantial amount in common. There is agreement that minority ethnic immigration in the postwar period was largely driven by economic factors, including the need to increase the labour force in Britain. There is recognition that significant upward mobility has occurred but that this varies between ethnic groups and owes much to their own efforts in often difficult circumstances. Racial discrimination, although given different emphasis and theoretical significance, is seen as a major and continuing cause of disadvantage to non-white minorities. Several key issues are widely recognised, including continuing discrimination in employment, extensive disadvantage experienced by the Bangladeshi community, and the high degree of discrimination and frustration experienced by African Caribbean youth.

These matters are serious cause for concern, but it is undoubtedly the case that members of black and Asian minorities are distributed across the British occupational class structure in a much more similar pattern to white people than 30 or even 15 years ago. This has been due mainly to the efforts of the minority ethnic communities themselves rather than to the benevolence of the 'host' society, but it represents significant progress in difficult circumstances. By overcoming class barriers partly by their use of ethnic resources, more successful members of minority ethnic groups have perhaps contributed to the widespread perception that class barriers are not so insuperable as they may once have seemed and that class is not such a singular source of identity.

Age/Generation (and the Division of Labour)

There are biological and social aspects to age. Sociologists focus on the latter but people aged forty years or more know in their hearts – and probably in other parts of their body – that anatomical decline is part of growing older. Human functions and faculties do not decline at an equal rate and some may not decline at all but the overall tendency to grow, mature and decline is without exception – so far. That said, to a substantial extent, society can shape or structure age stages, and even extend them. Most obviously, affluence has enabled many societies to extend childhood and youth greatly by introducing a lengthy period of compulsory education and expanding opportunities for postcompulsory education. People whom we now think of as part of 'youth' – some even in their thirties – are members of an age stage defined in modernity mainly through the massive expansion of further and higher education. In the medieval period, they were thought of simply as younger adults, generally in work like other adults but not yet married. Then, there was not the wealth to support the long period of youth (let alone a youth culture) or even a lengthy stage of childhood of the type that characterises modern societies. Other than the children of the elite, children and young people worked – generally alongside their parents.

It is just as necessary to consider age in social structural terms and particularly in relation to the division of labour as it is gender and ethnicity. A big part of the story of age in the twentieth century is the growth in the size of the dependent population of both old and young. The dependent population is that part of the population not in paid work, and the dependency ratio is the number of people not in paid work divided by the number of people in paid work. The dependency ratio has greatly increased during the twentieth century but this has been offset by a substantial increase in productivity per worker. Proportionately, far fewer people under the age of twenty are now in the labour force than at the turn of the last century and the number of nonworking older people has increased by several times. On this basis, it would seem that the contribution to labour and productivity of both these age groupings has greatly declined. However, as far as the young are concerned, the reason they have been withdrawn from the labour force into education is largely to enable them to be much more economically efficient and productive than they would otherwise be. On the other hand, many older people are sometimes perceived by managers as having outdated skills and even attitudes, and as lacking the flexibility or will to acquire newer and more relevant ones.

The anthropologist, Margaret Mead, has captured the axial position of youth in late modern society in her concept of a prefigurative culture. In her essay *Culture and Commitment: A Study of the Generation Gap* (1972), she distinguishes between three types of culture: *postfigurative, cofigurative* and *prefigurative*. A postfigurative culture gains its authority and 'knowledge' from the past and little change occurs from one generation to the next. The young learn traditional wisdom and fit into and reproduce established structures. The few tribal societies of the Amazon basin which have still not experienced the impact of modernisation are likely to be of this kind. A cofigurative culture is one in which significant change is occurring and contemporaries rather than elders are role models. Industrial society at its height – for instance, Britain in the first fifty to sixty years of the twentieth century – is an example. During this period the class and gender structures changed relatively slowly, but on a sufficient scale for children to take their parents, rather than their grandparents (the 'elders' of traditional society) as their working role models. A prefigurative culture is one in which the speed of change is so rapid that the culture must become anticipatory of the means, direction and effects of change. Mead's remarks have an obvious application to what Bell and more recently Castells refer to as the information society – the contemporary epoch.

If the massive changes brought about by the combining of electro-communications and computerised information is to be sustained and extended, it is obvious that young people must learn to operate and manage the relevant equipment and thought processes. The very rapid spread of computers and computer-dependent modes of information access and learning throughout education and in many homes has ensured that this is happening, at least to an adequate degree, to maintain and probably to accelerate the recent rate of change. As Castells and others have observed, there is nothing inherently egalitarian about the information revolution. On the contrary, unless it is managed in a way that ensures that the skills and means to access and use information are widely spread, the effect of the information revolution is almost certain to increase social inequality. There are clear signs that it is already doing so – and, in general, to the advantage of young adults, at least those of them that are skilled users. Young adults have excelled in areas such as financial trading and the production of media software in which computer skills are now essential. In contrast, significant numbers of middle aged males have been made redundant and taken early retirement rather than face the stress of 'reskilling' and the challenge of younger people to whom operating the new technology seems to come easily. Many advertisements for business and professional jobs now stipulate information skills as well as levels in general qualifications.

However, it would be a mistake to confuse the higher premium now put upon youthful skill and flexibility with a general shift in power and wealth towards the young. Other than in specific occupational areas, no such shift has occurred. Paradoxically, the much longer time the young spend in education weakens their immediate earnings and their power in occupational hierarchies but potentially increases both in the longer term. The massive investment of time and money in equipping youth, not only to operate the future economy but also to be able to innovate in a glob-ally competitive environment, places them in a relatively marginal position in terms of income and power in relation to older people in full-time employment. This statement needs to be qualified for class, gender and ethnicity which are characterised by their own inequalities but there is also an age/generation dimension to inequality and in general it operates against the young. Income from wages and investment increases steadily until about the age of fifty. In 1997, the under 30s got 19% of average net income which was 10% less than a decade previously. This sharp decrease occurred over the period in which further and higher education greatly expanded, with the result that far fewer of the age group were in full-time work. The income curve is at its highest between 30 and 50 years of age and drops somewhat between 50 and 60. Other than in some areas of finance and business, the salary structures of most full-time jobs, especially professional ones, are still graduated to reward experience, seniority and loyalty. Only a minority of highly qualified and/or talented young people can 'buck the system' and leap up the salary scale. Rather mislead-ingly, it is these that the press tends to feature disproportionately. After 60, average income drops sharply although there are particularly large income and wealth differences among older people (data cited in Observer Review, 15.11.1998:1).

It is the postwar baby boom generation that commanded attention in the 1960s which was domi-nant in the 1990s and likely to remain so for another decade or so. Sheer size is a factor although, rather evidently, it is mainly the highly educated middle class section within this age grouping that largely controls the economic and political heights. A relatively radical generation in their own youth, the now middle-aged have kept quite a tight grip on contemporary youth and have set the agenda for them to a greater extent than either generation may fully realise.

Despite the hugely increased social investment in youth and the future, it is not the case that all young people will benefit later from their education or training in the form of high incomes. Social scientists commonly estimate that perhaps as much as a third of the adult population of modern societies is not necessary for the functioning and prosperity of those societies (see, for instance, Will Hutton's 40, 30, 30, model of society: 1995). This is not a statement about human value but about who is needed to maintain a modern society. Significant numbers of young people leave education or training – even higher education – only to become largely or even entirely eco-nomically unproductive. Many others go into low paid work for which they are over-qualified. This is partly because of the loss of millions of well-paid skilled jobs in manual work and the growth of less well-paying jobs in areas such as personal services and retail-sales. Although some-thing approaching full employment is possible in modern societies it is likely that many jobs, par-ticularly of a routine service kind, will command only modest pay. It is against this background that young people feel the pressure to be competitive but often also feel insecure. It is even more the case than in the recent past that the rewards of career success can be enormous and the penal-ties of failure equally so.

The shift from an industrial to an information-driven service economy with all its consequences for the occupational structure is a universal feature of a modern or late-modern society and is not something likely to have been fundamentally affected by government. Whichever govern-ment had been in power from, say, the 1970s, young people would have had to come to terms with these changes as 'the way things now are'. However, the Thatcher administrations of 1979 to 1991 adopted policies towards youth of a highly directive, if not of an authoritarian kind, as it also did towards organised labour. Mrs Thatcher abhorred the permissive cultural climate of the 1960s and the progressive educational practices which she believed had perme-ated and undermined the educational system. She rejected the permissive cultural individualism of the 1960s and adopted an individualism based on its near-opposite – the work ethic and the self-discipline and competitive selection that went with it. The two recessions that occurred during her period as Prime Minister created very high levels of youth unemployment. As a result, young people were even more subject to government control than they might otherwise have been.

The Youth Training Scheme was introduced in the early 1980s in the teeth of recession. Much of the training offered was indifferent, especially among smaller employers, but YTS reduced the unemployment count and 'stored' those young people seen as most likely to be 'troublesome' relatively conveniently. Increasingly, the direction of policy was that young people should be in education and training and not on social security. In 1986, young people were removed from the protection of the Wages Council and lost legislative protection for pay and conditions. In 1988, 17 year olds lost the right to claim social security and this was later extended to 18 year olds. The main shift of 16 to 18 year olds out of full-time work occurred after the recession of the early 1980s. That of a large minority of 18-21 year olds occurred in the late 1980s and early 1990s following the second Thatcher recession. The Major and Blair governments have continued to pursue the policy of requiring those under 18 years old to be in education and training and not on social security and have also continued to expand access to higher education. The Blair government shifted some of the cost of higher education from the state/tax-payer to the consumer by imposing a partial fee-paying system.

Given the extent and considerable effectiveness of government control of youth during and since the Thatcher period, it is not surprising that youth political protest has been relatively quiescent and that youth culture has retreated somewhat to the margins, presenting a less direct challenge to the mainstream than the counterculture of the 1960s. Although not without pockets of social and political ideology and content, both Rave and Clubculture are mainly about having a good time – something that has always been a central feature of youth culture. As Steve Redhead has suggested there has been a shift from idealism to hedonism. However, even the pursuit of pleasure – admittedly sometimes loud and exhuberant – attracted official response. The 1994 Criminal Justice Act gave the police effective powers to stop raves although they judiciously seldom chose to exercise it. In the Act, the music objected to was famously described as 'sounds wholly or predominantly characterised by the emission of a succession of repetitive beats'.

Despite the redisciplining and retreat of youth, there are continuities as well as breaks with the 1960s. Some of the issues raised in the 1960s – particularly those concerned with the environment, sexuality, and lifestyle – are discussed more fully in Chapter 5.

Stratification and the Internet

This is a speculative section. Trying to gauge the effects of the new technology, particularly the internet, on stratification and inequality is fraught with difficulty. There is not a great deal of academic literature in this area and more informed journalistic coverage is not in agreement.

As far as class divisions are concerned – whether defined in Marxist or Weberian terms – the effects of information technology seem very likely to increase inequality. Already in recent years the gap between the wealth and income of the rich and poor has been increasing substantially. Both major individual shareholders and senior managers in multi-national companies have made private fortunes, in some cases running into billions. The high merger rate of international companies especially in banking and telecommunications has accentuated their accumulation of wealth. The term 'super-rich' has been coined to describe these individuals, echoing the term superstar coined a couple of decades ago to describe the new global stars of entertainment. Apart from a few exceptions, the wealth made by international business people is in a different league to that of entertainment stars.

At the more ordinary level of middle and working class people, information technology, including the internet, is also likely to accentuate inequality. Even in 2000, a majority of homes in Britain do not own a computer. Those that do are disproportionately middle class. For those inclined to get carried away by utopian notions of the world of high tech, a report by the London Skills Forecasting Unit (1999) will come as a shock. According to the report, one in five of young people in London have no computer skills. In his review of the report, Peter Kingston argues 'that this group risks becoming an unemployable IT 'underclass' '(Guardian, 5.10.1999: 13). In 1999 over 300,000 job vacancies in IT in London could not be filled due to a lack of qualified applicants. Another 300,000 employees in IT in the capital are considered by their employers to be under-skilled for their job. Outside the capital, worry among employers about levels of computer skills is even greater, two thirds as opposed to one third expressing concern.

It is not clear whether racial discrimination will occur in IT employment to the same extent that it has in other employment. Even without discrimination, the more working class minorities, such as African Caribbeans, are probably less likely to have easy access to home-based computer experience. In any case, as Kingston points out in his appropriately titled *Game Over for the Computer Underclass*, it would be a mistake to confuse young people's (mainly boys') 'lethal virtuosity with computer games or their mastery of the video machine for being competent on a word processor or with a spreadsheet' (*ibid.*:13). However, it is possible that in a new area of expertise in short supply a matter as irrelevant to job performance as colour will decline in importance. To that extent, sheer skill, regardless of class or ethnicity might over-ride prejudice more than in traditional areas of employment.

Whereas the IT revolution may well increase class inequality, it has the potential to erode gender inequality both at work and in non-work. Most of the available data is American where internet use, in particular is more widespread, and there women have steadily increased as a percentage of all internet users. In 1995 they were 27% and in 1999, almost 40%. However, as Liza Ramrayka points out in *Are women the future of the web?* the use of it is highly gendered:

> So what are women doing online? According to a study by the University of Hertfordshire, women tend to use internet to email friends, visit chat rooms and buy books or CDs on line. Men are more likely to spend their online time playing games, downloading software or reading newsgroup messages.
>
> (Guardian Online: 9.9.1999:2).

Clearly, a technological revolution does not necessarily lead to a social revolution. Even in employment where the shift from manufacturing to service work ought to have helped women, low to medium level wages persist in areas of heavy female employment, including those involving routine computer skills. Again, as may be the case in respect to racial discrimination, skill and the demand for it may lead to the breaking of gender barriers. At the current rate of change, these patterns of occupational and resultant social mobility should fairly soon become clearer.

Will the information age be the age of the young? Sometimes it appears so, but appearances may be deceptive. Certainly, images of 'city whizz kids' making – and sometimes losing – millions at their keyboards are striking. However, if the figures on computer illiteracy among London youth cited above are remotely correct only a minority of young people are computer competent, let alone making sizeable fortunes through their IT skills. Youth combined with aptitude for IT and the complementary qualities of character and intelligence will count for much in the information age but a fair quota of older people have all these attributes.

While there will almost certainly be shifts in the pyramid of social equality in the information age, the pyramid will remain in place and most probably become steeper. A later chapter looks briefly at those who are using information technology, including the internet, to try to confront international capital and governmental organisations on issues of global inequality and the environment. They are probably right to regard international capital as the generator of inequality and the new technology as a means that has the potential either to promote or oppose inequality (see pp. 219–20).

Conclusion: Modern or Capitalist Britain

The focus of this chapter has been on the social structure of contemporary Britain. The main areas covered have been the economic-technological and stratification. A detailed examination of issues of culture and identity, including individuality and agency, is held over until later chapters though brief reference has been made to them above. The view that will be sustained throughout this book is that Britain is best understood as a modern or, now, late modern society which is, nevertheless, a strongly capitalist one. In other words, it is closer to Giddens's approach which reflects that of Weber, than to a Marxist one with the qualification that more emphasis is given here to the enormous power and effect of contemporary capitalism to structure late modernity. To cut the difference between the two approaches, we live in capitalist modernity.

SUMMARY

1. This chapter focuses on late modern or postmodern society and the new sociology that is an attempt to understand it.

2. Three developments shape the structure of late modernity:
   ◆ Information technology
   ◆ Globalisation
   ◆ The decline of heavy industry and the rise of the service sector and the resulting consequences for class structure

3. LATE MODERNITY: The term implies that the above changes, though profound, occur within what can be termed the modern epoch. The term postmodernity implies that they have helped to bring about a new historical period – postmodernity.

4. LATE MODERNITY IS THE 'INFORMATION AGE'. According to Bell and Castells the control and use of information is fundamental to the structure and dynamic of contemporary society. Castells argues that control of information is mainly in the hands of transnational capital. However, individual states, the United nations and other international organisations, a range of non-governmental organisations and some highly decentralised groups are able to effect some counterbalance to the power of capital.

5. POSTINDUSTRIAL SOCIETY AND POSTFORDIST SOCIETY: Bell argues that the decline of heavy industry and of the industrial working class and the rise of the service sector and service class has brought about postindustrial society. Fordism refers to the large-scale and hierarchical way in which industry, welfare and consumption were organised in industrial society and postFordism refers to the more flexible and supposedly decentralised models of later modern society. Thompson and Lash and Urry argue that capital has become more powerful and less 'counterbalanced' by labour and government in the contemporary period.

6. THE CLASS STRUCTURE OF LATE MODERN SOCIETIES: has changed in a number of ways – some indicated above. What has become particularly conspicuous is the extreme inequality between the rich or 'super-rich' and the poor (variously referred to as 'the underclass' or 'excluded').

7 PATRIARCHY: has shifted from being a predominantly private system to a predominantly public one,

argues Sylvia Walby. This means that it now functions mainly in the area of paid work although it also plays a major role in shaping several other areas of society including the household and sexuality. Some improvements in the position of women suggest that gender relations are being reconstituted in a somewhat more egalitarian direction.

8. MINORITIES AND EMPLOYMENT: While there has been progress in the occupations situations of Britain's minority ethnic groups, substantial inequalities remain. Bearing in mind that these factors may apply to different degrees to different ethnic minority groups, factors that require to be considered in explaining their distributional pattern by occupation in Britain include:

   ◆ Differential cultural resources
   ◆ Class factors
   ◆ Racial discrimination
   ◆ Anti-discrimination legislation and its enforcement

9. AGE STRATIFICATION: in modern societies is often taken for granted or misunderstood. Like any form of stratification it is subject to change and has been changing in late modern Britain. While the new technology offers opportunities to some young people, the majority of them have been subject to increased social control via the education and training systems. The better off middle aged and elderly control a large portion of national wealth but the position of the impoverished elderly can be extremely bleak.

10. INTERNET AND STRATIFICATION: So far the evidence of the effect of the internet on stratification suggests that it may intensify rather than diminish established inequalities – but it is too early to say.

Chapter 4

Self and Identity: Structuralism, Poststructuralism and Postmodernism

Key Concepts:
contingent, discourse theory, essentialism, ideological/repressive
state apparatus, identity, relative, resistance, self,
signifier/signified/sign, text.

Introduction: The Identity Question

Identity is now one of, if not *the* dominant concept in sociology and it is an important thread of continuity in this book. 'Who am I' – as an individual – and 'Who are we' – as a species being – are questions that at some point or another occur to everyone, or, at least, to most of us. The fact that we are able to think about these questions at all indicates for many commentators the main direction of an answer to them: what is distinctive about human beings is a relatively highly developed level of consciousness, the ability to reflect on ourselves and others – 'reflexivity' in Anthony Giddens' term. However, this is rather to jump in at the deep end, and the significance of consciousness and other issues concerning identity is held over until later.

Stuart Hall's essay, 'The Question of Cultural Identity', sets out a useful framework for analysing the main issues. He points to three conceptions of identity: the sociological; the Enlightenment; and the postmodern. Here, I will simply give the basic definitions of these conceptions cited by Hall as they are amplified by constant reference throughout this chapter. He states that 'the classic sociological conception' of identity is that 'identity is formed in the 'interaction' between self and society' (276). He gives G. H. Mead's definition as an example (see below). In describing the dominant Enlightenment and postmodern understandings of identity, Hall refers to what he sees as a 'radically different conception of the individual subject'. He states that '(t)he Enlightenment subject was based on a conception of the human person as a fully centred, unified individual, endowed with the capacities of reason, consciousness and action, whose 'centre' consisted of an inner core'(275). Reason and a capacity to develop individuality were central to this conception. In contrast, the postmodern subject is 'fragmented; composed, not of a single, but several, sometimes contradictory or unresolved, identities ... conceptualized as having no fixed, essential or permanent identity' (276–77).

Hall's presentation of 'the question' of identity sharply underlines the disagreement between the Enlightenment and postmodernist view. As is described below, this debate remains fierce. Hall presents the sociological conception of identity as an outcome of the interaction of self and society. Hall's description of the Enlightenment understanding of identity is arguably somewhat over-simplified. In fact, the social interactive dimension can be found in the Enlightenment position. One would expect this to be so among contemporary defenders of the Enlightenment tradition such as Habermas and Giddens, but thinkers such as Rousseau and Voltaire were well aware that the character and capacities of the self are affected by social environment. To think otherwise would be astonishingly naive. Nevertheless, it is true that Enlightenment approaches do emphasise the innate human potential (developed in society) for self-consciousness and rational action. In this view, the self has the capacity to develop and sustain a coherent individual identity. Enlightenment positions on identity tend towards the individual/agency side of the dualisms and the structuralist/postmodern towards the society/structure side. It may be obvious by now that my own position is closer to the former and to that extent I disagree with Stuart Hall who, has been greatly influenced by the structuralist and poststructuralist thought that is discussed later in this chapter.

Sociological Approaches to Identity

A discussion of the sociological approach to identity prepares the way for understanding the Enlightenment and various 'post' views on identity and the individual subject although, of course, the later views have themselves entered sociological perspective.

As Hall points out, in Mead's conception, identity is the outcome of interaction between self and society. This approach underpins this section. It is important to remember, however, that the positivist tradition, going back to Durkheim, strongly emphasises – in my view, too strongly – the influence of society on the individual. The question of voluntarism and determinism in relation to individuality and identity will increasingly emerge as this chapter progresses. Within the interactionist tradition and in the thinking of 'modernist' sociologists such as Giddens, Habermas, and, more latterly, Castells, the self is influenced by society but has the capacity to mediate and negotiate, at least, some of those influences. This is assumed to be the case in relation to socially defined as well as individually defined identities, including specific social identities such as communal and collective identities.

In seeking a satisfactory sociological definition of identity, it is helpful to think in terms of the dualisms, particularly that of individual and society. As a starting point to defining identity, individual identity and social identity can be distinguished although both develop within particular cultures and are therefore influenced and to some extent integrated by culture. As has already been described, the interactionist tradition gives a fairly detailed account of the self as it develops identity (or identities) within cultural context . The Oxford Dictionary of Sociology usefully summarises how interactionists see this relationship:

> The self is a distinctively human capacity which enables people to reflect on their nature
> and the social world through communication and language.
>
> (1998: 294).

Within the interactionist paradigm, the I/Me distinction embodies the concept of agency ('I') and the social aspects of the self ('Me').' The use of the term capacity is important in this definition because it indicates that the self can to some extent construct individual identity and, for that matter, contribute to the construction of the social world.

Mead emphasised the personal and individual aspects of the self as well as those attributes shared by all members of the species. He recognised perhaps more than any previous sociologist the sheer variety of human individuality including that of intellect and imagination. Well before the postmodernists, he appreciated that identities are different. His section on 'the social creativity of the emergent self' in *Mind, Self and Society* recognises both that 'the character of the organism is a determinant of its environment' (as well as vice-versa) and that particular individuals can have an impact on society (215). For most this might be 'a slight effect' but persons 'of great mind and great character have strikingly changed the minds of the communities to which they have responded' (215–16). He goes on to illustrate his point with reference to Jesus, Buddha and Socrates. Mead's argument here is similar to Max Weber's, namely that the charisma of certain characters can act as a focus of social change. In general terms, Mead gives much more emphasis to agency and even self-creativity in explaining individual differences than do the postmodernists who see differences as predominantly or wholly socially inscribed or determined. Mead, then, is stating, contrary to the 'post' theories discussed below, that not only does an individual have a distinct self identity but that s/he can contribute to the construction of that identity.

Although for analytical purposes it is helpful to distinguish the personal and social aspects of identity, in fact they occur together in the same given individual. However, while it is impossible to separate the two it is clear that social identity pertains to the influence of external factors on the self. In a chapter titled 'Stigma and Social Identity' in his book on stigma, Erving Goffman refers to social identity as the way others categorise and evaluate an individual. He goes on to point out an important distinction between social identity and social status: the former involves the evaluation by others of 'personal attributes such as 'honesty' … as well as taking into account 'structural ones, like "occupation" '(1984: 12). The key point is that social identity is primarily defined by *others* although individuals may seek a given social status – say, a particular job, or role in the community. Equally, as Goffman points out, an individual may experience a conflict between her or his socially prescribed identity and the identity s/he aspires to. Anthony Giddens summarises Goffman's 'final' version of self in a way that makes clear the capacity of the self to overview or scan social context and to attempt to manage it in terms of personal experience – in other words to employ identity characteristics in an active way :

> The self consists in an awareness of identity which simultaneously transcends specific roles and provides an integrating means of relating them to personal biography; and furnishes a set of dispositions for managing the transactions between motives and the expectations 'scripted' by particular roles.
>
> (Quoted Williams: 156).

Manuel Castells gives a carefully considered definition of social identity which does justice to human agency as well as the socio-cultural input to identity and, in fact, combines the two aspects in the phrase 'social actors':

> By identity as it refers to social actors, I understand the process of construction of meaning on the basis of a cultural attribute or related set of cultural attributes, that is/are given priority over other sources of meaning (1997: 6)

Castells' important distinction between legitimising, resistance and project identities is considered elsewhere (see pp. 217–8). This distinction is made in relation to social movements but is of more general relevance. It refers respectively to dominant (legitimising) identities, resistance to them and the development of alternative (project) identities. It would be hard to imagine a more action-oriented definition of identity.

Sub-categories of social identity are *community identity* and *collective identity*. Community identity is characterised by a sense of belonging – defined variously as based on a network of relationships, beliefs, emotions or on place (and their symbolic expressions) or by all of these. Community identity in the sense of shared identity remains a crucial concept in late modernity and is discussed later. Ethnic communities, religious communities and 'supporters' of a given team are examples of communities. As used here, collective identity differs from community identity in that it implies a conscious effort of identification and often of organisation on the part of those who belong whereas initial membership of many communities is determined by birth and for a time, at least, not a matter of choice. Adopting a collective identity may involve formally 'joining' an organisation such as a church or trade union which has a communal aspect to membership or a more informal process of identifying with a particular body of people and their beliefs, such as a social movement. Whereas collective identity tends to be purposive and instrumental, communal identity is primarily emotional and an end in itself. However, often collectivities have a strong communal aspect to their identity.

Poststructuralism and postmodernism have sought to undermine the notion of a single and fixed individual identity or, as it is sometimes expressed, the idea of a unified individual subject. This issue has been perhaps the main 'battleground' of supporters of the Enlightenment tradition of the rational subject, such as Habermas and Giddens, and those, such as Hall, who argue that the 'postmodern subject' has been 'decentred' and experiences a variety of identities. An account of this debate unfolds below and in different contexts in the following chapters. It is one of the great intellectual debates of our time and though not new has been given new dimensions by the poststructuralist/postmodern challenge to the Enlightenment approach.

Finally, it is interesting to think of identity in terms of two of the dualisms. If the concept of identity is used as a lens to examine the dualisms of individual/society and agency/structure, rather more connections than breaks appear between them. Individuality and identity develop and find expression in society. Similarly, agency or action whether individual or collective has to relate to social structures even if the actor seeks to change or reject them. In my view, identity cannot be convincingly defined with reference to only one side of these dualisms.

Historical Concepts of Identity: Traditional, Modern and Late (or Post) Modern

Much of this book works within a framework of three broad historical epochs: the traditional, modern and late modern. This has been justified in terms of the different structural and cultural characteristics of these periods. However, this approach runs the risk of giving too simple a picture of matters, and particularly of the contemporary global situation. In late modern society, the traditional, the modern and late or postmodern exist together, sometimes uneventfully, sometimes even in harmony and sometimes clashing. A walk around the centre of almost any large town will confirm this by the historical and architectural variety of its buildings and design. Diversity occurs at the global, national and local levels. Many societies remain deeply influenced by the traditional world religions and some societies are run according to Islamic principles. Within Britain, a variety of cultural lifestyles exist which reflect traditional values and practices as well as modern influences. The multicultural ideal is that these differences can be positively accepted. An example of a clash of the modern and the traditional is the Blair government's reform of the House of Lords. The postmodern is most obviously apparent in artistic and intellectual life but some argue that the fragmentation that is said to characterise it is apparent in many urban landscapes across the globe and in the multiplicity of contemporary media.

Identity in Traditional Society

Given the above qualification, historically three broad concepts of identity can be delineated. These correspond to traditional, modern and late modern society. In traditional society, self identity tends to be defined by and even subsumed into community identity. Durkheim describes this as mechanical solidarity. Religion acts as a powerful unifying force – 'society worshipping itself' – and conscience and consciousness is primarily 'collective' with individuals having little opportunity and still less encouragement to develop themselves other than in socially prescribed ways. Severe retributional justice is administered to those who contravene social norms. Even such contravention rarely challenges the validity of the normative framework itself as does some political and philosophical non-conformity in modern societies. Religion also acts as a force against social change and towards social homogenisation. Members of traditional societies tend to assume that the social order is supernaturally ordained and will therefore remain static. People's roles are prescribed and they are expected to perform them in the same approved manner – individuality and difference would disrupt the assumed perfection and order of things.

Identity in Modern Society: The Renaissance and the Enlightenment

Modernity saw a shift in both how human beings saw or identified themselves in general – as a species – and, relatedly, in how self identity was perceived.

In traditional societies, identity was thought to be externally prescribed by God and King (in some cases, 'the God-King') and to be part of the divine order of things. In modern societies identity is more typically regarded as a human/social phenomenon. The historical context in which this change of perception occurred was briefly outlined in Chapter 1. Two great celebrations of humanity have occurred in the modern period: the Renaissance and the Enlightenment. However, whereas the Renaissance looked back to the then unequalled achievements of pagan Greece and Rome, the Enlightenment was future-oriented in its confident belief that human beings could create a better future for themselves. As Alex Callinicos puts it:

> The significance of the Enlightenment lies in large part in the fact that it broke with this assumption (that no new form of society could be created). It did so by formulating the idea of a new age which no longer seeks to derive its legitimacy from principles derived from the past, but rather offers its own self-justification. In Jurgen Habermas's words: 'Modernity can and no longer will borrow the criteria by which it takes its orientation from the models supplied by another epoch: it has to create its own normativety (customs/rules) out of itself.
>
> (1999:13). Note: Both brackets are mine.

Rousseau's famous remark that 'man is born free but he is everywhere in chains' illustrates Callinicos's point. It was Rousseau's intention, as it became that of many other radical intellectuals and activists, that 'man' would not remain in 'chains' to feudal and ecclesiastical law and hierarchy but would create a new, rational society.

Various alternative non-religious (but not necessarily anti-religious) theories of human beings' place on earth and in the universe were developed during the Enlightenment. Chapter 1 described how influential evolutionary thinking was in this respect. In turn, evolutionism was itself a part of the rise of scientific and materialistic explanations. Scientific explanations of the human species' identity have retained great prestige and, at least in the West, have probably gained increasing support throughout the last two centuries – though they have not gone without challenge. Rousseau himself was inclined to adopt naturalistic forms of explanation, arguing the natural potential of human beings was constantly frustrated through oppressive and unimaginative socialisation.

Human or natural rights theory was the most common framework in which the more radical thinkers of the French and American revolutionaries expressed their view on how society should accommodate human needs and aspirations. Natural or human rights are considered to be those rights which people have by virtue of their humanity rather by any external power, religious or secular. The American Declaration of Independence (1776) remains a powerful expression of the philosophy of universal human rights:

> We hold these truths to be self-evident: that all men are created equal; that they are endowed by their creator with certain inalienable rights; that among these rights are life, liberty and the pursuit of happiness.

Thomas Jefferson, who drafted the Declaration, got round the problem of the origin and justification of human rights by attributing them to a gift of God – something that future generations often found more difficult to do.

Alongside different general conceptions of humanity, a radical shift in how self identity or the identity of the subject was conceived also occurred during the Enlightenment. Again, there were disagreements and differences of emphasis but the general direction of thought is clear. From being simply a part in a greater scheme of things, the self was now seen as having certain capacities, including that of rational thought and action, and as having the potential for a coherent, integrated individual identity. Stuart Hall expresses this as follows:

> The Enlightenment subject was based on a conception of the human person as a fully centred, unified individual, endowed with the capacities of reason, consciousness and action, whose 'centre' consisted of an inner core which first emerged when the subject was born, and unfolded with it, while remaining essentially the same – continuous or 'identical' with itself – throughout the individual's existence. The essential centre of the self was a person's identity ... (T)his was a very 'individualistic' conception of the subject and 'his' (for the Enlightenment subjects were usually described as male) identity.
>
> (In Hall, Held and McGrew, 1992:275).

As will become clear poststructuralists and most postmodernists strongly reject the Enlightenment understanding of the individual subject. They particularly reject the notion that there is an *essential* human subject i.e., that the individual is born or 'endowed' with certain human capacities, including will, and so is able to sustain a continuous personal identity. The anti-essentialist view raises important issues and I will return to it later. However, it is questionable whether Enlightenment approaches are necessarily essentialist. The human rights supported by many Enlightenment thinkers pertained more to the political, civil and, in the case of Tom Paine, social conditions in which they considered people had a right to live, as much as to any fixed and 'essentialist' view of human nature – although what human beings have a right to and what they 'are' cannot finally be separated. Arguably, too, postmodernists have oversimplified the Enlightenment understanding of the autonomy of the individual subject. While the apologists of liberal-capitalism may have typically held an extreme view of individual freedom, among leading Enlightenment and post-Enlightenment intellectuals there was a strong awareness of the influence of the social on self development. The 'post' intellectuals have set up a 'straw man' version of Enlightenment thinking, the more easily to dismantle it.

Unsurprisingly, nineteenth century capitalist economists such as Ricardo and Adam Smith tended to have a positive view of the outpouring of individual energy and enterprise, even if they sometimes expressed concern about its social effects. Reflecting on these matters in the latter half of the nineteenth century, the founders of sociology often expressed more mixed views.

Identity in the Work of the Founders of Sociology

The founders of sociology all took the view that the way individuals perceive and experience their identities is profoundly affected by the culture they are born into. Where they differ is on the extent to which individuals cannot only contribute to the construction of their own identity but can intentionally and actively change the culture they live in.

1. Marx: Class Identity

Modernity saw a substantial change in the relationship between the individual and society – both as this was expressed in much political and social theory, and in social practice. The late eighteenth and the nineteenth century was a time of rapid change in which traditional bonds of feudalism were broken or undermined and many individuals felt relatively freer to choose and act – albeit that freedom in modernity has sometimes been illusionary. The founders of sociology each recognised these developments within their characteristic theoretical frameworks. However, as was discussed in Chapter 1, they were as much concerned with the social effects of modernity as with the greater individual freedoms that to some extent accompanied it. On the whole, their awareness of group conflict and exploitation and of the constraints of social institutions led them to be quite cautious about what some might now think of as changes in social identities but which they thought of more as changes in social relations and social structure. To establish how the founders of sociology understood identity requires some reinterpretation of their work in the light of contemporary priorities – always a difficult exercise.

The younger Marx shared the widespread belief of the Enlightenment in human potential, but unlike leading liberal thinkers thought that the potential of most individuals was frustrated under capitalism. While he condemned capitalist exploitation, his evolutionary approach to history led him to the view that capitalism brought some 'progress'. In comparison with the feudal period, Marx believed that capitalist society would change the behaviour of people and their self-perception. Although opposed to liberal capitalism, Marx recognised that it brought freedom of a kind for some – the capitalist class. He referred to this as 'bourgeois freedom' and he considered that it characterised society at the economic, political and ideological levels. He argued that capitalists sought a minimum of economic regulation and free trade between countries in order to maximise profit. They sought the dismantling of the system of government economic regulation that had existed under feudalism. The rigid master-serf relationship did not meet their needs for a mobile labour force which was also flexible in the sense that it could be easily hired and fired. A system of 'free' wage-labour was much more suited to the requirements of capitalists but offered little more than 'wage' serfdom for the working class. The development of a sharply gendered division of labour under capitalism further benefited capital in that it ensured that the cost of the care and maintenance of worker was not met by capitalists.

For workers themselves wage-labour, far from providing the opportunity for creativity and greater freedom, was profoundly alienating. The appalling housing conditions in which usually large working class families lived meant that housework was often the most back-breaking, least-fulfilling work of all. Economic laissez-faire ('do as you please') especially benefited Western business in the international context where it exploited markets and natural resources (including human beings – first, as slaves and then as low-paid wage workers). In Marx's time, the vote was extended to most of the middle class but only to relatively few of the working class. Unsurprisingly, he referred to this as 'bourgeois' democracy and we can never know whether his views would have become less politically revolutionary and more reformist had the universal franchise been introduced during his lifetime.

In current sociological parlance, Marx considered that the identity that workers had in capitalist society was restricted and oppressive of their potential. He argued that for this to change, they needed to become conscious of their position within the capitalist system and to act against it. In Weber's view, which I agree with, it is Marx's disregard of individual consciousness and the mechanistic way in which he defines collective or class consciousness that leads him to determinism. Marx distinguished between 'false' and 'true' consciousness: the former being the product of capitalist ideology and the latter the outcome of a socialist analysis of capitalism and an understanding of the socialist alternative. In effect, this analysis conflates individual and class identity – at least until the point at which socialism is achieved. The view that 'true' consciousness and, by implication, 'true' identity equates with class consciousness and are only achievable within a socialist framework has been a point of fierce debate within the Left since the time of Marx. Throughout much of the nineteenth and twentieth centuries, many working class people did adopt a collectivist and socialist identity, but many others did not and by the latter part of the century seemed less inclined to adopt socialism as a dominant, over-arching identity.

The above view is representative of Marx's later, more 'scientific' work rather than his earlier philosophical and humanistic reflections. The latter did not reflect a view of humanity based on natural rights theory but they did reflect an analysis of the 'species being' which argued that certain types of economic and social relations were more conducive to human happiness and development than others. The later Marx had become caught up in a theory of social evolution in which the immediate quality of human feeling and experience appeared secondary and subordinate to the process and pattern of historical change which Marx believed he had come to understand.

2. Durkheim: Communal Identity

Durkheim defined sociology and his study of it in such a way that he only really addressed the issue of identity at the macro or communal level. As a result, he leaves something of a vacuum at the individual and personal level of identity. He considered the latter to be more properly the territory of psychology than sociology. He was interested in the self as it was formed and penetrated by society primarily through socialisation and symbols of solidarity. Of course, Durkheim was aware that people would behave somewhat differently in modern than in traditional societies but his concern with this was at a general or societal level and more in terms of social order and solidarity than individualism and identity. He realised that people's consciousnesses would become more diverse and in that sense less social but, again, it was the social rather than the individual side of this development that pre-occupied him. Even his study of education focused more on its public function as a mechanism for fostering social solidarity and for preparation for fulfilling social roles, rather than as a means of individual development.

Durkheim's later work shows a shift in emphasis towards the analysis of the effect of ritual and symbol on collective consciousness and, by implication, social solidarity and conformity. In the *Elementary Forms of Religious Life* (1912) he shows how society is unified not merely by consciously understood codes of conduct but more profoundly at the level of communal expression. The early insights of psychoanalysis on the social structuring of unconscious instincts and fantasies through religion and other communal expression influenced Durkheim's work at this point. In turn, his analysis of symbolism has had enormous influence on the French structuralist tradition.

Durkheim was the only one of Marx, Weber and Durkheim to define himself professionally as a sociologist. He did so very much in the positivist tradition of Comte which ruled out subjective meaning and, in so far as it was considered at all, subjective identity, as irrelevant to sociology. The vacuum left by Durkheim in relation to individuality and identity had enormous and arguably negative consequences on the development of social thought in France because the 'space' was never adequately filled in the sense of theorised. On the contrary, as will be explained below, the French structuralist tradition sought to make that 'space' as empty of the individual subject as possible (p. 123).

Weber: The Social Actor and Individual Identity

Weber's legacy on the matter of identity is a mixed one. In his emphasis on individuality he is by far the closest of the three founders of sociology to the classic tradition of the Enlightenment. Theoretically, and to some extent methodologically, he conceptualised individuality much more fully than either Marx or Durkheim but his sociology also has a strong structural dimension. He considered that as a matter of historical fact modern organisational structures were developing in a way that repressed individuality and individuals. He regarded the corporate and government bureaucracy as the dominant organisation of the modern period – the 'iron cage' of his famous image. Whereas early capitalism had been characterised by dynamic if somewhat parsimonious individual and family enterprise, the early twentieth century saw the rise of the giant capitalist corporation and the development of huge government bureaucracies. Within these bureaucracies the roles of most individuals were sharply defined and narrow in scope. They offered little in the way of exercising personal creativity and judgement and not very much even in the way of employing institutional power. Although Weber did not sufficiently link his analysis of bureaucracy with stratification, he was well aware that in bureaucracies, as in society generally, the few at the top – the elite – benefited greatly in terms of wealth, privilege and power relative to the masses. At the heart of his despair, however, was his belief that the drive to bureaucratic hierarchy was irreversible.

Since Weber, the twentieth century has echoed with criticism of bureaucracy and its stultifying effects. No doubt most of this would have occurred had Weber not written his seminal analysis. The novels of Kafka, the folk-songs of Pete Seager, and the politics of Djilas, were doubtless spontaneous and individual responses to bureaucratic sameness and control. Within sociology, Charles Wright Mills is among the best known inheritor of Weber's theory of bureaucracy although Mills did make an explicit link between organisation and class theory absent in Weber. However, Mills did not find in this linkage any dynamic for social change. Rather, he found the mass of American society – a vast swath of middle and working class people – tied into the status quo by bureaucratic conformity and avid consumerism. Never one to miss the opportunity for social satire, Mills especially mocked the pretensions of the insecure white collar class (see p. 55).

Weber did not consider that individual identity was entirely frustrated by the routine and humdrum of bureaucratic toil. It was largely in the non-work area of life that Weber found that individuality flourished. The concepts of *status group* and *lifestyle* express this aspect of his thought. Whereas Weber considered class to be primarily an economic concept, he considered status to be a social one. People joined or were recruited to status groups because they had something important in common with other members. Thus, people of different class origins can and do belong to the same church – and share related social activities, or to the same sports or leisure club. In the context of a shared interest, however limited, people belong to the same community. Thus, in pursuing their own interests and/or beliefs individuals can create voluntary communities or, expressed otherwise, a common identity. People who share the same social activities develop similar lifestyles although inequalities of wealth set limits to this tendency. In fact, Weber, recognised that wealth itself is a source of status and shared social activity though not the only one. His analysis of the relationship between class, status and politics is more complex and less linear than that of Marx who, in contemporary terms, saw them as complementary parts of a unified identity in the 'truly' conscious individual. Weber agreed that work/class experience would often provide a basis for both communal and political activity but not always. The same was true of ethnic, religious and other major shared cultural experience. However, Weber regarded political activity as relatively autonomous and of central importance in directing the life of a society.

Identity and Culture in Late Modernity

Castells' argument that the shift from an industrial to an information basis of production has brought the world into a new historical period was presented in the previous chapter (see pp. 71–2). Whether we are in a new age or simply in a different phase of modernity, everyone agrees that the post second-world war period has seen profound changes. This section seeks to explore the response of social theorists to these new times, particularly their analysis of changes in culture and identity. The following is a summary list of the changes discussed elsewhere which provide the context in which they wrote:

The Information/Communications Revolution (see Chapter 3)
Globalisation (Chapter 7)
The (alleged) Decline of Class (see pp. 84–7)
The New Social Movements (see pp. 216–20).

Sociological theorists – indeed, a huge number of social scientists, cultural theorists, novelists and miscellaneous intellectuals – have tried to understand and interpret these changes in much the same way as their counterparts had engaged with the industrial and political revolutions of the late eighteenth century. In such periods, established ways of thinking are often overthrown or radically revised and new ideas and paradigms come to the fore. Questions of identity and culture are inevitably raised in these times of redefinition and redirection. The Renaissance, the Enlightenment and, arguably, the intellectual ferment around postmodernism of our own times are examples of such movements. However, while the artistic and intellectual achievements of the earlier movements are generally acknowledged, it is not yet quite clear what 'postmodernism' in its various forms has accomplished.

Identity, Culture and the New Sociology

The discipline of sociology changed greatly in the last quarter of the twentieth century. Of course, many have continued to work within the classic traditions or within the paradigms of the 'second wave' of theory which, with the exception of Symbolic Interactionism, largely grew out of classical sociology. Nevertheless, by the start of the 1990s, the subject addressed a substantially new and different range of issues and was beginning to take-on a different theoretical shape than in the 1950s/60s. This was partly driven by the speed and extent of social change and the resulting arrival onto the sociological agenda of the major issues listed above. In particular, new radicals – feminists, ecologists, anti-racists and others – pushed new areas of concern to the fore or sought to re-arrange priorities.

Among the theoretical developments in the subject there was a substantial shift in focus from structural matters, particularly established class and inequality issues, to cultural matters. The new focus was particularly on communication, consumption and identity. Fredric Jameson has referred to this shift as 'the cultural turn'. The cultural turn has been on a scale that has spread far beyond sociology. Thus, cultural studies and media studies, spawned mainly within sociology, are now run as separate subject areas in higher education. However, such breakaways have not resulted in a widespread return within sociology to traditional issues of structure and class. On the contrary, 'the cultural turn' remains very apparent within sociology itself and constantly challenges sociologists to extend the boundaries of the discipline and to review the adequacy of their theoretical and methodological practice. The next section examines the intellectual origins and content of 'culturalised' sociology. The impact of structuralism, poststructuralism and postmodernism on sociology and on many other disciplines has been enormous and to a large extent has shaped the development of the discipline in the latter part of the twentieth century. Intellectual movements on this scale invariably generate great controversy and that is certainly true in this case.

Rather than attempt a brief 'potted' review of a large number of structuralists, poststructuralists and postmodernists, I have chosen one or two of the most influential figures from each movement. This provides a basis for making some generalisations about these movements although considerable differences occur between particular thinkers.

Structuralism, Poststructuralism and Sociology: The Long Hello

It is important to distinguish between structural sociological approaches and structuralism. In the former case, the term structural refers to those sociological approaches which to a greater or lesser extent give precedence to social structure over social action/agency. Thus, Marx and Durkheim were structural theorists and the symbolic interactionists were not. However, the term structuralism refers to a specific intellectual movement which reached the height of its influence in the 1960s and 1970s and has had a lasting and profound effect on cultural studies and sociology. It is this movement that is the primary concern of this section although the critical comment made about structuralism and poststructuralism also applies more generally to those structural approaches which marginalise individuality/agency or reduce them to an effect of social structure. Both the specific movement of structuralism and structural approaches in general emphasize the influences which form an individual and de-emphasise individual will and choice which, in any case, tend to be seen as illusionary by many post-war structuralists and those they have influenced. Structuralist theory is notoriously complex and even obscure but its enormous influence not only on social science but on much of Western intellectual and creative life requires substantial presentation of it here. Structuralist theory has been imported into British cultural studies/sociology mainly by the influential Stuart Hall and has had a huge and, in my view, mixed impact.

The founder of structuralism as a specific theoretical movement is the French anthropologist, Claude Levi-Strauss (1908–). He was greatly influenced by Durkheim and by the Swiss linguist, Ferdinand de Saussure (see below). Another influential structuralist was the French cultural theorist, Roland Barthes (1915–1980), who popularised *semiology* – the science of signs. The best known sociological structuralists are Louis Althusser (1918–90) and Pierre Bourdieu (1930–) although it is the work of the former that is chosen for more detailed analysis here as it is rather more representative of the structuralist movement. It will be useful to start with a simple general definition of structuralism and then return to the development of the approach:

> Basic to the approach is the idea that we can discern underlying structures behind the often fluctuating and changing appearances of social reality
>
> (ODS:646).

According to Saussure, a universal set of rules underlie the variety of individual languages. He observed that while most people have little formal knowledge of what these rules are, they nevertheless practise them. In explaining how languages function, he distinguishes between *signifiers* (sounds/images) and the *signified* (concepts) which together constitute a *sign*. Thus, different languages have different words or signifiers for the concept of 'boy' which is what is signified by these various words. The material reality of a boy is not the same as the verbally expressed concept which refers to a boy. The reality that a sign refers to is known as the *referent*. Crucially, a sequence of signifiers/signified only make sense because each word/concept is different. Callinicos quotes Saussure's statement that '(i)n language there are only differences' (1999:267). It is because one sound/concept is not another one (i.e., is different from others) that sense and meaning can be built up. It is how sounds/concepts are related to each other in phrases and sentences that creates messages or meanings. Difference is at its sharpest in respect to binary opposites such as man/woman, good/bad, dry/wet.

In the structuralist analysis of language, one can see the beginnings of the postmodern emphasis on, and finally celebration of difference. A sequence of related signs has come to be known as a text. Within a given culture or subculture particular words and other signs mean more or less the same to most people. However, because signs can mean different things to different readers, texts, like individual signs can be 'read' or interpreted differently by different people.

The distinction made by Saussure between signifier and signified (together making up 'the sign') has been widely employed in sociology and cultural studies. Barthes applied Saussure's structural theory, including his signifier/signified/sign framework, to visual as well as verbal communication. To give an example, a raised forefinger can act as a signifier which in different contexts (i.e., in relation to various other signifiers) can carry different meanings e.g., one (in relation to numbers), first (rank order), out (cricket), 'get stuffed' (insult – in which context the index finger is more usually pre-ferred). His work has had a great influence on cultural studies in Britain especially through the Centre for Contemporary Cultural Studies (CCCS). The meanings of, say, the clothes of youth groups or the rituals of football supporters and much else from everyday cultural life have attracted this kind of analysis. One of the features of non-verbal signifiers, in particular, is that the concept or idea they signify may be rather diffuse or a single signifier may carry several meanings. Thus, a safety pin worn by a punk might signify aggression, sado-masochism, generally non-conformity, a desire to exclude or reject, poverty and so on. Of central importance to structuralism, is the fact that the individual may not be conscious of all the meanings/interpretations of any particular signifier or text with which they are associated e.g., a punk may not be aware of all the possible significations of wearing a safety pin or outfit of leather and pvc plastic. In addition to its specific methodological application within cultural studies, structuralism has influenced social theory in a more general way. Thus, its emphasis on the dynamic relationship between structures was adopted by Althusser in explaining how individuals understood or did not understand social processes.

Levi-Strauss applied the concept of structure to social analysis. He emphasised not the surface level of change but what he saw as the underlying structural realities located in the human mind. He argued that societies 'are limited to a choice of certain combinations from an ideal repertory, which it should be possible to reconstruct' (quoted Lane *ed.*, Introduction: 1970). Few, if any, leading structuralists have adopted the concept of 'ideal repertory' but the concept of deep struc-tures remained central to structuralism until Foucault broke with it. Levi-Strauss' contention that social relations can be understood in terms of binary opposites, though not original, was also influ-ential. Examples are, the asymmetry or 'opposition' between the one and the multiple, self and others, identity and difference, belief and reality, freedom and necessity (i.e., the limits imposed by need/order), nature and culture. Levi-Strauss and Durkheim differed on the nature and mean-ing of religious myths and symbols. The latter considered that belief systems such as religion and myth reflected and took their meaning from social reality. Thus, he stated that religion is 'society worshiping itself' i.e., unconsciously celebrating and reinforcing its own solidarity. For Levi-Strauss, the reverse was true. He argued that major social forms, whether religious or profane, reflected fundamental categories of the mind or universal human rather than social realities. Behind the great variety of cultural difference, Levi-Strauss believed it was possible to discover funda-mental human concerns. In this sense, he was a universalist whereas Durkheim was emphatically a relativist. It is decidedly Durkheim's *relativism* that most influenced later structuralism, including its main British manifestations. However, Levi-Strauss' belief in culturally transcendent categories of the human mind has a distinguished pedigree going back to Kant and passing through Karl Jung. What it doesn't seem to have is a place in sociology.

The work of Saussure, Barthes and Levi-Strauss established the intellectual basis for structuralism and applied the approach to verbal, visual, mythical and, by implication, all forms of sign systems. Two fundamental points about structuralism and its influence on poststructuralist and postmod-ernism and, ultimately, on sociology and other disciplines need to be made.

First, is that words and other signs are constructions which carry meanings in addition to and sometimes other than those which the author subjectively intends and that *the consciously held mean-ings of the 'author' of a text (virtually any social construction) cannot be privileged over other people's read-ings*. As indicated above and further explained below, these structures are unconsciously experienced and symbolically expressed (though symbols can also express consciously understood meanings). To access what these meanings might be requires the *deconstruction* of the relevant *text* or system of signs. This involves 'taking apart' (deconstructing) the text and analysing the relationships between its various parts and the relationship of the text to the wider context in which it is situated. In other words, *contextuality* is crucial in deconstruction. As stated above, the text may be verbal or visual. To give an example of the latter, a poster with a clenched fist on it may, depending on other signifiers and context, signify trade union solidarity or a boxing match.

Second, the idea of difference, which has become so central in poststructuralist and postmodernist thought, has its origins in the linguistic and cultural theory of the above authors. However, the 'post' understanding of the origin of difference is distinct from the liberal concept of individual difference. In the latter case the individual (or group) makes or constructs the difference whereas in structuralism the individual or group is made different by the effect of the structures of language and culture upon them. Structuralism and Marxism fit each-other so well because both argue that the meanings individuals profess may not be, indeed, routinely are not of their own making.

Althusser: A Sociological Marxist-Structuralist

Louis Althusser is, along with Bourdieu, one of the two major sociologists associated with structuralism. He describes three main social structures:

○ the economy
○ politics
○ culture/ideology.

Figure 4.1   Louis Althusser: His structural perspective reflected both Marx and the French structural tradition.

One of Althusser's main concerns was to illuminate how these structures relate to each–other. In doing so, he was motivated by a desire to quash Marxist humanism which had revived in the post-war period partly in response to the atrocities of Stalinism and the oppression practised by the state leadership in a number of other Communist societies. Althusser was convinced that a more intellectually robust and less sentimental response to Stalinism was to re-view and re-establish the 'scientific' Marxism of Marx's later years. He attempted to do this by developing an analysis of the relationship between the above structures which was both consistent with the tradition of scientific Marxism and relevant to contemporary capitalism.

A celebrated and controversial aspect of Althusser's refutation of humanism was his attack on subjectivism – the view that the individual subject can significantly shape his or her life and contribute to social change. He argued that the notion of the subject in this sense was a myth. Rather as Nietsche had pronounced the death of God, Althusser pronounce the death of the subject. Althusser's work contributed substantially to the concept of 'the decentring of the subject' which became a prominent theme in poststructuralist and postmodern thought.

Althusser argued that society cannot be understood on the basis of subjective meanings but should be analysed in terms of the relationships between social structures. In describing the relationship between the main structures he sought to avoid both crude economism and historicism (historical determinism). I will return to the latter shortly. The former refers to the view or doctrine that the economic base determines the superstructure – politics and culture/ideology. He argued that in contemporary capitalist society 'the relative autonomy of the superstructure' is possible but that the economy was 'determinant in the last instance' (which in some of his formulations is stated as 'never coming'). Althusser is thus attempting both to acknowledge that political and cultural/ideological action can occur which is not merely a reflection of the economic base and to reject the idea that such action alone can change the base. For capitalism to be replaced, the economic base itself must be in crisis whatever may be happening at other structural levels.

In stating the possibility of a relatively autonomous relationship between the main structures of contemporary capitalist societies, Althusser was partly recognising the increasing role of the state and the rise of the media. He distinguished between the *repressive state apparatus* – mainly the police, army, judicial and prison system – and the *ideological state apparatus* – mainly the education system and the mass media. Althusser contended that the education system prepared people for their roles in the capitalist occupational hierarchy and the mass media propagandised them as consumers. He emphasised the role of ideology in overall structural relations arguing that the bourgeoisie was able to reproduce its class domination through the mechanism of ideology, particularly via the media. Althusser used the concept of *interpellation* to describe how advertisements 'hail' or hook the individual by associating the product to be sold with, typically, sex or status. Chillingly, he states that it is at the moment a person feels most 'free', the 'moment of choice' – the moment of happily connecting with the advertisements appeal – that he or she is most fully enchained or caught by the system. Althusser presents the subject as being 'constituted' by the system rather than as capable of consciously responding to it and intellectually rejecting it. However, he considered that it was the role of scientific Marxism to analyse and clarify how ideology obscures the true and repressive nature of productive and social relations under capitalism. Executed in this way Marxist theory was objective as distinct from the subjective and deluded nature of other social theories.

Althusser's rejection of historicism is less convoluted and contradictory than his rejection of economism. He argued – as many have done – that the Marxist interpretation of history as unfolding in the form of predetermined stages was wishful thinking. Yet, he did not replace this notion with a view of history as significantly made by people. Like Foucault, he argued that historical change is unpredictable and a matter of contingency, accident and the unintended consequences of action. While these factors do play an unquantifiable role in historical change, many would argue that so, too, do the conscious intentions and actions of people.

Althusser can be located within the structuralist tradition in the following ways:

1. He gives priority to structure over action/agency (as did Durkheim)

2. He contends that there are structures which individual subjects are often unaware of but which profoundly influence their action and thought (for Saussure these structures are linguistic, for Levi-Strauss they are categories of the mind, and for Althusser, they are socio-economic).

3. It is the relationship between structures or structural relations that is the relevant level of analysis for explaining meaning or in Althusser's case, causation, not individual meaning.

Comment on Althusser

Any critique of Althusser is likely to give close scrutiny to his anti-subjectivist position and stress on underlying structural forces. Although his political inclinations were Marxist, sociologically Althusser is equally in the tradition of Durkheim. Arguably, he is even more 'extreme' in his structuralism than Durkheim. Although the latter considered subjectivity as irrelevant to sociology, he at least seems to allow the possibility that it could be studied within psychology and, therefore, presumably thought subjectivity does occur. In contrast, Althusser dismisses subjectivity and humanism as misleading tenets of liberal ideology that prevent people from seeing the deeper realities of structural relations.

Althusser's influence waned along with that of Marxism generally from the mid-1970s. Despite his routine rejection of Marxist historicism, his structuralism and anti-humanism also led him towards determinism. Many liberal and radical social theorists, including this author, would argue that subjective consciousness is a human capacity and that people inter-subjectively constitute society and have the potential to change it albeit within the limits of external conditions. There is more than a lingering determinism in Althuser's belief that he could restore Marxist theory to scientific status. Marxism may help to raise people's consciousness or understanding of their social situation but, in principle, it is no more valid or scientific than other social theories. Ironically, while claiming scientific status for his reading of Marxism, he sought to debunk the claims to objectivity of natural science, arguing that the practice of science always occurs within a political context.

As with several of the structuralist and poststructuralist theorists, there seems to be an unwarranted intellectual arrogance about Althusser. For him, ordinary individuals are too entramelled in the dominant ideology to initiate meaningful change. In envisaging the capitalist system as a series of structural relationships – understood only by a few Marxist intellectuals – Althusser closed the door on voluntary change. He replaced economic determinism with ideological-cultural determinism.

A comparison of the structuralist approach and symbolic interactionist approaches to language (preferred by Habermas) provides a sharp insight into the different emphases of the two theories. As was described above, the structuralist approach emphasises how the reader of a text (e.g. you or I looking at an advertisement or whatever) is 'spoken to' at the level of the unconscious. Communication is often aimed at manipulating the emotions to produce conformity rather than based on rational exchange. Thus actions that seem 'free' to the actor such as buying a product that has been heavily advertised or identifying with a dominant ideology are not a matter of rational choice. In contrast, Habermas argues that despite the obstacles put in the way of rational communication, it is nevertheless routinely possible to achieve it. Echoing Mead, Habermas considers that consciousness allows for meaningful inter-subjective communication. Distortions in communication can be put to the test and exposed in a variety of ways.

Given that the above interpretation of Althusser is highly critical it is fair to refer to a much more favourable and sympathetic review of his work. Ted Benton, writing from a close relationship to Marxism, finds several of Althusser's theoretical positions 'liberating'. These include his challenge to orthodox Marxism and his 'critique of economic determinism, and recognition of the relatively independent role played by non-economic practices in both maintaining and changing society which 'opened up a new set of possible ways about how change might occur, and who might bring it about' (Benton in Stones, 1999: 201). However, what *seems* liberating doubtless reflects the situation one is in. For non-doctrinaire thinkers these 'liberating' propositons must seem modest advances, particularly as Althusser appeared unable to take them further. Thus, he remained attached to the notion that the working class is the only agency of revolution and because of his anti-humanism, could never build on his rejection of Marxist-economic determinism.

Benton seeks to explain Althusser's anti-humanism. He argues that Althusser is not anti-humanist in the sense of being indifferent to human suffering (a fairly minimal moral achievement). However, he is anti-humanist in two senses. First, he opposes the Enlightenment and kindred projects based on the idea of human progress. Second, Althusser opposes what Benton refers to as 'voluntarist' approaches to sociological and historical explanation. Althusser certainly does that to the point of denying the operation of reason and will at all. Contrasting him with Althusser, Benton identifies the recent thought of Anthony Giddens as 'voluntarist' and refers, in particular, to '(t)he view recently advocated by Anthony Giddens of personal identity under conditions of 'reflexive modernisation' as the outcome of a 'project' of self-creation' as an example (196). It is surely an exaggeration to present Giddens as a simple voluntarist. Even the brief quotation from Giddens used by Benton himself shows that Giddens is well aware that human action, including the construction of personal identity, is influenced by social context, that of 'reflexive modernisation'. It is also not the case that all Enlightenment and modern liberal thinkers were simple voluntarists. Max Weber certainly was not.

Finally, Benton acknowledges that in rejecting the (supposed) 'voluntarism of the humanists, Althusser seems to have gone over to the opposite extreme of a 'structuralist' denial of human agency' (200). In a telling comparison of Althusser with the Italian socialist, Gramsci, Benton observes:

> By contrast, Gramsci had recognised the capacity of oppositional groups in society to challenge the hegemony (ideological sway) of the ruling ideas through cultural struggle in favour of an alternative ethical vision and way of life (200).

Bourdieu

Bourdieu is a prolific scholar and it is possible here only to deal with how he approaches the central issue of this chapter which is the relationship between the individual and agency, on the one hand, and society and structure, on the other. Fortunately, it is one of Bourdieu's main aims to integrate agency and structure and in broad terms his work can be read and assessed as an attempt to do so. In contrast to Parsons and Giddens, Bourdieu is strongly committed to grounding theory in empirical research and many of his key concepts and interpretations are buttressed by 'hard data' from surveys. In this sense, he advocates a social science of practice.

Habitus and field are the two key concepts employed by Bourdieu in his attempt to integrate the two sides of the dualisms. Habitus refers to the total context of social influences on an individual. He sees class as the dominant social influence and particularly stresses the way habitus forms cultural norms, attitudes, motives and competencies. Through their experience within habitus, then, individuals bring a socialised self to social 'fields'. A field is a distinct area of institutional power-play. The civil service, churches and denominations, business corporations, and larger institutional systems such as the polity or economy are fields of institutional power-play.

Bourdieu's close linking of habitus and fields is crucial to his scheme of integrating agency and structure. The concept that does much of the work in making this link is that of capital. There are various types of capital, including economic, but Bourdieu stresses the extent to which the possession or not of cultural capital, respectively advantages or disadvantages individuals in particular fields of activity. Bourdieu has empirically tested and illustrated this range of concepts in relation to the education system (1980). He argues that the cultural capital of middle class children greatly advantages them in the context of the middle class institutional ethos of the education system and that the lack of relevant cultural capital disadvantages working class children. Middle class children acquire further cultural capital in the education system and enter the field of competitive careers with the relative advantage enhanced. By the same token, children of working class origin have their disadvantages reinforced. Bourdieu describes examinations as mere rituals of legitimation which endorse these structural processes with the myth of genuine competition. He writes compellingly of the 'symbolic violence' meted out to the children of the working class. In his work on cultural practice, including aesthetic judgement and taste, Bourdieu further argues that practices which are widely viewed in individualistic terms in capitalist society are in fact class related (see *Distinction* 1984)).

So far, the above description of Bourdieu's work may seem to integrate the individual and society but very much 'on society's' terms. What is so far missing is an account of the role, if any, of the individual. Although, Bourdieu rejects individualistic explanations he does describe certain continuities of conduct-motivation shared by people in collective contexts. Objectively capitalist societies are structured in terms of social classes and within that framework people compete for domination and recognition (a concept which owes something to Weber's concept of status).

Like Althusser, Bourdieu strongly contends that sociology can achieve scientific objectivity. He argues that social scientists must constantly be reflexive in pursuit of objectivity. By this he means that they must monitor and remove any trace of bias from their work. On this basis, they are entitled to intervene in public in the making of public policy as Bourdieu himself has often done.

Comment on Bourdieu

How successful is Bourdieu's attempt to produce a sociology which avoids an 'either/or' emphasis on one or other side of the dualisms? It is difficult to avoid the conclusion that although Bourdieu did not regard himself as a structuralist, he is the last, if probably the greatest, of them. In other words his sociology is skewed towards an emphasis on social and structural factors at the expense of individual agency. Nevertheless, an account of capitalist society which describes people as competing for material goods and the recognition of others within a hierarchically structured social context will seem to many to cover much of human activity. Perhaps Bourdieu's major and distinctive contribution is his minute examination of how people seek recognition through cultural process and how in doing so they reproduce the social order. It is his emphasis on the psychological/social need for recognition that differentiates him from classical liberal and Marxist economic explanations of motives both of which stress interest (self or class) as the driving force of human conduct. Nevertheless, this selective if significant dash of Weber does not much dilute the overall Marxist-structuralism framework of Bourdieu's work.

To turn now to some more explicitly critical comments on Bourdieu. First, it is arguable that

Bourdieu's anti-individualism detracts from the overall balance of his sociology. To paraphrase Giddens' comments on Parsons, the stage is set, the script is written but the actors never get to interpret their parts. Along with Althusser and other structuralists, Bourdieu was determined to uproot French humanism and individualistic thinking. Both bitterly opposed the existentialism of Sartre which they associated with these characteristics. Sartre's emphasis on making moral and political 'choices' as a test of both integrity and being ('I choose there I am') did veer to the opposite end of the dualist polarity. Further, his rejection of the existence of the unconscious implied that the whole structuralist enterprise was based on an empty fallacy. One thing Freudianism in combination with structuralism has convincingly done is to illuminate how individual feelings, behaviour and thoughts are unconsciously influenced by cultural signs and images. Nevertheless, if existentialism is too simplistic, Bourdieu might draw from Weber a much richer account of action than he seems to want to contemplate.

A second criticism of Bourdieu needs to be carefully couched – Bourdieu's argument that sociology is a science. This approach may be taken to imply the controversial view that society is an appropriate 'object' for scientific study and can be explained in scientific terms. An alternative view is that society cannot be appropriately studied scientifically if this means adopting the same assumptions as natural scientists. This is because the actions of people are not predictable in the same way that the interactions of inanimate objects might be. Further, the study of meaningful action and motivation while requiring discipline is arguably a humanistic rather than a scientific skill. Those who accept the latter points tend to see sociology as part of the humanities or as a hybrid discipline. They also tend to take a much more modest view of the extent to which sociologists can claim an 'expert' relationship to the rest of society. In contrast, Bourdieu seems to assume that the social sciences can achieve a similar level of objectivity and certainty as the 'natural' scientists. Whereas Mills, Habermas and Giddens have made political and moral comment 'merely' on the basis of being concerned citizens particularly informed by their professional work, Bourdieu does so on the basis of what he claims is his 'scientific authority'. Ironically, this conjures up again the recurrent spectre in French sociology of the sociologist as 'high priest'.

Bourdieu's use of cultural concepts does, within his own terms, draw the individual closely into social processes. However, partly because he adopts a strong structural emphasis particularly in relation to class, his approach is clear and has a strong sense of direction. With Foucault, the pre-eminent poststructuralist, action and structure are collapsed into a single undifferentiated process in which the difference between the objective and subjective disappears.

Foucault: Poststructuralism

There are similarities and differences between structuralism and poststructuralism. As the term poststructuralism suggests, the view that there are 'deep structures' which underlie and shape, if not determine, the surface level of social interaction was not adopted. However, nor did poststructuralists shift to a more voluntarist or subjective interpretation of society. In the earlier and middle work of Foucault, the pre-eminent poststructuralist, the majority of people – individually and collectively – seem to be as much constituted by external forces as in structuralist approaches. However, what constitutes people in Foucault's approach is *discourse* rather than underlying structures (see below). It is only in his later work that Foucault raises the possibility of the conscious subvertion of dominant discourses and even then he does not do so unambiguously.

Foucault conceptualised power and knowledge as interdependent to the point of being part of the same indivisible process. Those who have power in any area – be it technical expertise, institutional or whatever – possess by virtue of that power the means to define what is important knowledge within their area of dominance and in so doing subject others – for instance, clients or subordinates – to their domination within their sphere of power. He expressed this controversial view quite unequivocally:

> There is no power-relation without the correlative constitution of a field of knowledge, nor any knowledge that does not presuppose and constitute at the same time power-relations (1977:27).

Foucault referred to the virtually circular relationship between power and knowledge as *power-knowledge*. The concept of power-knowledge can be viewed as an attempt to fuse the divide between the two poles of the dualisms and as poststructural in that sense. Given that Foucault considered that every social relationship was characterised by an element of power relations, the concept has wide application. Nevertheless, he argued that to understand particular formations of power-knowledge required detailed study. He advocated what he termed an 'archaeological' approach to disintering power-knowledge relations. This involved the historian immersing him or herself in the assumptions of a particular culture. In a further attempt to achieve an authentic grasp of cultural formations, Foucault advocated a geneological approach to pursuing information. This involved tracing the origin and development of ideas back through their evolution. The technique was intended to minimise the possibility of the researcher imposing his or her own cultural assumptions on the data. His own work covered institutions of power such as prisons, hospitals and asylums and social practices such as sexuality and patriarchy. In each of these cases he found that dominant groups explained and expressed their dominance by what he referred to as discourses. The Penguin Dictionary of Sociology gives a straightforward definition of *discourse* and provides a brief example of how changing historical discourses of 'madness' reconstitute the way madness is perceived and treated:

> This is a domain of language use that is unified by common assumptions. For example, M. Foucault ... describes discourses of madness – ways of talking and thinking about madness – which have changed over the centuries. In the early medieval period, the mad were not seen as threatening but almost as possessing an inner wisdom. In the twentieth century the discourse of madness emphasises the condition as an illness in need of treatment ... Sociological attention also concentrates on the social function of discourses, most importantly on their ability to close off possibilities. Within a discourse, there are literally some things that cannot be said or thought.
>
> (PDS: 120–21).

Foucault treated the professional expertise, authority and practice of twentieth century psychiatrists and other 'modern' professionals as just as much the product of discourse as earlier examples of power-knowledge. He particularly emphasised the extent to which specialist subject areas and professional practices based on modern science tend to exclude less powerful and established discourses (note, for instance, the struggle that psychoanalysis and faith-healing as well as other forms of less 'rational' and 'scientific' treatment have had in establishing professional 'respectabilty'). Within Foucault's framework of analysis the techniques of modern psychiatry, including surgery and drugs are examples of the application of power-knowledge relations reflecting a particular scientific discourse within which some have much more power than others.

The practical effects of discourse need to be noted. Discourses are not merely theories but ways of organising as well as perceiving the social world. For Foucault, the exercise of power and subjection to it can be highly physical. This is obvious in relation to some forms of modern psychiatric treatment referred to above (some of which are now discredited). In his *History of Sexuality,* Foucault illustrates how the body is organised differently – for instance, in relation to dress and posture – in ways that embody different concepts of what is required or acceptable. Thus, the Greco-Roman world was much more open in relation to nudity and homosexuality than most of the modern world. In general, modern bureaucracies, such as factories, the military, and large educational institutions, impose a variety of techniques of control and discipline on the body in the cause of producing their particular function. Foucault's concept of being *positioned* within a discourse describes how an individual or group can be 'captured' both psychologically and physically within a particular discourse – even though they may imagine that they are 'free agents'. Foucault's observations here might seem quite obvious but prior to his comments the body and its social organisation had been to a considerable extent ignored in social science, not least, sociology. This is much less the case now.

Far from sharing in the enthusiasm for the 'modern project of freedom', Foucault described the modern period as 'the age of discipline'. Discipline in modernity is characterised less by harsh physical punishment and restraint but by the potentially total surveillance and control facilitated by science, technology and rational organisation. Foucault's cited the nineteenth century reformer Jeremy Bentham's panopticon – a new type of prison – as an example of modern surveillance technique. The design of the prison was such that the gaoler could see any prisoner at any time. This also provides a vivid instance of Foucault's use of the term 'gaze' – with which the dominated can 'fix' the dominated. The technology of surveillance has developed rapidly even since Foucault's death. Videos, automatically triggered cameras and even computerised boss-employee communication sometimes used in modern surveillance and control can give the process an impersonal, even sinister feel ('Big Brother is . . .?). As Foucault noted in relation to psychiatry, modern techniques of control sometimes pursue mental as well as physical conformity.

Foucault's concept of discourse has been extended beyond the kind of specific applications illustrated above. He himself regarded the principle and practice of modern science as a general discourse which shaped particular discourses in given professional and academic areas. He used the terms 'discursive formations' to indicate that whole societies or cultures can be based on structures of knowledge or 'epistemes'. Thus, modernity is characterised by the dominance of rational/scientific thought and practice. Again, this discourse is not regarded by Foucault as 'objective' or, still less, as 'progressive' but as an example of power-knowledge relations reflecting and re-producing a particular 'regime of truth'.

Foucault's analysis of how social change occurs shifted towards the end of his life to a position somewhat less deterministic and to that extent less pessimistic than structuralists such as Althusser. His earlier/middle writings argue that systems of power-knowledge 'constitute' the subject ('the individual is an effect of power', 1980: 98) who is generally unable to envisage other ways of perceiving/acting in the world. The possiblity of conscious human action to change the world seems to be precluded. The self seems truly to be the product of discourse, lacking the capacity to effect events. Change occurs as a result of disruptions in the system by which one centre of power-knowledge becomes challenged by another. These may be quite *contingent* or unplanned. An example of what Foucault means here might be the immense social changes which emerged indirectly from the astronomical inventions and observations that brought the medieval religious model of the universe into doubt and contributed to the undermining of its social order.

Several recent commentators have stressed the considerable extent to which the later Foucault gives greater scope for resistance to dominant discourses and regimes of truth (Callinicos, 1999; Delanty,1999). In any case, he had always envisaged power as a two-way flow or as relational and as open to creative as well as destructive use. He argued that their are 'points of resistance' throughout networks of power. However, he continued to reject the 'illusion' of the possibility of 'freedom' outside power-knowledge relations either in an individual or collective sense. Instead he sees a plurality of resistance arising dispersed around the power networks. He describes three distinct kinds of struggle:

1. against wider forms of social domination such as racial, religious or social oppression
2. against forms of domination that take away from individuals the product of their labour (such as occurs under slavery and capitalism)
3. against subjection/submission to identities and positions within power networks imposed by dominant others.

Foucault sees considerable signs of resistance in the first area in contemporary society. Feminism, the gay movement, environmentalism and ethnic and religious revivalism are examples.

Comment on Foucault

Foucault's work is far-reaching and at times opaque. A brief comparison with the work of Habermas – his great intellectual antagonist – should help to clarify both the main direction of his thought and its intellectual impact. First, they differed in their attitude to modernity and the Enlightenment project. Habermas remains profoundly committed to the Enlightenment ideal of the creation of a rational society of free individuals, or at least as close an approximation to it as is possible. Foucault sees modernity as a particularly oppressive historical period and one which shows signs of fragmenting as the price of its own excesses become apparent (for instance, in anger in 'third world' and in environmental destruction) and as resistance increasingly occurs.

Second, they differed fundamentally in their approach to subjectivity. The premise of Habermas's thinking is that individuals have consciousness and are able rationally to communicate with each other. In contrast, in the bulk of his work Foucault reiterates rather than supersedes the broadly structuralist position that individuals are constituted by texts or discourses, the full content of which they are seldom aware of. Their respective approaches to language vividly illustrate this area of disagreement. For Habermas, language can be used consciously, creatively and truthfully to achieve a rational communication and a better society. For Foucault it is the other way round, people are virtual dummies and the structures are virtual ventriloquists.

Ironically, Habermas and Foucault both came to regard the New Social Movements of the Left as the most promising force for radical change. Towards the end of his life, Foucault became more optimistic about the possibility of becoming aware of the basis on which oppressive discourses were established and of the possibility of opposing them. Previously, he had suggested that historical change occurred mainly as a result of accident and contingency. To the small extent that he shifted towards voluntarism, he moved towards resurrecting the conscious subject within his theory but too belatedly to dispel the gloomy determinism that pervades his intellectual legacy.

John Sturrock in a not unsympathetic portrait of Foucault, shares an apparently quite widespread desire to rescue Foucault from the full extent of the intellectual consequences and perhaps even the personal despair implicit in his anti-humanism. It is worth quoting Sturrock at some length because what he writes could apply not only to Foucault but to the structuralist tradition in general. First, Sturrock acknowledges the comprehensive extent of Foucault's anti-humanism:

> Foucault meant to be recognised, as an anti-humanist, or as a militant in the war on subjectivity that was conducted so brilliantly during the structuralist years in France. Nothing that he wrote was quoted against him quite so insistently as his prophesy right at the end of *Les Mots et Les Choses* that Man was a 'recent invention of Western European thought' who, Foucault was ready to wager, 'would one day be erased like a face drawn in the sand at the edge of the sea. Quite what these ominous sounding words are threatening us with, I am unsure.
>
> (1998: 64).

Foucault's 'threat' is that what had been 'invented' – 'Enlightenment Man' – could in time disappear. Given that on the cusp of a new millennium, there is, for instance, speculation about increasing brain capacity by inserting micro-chips into it and downloading data and instructions, who can say that Foucault's speculation might not come to pass? But his is a bleak, not to say inhuman, vision. Here is part of Sturrock's paradoxical attempt to rescue a human element in Foucault's thought:

> For all this there is, inevitably, a certain humanism in Foucault. Had there not been, he could not have acquired the reputation he now has … He has come to be seen as the inspired enemy of a coercive normalisation in society, whether this operates in the sexual field, the psychiatric or the more generally behavioural. By calmly ascribing insidious powers of control to supposedly liberal societies such as our own, Foucault became the patron Saint of abnormality and deviance …

> (1998:65)

One can imagine Foucault spinning in his grave at the thought of 'Saint Michel' ! Be that as it may, the implied criticism of Foucault in the above – and it applies to most of the post/structuralists and postmodernists – is that, quite simply, they went too far in the application of their ideas. The Enlightenment may have claimed too much for 'man' and for reason and to have been afflicted by terrible hubris as a result, but these thinkers claim far too little.

Lyotard and Postmodernism

Lyotard is associated with the 'postmodern break' perhaps more than any other thinker. As John

Figure 4.2   Lyotard found flaws in the myth of modern progress … humanity might as easily destroy itself as endlessly progress.

Lechte puts it, having been a Marxist activist in the 1950s and 1960s, Lyotard 'became the non-Marxist philosopher of postmodernity in the 1980s' (1995: 246). First, Lyotard mounted a powerful intellectual attack on the credibility of *'metanarratives'* or systems of ideas which seek total explanations of how society 'works' and what action should be taken to change it . Second, he sketched out an alternative version of social interaction based not on totality and unity but on *plurality* and *difference*. He did this respectively in *The Postmodern Condition* (1979) and *The Differend: Phrases in Dispute* (1983). Part of the impact of Lyotard's approach was that it suggested a 'break' with both Marxism and liberalism. Marxism and liberalism were not only the dominant political philosophies of modernity but paradigms or worldviews which structured perception in every area of life – academic disciplines, creative work and even personal relationships. Much of Lyotard's work is, in fact, in the area of aesthetic/art theory and is often characterised by a certain postmodernist obscurity. That aside, Lyotard makes some powerful and even compassionate arguments which merit serious attention and have had a wide influence.

In a letter to a colleague, Lyotard tries to situate the debate about postmodernism by making three points (in Docherty; 1985 47-50). The first point he makes is basically the one referred to above about metanarratives but in the context of architecture – 'there is no longer any horizon of universality, universalization, or general emancipation to greet the eye of postmodern man, least of all to the eye of the architect' (47). Lyotard goes on to say that architects now have to work in the cramped spaces left by the grand and, in his view generally disastrous, designs of modern architects and planners just as people generally have to cope with the fragmentation resulting from the collapse of religious and philosophical grand designs. Secondly, Lyotard applies his argument about metanarratives and utopias particularly to technology:

> Technoscientific development has become a means of deepening the malaise rather than allaying it. It is no longer possible to call development progress.
>
> (49).

He goes on to state that the relentless pursuit of technological 'development' has divided humanity into two parts: those who are challenged by the complexity of technology (the rich West) and suffer from its fragmenting effects, and those who because they are left behind by technology and face the 'terrible challenge of their own survival' (the poor and excluded). He then makes the telling point that the modern project 'once applied in principle to the whole of humanity'. For Habermas and Giddens, it still does – but not with the innocent optimism of the early Enlightenment.

Lyotard's third point is that modernity should be constantly questioned and criticised rather than taken for granted as a time of progress and humanity. In the light of the species carnage that has characterised the twentieth century, few will disagree with that. Still, Lyotard makes the point a complex one. Following the model of art and aesthetics, he suggests by his examples, that criticism and dissent emerge more at the level of emotion and intuition than through critical reason. Here he is close to Adorno and at odds with Habermas who argues for the primacy of reason. It might seem a short step for the 'post' theorists to take, to accept that emotion, aesthetic response and even desire can and usually should be mediated by reason but such is their disenchantment with science, technology and the aspirations of the 'rational' mind, it is a step they do not take. However, on the matter of retaining a critical stance to modernity, Lyotard is surely right and to that extent is in agreement with Habermas and Giddens.

Lyotard's analysis had profound implications for the established sociological paradigms. He rejected the assumption that society could be understood as a 'unicity' or unity as in their different ways Marx, Durkheim, and Parsons had tried to do. Apart from the 'failure' of the metanarratives, he observes that the social groups and individuals who make up society increasingly do not share a common, 'legitimating' view of how it should be run or for what purposes. Social groups are different and they have different opinions. Postmodernity, then, becomes a time when different groups seek to pursue their own identity and view of the world in various degrees of tolerance and conflict. However, his thinking inclines less to volutarism than this basic description might suggest.

The intellectual underpinning for Lyotard's main argument is that all discourse, including the metanarratives of modernity, are relative or subjective systems which generate their own framework of self-reinforcing belief and language. Further, particular discourses involve power and action as well as beliefs and as a result shape or have impact on the social world. Thus, Marxism has a vast inter-related vocabulary of meaning and explanation which makes sense and provides a basis for further intellectual construction and for determining what positions/statements are 'correct' or 'incorrect'. In this sense, discourses are self-referential – one part/concept (say in Marxist class analysis) refers back to another and depend on each-other to build up the overall structure of meaning. Lyotard referred to the building of such self-contained intellectual systems as 'language-games'. At a more everyday level people 'play language games'' as they make sense of and explain their lives. There is clearly a great similarity between the Lyotard's concept of language games and Foucault's concept of discourse although the latter more fully encompasses the notion of practice.

The logic of Lyotard's argument leads him to take a pluralist position in relation to political ideologies and philosophical beliefs. Lyotard's pluralism and by extension postmodern pluralism differs from liberal pluralism in that he considers that there is no over-arching 'truths' accessible through communicative exchange whereas some liberals, at least, continue the pursuit of Enlightenment ideals or 'truths' while tolerating other discourses. So, whereas some liberals continue to adhere to certain philosophical principles, particularly about humanity, and (merely) tolerate differing views, Lyotard is saying that all views and discourses are of equal but relative status. Lyotard's analysis of science as a language game illustrates his own and postmodern relativism. In contrast, historically liberalism has regarded science as an objective, value-free means of establishing objective truths and laws through observation and experiment. Lyotard regards science itself as a discourse, characterised by distinctive rules and procedures not generalisable to other discourses. Science, too, is a 'language game' with its own internal, self-referential logic and not uniquely 'objective'. Lyotard stipulates several rules of science key, among which are that:

i. a scientific statement only exists in relation to other scientific statements which are validated by proof and argument and that therefore

ii. only those who share scientific knowledge can participate effectively in the 'language-game' of science which is detached from other narratives.

Lyotard argues that much of the practice of modern science is oppressive and threatening. It has become dangerously detached from external controls and is something of a juggernaut driving rather than being driven by human beings. This is partly because its sheer complexity puts it beyond most people's scope, but also because computerisation linked to modern technology provides new means of controlling human beings, including increasing and speeding up their work output (productivity). Whereas Foucault described techniques of bodily control, Lyotard generalises towards wide areas of technological dominance.

In making this point, Lyotard echoes a deep concern recurring throughout the twentieth century, notably in the work of Weber and the Frankfurt School, that instrumental reason undirected and unrestrained by moral motivation has the capacity to enslave rather than liberate human kind. However, in the light of his moral relativism, Lyotard might seem to have surrendered any basis on which to oppose this tendency other than at the level of sentiment and intuition referred to above.

Lyotard's refutation of Enlightenment 'idealism', of which liberalism and Marxism are variants, has bought him into disagreement with the pre-eminent defender of the Enlightenment ideals of reason, truthful communication, democratic consensus and progress, Jurgen Habermas. It is significant that Habermas uses a Meadean model of language as *consciously meaningful* symbolic communication rather than a structuralist derived model which sees language largely as the coding of often unconscious meanings which may easily undermine conscious intention. For Habermas language provides the main means by which all people can come to agreement through the use of reason whereas for Lyotard different groups 'play' different language games.

Another major postmodernist thinker, Baudrillard has extended similar analysis to the global media. This is discussed more fully in the chapter 7, pp. 203–5. Here it is enough just to indicate some consistency between his thought and Lyotard's. Baudrillard's interest is in visual signs or language rather than verbal or written discourse. In Baudrillard's view, signs in the modern media can come to 'mean' anything because they need not refer to any fixed material reality or event (i.e. they are not attached to fixed referents). Thus, an image of Che Guevara has slipped from indicating revolutionary sympathies to being a fashion accompaniment. According to Baudrillard this is a world of 'hyper-reality' in which the hype or the image may come to refer to anything or nothing. Pessimistically, he seems to believe that most people cannot 'see through' this world of surfaces and so cannot conceive of constructing something more substantial.

Comment on Lyotard

It is easy to sympathise and agree with Lyotard's criticism of metanarratives or ideologies which have the conversation of the world as part of their goal. Too much blood has been spilt in those kind of enterprises. In so far as liberal capitalism is implicated as one of these metanarratives, then Lyotard's criticism of liberalism are justified. The fact is, liberal capitalism is substantially implicated in this way because of its oppression and exploitation of many peoples and societies. However, that is an obvious if crucially important point to make. It does not in itself address the intellectual basis of the debate between liberals and postmodernists.

As a political philosophy and, it can be argued, increasingly at the level of practice, modern liberalism has developed in the direction of pluralism and tolerance. Thus, modern liberal nations accept the principle of multiculturalism both internally and in relation to other nations. The liberal Daniel Bell arrived at this conclusion in the nineteen fifties, some twenty years before Lyotard. However, in contrast to postmodern pluralism, liberal pluralism still adheres to broadly humanistic beliefs, principles and goals – albeit now much more pragmatically. To a certain extent the liberal humanist metanarrative does conflict with its pluralism. This is most obvious with reference to the area of human rights. The pursuit of what the liberal societies of Europe and America see as human rights sometimes prompts them to criticise and brings them into conflict with other cultures. For liberals, this is a tight-rope that has to be walked.

Liberalism, then continues to reject the moral relativism of postmodernism. Zygmunt Bauman makes an interesting reference to Lyotard's moral relativism. He quotes Lyotard to the effect that in relation to artistic criticism and, by implication, all criticism 'the objects and contents have become indifferent. The only question is whether they are 'interesting'' (in Hall and du Gay, 1996: 34). In place of judgement based on rational principles, we have response based on interest or desire.

Lyotard's critique of 'objective' science, and that of other postmodernists, has been the subject of a celebrated response. This was from a group of mainly American scientists who held the view that

Lyotard, Baudrillard, and Lacan (see below) had 'repeatedly abused scientific concepts and terminology: either using scientific ideas totally out of context, without giving the slightest justification ... or throwing around scientific jargon in front of their non-scientist readers without any
regard for its relevance or even its meaning' (Sokal and Bricmont, preface,1997: ix–x). Two of the
scientists constructed a spoof article from what they regarded as nonsensical would-be scientific
statements by postmodernists. They submitted this to the cultural studies journal *Social Text* which
duly published it as a serious piece. I am not in a position to adjudicate between the science of
these scientists and the 'science' of postmodernists so I will leave the reader to draw his or her own
conclusion. A comment by Sokal and Bricmont on Lyotard's model of what constitutes valid science is particularly thought-provoking:

> Finally, the 'model of legitimation' remains the comparison of theories with observations
> and experiments, not 'difference understood as paralogy' (whatever that may mean).
>
> (128).

Sokal and Bricmont's analysis of the 'science' of the postmodern 'guru', Lacan, is hilarious. They
particularly poke fun at his attempt to present the human penis in equation form as the square root
of minus one!

To some, the postmodern attempt to 'kill-off' the rational human subject is no better based than
their 'science' seems to be. Bauman cogently argues the contrasting position that as we seek to
construct sociological theory of modernity, '(t)he focus must now be on agency' (1992:190).
Again, however, readers will no doubt balance the arguments and draw their own conclusions. It
is important to note that Sokal and Bricmont do not dismiss that part of postmodernist thinking
in which they themselves have no professional competence'

> We make no claim that this (their 'science') invalidates the rest of their work, on which
> we suspend judgement. (x).

Ruptures in Modernity: Poststructuralist/Postmodern Propositions

Postmodernism is the most general term used to indicate the ideas so far covered in this chapter,
including postructuralist thought. Postmodernism asserts the view that there has been a break in
modernity on a scale that justifies conceptualising society, certainly Western but by extension
global society, as postmodern. The above pages have detailed some of the arguments to that effect.
The following list is a less detailed but more comprehensive and chronological summary of the
intellectual ruptures to modern Enlightenment thinking that together constitute the basis of the
postmodern framework of thought. One authority, Lacan, appears for the first time here and gets
slightly more than summary treatment.

Ruptures in the 'Unity' of the Identity of the Modern Subject

1. Freud and Lacan

i) Freud's 'discovery' of the role of the unconscious and of the instinctual in structuring behav-
    iour contributed to an undermining of confidence in individual reason and in the creation of
    a rational society. For many Freud's vision of the irrational and destructive depths of the
    human psyche was confirmed by the first and second world wars which saw slaughter on a
    mass scale and a sustained attempt at genocide. Freud also contributed substantially to the
    understanding of the importance of symbolic meaning and analysis through his pioneering
    work on the meaning of dream symbolism.

ii) Lacan, who can be classified as a structuralist (see below), brought together linguistic theory and an interpretation of Freud which emphasised the role of the uncounscious rather than the conscious ego in forming identity. It is through the unconscious that symbols enter the mind and, in Lacan's view, more or less structure it ('Man speaks . . . but it is because the symbol has made him a man' (quoted in Lechte, 1995:68). However, the subject is also constituted or made up of two other 'orders'. This trilogy is 'the real' (that which is 'always in its place'), the symbolic (linguistic/visual) and 'the imaginary' (the everyday life which the conscious subject 'imagines' is real but is structured by deeper, unconscious forces). In effect, Lacan reverses the commonsense assumption that everyday consciousness is focused on the 'real' by asserting that the dominant order is the symbolic which controls the subject, that the subject does not understand this, and therefore lives in an imaginary world which s/he mistakes for reality. Lacan, has had a huge influence on structuralism and French intellectual life and from there, more generally. His main impact was on psychoanalysis. Had he been more sociological in his thinking it would certainly have been necessary to devote more space to him in this chapter. However, his theoretical framework is clearly consistent with French structuralist thought covered above. He contributed to the growing emphasis in social theory on the role of the unconscious and the symbolic in the construction of identity differences – a line of thought further developed by Baudrillard (see pp. 203–5).

2. Structuralism and Poststructuralism:

i) Language and Symbols

Saussure and Barthes respectively developed a theory of language and signs which was later widely interpreted by structuralist influenced social theorists to demonstrate that human thought and action is entirely or mainly the product of language and signs rather than of human volition.

ii) Structural Marxism

Althusser's sociology gave precedence to social structures over the intention of 'the subject'. He argued that the subject in modernity is 'de-centred' to the point of non-existence.

iii) Foucault

The main direction of Foucault's thought, including his central conceptualisation of discourse theory, is relativistic. Individuals are caught in self-justifying and self-referential 'regimes of truth' which they can do little to change. However, if the body of Foucault's thought also implies the death of the subject, towards the end of his life he gave greater emphasis to modes of resistance.

3. Postmodernism

i) Lyotard argued with immense effect that the modern metanarratives of liberal and Marxist progress as well as the absolutist mode of thinking in general is at an end. What is left is difference – in discourse and identity. This, again, is relativistic but Lyotard's emphasis on difference moved the postmodern debate onto somewhat different ground – raising issues of the source and variety of differences and about the relations between the self and different others and the relationships between different identity groups.

ii) Baudrillard, reflecting the deterministic strand in the structuralist tradition, sees difference as the result of the influence of social, particularly media, imagery and symbolism. It is as if individual consciousness is a blank surface on which superficial and trivial images play (see Chapter 7) and connect only at the level of unconscious desire.

iii) By no means all thinkers influenced by postmodernism have adopted the pessimism of the French post/structuralists and post modernisms. On the contrary, social theorists such as Zygmunt Bauman and, on my reading, Angela McRobbie see a potential for creativity and celebration in a postmodern world liberated from the weight of totalistic ideologies.

The 'Two' Postmodernisms: 'Theoretical' Postmodernism and 'Popular' Postmodernism

To the frustration of some of those who have tried to interpret and critique postmodern thought, the postmodernism tradition seems to be based on two distinct and even contradictory analyses of culture and identity. Here I shall term these two tendencies, the 'theoretical' or intellectual and the 'popular' – although these terms are not entirely satisfactory. Cohen and Kennedy made a somewhat similar distinction in their use of the terms 'pessimistic' and 'optimistic' to describe basically the same two strands in postmodernism (2000). Theoretical postmodernism is the postmodernism of the French tradition of social theory described in this chapter and of the wide range of intellectuals it has influenced, many of them in universities in the United States. Its characteristic intellectual content is a tendency to cultural determinism. Individuals are described as 'hailed' or 'positioned' by 'ideologies' (Althusser), 'discourses' (Foucault), 'language-games' (Lyotard), or 'signs/images' (Baudrillard). In its more extreme formulations, identities seem to be described as projections onto the 'dead' human subject like images flickering across a blank screen.

The term 'popular postmodernism' is introduced to describe a quite different and largely opposite tendency in postmodernism which is the one quite widely adopted in the new identity movements involving youth, ethnic minorities and those concerned with exploring gender/sexuality. What many 'members' of these identity groupings and movements have taken from postmodernism is that they are relatively free to choose and change their identity from the seemingly vast array of identities available in contemporary culture. Consciously or otherwise, they have absorbed the postmodern axiom that belief in metanarratives or total ideologies is no longer compulsory and that instead they can select or perhaps even construct their own identities. This way of thinking and acting is characterised by a strong sense of agency in which 'multiple' identities, 'hybrid' identities, and 'fluid' identities and even 'new' identities are seen as available to individual choice.

There are two problems with 'popular postmodernism'. Firstly, it does not reflect what the major theoretical postmodernists said. Although Lyotard uses concepts such as 'plurality' and 'difference' to describe identities, he still sees them as the product of discourse into which individuals become enmeshed rather than as the outcome of their own volition. Theoretical postmodernism veers too sharply towards cultural determinism but 'popular postmodern is frequently naively voluntaristic – 'Thatcherism in drag' or 'left-wing Thatcherism' as it has been variously described. Secondly, 'popular postmodernism' – in its more extreme voluntaristic formulations – lacks an adequate sense of the constraints of social structure. Class and other inequalities of power, position and resources do not go away simply because people stop thinking about them. On the contrary, the effects of structurally produced inequalities, such as those of income and wealth, are likely to be all the greater when they are left ignored and unchecked. The extreme and growing inequalities of the contemporary world reflect great exploitation and provoke apparently growing if still fairly impotent protest.

In practice, the distinction I have drawn between the 'two' postmodernisms is not as sharp as suggested above. There are a number of intellectuals who could either be described as postmodernists or are influenced by postmodernism who emphasise the opportunity that contemporary culture offers consumers to make choices which shape their identities and lifestyles. Mike Featherstone and, though he is too independent a thinker to be labelled postmodernist, Zygmunt Bauman are examples. In introducing an element of agency into postmodern thinking, these commentators are generally well aware that there are social constraints on 'identity choice'. In particular, Bauman has stressed in his more recent writings the extent to which many are 'excluded' from the late twentieth century/new millennium consumer party (1998).

In my interpretation, the academic study of culture in Britain has unduly reflected the 'pessimistic' and over-deterministic thought of theoretical postmodernism. This is due mainly to the influence of Stuart Hall who has done more than anyone to introduce this tradition into Britain. In fairness, however, and despite his opposition to the individualistic tradition of the liberal Enlightenment, some sense of individuality – often frustrated – is seldom entirely absent from his work. It is almost as though he has found a form of expression which conveys both a sense of structure – very strongly – and of individuality – rather weakly. As a result, his language can be opaque and even carry seemingly contradictory notions. In his following musings on identity, including his own, he paradoxically speaks of what he 'could' have been and what he 'couldn't' have been as the same and he also states – what seems logically contradictory – 'I've become something I was all the time'. In the face of such complexity, it is perhaps not surprising that the 'popular' version of postmodernism has reverted to the simple:

> 'I don't think identity's fixed, the real, true self . . . It's constructed from historical processes: I am the sum of that boy called a 'coolie', the Rhodes scholar, the socialist from Jamaica. Every identity that feels so solid is the result of excluding things you could have been. I go back to Jamaica and I adore it, but I couldn't be a Jamaican. I ache for a parallel life I could have lived. I also couldn't disappear into Englishness. I understand Britain; but I'm only British in a hyphenated way . . . I never called myself black because no one in the Caribbean did then. I've come home to an identity I was never allowed to settle for; discovering I've become something I was all the time; a black intellectual, a migrant . . .'
>
> (Quoted: Guardian: 8.07.2000: Saturday review: 80).

Conclusion

The area that structuralist and, to some extent, postmodernist thought has explored is the influence of the structure of language and signs/symbols on individual and collective identity. Even though some of their work is obscure, there is no doubt that in excavating the deeper structure of human 'motive' they have developed a series of concepts and analytical tools of immense influence and usefulness. To deny this would simply be to contradict the evidence. The post/structuralists have re-written the 'rule-book' for the way many literary scholars now read texts and have influenced a far wider audience to look at 'objects' as constructed texts which, in their own gaze, they are (partly) reconstructing.

These are substantial and compelling achievements. However, in attempting to reconstitute the human subject as a text, as an object of linguistic/symbolic creation, they pushed their theoretical insights beyond reason into near intellectual anarchy. It may be invidious to say so, but some of the post/structuralists' own behaviour seems to taste of anti-humanist despair. Poulantzas committed suicide, Althusser murdered his wife and then apparently went mad. Foucault's sadomasochism was, of course, his own business, but he did seem to fiddle with the self-destruct button. These are perhaps no more than coincidences of biography and prove nothing about the quality of post/structuralist thought. Poststructuralist arguments must stand or fall on merit. In my view, they run second best to the still more impressive arguments of the Enlightenment tradition. The nub of the matter is whether or not human beings can significantly shape their own lives through consciousness, reason and will. Among the most impressive arguments to that effect are those of Habermas and Giddens and these are presented in Chapter 5. However, what is no longer tenable after poststructuralism is a naive and simplistic belief in the power of human reason of the kind not uncommon among Enlightenment thinkers.

The tendency of the structuralists to overstate their case is increased by their sometimes mechanical usage of the concept of binary opposites. The concept does seem to have much explanatory power. The tendency to see things in oppositional terms does widely occur not least in the primary social binaries of self/others and us/them. But it is surely equally obvious that there are ways of looking at phenomenon, including social phenomenon other than in the simple black and white terms of binary opposites. The spectrum has 'opposite ends' but there are all the colours in-between. The variety of social life is no less.

Despite the tendency to polarised thinking, poststructuralism and, especially, postmodernism has also become associated with an emphasis on difference and, if not quite variety, fragmentation. This is most clear in the work of the postmodernist, Lyotard. The logic of burying the 'grand metanarratives' was to acknowledge the possibility of smaller-scale levels of belief and identity. In his reference to 'language games', Lyotard seems to imply that discourses can multiply indefinitely. This may not quite amount to an enthusiasm for pluralism but some thinkers, such as Bauman have taken it in this direction. Treated in this more pragmatic way, postmodernism can perhaps enter the stream of radical liberal thinking of which Giddens and Habermas are the best known exponents. In any case, poststructuralists themselves often seem to hesitate before the prospect of finally signing the death certificate of the subject.

SUMMARY

1. DEFINITIONS OF IDENTITY: It is helpful to consider three definitions of identity: the sociological – in which identity is seen in terms of the interaction of the self and society; the Enlightenment in which more, though not necessarily exclusive emphasis is given to the capacity of the self to construct a coherent individual identity; the postmodern in which some see identity as a socio-cultural product and others emphasise much more that identities can reflect choice and for that reason may be subject to change.

2. CULTURE AND IDENTITY: What we now refer to as identity was experienced somewhat differently in traditional, modern and postmodern societies. In traditional society there was (and is) a closer fit between individual and communal identity to the point where a developed sense of individuality of the kind characteristic of modernity scarcely existed. In modernity the Enlightenment assumptions about the nature of identity became predominant both among intellectuals and at an everyday level. In late modernity, identity has become a highly contested concept with most major post/structuralist and postmodern theories rejecting the Enlightenment approach and seeing identities as social or cultural products. Confusingly, other postmodernists see identity much more in terms of personal/group selection – 'pick and mix'. These varied and somewhat contradictory approaches occur widely in popular culture.

3. IDENTITY, SELF AND SOCIETY: The founders of sociology all, to a greater or lesser extent, saw identity as the outcome of the interaction of self and society. However, their emphases were crucially different. Weber emphasised the role of agency and values and was closest to the individualistic strand of Enlightenment thinking. Marx insisted in the dominant role of the economic/class base in forming identity. Comte and Durkheim appreciated that there was a shift towards individualism in modernity but strongly insisted on the role of social structure in forming consciousness and conduct and established a powerful tendency towards deterministic social thought in French intellectual life which, in turn, has become globally influential.

4. STRUCTURALIST THEORY was built up by, among others:

Saussure: the underlying structures of language
Barthes: the underlying structures of signs, symbols and images
Levi-Strauss: universal categories of the mind – mirrored in myth and social structures
Althusser: the dominance of economic and cultural/ideological structures over the individual subject
Foucault: the dominance of discourse over the individual subject
Lyotard: the constitution of identity through language games (forms of discourse)
Baudrillard: the constitution of identity by the image saturated world of hyper-reality
Popular postmodernism: an everyday assertion and belief that the individual can 'choose identities' – sometimes accompanied by an appreciation that choices are limited and made under social influences.

5. THE POST/STRUCTURALIST AND POSTMODERN TRADITION:

Strengths
i)   It problematised simplistic notions of the 'autonomous' or 'free' self.
ii) It helped to establish the role of language and signs in structuring identity and individual/collective action.
iii) It clarified how the social, including the symbolic, 'structures' the unconscious and influences motivation and action.

Weaknesses
i)   It tends strongly to the deterministic.
ii) For humanists its anti-humanism is misguided and potentially dangerous.
iii) It is sometimes very obscure – perhaps because of the complexity of the area.
iv) Some of its leaders acquired a guru status not conducive to disciplined and reflexive thought.

6. RUPTURES IN MODERNITY – see text (presented in summary form)

7. (INTELLECTUAL) POSTMODERNISM AND POPULAR POSTMODERNISM: Confusingly, the predominant popular interpretation of postmodernism tends to the opposite of the intellectual tradition described in this chapter – i.e. to choice and freedom rather than cultural determinism.

Chapter 5

The Enlightenment Defended and Extended: Habermas and Giddens

> **Key Concepts**:
> communicative/instrumental rationality, discursive/practical
> consciousness, ontological security, public sphere, reflexivity,
> structuration theory, the third way.

Introduction

Habermas and Giddens both seek to keep alive the Enlightenment ideals of the progressive ame-lioration of the human condition and of the continuing expansion of opportunity for individual and social development. While they see serious dangers of the Enlightenment project coming apart, both remain optimistic to the extent that they still vigorously pursue it. Fortunately for the diversity of sociology, they approach their theoretical work in different and distinctive ways. Habermas works in the tradition of Marx, Durkheim and Weber, and particularly the first two, in that he seeks to build a comprehensive model of (Western) society. As well as his predecessors of the Frankfurt School, Habermas draws on Cooley and Parsons and also on a wide range of lin-guistic, psychological and political theory. Politically, Habermas is a radical with roots in Marxism and retains a strong commitment to greater social equality. However, he increasingly seems to envisage change and reform in the West as occurring peacefully albeit in part through the press-ure of radical social movements on the representative institutions of liberal democracy.

Anthony Giddens is as eclectic in the intellectual influences he draws on as Habermas. Having sur-veyed much of classical sociology in his earlier writings, Giddens seems now closer to Weber than any one else in his basic sociological approach. Like Weber, Giddens does not aspire to create a 'total', all explanatory model of society in the way that Marx and Durkheim did. Giddens tends almost to 'spin off' ideas, leaving it to others to further develop or empirically test them. This lack of dogmatism is characteristic of Giddens's political as well as his sociological views and the tone of his more recent writings has been increasingly liberal/social democratic (see p. 150). Writing of Giddens's more recent work, Dennis Smith suggests that 'the liberal baton was handed from Marshall (the major theorist of citizens' rights – my brackets) to Giddens' and that the latter is now among the main champions of the liberal reformist tradition (1998: 667). A pragmatic and cau-tiously incremental approach to theory has not inhibited Giddens from writing on virtually all the major contemporary sociological issues and he is substantially responsible for putting some of them on 'the sociological map'.

As critical defenders of the Enlightenment project, Habermas and Giddens have taken the full onslaught of the more pessimistic postmodernists. Against the view that capitalist culture has all but swamped not only dissent but almost the capacity for it, they continue to assert the possibility of independent thought and action and the continuing possibility of constructing a better society.

Jurgen Habermas

Jurgen Habermas: Communicative Rationality and the Public Sphere

Habermas's work is more sociological in its foundation than that of earlier members of the

Figure 5.1   Habermas has attempted to salvage the ideals and potential of the Enlightenment from the failures of capitalist modernity.

Frankfurt School. Habermas deliberately shifted the Frankfurt tradition towards social structural analysis while maintaining its characteristic concern with culture. Although a far more radical a thinker than Talcott Parsons, Habermas's structual analysis is in some respects closer to the latter's than it is to that of Marx. Like Parsons, Habermas thinks as much in terms of the social system and its sub-categories as of social classes. So comprehensive is the scope of Habermas's work that, along with Parsons, he perhaps comes closest to providing a 'total' model of society since the founders of sociology. Although Habermas shares Adorno's concern with the difficulties in which the Enlightenment project had become mired, he is committed to that project and his work can be read as an attempt to revitalise it. In this respect he stands in sharp opposition to those postmodernists who consider that the Enlightenment project is dead.

In presenting Habermas's thought, it is particularly helpful to understand 'where he is coming from' in the sense of how he understands the past and its relationship to the present and why he considers that the Marxist paradigm is an inadequate solution to the problems of capitalist modernity. I will deal with each of these matters in turn.

Although Habermas regarded the shift from traditional to modern society as progressive and potentially liberating, he considered that it also had fragmenting and alienating effects. Certain problems had become more acute during the twentieth century. As Habermas sees it, the unity of values, beliefs and practice of traditional societies had become separated in modernity into what he refers to as 'the life world' and 'the system world'. The life world is the world of lived experiences which is sustained by shared values reflecting custom and tradition. The system world refers to the large and complex array of bureaucatic organisations, including state organisations, which largely 'run' modern societies. Both the lifeworld and the system world have progressively changed and developed through rationalization. For example, in an aspect of his theory which parallels functionalism, Habermas states that both the life world and the system world have evolved and become increasingly complex and functionally differentiated. The life world has become differentiated into value or knowledge spheres – science, art (including aesthetics), and morality (including religion). In traditional societies these spheres greatly overlapped if, indeed, they were differentiated at all. The life world has also become characterised by greater reflexivity or conscious evaluation (both individually and collectively) and by the universalisation of beliefs as the values of modernity became widely diffused. The system had become more functionally differentiated with the development of more roles and institutions such as the economy, the state and the education system. While Habermas considers that this trend creates more opportunity for autonomy, he also emphasises the potential for social control and repression by the system.

A crucial part of Habermas's conceptualisation of modern society is the *public sphere*. The public sphere is the world of informed debate that originally grew up in the eighteenth and nineteenth century in which mainly middle class people participated. This exchange took place in inns, taverns and coffee houses and also in the burgeoning press. Especially for the rising middle class but also for the working class, the public sphere during this period was characterised by vital debate which, linked to various forms of political action, could influence the centres of power. The public sphere is virtually synonymous with civil society – that realm of society lying between the family/private life and the state but interacting with both.

In his first major book, *The Structural Transformation of the Public Sphere* (1962), Habermas argued that the twentieth century had seen a decline in popular democratic debate and participation – the public sphere. He shared the view of others of the Frankfurt School that the capitalist dominated mass media had taken up the 'space' previously occupied by a dynamic public sphere and that the capitalist state and corporations was increasingly controlling the life world. Habermas's 'project' can be most simply understood as an attempt to show how the public sphere could be revived through the means of communicative rationality. He did not believe that traditional Marxist thought was adequate to addressing and solving this issue although he retained a commitment to the humanistic and liberationalist values of Marxism. It is to this point that I now turn.

Habermas's Revisions of Marxism

Habermas firmly rejected the most ambitious scientific claims of the Marxist tradition, but just as decisively endorsed and developed its commitment to human liberation. Habermas's revision of Marx will be better understood after presenting his understanding of the purpose and disciplinary status of social science, particularly in relation to natural science. Habermas regarded critical theory as an alternative approach both to so-called scientific Marxism and to the positivist social science model of Comte and Durkheim, both of which had been based on the model of natural science. He also made an important though qualified rejection of Weber's view that social science should be value neutral, a concept also based on the natural science model. Habermas argues that it is the legitimate and rational purpose of social science to promote people's understanding of society and so enable them to increase their freedom of action. Logically, this approach involves a critical rather than a neutral or supportive attitude to the social status quo. It implies a focus on sites of conflict and areas of exploitation and an orientation to social change in the direction of greater human freedom and happiness. It is his commitment to continued human progress that is the basis of Habermas's claim to be an upholder of the Enlightenment tradition.

Habermas considered that the claims of Marxist theory to scientific prediction had been undermined by actual historical events and that the Marxist tradition was in need of substantial revision.

The fact that socialist-inspired revolutions had occured in the pre-industrial East rather than in the capitalist West was directly contrary to Marx's expectation. Further, the development of the welfare state in Western capitalist societies had served to blunt the potential radicalism of the working class as had the development of a culture of mass consumption. He argued that since Marx's time, state intervention in managing social dissent had increased in scope and flexibility. Like earlier members of the Frankfurt School he found little evidence to support the view that the working class was the likely agency of change.

Habermas's revision of Marx goes far deeper than simply an up-dating to reflect the realities of historical development – substantial though those revisions were. Habermas regards much of the conceptual basis of Marx's thinking as fundamentally misconceived. Whereas Marx sees human development in materialist terms, Habermas considers that what is most distinctive and valuable about humanity is its capacity to make rationally based moral choices. Whereas Marx famously stated that it is not the consciousness of people that creates their material conditions but their material conditions that creates their consciousness, Habermas contends that the quality of human life depended on people consciously shaping society according to their best moral values. For Habermas, historical progress is not defined primarily in terms of technological or other manifestations of material progress – important though those are – but in improvements in the moral and cultural quality of life. It is his belief in the possibility of progress – albeit defined primarily in moral and cultural terms – that locates Habermas firmly albeit critically within the optimistic tradition of the Enlightenment.

Habermas's rejection of historical materialism went to the very heart of Marx's own thought and allowed Habermas to shift cultural and moral analysis to the fore of his own thinking. At the core of Marx's materialist view of society is his analysis that changes in relations to the means of production are what drive social and historical change. Marx further believed that the capitalist economy was characterised by certain contradictions which would play a crucial if not decisive role in the destruction of the system. Habermas believes that the capitalist economy contains contradictions of this kind and argues that the management of capitalism – by the state as well as by business – may be effective enough to achieve the survival of the system. However, if human agency can engineer the survival of capitalism, it can also change it. Just as capitalism can be managed to prevent radical change, so it is possible – and necessary if change is to occur – for people to make the moral choice to change capitalism. Such a moral choice and continued commitment is only part of the process of change – it does not deal with all kinds of practical complexities – but it is a necessary part.

Nevertheless, it would be misleading to present Habermas as a simple voluntarist. He describes capitalism as an exploitative system and partly because of this as unstable and prone to crisis. He sees early capitalism as prone to economic crises – much as Marx did. In *Legitimation Crisis* (1973), Habermas argues that through political intervention and planning, relative economic stability was achieved in Western capitalist countries. Keynsian economic planning and the rise of the welfare state were largely responsible for this. However, capitalist economies remain unpredictable and crisis-prone and welfare policies are far from entirely coherent or effective. These weaknesses promote a rationality crisis of which a *crisis of legitimation* and a *crisis of motivation* are political and cultural expressions. Widespread public apathy and discontent are the result of the controlling and bureaucratic nature of modern capitalism as well as the intransigence of its inequalities. The consolations of the mass media and consumerism do not adequately compensate for lack of participation and autonomy. The motivational crisis is generated largely through tension between the system and the life world. To a large extent the system impinges on the life world in a disempowering way. Politically many do not feel they have the power to participate meaningfully in the decisions that affect their lives. Morally, there is a widespread sense that the system has lost a sense of purpose and direction and, at worst, is corrupt. Nor, as the New Social Movements demonstrate, has the system completely stilled protest. While managing more or less adequately to meet the material need of citizens, capitalism was failing to stimulate or even address their moral reason and imagination and their need for meaningful participation in the decisions that affect their lives.

The Crisis of Capitalism. Communicative Rationality

The key work in which Habermas develops his analysis of what might replace bureaucratic capitalism, is his two volume, *The Theory of Communicative Action* (1981, 1984). The core of his critique of capitalism and of his analysis of how change might be achieved is in his concept of rationality. Habermas distinguishes between *instrumental rationality* and *communicative rationality*. The former is the application of reason for practical, typically self-interested ends. The latter is reason employed in the genuine and shared search for moral truth and consensus which in turn can lead to rational, socially constructive action. What Habermas hopes for is a regeneration of the public sphere within which communicative rationality, and the moral and ethical debate which is part of it, can thrive and develop. Again, Habermas balances what he hopes for with an awareness of the structural realities of capitalism which militate against it happening. Communicative rationality can only fully occur in what he refers to as an *ideal speech situation* in which the cultural and material inequalities which prevent many people from developing their minds are abolished. Habermas is very much in agreement with the view common among 1960s radicals that for participatory democracy to occur people must be enabled to have the education and access to the information they need to practise it.

Habermas's concept of *communicative action* is the centrepiece of his theoretical model. He contrasts rational or non-coerced consensus with coerced or manipulated consensus. Coerced consensus is achieved by force or the threat of force and manipulated consensus by means of ideological influence or control. A rational consensus is arrived at through entirely open and democratic communication of a kind made difficult by the fact that the means of communication in capitalist societies are largely in the hands of a wealthy minority who use them to make money. Through rational communicative action the various claims to truth can be subject to *validity claims* by which others test them against their own perceptions of reality. Validity claims pertain to the objective (scientific), social and subjective areas of life and in each case Habermas maintains that individuals can reach moral and practical agreement. The ongoing process of rational communication and action is open-ended but would focus among other matters on the distribution of power and resources as well as on a wide range of identity and quality of life issues such as those raised by the new social movements. It is worth stating while Habermas considers that it is possible to establish a basic universal human morality (akin to human rights/responsibilities), he fully recognises that at the level of social ethics and practice a multiplicity of differences will remain between and within societies. However, in the public area – particularly the political and legal – communally binding decisions have to be taken and rules made. It is largely on the possibility of reviving rational communication/action in the public area that Habermas pins his hopes for further human progress.

Habermas's theory of rational communication and his desire for a revival of the public sphere are inter-dependent. The latter will not happen unless people are able to think in a rational way and communicate without being overwhelmed by the trivia of the commercially dominated modern media. Fundamentally, Habermas is concerned with revitalising democracy, and in his later writings, includes a wide range of activities and arenas as potentially involved in this process. Among these are rock concerts, party assemblies, church congresses and various ways of utilising the media. Nick Stevenson comments:

Habermas's (1996) most recent writing on the public sphere has sought more precisely to define its dynamic and spatially complex nature ... The primary task of the public sphere, therefore, is the detection and identification of public problems that need to be fed into the procedures of parliament and the state ... The domain of civil society, then, is much more than a well-scripted public relations exercise, but crucially involves the direct intervention of ethical communities, feminist campaigners, green networks, religious denominations, trade unions, ethnic organisations and parent groups. A societal-wide conversation is dependent upon the emergence of an 'energetic civil society' which is able to force issues and perspective onto the public agenda

(Stevenson, 1999: 42–3).

Habermas is neither a pessimist nor an optimist in his analysis of the outcome of the motivational crisis he describes and about the direction social change might take. He sees two possibilities. First, it may be that capitalism will continue its dominance operating largely through a technocratic, alienating and undemocratic institutional order. Second, he foresees a real possibility that those who seek to change the system will succeed in doing so. It is in the new social movements that Habermas finds the main basis for optimism. Movements such as feminism and the environmental movement although highly varied in their activities, already seek to live-out practically the participatory democratic and communal and communicative values Habermas espouses. The new social movements are not primarily motivated by material issues as was the working class movement but are concerned with 'quality of life, equal rights, individual self-realisation, participation and human rights ... The new politics finds stronger support in the new middle classes, among the younger generation, and in groups with more formal education' (1987:392).

Comment on Habermas

Habermas is currently the greatest – one is tempted to say 'last remaining' – 'totalising' and unifying social theorist. Whereas Giddens seems to aspire to provide an evolving framework of insight and debate, Habermas seeks to produce a comprehensive model of society. Like Marx, Durkheim and Parsons, if not Weber, he seems to want to put the whole of the jigsaw together. In fairness, however, he has changed and developed his model in the light of criticism and events. Far from being characterised by rigidity, his model has, if anything, increasingly reflected the role of agency and the values of cultural and democratic participation.

In his attempt to provide a more unified model of sociological theory, Habermas has drawn freely from the main sociological traditions. From Mead he drew much of his analysis of the role and scope of subjective consciousness and of inter-subjective action. In the tradition of Max Weber he conveys a deep sense of the dehumanising effect of 'the system' but it is from Parsons that he mainly borrows when describing its functioning and complexity. Habermas is noted as much for what he has abandoned from Marx as for what he has retained. Certainly, class greatly recedes in importance in Habermas's model – though the dominance of capitalism continues to be recognised – and the mechanistic Marx disappears altogether. Importantly, what he retains from Marx and the wider German philosophical tradition is a concern for truth, reason and human liberation. Abstract though these concepts may seem, Habermas makes them mean something significant and even conceivably achievable.

To turn now to some more critical comments on Habermas, it is arguable that over the years he has only partially acknowledged his slippage from a neo-Marxist to a more liberal or radical-liberal approach. The antagonism and polarisation between the life world of ordinary people and the system world of capitalists and bureaucrats described in Habermas's early writings gives way in his later work to a more open and potentially more responsive relationship between the two.

Although Habermas is enthusiastic about some of the New Social Movements – some of which act extra-legally – he clearly considers that in the longer term their actions will require mediation by the institutions of consensual democracy, including the democratic formulation of formal norms or laws. If Habermas has struggled in respect to defining the direction and content of his radicalism in the last quarter of a century, his experience is no different than that of the thinking left in general, including its intellectuals.

A number of criticisms have been made about Habermas's approach to rationality. Perhaps the most penetrating criticisms of Habermas relates to the central aspects of his thinking: communicative rationality and the ideal speech situation. The view that consensus will eventually form around the better (i.e. more rational) argument seem to be based more on hope than evidence although it is consistent with the determinedly constructive stance Habermas takes both to people and to change. Relatedly, it is a brute fact that individuals and social groups are not equal in their capacity to present and understand arguments. Patrick Baert accuses Habermas of 'a remarkable lack of sociological awareness' in relation to this point (1998:149). However, it is unlikely that a member of the Frankfurt School would be unaware of this matter. He looks to the new social movements to seek to inform the general public better, in a way that would enable them to address social and political issues more clearly and confidently. In any case, the movement towards more open and truthful communication is likely to take time and be dependent on social reform, including more genuinely egalitarian access to education.

Secondly, a somewhat different line of criticism of Habermas is that he over-emphasises the rational side of human beings at the expense of the emotional and personal. This is somewhat surprising given the strength of the Freudian tradition within the Frankfurt School and is in sharp contrast to Marcuse (see below). Perhaps he feels that others have adequately dealt with the destructive effects of collectively manipulated emotions and that his task is to raise more positive possibilities. Nevertheless, it is arguable that to some degree it is a normal function of language to enable a person to disguise or protect their emotional state rather than always truthfully to convey it. Although he insists on the importance of a free and open civil society, Habermas does not deal in detail with the relationship between the personal, including the emotional, and the social. In this respect, feminism and, among male sociologists, Giddens have done more to introduce a social perspective on the personal. In a different way, Habermas's emphasis on rational potential contrasts with postmodernists such as Baudrillard. The latter believes that 'hyper-reality' is the product of manipulation of desire and imagination.

Thirdly on the central issue of rationality, although Habermas insightfully explores communicative rationality, he does less justice to scientific and technical rationality which tend to get bundled together under the heading of 'instrumental rationality'. Apart from the obvious practical benefits brought about by science, there are, as John Lechte observes, more humanistic and arguably more sophisticated conceptualisations of science and technical reason than that often assumed by Habermas (1994). However, these remarks scarcely detract from the force of Habermas's critique of reason guided only by self-interest divorced from a wider moral purpose.

Finally, by postmodern standards, Habermas is 'old-fashioned' in working with the concept of an integrated subject. Despite all the confusing communication that bombards individuals, Habermas considers them as potentially capable of rational thought and action and as able to develop coherent and integrated identities. This is some way from the contingent, shifting and fragmentary concept of identity common among postmodernists. Again, how damaging this criticism may seem to be depends on which side of the argument one finds more convincing. As a defender of the Enlightenment project, Habermas remains committed to the possiblity of emancipated reason and of the rational subject. However, Habermas does acknowledge the 'de-centring' of the 'Western subject' and that the values and cultures of peoples beyond Europe will legitimately and substantially shape the future.

Habermas and Marcuse

Marcuse and Habermas share a common object of criticism: the misuse of technocratic/bureaucratic control and process in capitalist society. However, in articulating their images of what a more liberated society might be like, they make very different emphases. Paradoxically and with enormous power to shock, Marcuse envisaged liberation in terms of the construction of a new social reality or reality principle based on the pleasure principle. Utopian though such a vision appears, Marcuse was able to argue that a rational, material basis exists for such change and that in the 1960s certain groups were already beginning to demonstrate that it was possible. Notwithstanding these arguments, Marcuse was subject to passionate criticism, especially from leading American liberals. Complex though his theoretical thinking is, Habermas attempts no intellectual conjuring of the kind executed by Marcuse. His vision of liberation is based on the more familiar notion of reason directed by morality. What enthuses him in the new social movements is less their experimental hedonism and exploration of sexuality than their democratic and communal values. However, the fact that both Marcuse and Habermas draw some of their inspiration from a common source perhaps suggests a difference in emphasis rather than substance. It is possible to regard their thinking as complementary, with Marcuse exploring – perhaps to the limit – sexual-emotional liberation and Habermas looking for progress through communicative rationality.

Anthony Giddens

It is arguable that Giddens has explained or attempted to explain more about social life on planet earth in 'late modernity' than any other sociologist. Despite his commitment to rational progress, he has inculcated a sense of uncertainty in his writings by embracing the 'risk' theory of Ulrich Beck. Among his own major contributions to sociological theory is *structuration theory* in which he attempts to reconcile interpretist and structural theory. Structuration theory is typical of Giddens's open-ended approach to social theory in which he undogmatically sketches 'a big idea' which is then developed and perhaps tested by others. In the last decade of the twentieth century Giddens became internationally known for his espousal and development of globalisation theory. Following a period in California, he attempted to draw parallels between democracy in political and in personal life and seemed to imply that he supported a broadly liberal approach in both cases. His *The Third Way* (1998) and *The Third Way and its Critics* (2000) attempts to sketch a reformist way forward between Thatcherism and the 'old' Labour left (a fairly wide stretch of political turf!). As an occasional advisor to Tony Blair he has had some influence on its implementation.

Although Giddens would not wish to be thought of as a grand theorist in the tradition of Marx or Parsons there is a considerable consistency in his work and even a certain unity. This is especially so in retrospect now that his earlier critiques of Marxism, functionalism and positivism can be seen as preliminary to the fuller development of structuration theory, followed, in turn, by his development of globalisation theory. However, 'the unity', if that is not too strong a word, in Giddens's work is emphatically not one of detailed application and develoment of theory. There is relatively little specific use of structuration theory in his work on modernity, late modernity and globalisation. Rather, the unity of his work emerges through the increasingly insistent tone of his liberal-pluralist values and, relatedly, his commitment to a view of history and society in which agency is given ample and, as he would see it, adequate emphasis. However, it may be on his success or not in integrating the concepts of agency and structure that his reputation as a socio-logical theorist may well rest. Nevertheless, his wider political and cultural influence as a liberal intellectual in uncertain times may matter more in practical terms.

Structuration Theory

By the early nineteen eighties, Giddens's basic theoretical position and orientation was clear. He had already outlined his structuration theory in *The New Rules of Sociological Method* (1976, first edition) although his fullest presentation of it was in *The Constitution of Modernity: Outline of the Theory of Structuration* (1984). It is in his *A Contemporary Critique of Historical Materialism* (1981) that Giddens makes his definitive critique of both Marxism and functionalism and, less comprehensively, of structuralism. He sees both Marxism and functionalism as evolutionary theories of history/society which undermine human agency. Of Marx's materialist conception of history he states bluntly:

> No use is served in defending it in a blindly dogmatic way; it should be discarded once and for all.
>
> (1981: 105).

If possible, he is even more dismissive of functionalism. In the following quotation he gives several reasons for being so but his underlying point is that functionalism presents institutional adaptation and evolution as the core of sociological theory whereas Giddens sees a much more central place for human actors:

> The term 'function', I want to claim, is of no use to the social sciences or history; indeed it would do no harm at all to ban it altogether as any sort of technical term . . .
>
> I object to functionalism . . . on several grounds: that (like structuralism) it rest upon a false division of statics and dynamics (structure and change/process – my brackets) . . . that in stressing system needs, functionalist authors have been unable to see human beings as reasoning agents . . .
>
> I want to erase the notion of 'adaptation' (or any synonyms) from the vocabulary of social sciences just as that of function . . .
>
> (16–21).

Giddens offers his structuration theory as an approach which embodies both 'human beings as reasoning agents' i.e., as rational and conscious actors, and social processes. First, is his analysis of consciousness.

Structuration Theory: Consciousness and Rationality

Giddens's analysis of consciousness stands in sharp contrast to the thinking of structuralists and postmodernists on this matter, and is fundamental to his approach to social theory. Giddens stipulates a mental hierarchy of:

○ discursive consciousness;

○ practical consciousness;

○ the unconscious.

It is easiest to start with practical consciousness. This term describes the more or less unreflecting knowledge actors have of how to act. The taken-for-granted knowledge of how to carry out the actions that make up everyday life is necessary for effective action and interaction. Knowledge of how to eat with others, how to greet people, where to sit in a lecture room are all examples of practical consciousness. Practical consciousness is knowing how to act, and without it, social life would very quickly and disastrously degenerate into chaos.

Discursive consciousness is a higher form of thought because it entails the ability to reflect on practical consciousness. It involves the consideration of alternatives to taken-for-granted modes of action, a scanning and even a critical questioning of assumed knowledge. Giddens suggests that actors employ discursive consciousness in situations when, for some reason, practical consciousness is ineffective. A breakdown in normal routine or a disaster might prompt a resort to practical consciousness. However, Giddens does not consider that discursive consciousness is necessarily confined only to extreme situations. Some individuals, notably intellectuals, may think reflexively on a regular basis and in so doing make significant and even original contributions to human knowledge. On the other hand, some people may seldom think discursively but live most of their lives in an unreflecting, routine way. Given this, it becomes clear why, in this case in contrast to Weber, Giddens considers knowing how to act is what distinguishes the social actor rather than the capacity to act meaningfully. Nevertheless, as will be made clear below, the ability to perceive, think about and act upon options are capacities Giddens associates particularly with discursive consciousness (see also p. 194). To that considerable extent he distances himself from postmodernists such as Baudrillard who consider that thought and action are largely generated by external cultural forces.

There is a hint of a parallel here between Habermas's model of the life world/systems world and Giddens's practical consciousness/discursive consciousness, in that the latter term refers in both cases to a more abstract level of thought and relatedly more complex action. However, such a comparison seems to imply that the systems world and discursive consciousness are somehow superior which may well not be what either author wishes to suggest.

Giddens employs the concept of the unconscious in a distinctive way. He argues that human conduct is powerfully motivated by an unconscious need for ontological security. The latter occurs when actors take for granted that they have the knowledge to conduct their everday lives effectively. The link here with the other forms of consciousness is obvious: a sense of ontological security and practical consciousness are complementary but when the latter is challenged, discursive consciousness comes into play. Giddens does not imply that the scope of the consciousness of the 'knowing actor' is absolute: it is limited by social experience/context, by language and by individual capacity. Despite the usefulness of the concept of ontological security, Giddens perhaps misses an opportunity in not further developing his analysis of the unconscious. It is largely on their analysis of the action of the socio-cultural on the unconscious that the poststructuralists and postmodernists arrive at their deterministic conclusions and, to say the least, it would be interesting to see Giddens tackle them on their own ground. As it is, it is hard to find much mention of either Baudrillard or Stuart Hall in Giddens's work.

Structuration Theory: Beyond the Dualism of Agency/Structure

Giddens's structuration theory is an attempt to reconcile human agency with the fact that action is constrained and limited by social circumstances – and so is not entirely 'free'. Giddens rejects the approach which sees agency and structure as a dualism, as opposites, and instead proposes that they are two aspects of the same phenomenon: a duality rather than a dualism. He draws a parallel between social structuration and language. The parallel is between the structure of language (the underlying rules of grammar etc.) and speech – its use by active subjects, and social structure (rules and resources) and its use by active subjects. In using language, an individual operates within the constraints of vocabulary and grammar and at the same time achieves self expression. Both the use of language and the use of structural rules and resources enable actors both to reproduce and to transform, respectively, language and social structure. Giddens stresses that social structure is both the medium and outcome of action. We are used to language being transformed in use and it is the same with social structure. Young people, in particular, are especially inventive with language and similarly social structure can be reworked and reshaped.

Giddens sees a close parallel between action/structure and the use of language. The 'rules' and 'resources' which constrain action also, and primarily, *enable* intentional and communicative action to take place. Rules may be highly formalised such as traffic law, or informal such as the British habit of queueing. Giddens distinguishes between two types of resources: 'allocative' and 'authoritative'. The former refers to the availability of material resources to the actor, whether natural or man-made, and the latter refers to the power a person has, to get others to carry out her or his wishes. Putting all this together, knowledgeable action occurs by means of the critical use of rules and resources, simultaneously reproducing social structure.

The point at which structuration occurs is that of praxis (social practice) – the skilfull performance of conduct and interaction. The ability to tell the time, withdraw money from a cash machine, manage a company, run for political office are all practices which we need to operate more or less according to the rules, but the rules would not exist – and sometimes be subject to change – in the absence of human acts. However, importantly for the duality of Giddens's theory, structures do not exist independently of human action in some 'objective', 'out there' sense. Whereas for the poststructuralist and postmodernists, language and other sign systems are presented as causing human behaviour, for Giddens language and social structure are mediums for action. Really, the difference between the two views could not be greater and becomes the basis of two radically different approaches to understanding social life. Having refuted the deterministic implications in a number of earlier sociological traditions, Giddens finds it raising its head again in these later works.

Crucially for the social dimension of structuration, collectivities can share practices and these practices form and structure them. In fact, Giddens introduced structuration theory in relation to the reproduction of social classes in *The Class Structure of Advanced Societies*, first published in 1973. The two characteristics of groups that enable shared practice are enduring patterns of positions and relationships and defining structural features such as class or gender location. Collectivities may act together and as well as reproducing social structure may change it or transform it. Change may occur through conscious intention or unintentionally.

Comment on Giddens's Structuration Theory

Derek Layder makes a criticism which goes to the core of structuration theory. Layder has expressed his preference for treating each side of the dualisms, including agency and structure, as distinct albeit as also related. He warns that while he considers 'social practices to be one important focus for study' he 'thinks it unwise to allow it to monopolise our view of social analysis in the manner Giddens suggests'(8). Layder argues that his own more dualistic approach enables the particular issues relative to one or other side of a dualism to be focused on. Thus, in relation to individuality, issues concerning individual consciousness and meaning are very substantial and require to be dealt with primarily at the level of individuality – albeit that consideration of the social will inevitably be relevant.

In his *Modern Social Theory* (1997) Layder develops this approach further in the form of a 'theory of social domains'. According to Layder there are four principal domains: psychobiography, situated activity, social setting, and contextual resources. I will not pursue Layder's approach any further here other than to indicate its possible implications for Giddens's concept of the duality of structure. The four domains described by Layder indicate different layers of social reality each of which requires full recognition. The domain of psychobiography is closest to what is meant by the individual in the individual/society dualism. Situated activity is a level directly apparent in the dualisms considered in this book – that of face to face activity. Citing Goffman, Layder refers to it as 'response activity' (85). Social setting is fairly close to the level referred to by the agency/structure dualism. As Layder succinctly puts it 'social relations have a dual character in so far as they contain both 'reproduced' and 'free-form aspects' (110). Contextual resources refers to the various means available of achieving one's will.

Yet, Layder is emphatic that the domains overlap. He states flatly that 'the domains are completely interdependent' (77). Given this, his approach seems less incompatible with Giddens than he maintains. However, he criticises Giddens for rejecting the objective nature of structure implied in the dualisms (165). While particular social circumstances do represent 'objective' conditions for the individuals and groups that live within them, they were, nevertheless, constructed by other individuals and groups – sometimes long ago – and that (f)act is likely to be of relevance in dealing with them. Although Layder does not make the point in quite these terms, it is the case that in his near conflation of action and structure, Giddens strongly privileges action. It almost seems that he would like to abolish the term social structure along with 'function' and 'adaptation' and leave us simply with rules and resources and the use of and struggle for them.

A second criticism of Giddens is that he is sometimes accused of over-simplifying the theories of some of the targets of his criticism. There are defenders of Marx who would argue that his theory of historical materialism contains more of a balancing role for consciousness than Giddens allows, and others who feel he understates the emphasis in Parsons' work on meaningful action as opposed to functional necessity and cultural constraint. While it is true that Giddens is extremely emphatic in distancing himself from certain traditions of sociological thought, he is also at considerable pains to substantiate his accusations with reference to the texts in question as well as to detail his own positions.

Two related further criticisms of Giddens's structuration theory are often made. One is that structuration theory is obvious and the other is that it is so general that it is almost impossible to refute (see, for instance, Baert, 1998). What the theory comes down to is that people act – in various states of conscious awareness – in social contexts that constrain and enable their action. Perhaps the best defence here is an equally simple one – that it is better to be obvious and right than obscure and wrong. Sociological theories that are fairly easily accessible and do not offend commonsense surely have an advantage over those without these qualities.

The Institutional Structures of Modernity and Late Modernity

Despite its diverse nature, Giddens's recent thought is loosely integrated through his theory of modernity/late modernity and its extension into a theory of globalisation. It is as a critical apologist for liberal modernity that provides the main focus of Giddens's work in the last ten or fifteen years of the twentieth century. Giddens does not carry his structuration theory over into his work on modernity and globalisation in a sustained and rigorous way. However, the view that agents, individual and collective, and social structures at various levels are interacting in a flux of change informs his work. Again, if this is obvious, it needs to be.

With reference to which side of the dualism of modernity/capitalism best describes the present epoch, Giddens argues that the former term is the more appropriate, including the basic character of contemporary British society. Giddens takes this position not only in relation to Britain and the

West but in relation to the rest of the world (see his *The Consequences of Modernity*, 1990). Modernity has its source in Europe and has spread dynamically around much of the globe – although not without some resistance.

Giddens states that modernity has four institutional dimensions:

❍ Capitalism

❍ Industrialism (including bureaucracy)

❍ Surveillance

❍ War (Military).

While these institutional areas have a myriad of connections, they exist independently of each-other and have not caused each other. Together they make-up the institutional framework of modernity. Institutional frameworks are sustained and transformed over time through the processes of individual and collective structuration described above.

Giddens is closer to Weber than to Marx in the above characterisation although it is important that he includes capitalism as one of the major factors in creating modern society and ultimately the modern world. Weber sees the origins of modern bureaucracy in the practical application of the rational mode of thought, of which modern industry is only one, albeit a highly important, example. Although aware of the negative aspects of bureaucracy, Giddens dwells on them much less than Weber. It is central to his approach that rationality, including science and technology, is the basis of human progress since the Enlightenment and beyond. Like Weber, Giddens sees capitalism as having distinct origins from the bureaucracy, including industrial bureaucracy, albeit that the two became deeply interwoven in the West.

Giddens appreciates that, although capitalism is not the only conceivable economic system in late modernity, it has become globally overwhelmingly dominant – albeit in different forms (i.e. with a greater or lesser degree of state regulation and/or control/management). However, Giddens does not share either the neo-Marxist suspicion of capitalism of Habermas nor the cultural distaste for it of many postmodernists. His writings on globalisation emphasise the enormous power of capital and his analysis of risk in late modernity shows an acute awareness of the potentially environmentally destructive and socially disruptive effects of capital. He takes the view that global capitalism should be regulated by global institutions. Nevertheless, he regards the capitalist system as a highly successful creator of wealth which, in turn, provides a basis for considerable individual opportunity and cultural expression. He clearly regards global capitalism as 'here to stay'. Depending on one's own standpoint this may appear either fatalistic or realistic.

Giddens like Weber and Mills before him, gives ample place for the role of war and the military in his historical and social analysis. Weber even categorised some societies as 'military', in that power lay primarily with the military elite and Mills argued that in post second world America, the military elite had ascendancy over the political and business elites. As Giddens notes, the twentieth century has been a century of war and it is a simple matter to make the argument that war has independently and significantly changed the course of modern history. For example, war has been instrumental in changing national boundaries, in seriously reducing the male population – with massive social consequences, and in establishing Western domination over most of the globe. Giddens explains the frequency of modern war in terms of the rise of the nation-state and the high level of destructiveness of modern war in terms of the power of modern armaments and the industrial capacity to produce them in great numbers (the industrialisation of war). Giddens is optimist enough to entertain the possibility that the arrival of nuclear weapons may persuade people and governments towards peace – if only to avoid 'the unthinkable'.

Giddens's emphasis on surveillance – particularly by government – as a fourth fundamental institutional dimension of modernity reflects Foucault rather than Weber but it further distances him from the Marxist description of the last 150 years as 'the capitalist' epoch. A main purpose of surveillance is to impose discipline which, in turn, has the goal of achieving conformity and productivity. In modernity surveillance has to some extent replaced more physically violent forms of social control. As with the institutions of war and the military, Giddens notes that technology has played a major role in making the means of surveillance more efficient, and, in particular, has increased the possibility of covert surveillance. In 2000 an official proposal was made to allow M15 total access to communications on the internet. The explosion of information technology and communications has increased the potential (and reality) for centralising information storage and the overseeing of individuals and groups. The new means of surveillance are used by, among others, the state, business and organised crime. Although Giddens notes that people are highly resourceful in resisting surveillance – finding 'free space' and 'free time' – it is, of course, much more difficult to do so if the surveillance is covert and unperceived.

If Giddens is right in denying sole primacy to capitalism as the underlying causal and defining reality of the recent and contemporary West, then Marx was mistaken in doing so. To state a blunt conclusion to a complex problem, my own view is that Giddens's position is broadly right. Modernity is pluralistic or, as he puts it, *multi-dimensional* in its origins and in its institutional character. Basically this is also the view taken by Weber. The answers to understanding the con temporary world lie partly outside capitalism as well as partly within it. Weber perhaps makes the point more emphatically than Giddens, that bureaucracy has been the dominant organisational form adopted by states in fulfilling their functions, as well as by industry (though both have made some efforts to introduce different organisational forms if only in modification of bureaucacy). Of course, it would be quite easy to relate developments in bureaucracy, war and surveillance to capitalism and perhaps achieve plausible partial explanations of them on that basis. The premise of the Marxist paradigm goes further – arguing that within capitalism everything is explainable with reference to capitalism. I will leave readers interested in doing so to execute that particular circle.

Although the 'Weber-Giddens' model of modernity/capitalism seems theoretically and empirically sounder than the Marxist, the latter, far from being wholly redundant, in certain respects gained increased relevance in the last quarter of the twentieth century. Despite the inadequacies of the Marxist paradigm, the revival of free-market economics and politics in the Thatcher-Reagan period and the role of large-scale capital in globalisation in the last decade of the twentieth century gave a stimulus to Marxist scholarship. At the very least, capitalists and their supporters among politicians and social theorists were behaving – almost to the point of stereotype – very much as Marx had described. While, technological innovation contributed independently to the development of a postindustrial economy and the postFordist organisation of parts of it, it would be naive to think that capital did not promote, exploit and manipulate these trends, often at the expense of less powerful groups. Further, as will be discussed in the relevant chapter, the view that globalisation is driven by capitalism and that much of the content of global culture is capitalist in motivation and content is highly arguable. However, what does seem to have been conceded by most ex-Marxist theorists and even by most still writing more or less within the Marxist tradition is that the original Marxist model of change is now out-moded beyond convincing revision. It is not only the mechanistic or deterministic quality of the model and the sorry performance of Marxists in power that have discredited it. The agent for change itself, the traditional working class, has decreased in relative size and power and the 'new working class' has simply not taken over the mantle of 'collective agent of change'.

Late Modernity and the Wider Context

Giddens's use of the term 'late modernity' has already been introduced. Late modernity is a time of heightened modernity, when the consequences of humankind's relentless application of reason and science to the social and natural worlds are becoming more obvious. Reflexivity comes to refer not only to the capacity of human beings to reflect upon (and redirect) their actions but to the potential of the over-exploited natural world to 'strike back'. However, although Giddens by no means sees all the consequences of modernity as benign, late modernity still carries the promise of a good life for the many as well as the few. But he sees the risks of self-damage, of species-damage, as considerable and growing. In the tradition of Weber, Giddens tends to avoid drawing explicit moral conclusions from his sociological analysis. However, the implication of the sociologist of social action seems to be 'act quickly and rationally'. Putting his political hat on in *The Third Way* he counsels:

> Accusations of unnecessary scaremongering don't only come from the right, and many people lapse into the view that 'things will work out in the end'. Since by definition no one can count the risks, and future technological change is impossible to predict, no fully convincing scenarios can be drawn. Global problems respond to global solutions. We cannot leave global problems to the erratic swirl of global markets and to relatively powerless international bodies if we are to achieve a world that mixes stability, equity and prosperity.
>
> (1998:153).

'The Pure Relationship' (or Selfishness?) in Late Modernity: Anthony Giddens and Christopher Lasch

The purpose of this section is to provide a contrast between Giddens's rather optimistic view of the potential of relationships in contemporary society and the grim view of the situation of the human subject purveyed by many poststructuralists and postmodernists. Many of the latter have a view of the human subject that precludes meaningful relationships and so, quite logically, they do

Figure 5.2   Is the ultimate logic of Enlightenment individualism equality in love or narcissism?

not arise for discussion. In contrast Giddens has shown an increasing interest in the micro level of interaction during the nineteen nineties. In this respect his main relevant text is *The Transformation of Intimacy: Sexuality, Love and Eroticism in Modern Societies* (1992). This text may not be Giddens's most authoritative but it is an important contribution to his overall perspective.

Prior to discussing Giddens's contribution in this area, it will help to establish some relevant contextual trends. The development of the individual, or, in short, individualism is a central theme of the Enlightenment and certainly appears most strongly in modern Western society. This has happened in numerous ways. First, the relationship between the individual and society has changed. In traditional society, the main context of an individual's life was within a family that was closely connected to the immediate locality. Now, in late modern Britain, the majority of households have only one (27%) or two (32%) residents, figures that have risen steadily in the last quarter of a century. For a variety of reasons, these small households tend to be relatively more isolated from their immediate neighbourhoods than families with young children who provide a strong link with others (the proportion of 'traditional' households (a couple with dependent children) fell from 38% in 1961 to 25% in 1997). Those likely to be living singly or in couples are young adults, the divorced and the elderly. The first two of these tend to seek relationships – often partners or friends –outside of their immediate neighbourhood in the leisure areas of towns and cities. Their relationships tend to be spread laterally – across their own age-group – rather than deeply embedded in family and neighbourhood. The elderly living alone – of whom about 75 per cent are women – or in couples are less mobile and more likely to have some involvement in neighbourhood interaction but in a period when offsprings have been geographically highly mobile, the more vulnerable depend on state or private support or on occasional visits from family members. In contrast, the better off and more healthy elderly are a growing leisure market and are increasingly well catered for.

The above more individualised patterns of living and sociability are activity sought by some, and simply put up with by others through lack of choice. Giddens's *The Transformation of Intimacy* pertains more to the former. With regard to personal relations, as in most other areas, Giddens is inclined towards optimism. He argues that personal relationships structured by patriarchal power are being to some extent replaced by what he terms 'the pure relationship: a relationship of sexual and emotional equality, which is explosive in its connotations of pre-existing forms of gender power'(2). He detects a trend towards greater personal *autonomy* which he also endorses. As he defines it, autonomy involves a formidable degree of freedom, judgement and reflection or 'reflexivity' as he terms it in other contexts:

> Autonomy means the capacity of individuals to be self-reflective and self-determining:
> to deliberate, judge, choose and act upon different possible courses of action.
>
> (185).

Giddens defines such a relationship of sexual and emotional equality as 'the pure relationship'(2). He argues that both partners must retain ultimate autonomy in a relationship, although while it is on-going complete autonomy is held in abeyance by mutuality. He makes the classic modern radical link between personal and political life. He argues for democracy and equality in decision-making. In Walby's terms, this is an assertion of the desirability of the complete eradication of patriarchy in the private sphere. He refers to the everyday democratic negotiation in a relationship as 'life-politics'. Mirroring democratic politics, life-politics is based on three core qualities:

○ Equal decision-making power within a relationship

○ Openness and trust

○ An equal and fair balance of rights and duties

A condition of the democratic relationship is that those involved want it and continue to want it. Giddens accepts that once a person has clearly lost commitment to a relationship s/he has the right to withdraw from it. Typically, he accepts the consequences of the modern, liberal revolution in personal and sexual relations now largely embodied in marriage and sex equality law. If the autonomous self and the significant other come into serious conflict, the autonomous self can move on. The proviso that Giddens makes is that adequate and proper provision must be made for any children involved in the ex-relationship.

There is no doubt that the trends to which Giddens gives such liberal articulation run deep in modern society, particularly Britain and America. Individuals are increasingly opting either not to marry or to marry later and to have fewer children. The average age at which a woman gives birth to a first child has been getting later and a large minority of women of child bearing age (about 1 in 5) say that they do not intend to have a child at all. Clearly, more people are preferring to spend their time on their 'life projects', including their relationships, and often see the work and responsibility involved in bringing up children as an encumbrance to this.

Giddens's concept of the pure relationship can be viewed as a particular attempt to extend the Enlightenment belief in individual freedom and equality to women although he is comprehensive in acknowledging that the rise of the 'pure relationship' lies in the ideal of romantic love, particularly favoured by women.

There are many social commentators, other than postmodernists, who regard the above developments concerning families and relationships much less positively than Giddens. Among the most bleak of assessments is Christopher Lasch's *The Culture of Narcissus* (1980). Narcissus was the mythological character who saw his own reflection in a lake and fell in love with it. The implication is obvious: individuals in modern society are self-obsessed. Lasch covers much the same ground as Giddens but comes to dramatically different conclusions. The developments that Giddens see as providing the possibility for greater freedom, equality and mutual expression in relationships, Lasch sees as creating an impossible burden of expectation and performance – for which children often carry the flack:

> This appearance (of intimacy – my brackets) is an illusion. The cult of intimacy conceals a growing despair of finding it. Personal relations crumble under the emotional weight with which they have been burdened . . . (T)he deterioration of marriage contributes in its own right to the deterioration of care for the young.
>
> (320–21).

One way of reconciling Giddens and Lasch is to see both the possibilities for expression and development in personal relationships and the many risks and failures inherent in the loosening of social controls on relationships in late modernity and the shift to greater choice and autonomy. Individuals have greater freedom and choice in personal relationships and 'win or lose' the stakes are high.

Giddens and 'The Third Way': Politics and Policy

Anthony Giddens's books, *The Third Way: The Renewal of Social Democracy* (1998) and *The Third World and its Critics* (2000) together present perhaps the fullest statement of the Third Way philosophy. It is highly indicative of Giddens's thinking that he titles the chapter in his 1998 book that would usually be referred to as 'social policy', 'The Social Investment State'. In his first paragraph on this topic, Giddens argues that government has an 'essential role to play in investing in the human resources and infrastructure needed to develop an entrepreneurial culture'(1998:99). Both Blair and Giddens clearly believe that where it is reasonably possible, those who take something out of the state should put something back.

Giddens goes on to claim that equality is the basic principle of the Left. He defines equality in original if arguably radical terms, as social inclusion and inequality as exclusion. In more detail he states:

> Inclusion refers in its broadest sense to citizenship, to civil and political rights and obligations that all members of a society should have, not just formally, but as a reality of their lives. It also refers to opportunities and to involvement in public space
>
> (1998:102–3).

Giddens points to education and work as two opportunities necessary to inclusion in modern society. Although Giddens does not specifically mention social rights they are fairly clearly implied in this statement although the coupling of rights with obligations seems to indicate that the full rights of citizenship are contingent on fulfilling the responsibilities of citizenship. In the past it has been the case that individuals may have their rights curtailed if they commit certain crimes. New Labour has virtually made the right to social security dependent on accepting the responsibility to work if reasonably suitable work can be found. Such a practice could be seen as consistent with, if not implied in, Giddens's close coupling of rights and obligations.

Giddens lists the main characteristics of the inclusive society:

- Equality as inclusion
- Limited meritocracy
- Renewal of public space (civil liberalism)
- 'Beyond the work society'
- Positive welfare
- The social investment state

What Giddens means by equality as inclusion has already been explained. The reason why meritocracy must be limited is, as Giddens graphically illustrates, that the free market can create such enormous inequalities, including income inequalities, that there needs to be public mechanisms for reducing them. Some have criticised the Blair Labour government for not reducing inequality, particularly income inequality, enough. Some of Giddens's most interesting comments relate to the third point – 'renewal of public space'. By this he certainly means that money should be spent on urban and rural public amenities, facilities and buildings in a planned way but also on the core welfare services such as education and health. The purpose of this is to meet the needs of the disadvantaged but, crucially, also to retain a stake in the public services for the middle classes and so to retain their interest and active involvement in civil society. Here Giddens echoes the vision of Mills and Habermas of a revitalisation of public life. In what he calls 'this basic sense' welfare concerns what the better off – Giddens actually says 'the rich' – need from and can give to the wider community as well as the needs and contributions of the less well-off: the 'welfare society' rather than 'the welfare state'.

Giddens's fourth point, 'beyond the work society', needs careful interpretation. He emphasises as much as Labour has come to do, that Britain needs an educated and trained workforce and that those of sound body and mind should work. What he means by 'beyond the work society' is one in which educated and productive individuals realise that work and money are not everything and in which they develop the imagination and compassion to provide for those who cannot work. This is ambitious but in a society which now spends more on leisure than food – the most basic necessity – and which is media-communications saturated, quality of life issues are not merely matters of marginal speculation, they are a public and individual priority.

Giddens's view that welfare should be part of and contribute to a dynamic society picks up momentum in the sections on 'positive welfare' and 'the social investment state'. In the section on 'positive welfare' he constructively confronts many of the criticisms of the postwar welfare state whether from the Right or Left. These include excessive bureaucracy; waste; fraud; dependency; and inefficiency – in the sense of failing to relate cost to productive outcome. He also makes the interesting and controversial point that the welfare state 'is a pooling of risk rather than resources' (1998:116). The relevance of this observation is partly that the burden of risk can shift – for instance, to a particular generation as it ages and needs more social security – but also that risk can be positive, as in entrepreneurship, and to that extent risk-taking should be encouraged.

In his section on 'social investment strategies' Giddens seeks to restructure conceptions of welfare in positive social rather than dependent statist terms. To illustrate his point he takes two examples: provision for old age and unemployment. He observes that the term 'pensioner' is an invention of the welfare state which largely glosses over the vast differences of wealth, health and capacity to contribute to society, of older people. Many of these could still do full-time work and Giddens suggests that instead of retiring ('making redundant') fit and able people early, the fixed age of retirement should be abolished and the timing of retirement made more flexible to individual circumstances. Without being specific he also indicates the need for pension reform in a society in which a substantial number of older people are wealthy or comfortably off but many others are poor and need to draw social security as well as the state pension which has steadily declined relative to average earned income.

It might seem facetious to say it but Giddens's solution to unemployment is employment. He says almost nothing about policies aimed at ameliorating the condition of the unemployed other than those related to job creation. His survey of such policies is quite substantial and eclectic and includes the possibility of cutting the length of the working week in specific industries, mainly those with a contracting labour force. He also advocates support for entrepreneurial initiatives involving technological innovation and small business start-ups (both of which have since been implemented by the Labour government). He also refers to another policy adopted by Labour – public-private partnerships, involving projects of value for the community carried out by private enterprise. Typically, it is only when Giddens has described how wealth might better be created that he indicates how it might better be spent. In this respect he argues for two policies which would both help many individual employees and create more labour flexibility – more pension portability between employment sectors and family friendly workplace policies.

Giddens ends his chapter on the social investment state by turning Beveridge's five evils on their head:

> 'Positive welfare would replace each of Beveridge's negatives with a positive:
> in place of want, autonomy;
> not disease but active health;
> instead of ignorance; education as a continuing part of life;
> rather than Squalor, well-being;
> and in place of Idleness, initiative'

(1998:128).

The scope of Giddens' writings is vast and *The Third Way* can be seen as one expression of his commitment to autonomy, democracy and creativity in personal as well as public life. However, if this seems visionary, there is a typically New Labour emphasis on responsibilities as well as rights in *The Third Way*. The welfare society Giddens advocates would involve a cultural shift of considerable dimensions which, on balance, seems to favour freedom more than security. Some of the review comment on *The Third Way* was critical of the lack of specific reforms suggested by Giddens (see, for instance, John Dunn, *All Zest and Little Nerve*, THES, 25.9.99:23). It is debatable whether this is an accurate criticism but, in any case, it is a mistake to judge this book mainly in terms of practical suggestion. This is a work of ideas and ideas can often be concretely expressed in more ways than one. One test of Giddens's book, though not the only one, is the extent of its influence on the Labour government. In the end, Giddens's work on the Third Way is likely to be seen as a contribution to the theory and practice of liberal social democracy rather than as anything more novel.

Comment on Giddens

Comment on Giddens's structuration theory and 'The Third Way' has been given above and his analysis of globalisation follows below. Technical criticisms of his theoretical work aside, what is worth stressing here is the remarkable extent to which Giddens has emerged as a main representative of liberal/social democratic sociology in our time. He reflects Weber's emphasis on the acting subject and on social plurality but also the applied social reformist of British sociology (notably developed at the London School of Economics at which Giddens is Director). Marxists see him as insufficiently radical in his treatment of capitalism whereas free-marketeers dislike his support for socially interventionist government and regulation of the capitalist economy.

Conclusion: Habermas and Giddens: The Dualisms

Habermas and Giddens are both notably involved in creating social theory that is not over-balanced towards agency or structure and so is neither wholly voluntaristic nor determininistic. It would seem obvious that neither of these extremes would provide an adequate basis on which to build any kind of social science but that has conspicuously proved not to be the case. In general, however, Habermas and Giddens have needed to do more work rescuing agency, rationality and subjective meaning than on the structural side. This is because within sociology there is a tendency to emphasise the impact of the social rather than that of the individual agent. Arguably, in Marxism and functionalism even collective agents get moved by the social system rather than vice-versa. In classical economics, the emphasis tends to go to the other extreme, and the individual consumer or entrepreneur is presented as the sole moving force of the economy and even society. However, neither Habermas nor Giddens has any intention of returning to simplistic subjectivism.

In this respect, an extremely important parallel in the work of Habermas and Giddens is their analysis of language as the means by which subjectivity is permeated with a consciousness of others, and so, in effect, always has an inter-subjective dimension. For Habermas language provides the means to rational (or distorted) communication. Giddens argues that language is publicly accessible and provides a means for sharing knowledge and discourse. Both would easily accept that part of self-identity draws upon socially constucted categories of language, while considering that the individual can mediate these. Given the immense richness of language and imagery, they stress that identity construction is enabled rather than limited by language. Nevertheless, it is true that not all social actors are equally skilled in language and inter-subjective communication.

Habermas's attempt to analyse links, including potentially more meaningful links, between the life-world of everyday interaction and the systems world has similarities with Giddens's theory of structuration linking action and structure. The difference is that Habermas is outlining what is virtually a political project of repossession of the remote systems world by the people, whereas Giddens is arguing that structures and systems are made by actors although some may have the resources to use them to oppress others. Without pursuing a quite complex matter in detail,

Giddens considers that system integration or the lack of it is best theorised in terms of structuration rather than institutional functioning.

Both Habermas and Giddens would like to see a society more subject to reason and humanity and, in fairness, they have both gone to great lengths to describe what these fine words might mean in practice. Habermas advocates the use of every appropriate democratic and educational device available in liberal democracy to raise the level of communication and debate, as well as being broadly supportive of the radical social movements of the left. Giddens is now closer to the liberal or social democratic political centre or, as he might prefer it, centre left.

SUMMARY

1. Although working in very different traditions, Habermas and Giddens both make qualified defences of the Enlightenment principles of reason and individuality. However, both consider that unregulated capitalism is destructive of community/society.

2. HABERMAS
    i)   INFLUENCES: Habermas's work reflects a wide range of influences including Marx; the Frankfurt School – of whom Habermas was the major figure of the second generation; Weber; Mead; and Parsons. Habermas's eclectic, undogmatic and humanistic neo-Marxism can be contrasted with the so-called 'scientific' and materialist Marxism of Marxist-Leninism.
    ii) THE PUBLIC SPHERE: Habermas's early work explored the decline of the public sphere of democratic inquiry, debate and action.
    iii) REVISIONS OF MARXISM: Critical theory is further developed as an alternative to Soviet Marxism. The central importance of the working class as the agency for change is rejected. Moral choice and consciousness are emphasised and historical materialism de-emphasised.
    iv) COMMUNICATIVE RATIONALITY AND ACTION: These concepts are central to his overall theory of social change. Unless people can understand each other and effectively express themselves, a better society than contemporary capitalism is not likely to be achieved.
    v)   STRENGTHS AND WEAKNESSES:
    Strengths:
    He has constructed a complex and integrated 'total' model of contemporary capitalism
    He has defended communicative rationality and indicated how it might be practiced
    He has analysed the 'crises' of contemporary capitalism
    He has indicated how a new, more equitable democratic consensus might be formed
    He presents a 'balanced' account of modernity in that he recognises both achievements and failures

    Weaknesses:
    He underestimates the problems in achieving communicative rationality
    He underestimates the emotional side of human beings and over-emphasises the rational side
    He is somewhat unfair about scientific and technical rationality
    For postmodernists, his defence of the integrated human subject is mistaken.

3. GIDDENS

    i). The scope of Giddens's theoretical work is immense, encompassing an early engagement with classical and 'second wave' theory through the development of structuration theory to globalisation theory and, recently, the Third Way. However, he disclaims any attempt to produce a 'total' theory, preferring instead to promote and provoke constructive theoretical debate.

    ii). STRUCTURATION THEORY: This is an attempt to overcome the polarisation of the agency/structure dualism by replacing it with the process of structuration which is reflected in the duality of structure. Structuration refers to the fact that as the individual or collectivety employs the rules and resources of structure, so structure is sustained albeit sometimes changed. Giddens presents a robust view of the potential of human actors or agents while not simplistically implying that all attain the same level of social effectiveness. The consciousness of the agent – practical, discursive and unconscious – is complex and potentially powerful in Giddens's description of it. The concept of discursive consciousness prefigures the concepts of reflexivity – the critical scanning oneself and society – important in Giddens's later work. The various criticism of structuration theory frequently focus on the way it might appear to 'flatten' out the tension and conflict between agency and structure – although Giddens emphasises that structural power is not equally shared.

iii). THE INSTITUTIONAL STRUCTURES OF MODERNITY: These are capitalism; industrialism; surveillance; and war. The key point of theoretical debate is that Giddens, unlike Marxists, does not prioritise capitalism in explaining the emergence and character of 'modernity/late-modernity'.

iv). THE 'PURE RELATIONSHIP' IN LATE MODERNITY: In *Transformation of Intimacy* (1992) Giddens deals in more detail with the personal and emotional side of life and its connections with the social in greater detail. He argues for democratic, equal and trusting – but voluntary – relationships. Globalisation (see chapter 6).

4. THE THIRD WAY: This is an attempt to indicate an alternative radical politics to the 'Old left' and the New Right.

5. HABERMAS AND GIDDENS

Although their work goes beyond those of the Enlightenment intellectuals in its scope and the issues they raise, in their defence of agency and consciousness they stand within the Enlightenment tradition.

Chapter 6

Identities in Late Modernity

> **Key Concepts**:
> consumerism, counter-culture, determinism/voluntarism,
> hegemony, homology, hybridity, masculinities, risk, sexuality,
> subcultural.

Introduction

This chapter critically reviews some applications to specific areas of society of the 'post' theories discussed in previous chapters. These are youth, gender and sexuality, and 'race'/ethnicity. The global environmental movement is dealt with in the later part of Chapter 7. The cultural material covered in this chapter complements the more socio-economic analysis of several of these topics given in Chapter 3. This chapter also discusses a number of general cultural themes relating to late modernity.

Part of the background of the emerging 'identity movements' of the postwar period covered in this chapter was the decline of traditional class cultures. This was most clearly demonstrable in relation to the industrial working class but 'respectable' middle class culture was also eroding and the confident superiority of the established upper class was under challenge, both from the newly rich and from a less respectful and deferential general population. Of course, new cultural and status hierarchies have taken shape reflecting profound changes in socio-economic structure (see pp. 77–84). Nevertheless, according to some thinkers, class as the basis for social theory and the wider political 'working class project' had, in Lyotard's terms, lost 'credibility'. People were looking for new developments and, in fact, were beginning to create them at some pace and on some scale.

However, it is important not to exaggerate these developments or people's awareness of them. In fact, Hall and Jefferson's account of postwar youth (1975) which is presented below, gives great emphasis to class in shaping the lives and actions of youth. Again, as was previously discussed, if class cultural differences do seem now to be less dominant in people's lives than, say, in the 1930s, there is plenty of evidence that both the material realities and consciousness of class remain significant.

The 'Post' Conceptual Tool-kit of Cultural Analysis

The poststructuralist, postmodern and other thinkers analysed in previous chapters have contributed to a fundamental reappraisal of contemporary Western culture and, in some cases, to our understanding of the West in relation to other cultures. The debate about structure and subjectivity and, by implication, identity analysed above gathered pace during the 1960s and 1970s. This debate, both reflected and affected social change, including the actions of radical activists. The influence of these thinkers is apparent in the various analyses of the key areas of identity given below. In particular, Stuart Hall disseminated into Britain some of the central ideas of these, mainly French intellectuals. Michelle Barrett exaggerates when she states that Stuart Hall '*is* cultural studies in Britain' (1999) but her remark indicates the immense and merited respect he has achieved and the huge influence he exerts. Nevertheless, aspects of his thinking are open to formidable criticism.

As is recorded below, Hall introduced a substantial body of cultural theory and analysis into Britain. The content of this theory evolved over time as did Hall's own thinking. The point of the list below is simply to indicate some of the main terms and related approaches Hall played a major part in importing. It is simply intended to recall some important concepts presented in more detail above and to be of practical use in understanding the rest of this chapter.

- essentialism
- Enlightenment subject
- decentring the subject
- semiology
- sign/signifier/signified
- referent
- text
- read (in reference to texts)
- deconstruct
- discourse
- difference

Note: For brief working definitions of these terms, see glossary.

Youth Culture

Youth Began It: The 1960s

This section will begin with an analysis of the 1960s radical youth movement and then proceed to an analysis of 1960s youth culture in general. A comparison is then made between 1960s and 1990s youth. This is no small task but the 1960s is the seminal decade for understanding developments in culture and identity throughout the remainder of the century. The sixties brought about a significant break with the past in terms of the opportunities for constructing identities and in how identities are conceived – a change which some consider superficial and others, including myself, profound. The changes in the way certain individuals and groups began to think about themselves owed more to their response to changes in society than to the work of the intellectuals discussed in the previous section but there was important interchange between radical ideas and radical action.

The 1960s Middle Class Radical Youth Movement

The initial group to be considered, the young radicals, includes all those who in some way took part in the 1960s radical movement – in both its political and cultural manifestations – which had its origins in the United States and Britain and reverberated throughout the world. Most of those involved in the movement were from middle class backgrounds, prompting the observation that their's was the radicalism of affluence. The worldwide youth movement of the 1960s addressed many of the issues referred to earlier and in some cases drew directly on the thought of prominent social theorists. In turn, many radical thinkers, notably Mills, Marcuse and Habermas, responded to the the movement and incorporated an analysis of its activities into their work.

One of the lasting themes of 1960s radicalism was the aspiration to bridge the divide between the political and the cultural and relatedly between the political and the personal. The basic motive here was to achieve a transformation that embraced both people's lifestyles and personal relationships and the realm of politics. What was sought was radical change rather than simply a superficial political 'fix' or compromise. The idealistic and uncompromising nature of the 1960s movement is easily seen in some of the popular slogans it generated as well as in some of its activities. Slogans such as 'Love is the true radicalism', 'Freedom Now' ('Now' was the timescale for much sought-after change!), and 'We are the people our parents warned us about' were not the language of mainstream politics. Nor were sit-ins, communes and the paraphanalia of psychedelia the stuff of convention either. My own characterisation of the 1960s radical youth phenomenon, at least in its core American manifestation, is that it was a romantic or idealistic movement although this terminology does not capture its more structurally oriented socialist/Marxist strands (Ph.d., Keele University, 1974. For a similar interpretation, see also, Kumar, 1995).

Although it is easy retrospectively to pick out dominant trends in the 1960s movement, at the time events moved so rapidly and across such a variety of fronts that it was not at all clear what the connections, if any, were between them. Further, though some common themes are clear, it is important not to try to homogenise these events into an artificial sameness. I will briefly outline the main events in the political and cultural trajectories of the radical movement in turn, although many individual and groups fairly seamlessly participated in both, often seeing them as aspects of the same social transformation. Politically, the Campaign for Nuclear Disarmament (CND) was well established in Britain by the mid-1950s and anti-nuclear movements also appeared in the United States during that decade. The black civil rights movement peaked in the 1960s but was well under-way by the late 1950s. Among other things, the civil rights movement established a wide preference for non-violent political strategies across the movement although this was effectively challenged by both the Black Panthers and the neo-Marxist Weather-people in the late 1960s. The cause which attracted most mass political support was opposition to the Vietnam War. The anti-nuclear/peace movements fed into the anti-war movement but a key factor in explaining its popular support was the compulsory draft in the United states which many thousands of young men sought to avoid, some legally, others illegally ('Hell no, we won't go!').

The cultural radicalism of the 1960s has more immediate relevance to identities which is a main topic of this chapter. The two main early examples of cultural radicalism were the 'Beatniks' or 'Beats' of the American West Coast and the folk-song revival led by Bob Dylan and Joan Baez in the United States and, somewhat derivatively, by Donovan and Julie Felix in Britain. The Beats were the original 'drop-outs' or alternative lifestyle 'freaks'. They sought lives in which pleasure took precedence over paid work. Sex, poetry and literature, jazz, drugs and adventure, in no particular order of priority, were favoured activities. It is seldom mentioned that the Beats often had a caring and conservationist attitude and approach to nature and the environment, even though some indulged in prophesies of eco-disaster which, at best, have proved premature. Their favoured drug was cannabis and its use later spread to the sixties counterculture and into mainstream life. The folk-song revival was intimately connected to the political events referred to above. In fact, in the early 1960s the term 'protest music' was more often used to describe this genre and Dylan directly addressed issues of racial equality and peace in his early songs. As the 1960s wore on and the political mood became more confrontational and violent, a split emerged which divided the political and cultural wings of the movement (although there were always some who sought to bridge the divide). The counterculture sought to achieve change through establishing lifestyles, personal and in some cases communal, which embodied principles in opposition to mainstream society. Typically, these principles involved a greater emphasis on personal openness, sharing and pleasure. Of course, the reality often mocked the ideal but real experiments in 'revolutionary' lifestyle and relationships were attempted, the influence of which continues in some of the contemporary New Social Movements. The role of psychedelic drugs in the counterculture was immense. What the more powerful of these drugs did was reinforce both the experience and vision of a society or way of life based on a morality of mutual openness and sharing and on pleasure rather than repression. If this sounds too good to last, so it proved. Not only was there a political/cultural split in the movement but the counterculture itself fragmented – some 'dropping out' entirely, some going religious, and others struggling to maintain links with the increasingly angry political radicals.

The above account of 1960s cultural radicalism is based almost entirely on what happened in the United States rather than Britain. This reflects the balance of influence between the two countries. The mid-1960s British popular music 'invasion' of the United States was a major commercial phenomenon but it involved the diffusion of few radical ideas. The Beatles may have gone to the United States as 'conquering heroes' but they arrived back as 'turned on' hippies convinced that 'Love is all you need'. From then on many British and American rock groups explored, often fleetingly, in their lyrics issues of social, political and cultural change. Undoubtedly, groups such as the Grateful Dead and the Beatles, particularly John Lennon, were dynamic participants in the radical movement of the 1960s. Even their struggle to retain integrity and radicalism in the face of their massive earning capacity in the capitalist market was reflected on a smaller scale in the lives of many 'ordinary' 1960s radicals. In 1969 the American magazine, 'Fortune', found that as many as 39% of American youth had radical or countercultural values. A generation on, however, and most now seem to be esconced comfortably or otherwise in 'the system'. Nevertheless, as will be described later, the radical movement of the 1960s raised issues and generated insights of lasting importance.

Stuart Hall and Tony Jefferson in the edited collection *Resistance through Rituals: Youth Subcultures in Post-war Britain* (1975) make a somewhat different emphasis in their interpretation of the above movement. This volume dealt mainly with the working class youth subcultures more typical of Britain but Hall and Jefferson adopt a neo-Marxist, class-based interpretation of both. Their then still relatively traditional class framework of analysis leads them to underestimate the radical potential of the largely middle class radical youth movement. They see the movement as a conflict occurring within the middle class in which the younger generation were exploring the expressive potential of a new, more affluent phase in capitalism not yet recognised by their parents. They anticipated that eventually the more expressive and hedonistic behaviour of the counterculture would diffuse, doubtless in modified form, to the middle class as a whole though not to the working class unless social revolution occurred: 'the middle class countercultures ... prefigure, anticipate, foreshadow – though in truncated diagrammatical and 'Utopian' forms – emergent social forms'(69).

This analysis clearly has similarities to the one given here but my difference of interpretation from Hall and Jefferson is nevertheless substantial. Briefly, their Marxist frame of reference leads them to underestimate the radical potential of the mainly middle class radicals and to overestimate that of the mainly working class youth subcultures (even though they are cautious in relation to the latter). What I shall contend – along with many others – is that a theoretical framework which prioritises class can lead to a distorted interpretation of movements in which generation, gender, race/ethnicity and other aspects of identity are prominent and, in my view, sometimes of equal if not greater importance. It is arguable that what Hall and Jefferson saw as the 'utopian' aspirations of the middle class activists had more potential for radical change in late modernity than the rather 'old left' mode of thinking that they themselves maintained in the 1970s and which, in certain respects, Hall still retains. In importing Althusser rather than Mills and Marcuse into British intellectual life, Hall stayed with a model of Marxism which was relatively conservative in its determinism and 'scientism'. This point of disagreement is further explored below.

Working Class Youth in the 1950s and 1960s: Subcultural Theory

Not only campus-based youth but Western youth in general experienced substantial change in the postwar period and to some extent this has been 'globalised'. There are countless surveys which show that in recent decades a majority of British youth has never been very radical (two examples appeared, respectively, in 1974 (National Children's Bureau) and 1996 (*The Independent* newspaper). In both Britain and the United States, political radicalism was mainly a phenomenon of middle class, campus youth. The 'mass' youth 'revolution' of the 1950s and 1960s was one of consumption and style. It was partly a response to increased affluence and leisure and to new opportunities for consumption and partly an expression of creative imagination and genuine, if rudimentary and sporadic, social awareness. The change in leisure habits included youth from all social backgrounds but factors such as class, 'race' and sex/gender influenced particular cultural and subcultural formations.

If increased affluence and leisure was the context, the spark to the 'teenage explosion' was music. Partly politicised folk music was a powerful focus and motivator for many students but had brief and limited influence among the rest of youth. The genre that really set things moving was rock and roll. Again, the origin of rock and roll was American and the organising drive behind its commercial exploitation, including its export to the British market, was the large American music companies. Bill Haley's hit single 'Rock around the Clock', and film of the same name triggered youthful hysteria across both the United States and Britain. Many of 'the older generation' duly registered 'shock' but to little effect. Elvis Presley seldom, if ever, expressed a political opinion but his celebrated sexuality and sensuality contributed to a general relaxation of social mores. Prior to the Beatles, Britain's own earlier rock and rollers were mostly pale imitations of their American counterparts but they helped to change the tone of popular music in the direction of noise, beat, excitement and youthfulness. As a contemporary commentator Mark Abrams noted, teenagers particularly benefitted from the full employment and relatively high wages of the early postwar years (Abrams, 1958). The 'youth market' was soon firmly established and youth began to impact in an increasingly colourful and expressive presence on the national scene.

The above developments indicate the broad context in which specific strands in British youth culture can be further analysed. In Britain, sociologists initially concentrated on male working class youth although a substantial amount of work has now been published on black youth and young women. The Centre for Contemporary Cultural Studies in Birmingham developed an approach which became the dominant model for theorising youth although it has been increasingly criticised during the 1990s (see below). The basic position of the Centre, as it has been refined and extended over a period of time, is that fundamental structural factors such as class, 'race'/ethnicity and patriarchy contribute to the cultural formations and style of youth. (Hall and Jefferson *eds*.: 1974; Gilroy,1987; McRobbie, 1991). A key theoretical concept developed by the Centre is 'cultural resistance'. The concept was mainly developed in the early 1970s in relation to subcultures of working class boys but, with qualifications, was given wider application. Cultural resistance refers to actions, including the use of language and symbols, by subcultural 'members' which consciously or otherwise disrupt or oppose the control exercised over them. It was not difficult to show that gangs of working class boys sometimes opposed the authority of the likes of teachers and the police in words and actions which were quite unambiguous. Similarly, the dress style and much of the leisure activities of 'the lads' had a provocative as well as a celebratory element about it.

In 1975, the CCCS published *Resistance Through Rituals: Youth Sub-cultures in Post-war Britain* – a title which succinctly announced the theoretical linkage of cultural resistance with youth subcultures. The book is an impressive collection of theoretical and ethnographic pieces. The latter examined a series of working class youth subcultures in terms of their relationship to particular structural, often class issues or problems.

Thus, Tony Jefferson sees the Teds as concerned with the defence of space (against immigrants) and status. He suggests that their adoption of the bootlace tie often worn by American gangsters symbolically captures both their (defensive) aggression and social aspirations. Dick Hebdige's reading of 'the meaning of mod' sees them as re-working the meanings given to objects in the dominant culture in a way that expressed their own subcultural values. This usually involved a subtle or not so subtle change in the 'ex-propriated object': the 'neat' hair-cut deviated slightly from the short-back and sides, the smart suits were just a little on the showy side of straight; and the conversion of the union-jack into various items of clothing was openly iconoclastic. Hebdige is careful to stress how dazzled Mods tended to be by the dominant consumer culture. Their attempts at originality and assertions of independence are fragile and easily absorbed into the dominant culture. In his later work, *Sub-culture: the Meaning of Style* (1979), he introduces the concept of *incorporation* to describe how youth sub-cultures generally are vulnerable to such absorption. This can take the form of ideological or commodity incorporation. The commodity form involves 'the conversion of subcultural signs (dress, music, etc.) into mass-produced objects' and the ideological form is 'the 'labelling' and redefinition of deviant behaviour by dominant groups – the police, the media, the judiciary' (94). An example of the latter cited by Hebdige was the way that in the summer of 1977 *The People* and *News of the World* carried features on 'punk babies, punk brothers, and punk-ted weddings' (98).

The main theoretical piece in *Resistance through Rituals* is Stuart Hall and Tony Jefferson's lengthy introduction to the collection. Here they spell out the theoretical framework for the analysis of youth on which the authors of the book are broadly agreed. They state that class is the fundamental structuring reality in capitalist Britain and that youth sub-cultures are situated within and reflect this context. However, there are generational aspects both to the problems and attempted solutions of youth. They see both working and middle class youth subcultures as seeking solutions to real 'problems' but frequently in an 'imaginary' way through cultural rituals and style statements. Hall and Jefferson cite two social theorists, Antonio Gramsci and Roland Barthes. They adopt Gramsci's concept of *hegemony* to argue that in Britain 'the ruling class' has achieved a degree of widely accepted authority partly through an ideology of affluence, consumerism and opportunity that enticed working class compliance. The concept of hegemony embodies the notion that cultural ascendancy is liable to shift and challenge. Members of the adult working class both challenge ruling class hegemony politically and industrially and also find some respite from it in their own cultural pursuits and institutions. The resistance of working class youth tends to be mostly in the area of leisure and to take symbolic or ritualistic form and provides 'imaginary' and even illusionary solutions. In interpreting the cultural symbolism of youth, Hall and Jefferson acknowledge the influence of Barthes who, as we saw, outlined a methodology for interpreting signs. It is worth quoting at some length Hall and Jefferson's interpretation of the Teds and the Mods referred to in the studies above:

> They (members of working class youth subcultures) 'solve', but in an imaginary way, problems which at the concrete material level remain unresolved. Thus the 'Teddy Boy' expropriation of upper class style of dress (e.g. Edwardian suits) 'covers' the gap between largely manual, unskilled, near-lumpen real careers and life-chances, and the 'all-dressed-up-and-nowhere-to-go experience of Saturday evening. Thus, in the expropriation and fetishisation of consumption and style itself, the 'Mods' cover the gap between the never-ending-weekend and Monday's resumption of boring, dead-end work
>
> (Hall and Jefferson, 1975: 48)

Invisible Girls?

A criticism often made of the CCCS is that it neglected young women and black youth. There is some truth in this criticism but less than is often assumed. Really, this criticism applies better to work in the field of youth prior to 1968, the year Stuart Hall, himself of African Caribbean origin, became Director of the Centre. In fact, there were two articles on black youth and one on young women in *Resistance through Rituals*. These articles and later ones from members of the CCCS provide a basis for saying that the feminist and black critiques of the Centre's emphasis on white male youth was significantly an internal one. *Girls and Subcultures*, by Angela McRobbie and Jenny Garber argues that the subcultural model is inappropriate for analysing the situation of young women. Instead, they offer as their central theoretical concept, that of *structured secondariness* (209). The basic idea behind this concept is now familiar and widely accepted: that women and girls tend to play subordinate and marginalised roles to men and boys throughout society. As far as leisure activity is concerned McRobbie and Garber stress the time teenage girls spend together in smaller numbers of two or three often listening to pop music, reading romantic 'teen' magazines and chatting together about feelings and relationships. Girls do appear to some extent within the subcultures but usually as adjuncts to the boys status and sexual needs. The exception was the more 'feminised' Mod subculture in which the girls achieved a more prominent and equal place.

Black Youth: Resistance. But resistance to what?

One of the strongest statements of the 'resistance' thesis occurs in *Policing the Crisis* edited by Stuart Hall and others and published in 1978 on the subject of the moral panic about the supposed outbreak of mugging by black (male) youth in the early and middle 1970s. It is certainly the case that black youth – by which Hall means African Caribbean youth – had a stronger case for resisting the dominant society than any other section of youth. From the point of view of elaborating the 'resistance' thesis, the most relevant chapter is the one titled 'The Politics of Mugging'. Hall argues that the black minority in Britain are a *fraction* of the working class but that they have also been subject to the additional problem of racism. The second generation of migrants were less willing than the first to put up with racism. Further, young black men had few illusions about the type of work they were likely to be offered, if indeed, they could get work at all. While being cautious about the statistical basis of 'the mugging outbreak', the book's authors discuss the possibility that crime is one 'strategy of survival' for young black people although they insist that mugging is carried out only by a minority. In Jamaica the hustler is regarded by some as a figure of status who is not a mere criminal but as someone who is making a living on the strength of his wit and knowledge. These considerations lead to the question of how black crime relates to wider political issues:

> But *can* crime provide the basis of a resistance which is capable of transforming or even modifying the circumstances which force more and more young people to enlist in its ranks? Is hustling and petty crime the basis for a viable class strategy? Or is the 'criminal consciousness' destined to remain a quasi-political form of consciousness only . . . (361)

Hall's answer is basically that hustling has the potential to develop into a strategy for change. Over twenty years on from when the above questions were asked, the evidence suggests that a negative answer is more accurate. Crime and later disorder in some areas of black concentration may have alarmed liberal politicians into some measures of reform more or less of benefit to black people, but in the medium and longer term it seems to have made little obvious positive contribution to the wellbeing of black people generally or to the development of black politics of any kind. The majority of black voters voted Labour in the 1970s and that was also the case in the 1990s. Black crime and disorder probably did not affect this one way or the other. The Marxist framework adopted by Hall and his colleagues at the time led them to over-theorise crime as potentially radical class action. While there is plenty of evidence of cultural resistance and some political radicalism among young black people there is little to suggest that many connected it systematically to class exploitation or saw radical or revolutionary socialism as a solution. More likely, what most wanted was a fair chance to compete in Britain's capitalist society. Their concern and anger about racial discrimination was just that and not, as the authors suggest, a way of responding to their particular experience of class oppression. In his more recent work Hall himself has moved away from Marxist formulations of "race"/ethnic and youth issues, and gives fuller acknowledgement to the validity and relative independence of identities other than class (see below, p. 178). However, his work is still characterised by a distinct tendency to describe people as 'motivated' or, more precisely, influenced, if not controlled by external structures, now more often seen as cultural, along the lines of French structuralists, rather than class, along the lines of Marx.

Comment on Subcultural Resistance Theory: and Youth 1980–2000

Before recording some criticisms of the work of the CCCS in the area of cultural studies, particularly subcultural analysis, it is important to indicate the extent of the Centre's achievement. At a theoretical level, the Centre introduced the structuralist mode of 'reading texts' which has greatly contributed to the understanding of symbolic meanings and the signification process. In my view, this has been somewhat at the expense of giving due emphasis to literal meanings and conscious communication but the usefulness of the post/structuralist approach in revealing how emotions and the unconscious can be manipulated is now widely accepted. Members of the Centre have, with many others, also contributed to the dissemination of postmodern theory and modes of analysis.

It is easy to take for granted the extent to which the work of the CCCS has left its imprint on sub/cultural analysis. Concepts such as the following have been introduced and/or popularised by the CCCS and its ex-members (many now encamped at Goldsmith's College, London):

○ encoding/decoding cultural messages
○ the cultural circuit (i.e. the various transformations in cultural transmission)
○ the meaning of style
○ homology (the cultural fit between argot (jargon), dress and demeanour)
○ cultural resistance
○ hegemony (Gramsci)
○ de-centring of the subject
○ interpellate (one of Althusser's more useful terms)
○ inflection (or shift in the cultural meaning of a word/action)
○ read/text
○ difference

Note: Working definitions of the above terms can be found in the glossary.

If, as Richard Hoggart, its first director has suggested, the CCCS has made cultural studies 'very theoretical', then that may have been almost inevitable and, in view of the advances made, a price worth paying.

A first and among the most common criticisms of the CCCS's analysis of youth is that the term 'subculture' too sharply distinguishes between the supposed 'members' of spectacular subcultures and 'ordinary' youth. This criticism is associated with Steve Redhead (1990) and has recently been strongly re-stated by Andy Bennett:

> In my view ... the term 'subculture' is deeply problematic in that it imposes rigid lines of division over forms of sociation (i.e. interaction – my brackets) which may, in effect, be more fleeting, and in many cases arbitrary, than the concept of 'sub-culture' with its connotations of coherence and solidarity, allows for.' (Bennett, 1999).

Bennett sees youth culture as much less characterised by subcultures and uses the term 'neo-tribe' to describe how a much larger and less class–differentiated number of young people move in and out of various style and consumer trends without necessarily attaching much meaning to them.

My own view of Bennett's neo-tribe model is that it applies much better to the last 15 or 20 years of the century than to the 35 years following the second world war which was the period Hall and Hebdige were writing about. The lines of class were much more obviously and sharply drawn during that period – not least, culturally. Whether or not they were 'members' of particular sub-cultures – and Hall and Jefferson do not suggest most were – it was generally still fairly easy to pick out a working class from a middle class youth. It is also true that the class roots of the earlier sub-cultures were fairly identifiable even if later their various styles were marketed and adopted more widely. In any case, Hall and Jefferson recognised that youth subcultures could be 'loosely or tightly bounded'(14). They also recognise that youth subcultures can be fleeting. An issue which they do not address is the relationship of 'ordinary' working class youth to the subcultures other than in McRobbie and Garber's argument that the model does not apply well to working class girls. On balance, it does seem that a subcultural model of youth, granted that many young did not participate in the 'spectacular' subcultures, is appropriate to the period to which the CCCS applied it. As will shortly be discussed, a different model is required for youth at 'the end of the twentieth century party', to use Redhead's term.

A second criticism of the CCCS model is that it exaggerates the extent to which the 'subordinate' subcultures were 'resisting' the 'hegemony' of 'the dominant culture'.

Again, however, a close examination of what Hall and Jefferson actually wrote indicates that they were quite limited in the claims they made for the nature and effectiveness of the resistance of the subcultures to the dominant culture. Like their parent culture, working class youth subcultures could 'win space' for self-expression – of the kind described in the quotation about the Teds and Mods above – but this resistance to domination was typically ill-targeted and ineffectual:

> There is no 'sub-cultural solution' to working class youth unemployment, educational disadvantage, compulsory miseducation, dead-end jobs, the routinisation and specialisa-tion of labour, low pay and the loss of skills. Sub-cultural strategies cannot match, meet or answer the structuring dimensions emerging in this period for the class as a whole ... They 'solve', but in an imaginary way, problems which at the concrete level remain unsolved.
>
> (Hall and Jefferson: 48)

Black youth aside, Hall and Jefferson claim so little for subcultural resistance in terms of its ideo-logical coherence, targetting and effectiveness, that it raises doubts as to whether the subcultures are actually resisting the dominant system even in an 'imaginary' way. If not, the question must also be raised as to whether the substantial theoretical apparatus they erect in order to analyse 'resistance' is not redundant, or more specifically, whether their basically Marxist class conflict model, leads them to see resistance where there isn't any or, at least, not the resistance to class hegemony that they imply. A feasible alternative explanation to 'the lads' behaviour is that it was simply anti-authoritarian and defensive-aggressive towards outsiders i.e., they were mainly con-cerned with territory and power. They were more likely to express their resentments against vari-ous authority figures and against 'foreigners' than in class terms. Predictably, such attitudes would be expressed in the lads' style, demeanour and language (in other words, culturally). The lads anti-authoritarianism can be explained, structurally, in generational as well as in class terms (although Hall and Jefferson give precedence to the latter). In the 1950s and 1960s working class youth was still quite overtly – and not infrequently physically – controlled by numerous agents, prominently teachers and the police. However, the new affluence and leisure both fuelled a sense that life did not have to be so oppressive and provided opportunities for 'escape', consumption and 'fun'. The 'embourgeoisement' thesis had more relevance to the spectacular subcultures than Hall and Jefferson wanted to allow. Alongside the traditional working class values of toughness and being macho of groups such as the skinheads, was more confident self-assertion, consumption and display.

A third, and the most fundamental criticism of Hall and Jefferson, is that they impose their own interpretation on the action of the 'lads' at the expense of that of the 'lads' themselves. Their neo-Marxist theoretical class radical framework leads them to overestimate the importance of class in relation to youth in the 1960s. For them, the final or objective significance of the ferment of youthful activity in the 1960s was defined in terms of – an admittedly highly sophisticated account of – the capitalist class system. That is why they conclude their discussion of the middle class youth movement with the stark sentence: 'Answers lie elsewhere'(71) i.e., in class based rather than generational action. However if Lyotard is correct, the Marxist narrative in which capitalism is abolished is simply just another point of view and one with declining appeal. In practice, women, gays and lesbians, environmentalists, as well as the more radical young and others have acted to oppose the immediate structures that oppress them – sometimes linking them to class, sometimes not – and to explore and develop their identities without necessarily feeling that doing so depends on any 'final' solution to the problems of capitalism. As for the 'lads', Hall and Jefferson, despite their qualifications, read too much into what they were doing. What they were 'up to' is probably much the same as what lads under the knuckle of authority perenially 'get up to' – only more so because the pressure from authority was slightly weakening and the opportunities for having fun seemed to be increasing.

Finally, the influence of structuralism on the CCCS, as well as Marxism, had mixed results. On the positive side, the use of Barthes to analyse 'the meaning of style' and ritual led to new ways of looking at subcultures and revitalised British cultural studies. On the other hand, in my view the influence of structural Marxism, particularly on Hall's thinking, led at times to rather laboured and formulaic analysis. In the nineteen seventies and early eighties, the notion of class as the 'determining' (the word was sometimes used) structure always lurks behind his analysis and largely dictates its framework and conclusions. Even in his later work (see Chapter 8), Hall continues to be drawn to theoretical frameworks characterised by a tendency to structural determinism. In the 1997 textbook he edited on 'representation', he favours a relatively socially determined approach to explaining language and other cultural forms. He presents three models of representation: the reflective in which language or other forms of representation are taken to express only what objectively exists 'out there'; the intentional in which they are taken to express only what the speaker or author wants to express; and the constructionist in which representation is seen as 'constructed in and through language'. Hall then goes on to concentrate almost exclusively on the constructionist approach. Unlike many authorities he interprets constructionism in highly post/structuralist terms. Intentionality is seen as something outside of constructionism and in Hall's account largely ignored. It is possible to find some acknowledgement in Hall's work of the view that a social actor or author can use language and other representational forms to construct meaningful communication but the clear and consistent emphasis of his work is that 'structures', linguistic or otherwise, 'speak us'. There is some truth in this but overemphasis and exaggeration obscures a greater truth.

Diaspora from the Centre: Different Interpretations of Difference

It was not until the late 1980s and 1990s, that several individual ex-scholars at the Centre published work which clearly broke with the principle that class is the fundamental reality into which age, gender and ethnicity must 'fit'. Paul Willis' *Common Culture* (1990) and, particularly, Angela McRobbie's *Postmodernism and Popular Culture* (1994) give class no more 'essential' priority than age, gender or ethnicity. It is the inter-play of these factors and the construction of hybrid and changing identities that become the focus of analysis in the 1990s. Although structural influences on action are attended to, the significance of action is also interpreted in terms of actors' meaning rather than exclusively in terms of some external, objective reality.

McRobbie's article, 'Different Youthful Subjectivities' (1996) seeks to pursue some of these newer themes further. She explicitly sets aside the 'class-youth' couplet and instead focuses on the 'constellations of 'different, youthful subjectivities' particularly in relation to ethnicity and 'changing modes of youthful femininity and masculinity'. Now her emphasis is on hybridity, flux and change and in outlining an agenda for the further study of these areas she argues that 'it would be necessary to pay greater attention to the space of interracial, interactive experience and to explore the processes of hostility, fascination and desire which penetrate and shape the nature of these encounters'(39). Here, McRobbie is partly referring to the apparent burgeoning of 'mixed-race' relationships in late twentieth century Britain – a development doubtless full of challenge but which is inestimably more interesting and promising for 'race'/ethnic relations (i.e. human relations) than cultural separation or, perish the thought, segregation (see also, O'Donnell and Sharpe, Routledge, 2000).

McRobbie deals with the issue of structure and agency in relation to the creation of these cultures by, in effect, arguing that they occur simultaneously and inseparably:

> there is no clear sociological divide between 'lived' experience and 'texts and representational forms'. The one is always merging with the other, sometimes socially, in the club, listening and dancing to the music, at other points alone, in front of the television, or else with a book or magazine in hand. The sounds and images addressed almost exclusively to young people represent identity-formation material, the success of which lies in its ability to reach into the adolescent unconscious and literally form a generation through the shared experience of particular books, records, films, videos, TV programmes and social activities such as dance (43).

The extent to which McRobbie considers that young people act upon the cultural 'material' as well as being formed by it is not absolutely clear but there is perhaps a shift in that direction in comparison to her early work at the CCCS. It is a shift that certainly needs to be made. A more action oriented emphasis, including a thorough theorisation of action as well as structure, would strengthen the influential tradition of cultural analysis popularised by the CCCS. I will return to this issue later.

Gender Relations and Identities

It was second wave feminism that brought gender relations to the fore in the postwar period. One of the immediate causes was the chauvinism that many politically conscious women found in the radical movement of the 1960s. It did not take long to occur to many women that if they were expected to 'make the tea', 'do the typing' and support their invariably male leaders in a radical movement, then it was more than likely that the rest of society was also highly inegalitarian in terms of the gender relations. Soon a stream of feminist literature was published including Kate

Millet's *Sexual Politics* (1970) and Germaine Greer's *The Female Eunuch* (1971) which sought both to analyse this inequality and to mobilise women against it. The broadly agreed term to describe the near universal phenomenon was patriarchy. The feminist challenge to men was to seek to understand and to act to stop their exploitation of women. The gender section in Chapter 3 concentrated mainly on women, the next section focuses on how men have redefined themselves under the impact of the feminist challenge, when, indeed, they have done so.

Masculinities

There have been few, if any, more powerful and influential movements in the latter part of the twentieth century than feminism. During the last quarter of the century, the issue of gender equality has seeped into the Western 'psyche' and arises in every area of life. While, as Walby notes, progress to greater economic and political equality is slow and uneven, it seems that the cultural impact of feminism is irreversible. The disruption in patriarchal assumptions and the redefining of gender relations initiated by feminism have proceeded too far for a return to unquestioned and stable patriarchy to occur. This is not only because women have significantly undermined the system of patriarchy – through their educational achievements, through their contribution to the regendering of family/paid work norms – but because the unreflective confidence of many men in the 'naturalness' of patriarchy and 'male superiority' has also been undermined. Patriarchy has not been just or even mainly undermined in material and practical terms but as an ideology and belief-system. Patriarchal structures persist in many areas of life but they are often transparently 'wobbly' and those who 'man' them no longer seem quite in control.

Unsurprisingly, men's entry into the gender debate and gender politics has been uncertain and at times awkward and defensive. After all, they have been the butt of much female anger and some ridicule – an understandable reaction to centuries in which women have been primarily presented as either objects of sexual desire or as creatures of domesticity. The men's movement in Britain and the United States which arose largely in response to feminism generally accepted and focused on the premise that men are the oppressors and beneficiaries of patriarchy. Often the ethos of local men's groups was to change patriarchy at the level of personal relations as this seemed the most accessible area of action. It is difficult to quantify it, but this did seem to result in a fairer division of labour between some of these men and their partners. The idea of 'the new man' was born. However, the men's movement never involved more than a tiny minority of men and never achieved the kind of public profile or wider influence of feminism. The 'new laddism' of the 1990s which defensively and confusedly reasserted chauvinistic values in terms of 'beer, football and girls' was probably closer to the popular mood among young men than the radical men's movement.

The successes of the heterosexual men's movement in the 1970s and early 1980s were mainly at the level of personal relations and it added relatively little to the theory of gender relations. It was not until the latter part of the 1980s that men and masculinities began to be conceptualised in a less guilt-ridden and defensive way in relation to women and feminism. What was needed was an approach which shifted the emphasis from an almost exclusive concern with patriarchy and even from its well documented oppressions to an overall analysis of gender relations. By far the most influential contributor to the development of a body of theory that has begun to do this is R. W. Connell. The latter's two major general works on gender theory are *Gender and Power* (1987) and *Masculinities* (1995). Connell's model is quite comprehensive and complex but perhaps his major achievement has been to develop the analysis that masculinities and femininities are social constructs and that men's power and experience within gender relations varies enormously. Connell adds to the feminist analysis of women's oppression an exploration of the variety of men's gendered experience, including their own frustration, pain and oppression.

Connell's model is a structural one but it strongly reflects the more flexible concepts of structure of late/postmodern theory. He uses the terms 'gender order' and 'gender regime' to describe the general structure of gender relations. He defines a gender order as 'a historically constructed pattern of power relations between men and women and definitions of masculinity and femininity prevalent throughout an entire society'(99). Nearly all known societies have been more or less patriarchal i.e., men have had more power than women, but matriarchal or roughly egalitarian gender orders are possible. Connell employs the concept of 'gender regime' to 'describe the state of play' in gender relations 'on a smaller stage'. The latter could be a family, classroom or peer group. He states that there are three main institutional areas that structure gender relations:

1. power relations
2. production relations
3. cathexis (sexual/intimate relationships)

The second area, production relations, was considered in Chapter 3 and is a crucial area of masculine dominance. In this chapter the focus is on the cultural aspects of gender relations. Despite separately categorising power relations, Connell recognises that inequalities of power occur throughout society and apply to cathexis/culture as to production relations as well as to political systems. A common illustration of gendered cultural domination is the widespread presentation in the West of women as objects of men's desire – a cultural practice which also illustrates Connell's third structure of the gender order, cathexis. Connell argues that *emphasised femininity* is the commonest form of subordinated femininity as it is based on women presenting themselves as objects for men's desire. Many women have reached the same conclusion and now present themselves much less as objects for men's sexual consumption. Other women retain a feminised self-presentation without wishing to imply either a general sexual invitation to men or that their own sexuality is the only aspect of them meriting a response.

Connell describes both power and cathexis as areas of patriarchal dominance despite many acts of challenge and resistance – some successful – at the local level. However, one of Connell's most useful contributions is his analysis of the extent to which masculinities interact with other factors, notably class and 'race'. As a result, a wide variety of masculinity types occur.

Connell refers to two main categories of masculinities: *'hegemonic'* and *'subordinate'*. His description of hegemonic masculinity makes it clear that this can change historically:

> Hegemonic masculinity is not a fixed character type always and everywhere the same. It is rather the masculinity that occupies the hegemonic position in a given pattern of gender relations, a position always contestable (1995:76).

In the contemporary West and in much of the world, the hegemonic figure is able to live out gender relations in a way that embodies and reproduces patriarchal norms. Aware that individuals rarely entirely correspond to general characterisations, Connell avoids giving examples but perhaps Rupert Murdoch, the media mogul, comes close and in the celluloid world, John Wayne.

To the extent that men's masculinity fails to incorporate the dominant pattern, they are likely to be subordinated:

> Within that overall (hegemonic – my brackets) framework there are specific gender relations of dominance and subordination between groups of men.
>
> The most important case in contemporary European and American society is the dominance of heterosexual men and the subordination of homosexual men' (78).

Connell points out that homosexual men have been negatively stereotyped and greatly discriminated against in Western culture because they do not conform to the dominant model of what a man should be (see below).

By marginalised masculinities, Connell means those forms of masculinity which are less powerful because the men concerned are of subordinate position in class or 'racial' structures outside the gender order. To give a deliberately challenging example, an elderly black man in irregular employment clearing litter is far less wealthy and powerful in class terms than a rich, young and successful woman business executive. What little advantage he may gain from the *gender dividend* is unlikely remotely to compensate for class, racial and probably generational disadvantage – which, in any case, tend to be intensifed when they occur together. It is the apparently increasing occurence of such cases that suggests that it is appropriate to review gender relations to take more into account the changes of the last quarter of a century.

Changing Gender Relations in Late Modernity

On the face of it, that is if we look at gendered structural inequalities, women still appear to be, and to a considerable extent are, disadvantaged by patriarchy. At best, the pattern of progress is mixed. There are more women in the higher reaches of business and the professions than forty years ago, and, thanks in part to Labour Party policy, there are many more women MPs and Cabinet members and more women in political and public life generally. Yet, the absolute percentages of women compared to men in all these areas remains quite small although gradually increasing. Surprisingly, one important measure of progress – the average wage of women compared to that of men – has hardly improved at all, fluctuating around 25% less than that of men for many years.

However, as was detailed earlier, Walby makes the important point that women are increasingly occupying different positions in relation to patriarchy and to the capitalist socio-economic system (see, pp. 87–90). This point can be extended to many areas of life. Young women tend to be much better educated and to have better career opportunities than older women. A far larger number than in the past will have either no children or just one or two – 'freeing' them to pursue full-time, longterm careers. It will take a generation or two for these changes to feed through into substantially increased economic equality between men and women but such an increase does now seem to be 'progammed into the system'. However, older women, particularly poorer ones, do not participate in the benefits of these changes and their situation requires a specific and robust public policy response. Women single parents are also particularly vulnerable to poverty and again can miss out on the gains many other women enjoy. The diverse situations of women does not lead Walby to relax her opposition to patriarchy but she does indicate that feminist strategies in the future will have to accommodate radically different needs among women.

Working from a different theoretical tradition than Walby, the diverse situations and, in particular, different identities of contemporary women have been emphasised by postmodern feminists who focus predominantly at the cultural level. Not only do postmodern feminists emphasise diversity, they themselves are quite diverse in their theorisations. The basic argument here is that given that there is no essential gender or, according to this view, sexual identity, there is no reason why women (or men) should be limited to traditional concepts of gender identities and roles. Postmodern feminism, then, in common with postmodernism generally, emphasises difference and plurality. A central point of postmodern feminism is that second wave feminism has tended to be dominated by middle-class Western women and has inadequately dealt with and conceptualised the experience of other women. Thus, bell hooks has prominently argued that the sex/gender experience of women of African descent has been significantly shaped by 'racial' oppression to an extent that required different theorising and action. In some cases, white women had been party to the oppression of black women. Elizabeth Spelman in *Inessential Women* contends that it is absurd to argue that it is possible to extract some essential general attributes of women from the reality of the flux of class, 'race', age and other identities that are experienced differently by individual women (1988). These different identities are likely to involve different relationships and lines of action, including political action, and in some contexts, involving men.

Although the diverse situations, experiences and identities of women are now more fully acknowledged, at a practical level many feminists have become concerned that postmodern feminism will fragment the feminist movement before it has achieved its goal of equality for women. To achieve equality requires that women continue to act collectively – as they have had to in order to achieve many of the gains made so far. The obvious relevance and cogency of this point has prompted a number of postmodern feminists to develop suggestions as to how feminists might both accept the immense diversity of women while retaining a collective strategy and identity. An article to this effect occurs in Nicholson and Seidman's edited volume, *Social Postmodernism* (1995). This is an important volume because it is a collection of attempts by a number of authors to rescue postmodernism, including postmodern feminism, from fragmenting into a proliferation of unconnected discourses and differences. In her article, 'Women as seriality: thinking about women as a social collective', Iris Young states: 'Feminist politics evaporates . . . without some conception of women as a social collective'(193). Young's argument is that despite their differences women can be regarded and can act as what, following Sartre, she terms a '*series*'. She distinguishes a series from a group. She describes a group as forming actively and self-consciously around given objectives whereas a 'series' is made up of individuals who, though they have common interests, may not be aware of them. She suggests that women are a series in that they still do have common interests mainly because they are all still liable to discrimination through patriarchy. Feminist groups should keep in mind the wider concerns of all women and address specific issues where relevant. She argues that 'feminist politics must be coalition politics' because although all women have common interests around which they need to combine, different groups of women also have different interests and identities (212).

What about men and boys in late modernity? Following the challenge of second wave feminism, they and their masculinities present an oddly inconsistent picture.

On the one hand, many men profess to believe in gender equality and a number even seem to feel some collective guilt at the oppression of women. However, most hang onto what power and privilege they can – and this remains so substantial that it is still premature to assume the inevitable end of patriarchy. Though alive, however, patriarchy does seem a little sickly. In the past two or three decades, millions of working class and middle class men have 'taken early retirement' or simply been made redundant from the full-time, 'jobs for life' that were often the basis of their status and masculine self-esteem. To the extent that the economy has been 'feminised', some have been replaced by women although the latter have usually experienced poorer working conditions and received lower pay. In the last decade of the century, boys have regularly (if not always accurately) been presented in the media as lagging behind girls, both in school-work and even in terms of career prospects, and as somewhat prone to deviant and anti-social behaviour.

The response of many men and boys to the above developments has, understandably, not been entirely confident. Mac an Ghaill (1994) has usefully suggested that there is a crisis in both middle and working class masculinity which, it can be suggested, amounts to a generalised crisis of masculinity. Increasing numbers of middle class men have had to respond to the demands of articulate, educated wives for a fair share of work and rewards in relation to paid and domestic work.

Yet, what Anthony Giddens refers to as the democratic relationship is not easily achieved – as high divorce and separation rates show (see pp. 148–50). Working class men and boys have been faced with a collapse of the industrial and extractive work around which they built their culture (*Coal is Our Life* is the evocative title of Dennis *et al's* book of 1959). The government's 'welfare to work' policy may turn out to be better than a life on and off welfare but it cannot provide the sense of security and identity of the stable jobs of the high industrial period.

While it remains supremely relevant to treat gender in terms of the system of patriarchal oppression, it is increasingly important to examine the complex changes affecting patriarchy and the related shifts in gender relations. Patriarchy is a system of masculine domination but not all relations between men and women are characterised by the dominance of men. In some situations, and probably the number is growing, women have more power than men and may use it for self-interested purposes of control and domination.

The possibility that the gender gap is closing or may close suggests the interesting speculation that it may disappear altogether. This is the underlying notion behind John MacInnes' *The End of Masculinity* (1998). He suggests that as women increasingly occupy roles previously in the preserve of men and vice-versa, the characteristics associated with masculinity and femininity will become much more equally spread across the sexes and lose their particular association with one or other sex. If gender is socially constructed then it may disappear or diminish under the influence of social change. Reassuringly perhaps, MacInnes does not think that sex will disappear with gender – although one can speculate that sex may be expressed somewhat differently. But that is another story!

Sex and Sexuality

There has recently been a considerable change in the way sex and sexuality are theorised within sociology and social theory. It used to be common to distinguish between differences of sex which were seen as biologically given and differences of gender which were seen as culturally constructed and as therefore open to change. For many feminists, sex differences were often then bracketed off as either beyond the concern of sociology or as having no inevitable substantial or negative social consequences for women that could not be dealt with in the context of gender fairness and equality. Thus, while women conceive and bear children and men do not, social reform could remove the possible disadvantages for women. However, this pragmatic approach did not directly address whether and to what extent males and females are biologically different. Further, the quite widespread use of the originally functionalist concept of sex-roles seemed to imply that the traditional division of labour between men and women was somehow determined by their sex.

More recently, two views have come into prominence which reject the sex/gender division. The first view is that sexuality is a personal/social construct and is not biologically determined. In this analysis, a person's biological sex does not determine their sexual identity. This is a social constructionist approach. The second view is in part a response to the constructionist approach. It accepts that – for whatever reason – men and women are in certain significant ways broadly different and that this might not be a bad thing. Implicitly or explicitly, the argument is often made that the way women think, feel and behave is better – more co-operative, helpful and less competitive and destructive – than the way many men behave. That perennial feminist wild-card, Germaine Greer argued in *The Whole Woman* that liberation for women would not be achieved by becoming like men – whom, by and large she does not see as such exemplary role models:

> Liberation struggles are not about assimilation but about asserting difference, endowing that difference with dignity and prestige, and insisting on it as a condition of self-definition and self-determination.

> (1998:1)

Although the view that men and women are significantly different does not depend on there being a substantial biological basis for sexual difference, it would obviously be strengthened if that were the case. Much, though not all, recent biological and evolutionary theory, especially in its more popular expressions, tends to emphasise the extent to which human behaviour, including male/female behaviour differences, is genetically pre-programmed. This work lurks behind the recent wider revival of the concept of sexual difference. Clearly, this view constitutes a challenge to the view that sex/gender inequalities are socially constructed and can be changed.

The constructionist understanding of sexuality has its modern or postmodern roots in the 1960s. Although, initially the 'sexual liberation' of that period was enjoyed mainly by heterosexual men, it quite soon extended to heterosexual women (who initially were perhaps more objects of desire and lust than fully active and equally initiating participants), homosexuals and lesbians. Throughout the 1970s and 1980s, 'the gay rights' movement sought to end discrimination on grounds of sexual identity/preference and to achieve equal status and opportunity with other people. By the end of the century the movement had come close to achieving legal equality. Prejudice and discrimination against gays seems to be decreasing but still occurs widely, sometimes in quite vicious forms. As Bob Connell, who adopts a constructionist approach, points out, those who identify with hegemonic masculine identity may see a challenge and feel insecure in the face of an identity which they perceive as so different from their own. Just as the black liberation movement redefined the term 'black' positively, some gays have attempted to mock dominant definitions of their sexual preference by adopting the label 'queer' as a self description. In doing this, they rejected the statement implicit in the term that their identity is somehow deviant or abnormal.

Peter Gatter in *Identity and Sexuality* (1999) puts the case for regarding sexual identities as socially constructed with exceptional clarity and balance. First, he recaps the theoretical reference of this approach:

> The view that certain identities did, and could only emerge in specific historical circumstances, is most closely asociated with Foucault's work. Many other scholars have taken up his framework in looking at the historical rise of sexual identities in the West . . .

> Contemporary anthropology and interpretive sociology tend to the view, not that there are natural laws of society (as early sociologists such as Durkheim held) but that the social and cultural, in line more widely with late modernist and postmodernist thought, have to be understood as reflexive products of human consciousness.

> (1999:24–5)

Gatter's second point is an empirical one:

> The ethnographic record shows that various aspects of persons are considered very differently in different cultural settings. To take an example pertinent here, the apparent incidence of homosexual behaviours, how they are regarded, and the senses in which they are associated with particular identities are highly culturally variable. (25)

Gatter then goes on to cite an example of a cultural rite of passage in Sambia which, if it were to occur in the West would be regarded as an extreme example of homosexual paedophilia. The rite is the culmination of quite a complex initiation from adolescence to adulthood. During the more secret part of the rituals, the elders blow flutes which represent penises and similarly, the initiates must suck the penises of the elders. By taking in semen, the boys become transformed into men able to impregnate women and, in turn, inseminate other younger initiates. As, Gatter states, semen is thought to be the actual and symbolic location of male power – thus, the significance of the ritual. These activities are not considered to be homosexual and for the majority are actually a crucial step on the route to heterosexual relations.

There are many examples of sexual rituals and practices in other cultures which appear strange to Western eyes. Similarly, sexual practices change, at least in their acceptability and relative visibility in the West. This strongly suggest that sexuality is very 'plastic' or flexible. It also suggests that in a society which greatly values freedom of choice and expression, a great variety of sexual practice and invention is likely to occur. However, no society that does not wish to invite chaos and ill-health would allow irresponsible freedom.

Jeffrey Weeks, one of the scholars Gatter refers to above, is among the most prolific and passionate advocates for 'choice' rather than 'destiny' in matters of sexuality (1995). For choice to be possible there must be tolerance of difference. Weeks rejects biological essentialism arguing that it is the meaning given to sexual identities that most matters. Meanings can be socially imposed or learnt but they can be challenged and changed. He argues that in modernity sexual intolerance and persecution have often occurred under the various worthy banners of 'Nature, Science and Truth'(26). The purpose of imposing such a narrow morality and range of sexual behaviour was to achieve social regulation and control. While recognising that choice has always been an aspect of liberal philosophy, he argues that 'under the condition of postmodernity it has assumed a new significance' and could achieve greater and fuller expression.(28) He states that choice need not stop at the market place but that relationships, including their erotic aspects, are a 'major site for seeking authenticity' (66). However, he emphasises that choice cannot be made in a moral vacuum guided only by the desire for self-gratification. In fact, as the title of his book, *Invented Moralities*, indicates, he is as much concerned with morality as sexuality or rather with the relationship between the two. He wants to get beyond the simplistic attitudes and practice based on either side of the binary of liberation/repression. What his moral suggestions seem to come down to is that relationships involve responsibility and belonging as well as pleasure and that the framework of choice involves the freedom to leave as well as embark upon a relationship but neither without bearing in mind the legitimate needs of others.

However, he is neither prescriptive nor sanctimonious and recognises that experimentation and practice are necessary for people to discover and test the principles that they might live by.

On a wider scale, Weeks sees the possibility of a new radical rather than merely liberal individualism becoming the 'dominant theme of the age'. In saying this, he is seeking to rescue postmodernity, including its sexual practices, from the chaos of relativism, amorality and irresponsibility. Beck and Giddens have referred to late modern society as 'risk society' and it is pertinent that the sub-titles of Weeks and Gatter's books are, respectively, 'Sexual values in an age of uncertainty' and 'Aids in Britain in the 1990s'. If the 1960s was about 'freedom now' what they are suggesting is 'freedom with care' – for self and others.

Ethnicity

In the postwar period, ethnicity is the collective identity which appears internationally to have had the strongest and widest appeal. To say that the appeal of ethnic identity is almost universal would be to exaggerate – but only slightly. For many it seems to be a base identity, stronger even than that of class or nation. Across the world peoples are often prepared to fight with an intensity they reserve for little else in order to establish what they see as their ethnic identity. Ethnic conflicts sometimes occur within and sometimes across national boundaries. Throughout much of the old Russian Empire, in many parts of post-colonial Africa, in the ethnic jigsaw that is Indonesia, and even in the 'more stable' nation-states of Western Europe ethnic tension and struggle is commonplace. Inevitably, as one contemplates ethnic bloodbath after ethnic bloodbath, the question 'why?' occurs.

Of course, answers are not quite so simple as the previous paragraph might be taken to imply. Ethnic conflict is not always, and may be seldom, caused simply by the fact that two peoples see themselves as irreconcilably different. After all, there are probably more cases of Jews and Arabs, Turks and Kurds living in reasonable harmony side by side than the more publicised contrary cases. Most ethnic conflicts are not merely about identity but about the control of power, resources and territory by one group at the expense of another. All the conflicts indicated above have a strong basis of material interest – typically territorial or relating to political power and patronage. On the other hand, it would be a mistake to see the identity and ideological aspects of these conflicts as necessarily secondary to the material. Once two ethnic groups develop a history and mythology of conflict, once they 'demonise' each other, the conflict takes on its own cultural momentum. For instance, this was the case with the Serbs and Kosovan-Albanians. It is also clearly the case in Northern Ireland where each 'side' celebrates its history and identity at the expense of, and sometimes provocatively in the face of, the other.

Given the sombre opening to this section, it is important to emphasise that the story of ethnicity, including ethnicities in the contemporary world, is not all grim. The story of ethnicity is in large part, the story of the human 'race', of its varied achievements as well as its vile intolerance. There is a major ethnic component to many of the great historical collective expressions of culture – such as the Italian Renaissance, the Scottish Enlightenment and contemporary black music. Equally, or, rather more important is the dynamic inter-action of one ethnic culture with another, or of multiple ethnic cultures which Stuart Hall rightly sees as one of the more positive cultural developments of late modernity.

Britain: A Darker Shade of Pale: 1945–2000

In the nineteen fifties, cultural considerations were secondary to economic ones in relation to immigration policy. As was examined in a previous chapter, the reasons for mass immigration from Britain's colonies and former colonies in the 1950s and 1960s were overwhelmingly economic. This was true from the point of view of both the 'host' nation and immigrants. However, negotiations and struggles between the majority and minority ethnic groups over *cultural identity* occurred from the start and built up as later generations of minority ethnics variously asserted themselves. These interactions involving issues of identity were not abstracted from material issues but were related to and rooted in a struggle for power in all major areas of British society. At issue was the cultural identity or identities of the people of Britain. Among the politico-cultural formations that characterised interactions between some of the majority and minority ethnic groups were:

○ Assimilationism

○ Multiculturalism

○ Anti-racism

○ White cultural hegemony

○ Cultural resistance

○ New Ethnicities

The first three of the above terms were widely used by policy makers whereas the last three are sociological descriptions of more diffuse, less formalised tendencies. All involved issues of power and identity.

Assimilation

Although early postwar immigration was driven primarily by mutual self-interest it was made possible by the principle of equal citizenship although this ideal was swiftly paired down once it was widely acted upon. The 1948 Nationality Act enabled citizens of the Commonwealth to live in Britain with virtually full rights of citizenship. In practice, equality was not achieved due to substantial and well documented prejudice and discrimination on the part of some white Britons. At 'street level' discrimination occurred in every area of life with the sign 'No blacks need apply' and its equivalents appearing quite commonly. The official view was that the immigrants would eventually 'assimilate' to 'the British way of life'. However, initially very little was done by government to facilitate this process. One early intervention – bussing children to schools outside their neighbourhood to achieve a 'more balanced racial mix' – was ill-thought through and was as likely to exacerbate social tension as to relieve it. Much more helpful was the policy pursued energetically by some local education authorities of teaching English as a second language to immigrant children who did not speak it and, in some cases, to adults. However, records of Cabinet meetings reveal that by the mid-fifties the Tory government was becoming increasingly concerned at the social conflict and disorder that it saw developing between some white Britons and new immigrants, particularly young white and 'West Indian' men.

In fact, the first postwar immigrants from the new Commonwealth were predominantly young African Caribbean men. For a number of reasons these young 'black' men often did not 'assimilate' as many white Britons rather vaguely hoped. From a sociological perspective - and with the help of hindsight – this is not surprising. First, the extent of the racism many experienced caused some to react against the majority culture as racist. The contrast between the 'accommodation' of the immigrant generation of African Caribbean men and later generations can be overdrawn. In 1959 sizeable 'race riots' occurred in London's Notting Hill area and in Nottingham. It was perhaps the fact that, in a time of labour shortage most of the immigrant generation did get work, that prevented conflict developing on the scale that it did in the 1980s. Despite the above problems, the foothold on the occupational ladder that many African Caribbeans did achieve in the longer run enabled a significant middle class to develop. On the other hand, not everyone was able and some did not want to take this hard route and what some have called 'a black underclass' also developed (Rex and Tomlinson, 1979). A second reason why the assimilation of young African Caribbeans did not quickly or comprehensively occur was that they possessed a culture that was itself powerful and resilient and, perhaps most importantly, provided meaningful expression for them. This issue was discussed earlier in this chapter (pp. 162–3).

Multiculturalism

The second half of the 1960s, saw the development and clarification of four broad politico-cultural approaches to ethnic or what were then more widely called 'race', relations. These were multiculturalism, anti-racism, white-cultural hegemony (shading into racism), and, what Stuart Hall has termed, cultural resistance. Following the election of a Labour government in 1964 the official position quickly became multiculturalism. The theory of multiculturalism is to accept and respect the equality of all the ethnic cultures in a given society and to enable them to be freely expressed in a context of mutual tolerance. In order to support the development of such a society, the government passed legislation to make illegal incitement to racial hatred (1965) and discrimination in the key areas of public life, including employment and housing (1968). Multiculturalism has had some success in promoting ethnic cultural interaction and understanding but it did not address the central issue of white dominance of institutional power. This was the main criticism of multiculturalism raised from the anti-racist approach.

Anti-racism

Anti-racism is predominantly a structural rather than a cultural approach to racism and discrimination. It seeks not just an egalitarian sharing of cultures but an examination and acknowledgement that white people have oppressed black people both historically and in contemporary society and action to put an end to the latter situation. The concept of *institutional racism* is central to anti-racism. A distinction is made between individual and institutional racism. The latter occurs when the rules, practices and cultural ethos of an institution lead, either intentionally or unintentionally to discrimination against black people. One policy for dealing with institutional racism is to set target dates for recruiting and retaining staff from minority ethnic groups proportionate to their presence in a particular population. Although it was considered by some to be a radical approach in the 1970s, the basic principle that there is a structural and institutional dimension to racism became widely accepted by the 1990s. The Labour government elected in 1997 after 17 years of Conservative rule insisted on the adoption of anti-racist policies by the London Metropolitan Police Force and by the fire-service. If – and it is a big 'if' – these policies are effectively enforced there is a possibility that these services will operate substantially in a 'racially' egalitarian way. The strategy of adopting a target figure for minority recruitment was adopted by the Patten Report on the Royal Ulster Constabulary published in 1999. In this case the aim was to achieve a more representative balance of Catholic and Protestants in the force.

White Cultural Hegemony

Unlike multiculturalism and anti-racism, the white cultural hegmonic position sought to privilege the majority 'white' culture over minority ethnic cultures. This view has been held and expressed with highly varying degrees of intensity throughout the postwar years. The assimilationist view itself often unproblematically assumed the superiority of British culture and was held by many well meaning if not always well informed people. Assimilationists at least accepted the possibility of the new immigrants remaining in Britain even if they wanted their culture to 'disappear'. Others expressed much more virulent views. The response of one Conservative mid-sixties by-election candidate to the Labour government's multicultural approach was the slogan: 'If you want a nigger for a neighbour, vote Labour'. Leading Conservative politician, Enoch Powell sought to avoid language that would make him legally liable for 'incitement to racial hatred' (1965 Race Relations Act) but tested the limit with his powerful rhetoric of cultural separatism, repatriation and warnings of social disorder following upon black immigration. His notorious 'rivers of blood speech' led to him to being sacked from the shadow cabinet by Edward Heath.

When Margaret Thatcher defeated Edward Heath in the contest for the leadership of the Conservative party, Britain had a Prime Minister in waiting who adhered to a mono-cultural rather than a multicultural notion of 'British' culture and announced this in language which while it lacked the incendiary quality of Powell's was perhaps more offensive:

> People are really rather afraid that this country might be rather swamped by people of a different culture ... the British character has done so much for democracy, for law, and done so much throughout the world , that if there is any fear that it might be swamped, people are going to react and be rather hostile to those coming in. So if you want good race relations, you have to allay people's fears on numbers.
>
> (1978)

This apparently oppositional juxtaposition of British culture and the culture of immigrants risked alienating Britain's minority ethnic communities but what was primarily responsible for the 'racial' conflict of the Thatcher period was the deep recession that occurred during her first administration (1979–83).

Although the urban disorders of 1981 and 1985 involved white as well as black participants, they expressed a strong element of black disaffection, particularly on the part of young black males. Conflict – both cultural and physical – had long been an element in black/white relations. Given the experience of slavery and substantial 'racial' oppression following slavery in both the United States and the Caribbean, this is not surprising.

Cultural Resistance

Resistance was not the only response to white brutality and racism but it was a common one. The tough, proud, confrontational lifestyle of the Jamaican hustler provided a ready role model for black British youth once relations with whites soured. As early as the 1960s, young black males in Britain widely adopted the Jamaican Rude Boy style. Like black hip-hop music of the 1990s, their favoured musical style of reggae was full of abrasive, racially sensitive lyrics spiced with macho posturing and aggression. In the hands of Bob Marley, the reggae beat was slowed and deepened to embody more pacific and racially conciliatory sentiments. Even Rasta, however, of which Marley was the acknowledged interpreter ostensibly sought separation from, rather than integration with, white people.

Young African Caribbean males carried resistance into every area of life. Their conflicts with teachers and with the police have become a feature of everyday life in Britain. I have no intention of raising the issue of 'blame' here. As far as explanation is concerned, however, the historical context of racism and the vicious circle of conflict created between black youth and the agencies of social control as a result of mutual negative experience and labelling are prominent factors (for an analysis of the 'vicious circle' explanaton, see Young and Lea, 1984).

Although the term cultural resistance rightly implies that black youth culture has a strong theme of defensiveness, it would be a mistake to see it exclusively in those terms. Proudhon's famous maxim – 'the destructive urge is also the creative urge' – would seem to apply. The desire to destroy racial oppression and restriction has been accompanied by great creativity and assertion. It is a cliche that sometimes the best art and most creative action is generated out of oppression and suffering. If so, black people have had plenty to go on. In the nineteenth century they created the blues and gospel and more recently jazz, reggae and hip-hop. Sometimes hip-hop and the rap that goes with it has been more about macho posturing and rivalry rather than the social and religious-philosophical commentary of some earlier forms. Reflecting a dynamic of destruction between black males, it has been associated with a number of maimings and killings, including the 'execution' of leading rap singer, Big Daddy. There has always been a tension between the vast fortunes made by some black performers and the desire of many of them to keep their work relevant to 'the street'. Arguably, Bob Marley managed this more consistently than many of the rap artists, such as Puff Daddy. As black artists and black youth in general increasingly established their cultural and stylistic presence in the 1990s, the political undercurrents of the 1970s and 1980s receded or became merely cultural rhetoric.

The creativity and style of black youth has earned them a dominant position in youth culture. 'Black' music, argot, demeanour and dress style are regularly adopted by white and increasingly Asian youth. They are more responsible than youth of any other ethnic group for the cultural hybridity that is breaking down ethnic separateness – although the flow occurs in all directions.

Part of this cultural exchange involves mixed ethnic relationships and partners and self-evidently will result in more 'mixed-ethnic' offspring. It is more in the cultural than in the political sphere that youth sets the pace and pattern of change. This is even true of black youth which has nevertheless always had a sharper political message to deliver than most.

New Ethnicities

Stuart Hall first put forward the 'new ethnicities' analysis in 1988, ten years after the publication of his co-authored book, *Policing the Crisis*. It signalled an influential, postmodern turn in his thinking. He argued that minority ethnic groups needed to respond to the hegemonic white version of British cultural identity being put forward by Mrs Thatcher and others on the political right. He contended that British minority ethnic groups had every reason to be proud of and to celebrate their own identity and that this was one way of challenging a racist mono-cultural hegemony. More recently still he has begun to recognise and respond positively to the extent that cultural hybidity increasingly characterises British culture, especially among the young (see p.163).

A Note on the New Social or Identity Movements

Although it has not been the main object of this chapter to describe the new social movements, in fact, this has to a significant extent been done. The new social movements are those that have arisen independently of the 'old' working class movement and around the issue of self/collective identity. The sixties youth movement gave an impetus to many of these although the women's movement, gay movement and black liberation movements had independent origins and have emerged as huge movements in their own right. The movement missing from this chapter is the one that some would consider the prototypical new social movement – the 'Green' or environmental protection movement. This is because I have decided to deal with this movement in a global context – which is the one to which it best belongs. Perhaps more now than 'members' of the other movements mentioned above, many 'greens' remain outside the system – in so far as it is possible to remain outside global capitalism. Or, it is perhaps more accurate to say that they relate to the system from a clearly articulated position of difference – namely, conservation of and continuity with nature.

Cultural Themes in Late or Postmodernity: The New Sociology

One of the problems in making sense of postmodernity is that many postmodernists do not consider that ours is a very coherent age. In fact, they consider that the contemporary period is one of fragmentation and confusing and rapid change. Further, their own theories to some extent reflect this. Whereas classical and 'second wave' theorists at least aspired to present rational analyses, some postmodernists deliberately express themselves almost dramatically, using irony, humour and shock tactics to make their points. This is partly because they wish to demonstrate the relevance of the irrational and emotional in social life. This aspect of their approach should become clearer in the next chapter. Anthony Giddens is more classically rational and systematic in his theoretical approach but in his case, the sheer scope of his writings can leave one searching for the connections. What follows, then, is not an attempt to make full sense or even fully to tabulate the content of the new sociology but simply to give an indication of its scope and to signal where more detailed analysis of specific points can be found in this book.

In fact, it is in Chapter 7, which deals with globalisation that the main themes of the postmodern critique of capitalism are given fuller analysis. These are:

○ The profit motive

○ The global cultural hegemony of the United States

○ A Superficial or 'Surface' Global Culture

○ Hyper-reality

○ The Collapse of the Cultural into the Economic

○ The Convergence of High and popular Culture

○ Critiqueing the West's Construction of 'the Other'

The first four will not be dealt with further here. The first two are familiar enough and can be assumed for the purposes of this brief section and the second two and the seventh are complex and require the more extended presentation given in the next chapter.

The proposition that the cultural is collapsing into the economic is a fascinating one and is at the heart of postmodern thinking. The relevant section here is simply to give more general and empirical arguments for this view than the specific ones cited by Jameson in Chapter 7. The same motive is behind introducing here the issue of whether the distinctions between high and popular culture are collapsing. Other points raised below occur elsewhere in this book but also require discussion here.

Introduction

Control and Choice: Cultural Production and Consumption

The centrality of culture in late modern society and the commodification of much cultural production and consumption does not imply that traditional cultural issues, including those of cultural control and cultural quality, are no longer relevant or are in some way closed. These questions are only closed to those who imagine they have the exclusive 'right' answer to them.

It is obvious that the control of the production of much of popular culture, from 'movie hits' to branded clothes and trainers, is in the hands of multinational corporations. It is equally obvious that producers want to sell their products and often market them aggressively through the mass media to consumers. Fundamentally, this is the same situation that has prevailed throughout modern capitalism although the 'space' of culture is larger and the number and apparent variety of cultural commodities greater. There is a long tradition of cultural analysis within Marxist sociology which is pessimistic about the effects of the media and consumption under capitalism. A major example of this is the Frankfurt School (see pp. 35–7). This approach is continued in the postmodern pessimism of Baudrillard which is discussed in the next chapter in the wider context of globalisation. More recently, however, a number of researchers have conducted micro-level research which shows that a variety of responses to media output can occur even within the same household. However, these responses are not presented as wholly 'free' but are structured by, for instance, gender and age (see, Silverstone, 1990).

If the basic debate about media 'effect'/response is familiar, there are a number of significant new developments which frame the debate rather differently – particularly in relation to choice and quality. First, as ever, is the new technology. Technological innovation has made possible the proliferation – potentially limitless – of television channels. Second, in the United States and Britain, this development has been implemented overwhelmingly by private enterprise although the BBC has launched a new educational channel, BBC 3 and has further expanded its channels as a result of digitalisation (which enables more channels and better reception).

Have the above developments in Britain led to greater choice? The answer is less clearcut than might be assumed. In a simple quantitative sense, those people who have rented access to SKY or cable channels have more to choose from. However, they and their families represent only about a third of viewers. The rest have probably had their choices marginally reduced, at least in the area of sport, where many of the main events are bought up by SKY or pay per television. Even those who do have SKY or cable often complain about the pricing structure of channel 'packages' which both makes the more popular channels (sport and premium films) expensive and encourages people to buy access to channels they are not much interested in (by including them cheaply in packages with more popular channels). Despite these commercial manipulations and constraints, it would be blinkered to deny that for those willing to pay for it, the above developments provide increased choice. There has been an increase both in the quantity and variety of sport, business, travel, soft porn, and films.

The Collapse of the Cultural into the Economic: The Erosion of Work/Leisure Divide

There are several developments that lend support to the view that the economic is becoming more concerned with the cultural and that the cultural is increasingly part of the economic. Most obviously, the relative proportion of production devoted to cultural goods as distinct from goods intended to meet basic needs has greatly increased. Production now is substantially devoted to feeding cultural consumption. Cultural commodities, or commodities with a substantial cultural element probably now account for most of the global economy. Tourism is now the world's major industry. Huge multinational organisations, tiny companies and even individuals generate a vast output of words, sounds, images and objects which they hope others will buy. What this process of commodification does to the quality of culture is hotly debated. Second, increasingly the means of production – information technology – is concerned with language and image – the core of culture. The information and communications revolutions and their effects have propelled cultural and economic change in late modernity. As was argued in Chapter 3, these revolutions have permeated the whole of social life, reshaping both production and consumption.

Further, the work/leisure divide is increasingly eroding. In the industrial age, the brute physicality of factory life and the sharp division of the day into '9 to 5' and after, clearly separated work from time spent in leisure and personal organisation. Both factory and office workers knew when they were 'finished' at work and usually felt pretty good about it. Economic/work activity is now less clearly separated from cultural, leisure and home-based activity though the old patterns persist for many. There are several reasons for this shift, most of them related to the revolution in information and communications. The first four reasons pertain to the actual or potential uncoupling of employees from large sites of employment, pre-eminently factories and office blocs. First, the production of physical commodities no longer requires large numbers of people to be in one place for the same shift, many of them repeating the same action over and over again. The automation of production has accounted for the loss of millions of jobs in the traditional 'smoke-stack industries. To the extent that men were more often employed in this type of work, its decline predominantly affected 'masculine' experience and contributed to what is arguably a generalised crisis of masculine identity. Second, the now dominant service sector does not require employees to be based en masse in the same place to the same extent as did the Fordist industrial economy. The production of services can take place with a more physically decentralised labour force although office work is still sometimes organised on the factory model for reasons of control and perceived convenience. The PostFordist economy has facilitated the bringing of more women into the labour force and while it can provide 'flexibility' for employer and employee, it can leave the latter isolated in part-time or temporary, perhaps home-based work, and vulnerable to exploitation. Third, a factor which further facilitates labour decentralisation and flexibility, is ever increasing ease of access to the new means of production – the vast and expanding array of information/communications technology. A small room or part of a room in a person's home can be more than enough space to do the bulk of many, perhaps most, jobs in postindustrial society. Fourth, the information required to do work is both more easily accessible and of greater quantity and, often, quality. For instance, the internet is increasingly used as a means to execute economic activities, including making money, as well as for leisure communication and fun. Indeed, one person's fun is often another person's means of making money.

A further point refers to the rapid global growth of the cultural economy itself. Fifth, and finally, cultural production has a significant and growing global dimension although the Western origins of much globalised culture and the fact that most of the profit from it goes to the West is often resented and contested. As Giddens frequently stresses, globalisation is not merely about the West or resistance and responses to the West. Islam is an expanding culture of global dimensions and 'black Atlantic' culture has some roots outside of the West and elements of its content are highly critical of the West. Arguably, however, these more traditional cultures are less commodified than that of the West.

The Convergence or Elision of 'High' and Popular Culture?: The Quality Question

The issue of what is 'high' or 'poor' quality in culture has always been complex and has been further problematised by post/structuralist theory. The logic of structuralism is that there is no single inherent or privileged meaning to a text but that different individuals will read it differently i.e., find different meaning in it. Thus, feminist and anti-racist readings of those texts seen as presenting the relevant groups as subordinate and/or inferior are almost certain to be different to those who do not share these discourses, including, perhaps that of the author of a given text. *Relativising* the meaning of a text is not quite the same as asserting that there are not and cannot be general or consensual standards on which its quality can be judged. However, it is not possible within the confines of this book to do more than indicate what the basis of judgement about cultural quality might be.

Achieving consensus about quality is not impossible. There are many areas of activity where the basis on which quality is judged is explicitly or implicitly agreed. However, consensus judgements about quality need not be based on the intrinsic worth of an object but simply on the criteria on which a group of people agree to make a judgement. For instance, student texts (course work, exam essays), are often assessed – in effect, judged – by widely, if not universally, agreed criteria. As far as television programmes are concerned it is not difficult to establish basic criteria on which to judge technical quality and quality of performance (e.g. how well a person acts in or anchors a programme). It is certainly arguable that as more and more people are employed as newscasters and presenters that quality in these respects has become less professionally even.

It is a much more difficult matter to establish that one cultural product is inherently of superior quality to another. Such a judgement implies that there are objective or inherent cultural and artistic standards which some cultural products achieve and others do not, to the same extent. For instance, on what basis can it be stated that there has been a decline in the intrinsic quality of television and modern culture generally or, even that certain cultural products, say Shakespeare's plays, are intrinsically of 'better' quality than others, say for example, the many soaps and serials that make up the core content of television drama.

A longterm development that has contributed to the shift away from making confident 'objective' judgements about cultural quality has been the shift in the focus of artistic control from the traditional upper class to modern capitalists. With this shift has gone the 'aura' of high art as something inherently superior and different to popular art. If classical music and literature can be pack-aged and marketed for a mass audience, it very often is. Classic FM and 'even' Radio 3 can attract bigger audiences by playing mainly 'the good' (easy?) bits from often long works, then, sometimes, some would say, too often, they do. It is developments of this kind that prompt the accusation of 'dumbing down'.

There is some recent empirical evidence that claims to show a decline in the quality of television current affairs and drama. In 1999, an independent study commissioned by the Campaign for Quality Television concluded that a gradual 'Disneyfication' of British television culture is occur-ring 'where the bright, safe, glossy and formulaic guaranteed rating successes are replacing more challenging and enlightening approaches'. The report stated that the number of single dramas had halved since the 1970s while that of soap operas had increased by five hundred percent in the same period. Soaps are now 63% of all drama. However, many writers of high repute have written for soaps and many consider the best of them to be good and relevant drama. The charge of the report on news and current affairs was that quality is being sacrificed to save money – partly by not broad-casting demanding, indepth programmes at peak times. It was hotly contested by leading figures involved in the industry (see, for instance, an exchange between Steve Barnett, one of the report's authors and David Lloyd of channel 4, Guardian, R.S. 30.10.1999: 2). It has to be said, that in comparison with such factually based arguments, postmodernist assertions tend to be more general in nature.

Identity: Pluralism, Fluidity and Hybridity

A frequently expressed view among those influenced by postmodernism is that popular culture has become very fluid and hybrid (made-up of influences and/or signs of different cultural origin) (Hall, 1992). The monoculturalism of traditional and even some modern societies has been chal-lenged by cultural pluralism. Initially, postmodernism hailed a break from the cultural drabness and 'sameness' of modernity and the apparent proliferation of cultural difference. Then, came a grow-ing realisation of the permeable nature of cultural boundaries. In the global village 'pick and mix' and hybridity in relation to cultural style became increasingly common. However, cultural trends often produce reactions, and there are many cases in which established national, ethnic and reli-gious frames of cultural reference have been reasserted in the face of the seeming cultural chaos and promiscuity of postmodernity.

One of the strongest indications that 'ordinary' people are not mere 'cultural dopes' is that they 'put together' cultural combinations that do not initially exist in the market place (until and unless they are copied and produced by business). The youth styles discussed earlier began not in the design department of a fashion house but 'on the street'. The Teds and the Punks were both very eclectic in the way they constructed, deconstructed and reconstructed their on-going styles – and crucially the signified meanings that went with them. Some of these stylistic changes have a specific purpose – often to shock, in the case of the Punks – and many seem to be motivated by a more general desire to 'be original' or, at least, 'different' for as long as it can last. 'Nineties youth' refer less to class and less even to traditional ethnic identities in their stylistic formations. Style has become more of an end in itself or, like 'techno', is related to a particular type of music. Social and political implications are less obvious (even rap now seems to refer more to sexuality and machismo than to racism or 'ghetto' life). The eclectic nature of much youth style and the speed with which it changes can create an impression of fragmentation but those involved can usually make sense of what is happening and 'find their way around' the relevant 'scenes'.

The Personal 'Price' of Capitalist Culture: Risk and Stress

The culture of capitalist modernity is highly materialistic and competitive. Even for the successful, the price in terms of stress and personal life can be high. For 'the excluded' or those who find they cannot cope, the price can be very high. Anyone with minimal imagination knows that the prospect of disaster or 'failure' is close enough occasionally to feel uncomfortable or insecure. Small things can bring the situation home. I was shocked to read in the December 1999 issue of the Voice's 'Journal' that 'one third of the UK's elderly citizens will have to choose between heat and food this Christmas' (Vol 4). And living longer is 'a good thing'? A similar 'stray fact' is that there are more people over 50 than under 26 sleeping rough on the streets of Britain. Some apparently who seemingly coped very well for a while and then didn't. There but .... It is incongruous that in an affluent age, welfare does not seem to stretch as far as it used to. Perhaps what the 'old', patriarchal welfare state of Beveridge gave was only the illusion of security but, if so, it is an illusion now gone.

Giddens points to risk and insecurity in late modernity on a still larger scale; the unintended sequences of modernity. The effects of the unwise use of science on the environment, in war, on food and nutrition can be catastrophic. He is no Jeremiah but the warning is serious.

CONCLUSION: Identity Politics in the Wider Context

The scope of this chapter has been considerable. The scope of the next chapter is larger still because it takes up some of the issues raised above in a global context. This chapter has examined several fast-changing postwar identity movements and looked at some general issues prompted by developments in the theory and practice of identity.

Discussion has mainly focused on Britain and the West. But identity is a global issue. The impact and dominance of the West has forced other cultures and individuals to address their own identities – as well as their power and resources – in relation to the West – either to reject, to imitate, to select or to assert their own cultural values and perspectives. The identity movements discussed above have their resonances worldwide, especially those concerned with gender and racial/ethnic liberation.

The present period is still one of overwhelming Western military, political and cultural dominance but it threatens soon to be one of reckoning. Across the globe, Western political and commercial power is challenged. The challenge is no longer that of the 'big alternative', Communism, but comes from those who, for one reason or another, have objections or reservations about what the West has done. Some articulate their dissent in terms of affronted tradition. This includes some Muslim leaders and their followers. Others, such as the environmental activists, are concerned with the possible effects of break-neck development on the environment, the climate, nutrition, and ultimately, on the planet and its people.

SUMMARY

1. IDENTITY MOVEMENTS: The slow apparent decline in the subjective importance attached to class and to class based movements in the post-war period provided the context for other sources of identity and action to develop. These included youth, ethnicity, gender and sexuality. These identities were located less at the point of production and more widely in both personal/lifestyle and public/political arenas and in the links between them. (See the 'post' conceptual 'tool-kit, p. 156).

2. YOUTH: The contextual factors for the rise of post-war youth were affluence; greater leisure; more

opportunities for consumption especially in respect to fashion, music and the media; and a tolerant and liberal climate. As far as middle-class and more educated youth was concerned, the expansion of higher education provided a basis for collective experience which stimulated both radical political action and the emergence of a counter-culture – together referred to as 'the (sixties student) movement'. The continuing objective influence of class on youth is illustrated by the extent to which the foci, concerns and styles of the more working class youth subcultures were distinct from those of middle class youth – though there were many 'cross-overs'. However, the concerns of African Caribbean youth seemed mainly to reflect ethnic pride and identity and resistance to racism. The patriarchal contradictions of the youth movement helped to stimulate second wave feminism which emerged with a powerful agenda for change and a variety of ideologies and practices ('feminisms').

'Eighties and nineties' youth has a broadly distinctive character somewhat different from that of the previous generation, now 'in power'. In the vortex of an age of consumption and media explosion, the extent to which this generation is politically passive and primarily concerned with hedonism can be overdone. First, is has had to live in a period of political and cultural backlash begun by Thatcher and which seems to linger under a cautious Blair. The New Social Movements are largely the product of the energy and imagination of contemporary youth.

3. GENDER RELATIONS: From about the 1980s onwards feminists have increasingly recognised that women and girls will seek their identities in a variety of ways. Nevertheless, feminists still want gender change to move towards greater equality and freedom for women and for patriarchy to be further undermined. Men have responded to the feminist challenge in various ways. The work of Bob Connell provides perhaps the most detailed model of patriarchy and of masculinities, including how masculinities are socially re/constructed. Connell's *Masculinities* (1995) describes the dominant or hegemonic form of masculinity in the West as competitive and egocentric. He also describes the subordinate masculinity of homosexuals and marginalised masculinities reflecting 'race' and class disadvantage. Connell and, particularly, Mac an Ghaill (1994) suggest that hegemonic masculinity is in some degree of crisis – partly reflecting the challenge of feminism. New forms of masculinity – some defensive, some egalitarian and more emotionally open – are developing. In time the way human beings feel, think and act may not be gendered in any clearly identifiable way at all.

4. SEXUALITY: Perhaps sociologists are too prone to be dogmatic about what many of them believe to be the minimal effect biology has on sexual preference and identity. However, it is easy to illustrate a very wide range of sexual practices and identities throughout the world, many at variance with Western sexual norms which have themselves tended to change and become more diverse in the postwar period. Jeffrey Weeks sees virtue in this variety, arguing that greater tolerance to different others, and greater choice and freedom – as long as accompanied by responsibility and affection – are culturally and morally enriching.

5. ETHNICITY: Ethnic identity, like national identity, is very powerful. Historically, this source of difference between peoples has led to conflict and carnage as well as some mutual appreciation and celebration. Ethnic identity, like other identities, is not fixed and within one ethnic group there may be many different interpretations of ethnic identity. In Britain African Caribbean cultural identities have been formed through interaction with the dominant culture, varying in kind from assimilationist to resistance.

6. CULTURAL THEMES IN LATE OR POSTMODERNITY: The unifying feature of the various 'postmodern themes' presented in chapters 6 and 7 is the theory of identity shaped or even formed through the consumption of signs – the key debate being around the extent to which people are cultural agents (active) or cultural 'dopes' (passive).

Chapter 7

Britain in the Global Context: Structure and Culture

> **Key Concepts**:
> decentring, globalisation, human rights, hyper-reality, new social movements, (the) other, world system

Introduction

What is globalisation? What is Britain's involvement in it and how has it been affected by it? By any measure these are big and complex questions and it is not surprising that they have excited controversy and provoked sometimes conflicting answers. This book has constantly illustrated that sociologists reflect the concerns of their time and this is certainly the case with globalisation.

In explaining and interpreting globalisation the lines of disagreement are again partly drawn between those who take a relatively pluralist approach and various neo-Marxists and postmodernists who tend to see globalisation as caused and dominated by capitalism. Among the former are Robertson and Giddens and among the latter Wallerstein and Jameson. It would be simplistic to suggest that the former are necessarily positive in their assessment of globalisation – most are fairly mixed – but the latter are generally very negative about what they term 'capitalist globalisation'. In framing globalisation in terms of these two broadly different approaches I am deliberately maintaining the liberal/postmodernist debate of the previous two chapters. Others would frame the issue of globalisation differently and, indeed, some do not consider that any such process is occurring (see below). The threads of the debate between the two general but profoundly different, positions I have indicated run throughout this chapter, surfacing particularly strongly in the concluding section on political globalisation.

Globalisation, Globality and Globalism: Definitions and Debates

There are so many aspects to globalisation – economic, political, cultural – that it is easy to overlook what is the fundamental character of the process itself. At the least, globalisation must involve an increasing trans-national dimension to social life. If globalisation of any kind is occurring, something must be happening or being experienced across national boundaries. Malcolm Walters' definition of globalisation captures this central aspect:

> A social process in which the constraints of geography on social and cultural arrangements recede and in which people become increasingly aware that they are receding.'

> (1995:3)

Anthony Giddens's definition stresses not only the erosion of old boundaries but the greater interdependence characteristic of globalisation:

> The world has become in important respects a single social system as a result of growing ties of interdependence which now affect virtually everyone. The global system is not just an environment in which particular societies – like Britain – develop and change.

The social, political and economic connections which cross-cut borders between countries decisively condition the fate of those living within each of them. The general term for the increasing interdependence of the world is globalisation.

(1997:63-4)

Given, as Giddens states, that globalisation is occurring in the economic, cultural and political spheres, then one would expect to find relevant evidence of it in each sphere. Thus, economic globalisation might be reflected in multinationals having factories and branches across the globe and in the worldwide availability of certain consumer products; cultural globalisation in the multi-national and media-driven spread of leisure and fashion styles and images across national boundaries; and political globalisation in the rise to power of such institutions as the United Nations and the increasing tendency of nations and groups of nations to act with global awareness and effect. If globalisation is occurring in these areas, then one would also expect to see engagement with it at all levels from the individual to the nation-state and beyond to the regional-bloc level. For example, in respect to cultural globalisation, one would expect to see national governments attempting to respond to and perhaps regulate the massive increase in information and images crossing 'national boundaries' although attempts to block or seriously inhibit their flow at 'national boundaries' appear formidably difficult because of the ease with which they can be transmitted and the apparent demand for them.

The term 'globality' describes how every locality or, simply spaces, has been or is liable to be affected by globalisation processes. Ulrich Beck defines the term as follows:

> *Globality* means that *we have been living for a long time in a world society* in the sense that the notion of closed spaces has become 'illusory'. No country or group can shut itself off from others ... 'World society', then denotes the totality of social relation-ships which are *not* integrated into or determined (or determinable) by national-state politics

(2000:10)

The term 'globalism' has a very precise application. According to Beck's definition it refers to 'the view that the world market eliminates or supplants political action – that is the ideology of rule by the world market, the ideology of neo liberalism'. Put otherwise, globalism is an undiluted commitment to a world run and dominated by capitalism.

Networks, Scapes, Flows and Hybrids: Speeded Up Globalisation: Manuel Castells and John Urry

Writing independently, Manuel Castells and John Urry have greatly contributed to the current reconceptualisation of sociology in the light of globalisation. Both adopt the term *network* as a key concept. They consider that a minimal requirement of globalisation is the creation of networks of communication, many interlinking and criss-crossing the world. In the ancient, medieval and early modern world, the means of communication over long distance were limited. People either travelled under their own energy or used animals or sail. Then, the web of communication – if it merits the description – was spun thin and slow and until the modern period did not encompass the full extent of the globe. By the high modern period – say, around the turn of the nineteenth century – rail, improved road, mechanised nautical, and, shortly afterwards, air travel was revolutionising trade and travel, and the telephone and 'electric' telegram enabled rapid personal communication to occur without the necessity of travel. As Robertston puts it, the conditions were in place for globalisation to 'take off'.

It is Manuel Castells' argument that information technology has provided the means to produce global networks of communication on a scale and of such quality and efficiency that new sources of power (knowledge is power), influence and control are available. He considers that a new epoch – the information age – has emerged in which the dominating and formative influence is *networks of communication*. Government, business, including the entertainment business, and ordinary people via the internet, have access to and can contribute to the content of these networks. However, they do not have equal access to the most powerful technology and networks of communication nor, therefore, to the most potent information and knowledge. Who controls the new networks and in whose interest, is highly relevant – unless the information age is assumed to be a free for all. These issues constantly surface in the following discussion of the various areas of globalisation.

In his paradigm challenging book, *Sociology Beyond Societies: Mobilities for the Twenty-first Century* (2000), John Urry further extends the conceptual vocabulary of globalisation. He quotes Castells to the effect that in *networks* there now exists 'a new material basis for the performance of social activities throughout the social structure ... shaping social structure itself' (34). In defining and explaining networks, he draws on a number of authors:

> Castells defines a network as a set of interconnected nodes (points of contact or communication – my brackets) the distance between social positions are shorter where such positions constitute nodes within a network as opposed to those which lie outside the particular network ... Networks thus produce complex and enduring connections across space and through time between people and things (see Murdoch 1995:745). They spread across time and space which is hugely important, since according to Law, if 'left to their own devices human actions and words do not spread very far at all' (1994:24). Different networks possess different reaches or abilities to bring home different events, places or people ...' (34).

Urry goes on to introduce the terms *scapes* and *flows*:

> Scapes are the networks of machines, technologies, organisations, text and actors that constitute various interconnected nodes along which flows can be relayed (35).

What Urry means by this becomes clearer when he lists the main scapes:

○ transportation of people by air, sea etc.
○ transportation of objects by post etc.
○ wire and co-axial cables
○ microwave channels used by cellular phones
○ satellites for radio and television
○ fibre-optic cable for telephone, television and computers.

Scapes, then, refer to particular types of networks in their totality.

Flows are what pass through or are transported or conveyed by networks – for instance, people or information. As Urry puts it:

> By contrast to structured scapes, the flows consist of peoples, images, information, money and waste, that move within and especially across national borders and which individual societies are often unable to or unwilling to control directly or indirectly (36).

Urry emphasises that the increase in the numbers and rapidity of flows creates hybrids or phenomena that are the product of two or more phenomena combining. This is particularly apparent in the area of culture and has been explored earlier in this book (see p. 182). Of course, all or virtually all cultures constantly change but it is the case that whereas traditional cultures tend to change slowly or to resist change globalisation tends to create pressures towards change.

It is the contention of Castells and Urry and of Bell before them that the massive increase in trans-global flow of information is playing a fundamental role in restructuring society at every level. This is illustrated in the sections that follow.

Actors and Levels of Action in the Global Context

It is crucial to note that globalisation is not a one-way flow of influence and effect wholly dominated in a top-downwards way by the multinationals. Simply in terms of understanding the range of responses to the multinationals, it is useful to think of action in relation to them both in terms of various levels and also in terms of particular agencies and movements, although in practice this distinction is less obvious. There are other levels of effective action as well as the global – not least the national – and other organisations as well as the multinationals are able to act in a global context. It is helpful to list the main levels at which other agents or organisations interact with – sometimes to oppose – the multinationals. The multinationals do now permeate every level of social life but at every level, there is some potential to resist or to modify their influence. It is important to note that these levels indicate the social, political and personal identities of the actors involved as well as the geographical basis of action. Thus, an attempt by a national government to control a multinational may reflect a sense of national independence and pride. It must be remembered, however, that partly because of the investment power of the multinationals and their skill in marketing their consumer products, they achieve a lot of acceptance and support at all levels. It is because he believes that there has been a decisive shift to the global level that Beck writes of a 'Second Modernity'. The first modernity was defined in terms of modern nations, the second in terms of the global.

Institutions, organisations and individuals – the latter often acting collectively – may conceivably act at any level although the less powerful the agent, the less scope there is likely to be to effect change (see figure 7.1). Thus, an individual acting alone will have less chance of changing the policy of a major oil or auto company than a global organisation such as Green Peace. Some of the New Social Movements (NSMs) such as the environmental movement and the human rights movement – themselves 'made up' of a myriad of independent organisations and agencies – are a major source of criticism and in some cases active opposition to the multinationals. Certain nation states or members of a particular ethnic or religious groups, are critical of the lifestyle and sexual content of many media products exported by Western multinationals and reject or regulate them accordingly. Islamic values and beliefs have inspired many such cultural as well as political conflicts of this kind. Thus, Muslim anger and revenge at Salman Rushdie's *Satanic Verses* – regarded by some Muslims as blasphemous – was targeted against the publishers as well as the author. Further, the economic and financial autonomy and power enjoyed by multinationals has mainstream critics as well as enthusiasts in the West. Thus, the financial crisis of 1998, led many political and economic experts to call for a strengthening of political control over the global movement of capital. Individuals are not without access to power at various levels. Many individuals have appealed successfully against both multinational action or national law to the European Court of Human Rights although such cases may be more affordable and sustainable if pursued as 'class' or collective actions. The Human Rights Act which came into force in 2000 provides a potential basis for such challenges within the British legal system.

Globalisation, then, should not be seen as a process carried out by and entirely on the terms of multinationals but should be understood to include the responses of others to the multinationals

Global e.g., Microsoft, Green Peace

Bloc (or Regional-Bloc) e.g., European Union

National

Regional e.g., North East England

Local (Community) e.g., small estate, village

Individual

Figure 7.1   Levels of action and actors within the global context

and to globalising processes in general. Undoubtedly, the multinationals have 'set the pace' but there are other significant players in shaping late modernity, some of whom are motivated by very different values to the top executives of multinationals.

Globalisation: Accounts and Evaluations

Two broad types of accounts of how globalisation developed are given below: liberal-pluralist and Marxist. The former is presented in somewhat different but not generally contradictory accounts by Roland Robertson and Anthony Giddens and the latter mainly with reference to Emmanuel Wallerstein and later in the chapter, Fredric Jameson and Baudrillard. It is important to be clear about the values upon which these accounts rest. At the risk of over-simplification, underlying the liberal-pluralist accounts tends to be the view that, despite the many atrocities associated with the expansion of the West which has played a major role in globalisation, the humanistic legacy of the West is worth preserving and building on across the globe. In particular, both Roland Robertson and Anthony Giddens take the view that the ideals of the Enlightenment – reason, equality before the law, liberty, and human happiness and fulfilment – are worth securing throughout the world. Neither, however, assume that globalisation will guarantee this, particularly if it is dominated by unfettered capitalism. Without denigrating or seeking to undermine other cultures they continue to subscribe to these core cultural values of the West. However, it needs to be made clear that both, and especially Giddens, see globalisation as more than just the product of Western expansion and Westernisation. Nevertheless, other approaches stress much more the extent and opposition to Euro-American global hegemony. Thus, Stuart Hall writes of 'the decentring of the West'.

Marx's own account of the expansion of Western capitalism was itself influenced by the optimism of the Enlightenment, in that he thought that capitalism was creating a basis for socialism. To that extent, he and later Lenin believed that capitalist imperialism would eventually prove a stepping stone to progress. Marxists and neo-Marxists of the twenty first century are much less likely to share Marx's optimism about the arrival of socialism but they certainly share his criticism of capitalism. Wallerstein gives a powerful description of what he refers to as the *capitalist world system* but offers no strategy for change comparable to the now outdated one put forward by Marx himself. From the Frankfurt School onwards, there has been a profound strain of cultural pessimism in Marxist thinking based on a negative critique of capitalist consumer culture. This tradition of anti-capitalist cultural analysis has been continued in the thought of ex or neo-Marxists such as Jameson and Baudrillard, now more often referred to as postmodernists. Their work is presented in the section on cultural globalisation.

Two other accounts of globalisation should be introduced here, particularly as they are referred to recurrently rather than dealt with in a separate section of the chapter. One is the celebratory account of Western imperialism and capitalist globalisation itself, more or less assumed by some of those companies and governments responsible for them. Those who have taken 'Western civilisation' to the rest of the world through either war or commerce, not to mention religion, tended to believe that their culture was superior to others – where, indeed, they thought beyond their own immediate self-interest at all. This view reflects the central principle of classical liberalism that economic freedom (freedom to pursue business and trade) and political and cultural freedom are indivisible i.e. you cannot securely have one without the others. Capitalism itself is seen as the means by which these freedoms are achieved and is virtually identified with them. The term *globalism* describes the ideology which seeks to legitimate capitalist global hegemony.

Classical or capitalist liberalism differs from radical or reformist liberalism in that the latter approach seeks to use government to regulate capitalism and to achieve, promote and protect human rights, including now basic material rights, to an extent that classical liberals oppose. The difference is roughly indicated at the British domestic level by that between Thatcherism and the liberal social democracy of the Blair government or between Thatcherism and the reformist Jospin government in France. At the world or global level, the difference is reflected in, for example, those multinationals which seek business in any country more or less regardless of the nature of the regime and Amnesty International and the human rights movement in general which put the issue of such rights ahead of commercial interest. Classical liberalism and liberal social democracy or radical liberalism are not necessarily mutually contradictory, in that classical liberalism is not necessarily antipathetic to human rights and radical liberalism is not in principle opposed to capitalism. However, because different ideas and beliefs do produce different outcomes, in practice the difference in emphasis can be crucial.

The final account of Western imperialism and capitalist-led globalisation to be mentioned here is that of 'the victim' or, more precisely, victims. These processes were led first by Western European countries and then by the United States. American consumer culture has fundamentally altered if not destroyed some cultures but it has not done so without sometimes provoking defensive and angry reaction. For instance, while some Islamic societies, such as Saudi Arabia, have adopted some aspects of American culture, others such as Iraq have bitterly opposed Western lifestyle. China has taken to Western consumerism but it remains unclear whether it will adopt political institutions that would be regarded as democratic in the West. Non-Western accounts of globalisation often reject the Euro-American perspective – they see with a different eye and tell a different story in which Western values and the Western subject are perceived as intrusive and oppressive. Thus, many Muslim societies put their own culture and people at the centre of their concern and to that extent the Western subject is *decentred*. Often non-Western accounts or *narratives* are of unwanted Western domination and destruction and they tell, too, of legacies of longterm bitterness and distrust. Against some of the grimmer realities of Western relations with the rest of the world, the radical liberal project of global citizenship based on material sufficiency and political and cultural freedom attracts some scepticism in the rest of the world. This does not mean it is not worth achieving – though through negotiation rather than coercion – but it does mean that the trust required to achieve it is largely lacking (see the account of the World Trade Organisation conference in Seattle in 1999, pp. 218–20).

Liberal Accounts of Globalisation

(1) Roland Robertson

Although globalisation has developed rapidly in the information age, according to Robertson, it has a significant pre-history. Roland Robertson argues that there have been five phases of globalisation. He suggests that the *germinal phase* occurred between 1400 and 1750 with the rise in

Europe of a scientific understanding of human beings place in the universe, to some extent at the expense of a religious one. Driven by curiosity and the desire for wealth and power European traders and armies carved out world empires. Superior technology gave them a navigational and military advantage. As far as Robertson is concerned the germinal phase largely pre-dates capitalism although the economic motive played a role in it.

The second phase, the *incipient phase* (1750–1875) saw the establishing of modern nation states and, crucially, their conflictual and competitive relations in the international field. The third phase, the *take-off phase* (1875–1925), the conceptualisation of the world in terms of four globalizing reference points

○ the individual

○ the nation-state

○ an international system of societies

○ and a single humanity (initially, gendered as masculine)

According to Robertson, these concepts became increasingly adopted and applied as guides to behaviour throughout the world. He also observes that international sporting and cultural links also increased during the third phase. The fourth phase, the *struggle for hegemony* (1925–1969) saw further trends towards internationalization, such as the founding of the League of Nations and the UN but also ideological-military struggle for predominant influence over, if not control of, the world. The fifth phase, the *uncertainty phase* (1969–1990s . . . onwards) is characterised by a rising awareness of the globe as a social entity and attempts to define rights and identities, for instance, individual and communal, with reference to universal humanity (no longer unequally gendered).

The third phase is crucial in defining the basic elements of globalisation because it established what Robertson sees as the four main points of reference in the '*global field*'. These reference points bear comparison with the levels of action/identity indicated in the previous section and in two cases – individual and nation-state – the same term is used. However, Robertson is less concerned to state that other levels of action can be a check on globalisation than to stress that the values of individualism and nationalism have become increasingly adopted globally and that the universalisation of these values is central to the process of globalisation.

Robertson's fourth phase sees developments beyond the merely international, narrowly defined and may be preliminary to globalisation. In his scheme and in general usage, the term 'international' indicates relations between national states and is a global system of relations although falling short of the substantial 'pooling' of national powers and sovereignty that developed globalism would seem to require. He regards bodies which go beyond practical cooperation between nations to seeking to promote and implement universal values as tending towards the global. The United Nations is the most prominent example of these.

Robertson's fifth phase, is one in which a genuinely global dimension is considered to have emerged both in practical terms and in terms of people having developed a global consciousness. Now an awareness of a common humanity with shared basic human rights occurs across the globe.

Although Robertson considers that the global field as indicated by the above four reference points has been emerging for most of the twentieth century, he argues that it is only in the last quarter of a century or so that globalisation has actually occurred. Globalisation is characterised both by specific developments – such as a globalisation of the media and aspects of consumption – and an awareness that this is happening. Only very recently has a widely shared 'consciousness' of global identity emerged. A global consciousness goes beyond internationalism – which is based on distinct nations acting together – to an awareness of processes that transcend national boundaries.

Thus, globalisation can be seen to be occurring in so far as pollution or nuclear proliferation are seen in planetary terms; or in so far as a major economic or financial crisis is conceptualised in global terms.

Robertson argues that globalisation began prior to modern capitalism and does not single capitalism out as its only or major cause. His approach to explaining globalisation is pluralistic and in so far as it is sociological at all more resembles Weber than Marx. His emphasis on consciousness and values in the development of globalisation is rather culturalist but he also stresses the role of nation states in exploring and 'connecting up' parts of the world and he acknowledges the importance of technology in making globalisation possible.

Robertson's historical account of the development of globalisation gives a central place to human rights and to the development of a global humanistic consciousness. To that extent it is a culturalist account. While this reflects a major theme in contemporary global politics and culture, it is also one of profound concern to Robertson himself. His cautious optimism that the global level of consciousness and action could generate an extension of human rights is one of the more positive interpretations of globalisation and contrasts sharply with most Marxist accounts which see scant prospects for a serious and substantial commitment to human rights in the face of the self-interested dominance of the multinationals. However, Robertson himself is in no doubt that it will be immensely difficult to implement human rights universally and always a struggle to maintain them (Conversation with the author: 2000).

Robertson refutes the criticism that he is suggesting that non-Western nations are bound to succumb to Western culture. He clearly sees the cultural values underlying human rights as universally human. Otherwise, he accepts that some nations may seek to define themselves as different from and independent of the West. However, he argues that in doing so they necessarily 'relativise' themselves by having to define themselves in relation to the West. However, the view that non-Western 'others', define themselves to a considerable and meaningful extent in transnational religious-cultural terms is a cogent one. There is a sense in which the international community of Islam, despite some deep differences and divisions, represents an alternative frame of reference to global humanism. Huntington (1996) divides the world into distinct and not necessarily compatible cultures in which context an ideology of human rights may be less than overwhelming.

Malcolm Waters summarises four key substantial propositions about globalisation from Robertson's work:

1. globalisation has already happened and is accelerating
2. new concepts are required to analyse globalisation
3. the process is reflexive and cultural in character
4. 'globalisation follows the path of its inexorable logic' (Waters: 46).

Giddens would probably have little difficulty agreeing with the first three of those propositions although he might stress factors other than the cultural structure globalisation. If the fourth factor implies any evolutionary inevitability, then, Giddens would reject it as he rejects all evolutionary and 'inevitablist' schemes. Giddens sees globalisation as the outcome of a variety of processes and events and as a negotiated process in which both globalisation and the management of it are contested.

(2) Anthony Giddens

Whereas Robertson writes in the style of a cultural and political historian, Giddens explains globalisation in more characteristically sociological terms. However, despite Robertson's culturalist inclinations, both are pluralist in their approach to causal explanations. As he does in explaining the emergence of modernity, Giddens adopts a *multi-dimensional* approach to explaining globalisation and argues that four main factors underly its development:

1) Capitalism

2) Industrialism (including technology)

3) The inter-state system, i.e., relations of nations

4) Militarism

In effect, for Giddens, globalisation is modernity writ large – although the dominant, Western, version of globalisation can be resisted. Two of the three factors he cites in explaining modernity – capitalism and industrialism – also explain globalisation. A third, militarism is simply a routinised ability to wage war – the latter being the third factor he mentions in the formation of modernity. The fourth factor – the inter-state system – is different and he makes the point that is central to Robertson's analysis – that the nation-states of the world have increasingly, albeit with great difficulty, moved to act together in a regional and global context. Giddens gives particular emphasis to the convergence of several of the factors mentioned above in the form of the highly nationalistic, industrialised, militarised and bureaucratised European nation states whose expansionist activities began to bind the globe together. He also points out the relevancy of a historically contingent factor – that the long period of relative peace in Europe in the nineteenth century enabled the attention and resources of the European nations to be turned outwards to wider possibilities. One can add, that being an island and naval power were related contingencies crucial to the major role Britain played in the earlier stages of globalisation. Now, the process is profoundly influenced, some would say dominated, by American commercial and political-military power.

In differentiating capitalism from industrialism, Giddens deliberately distances himself from Marxist interpretations of globalisation which strongly argue that the character of globalisation is defined by capitalism. While agreeing that capitalists control much industrial technology, Giddens points out that technology has important functions and effects regardless of whether it is owned by capital or by the state. Thus he stresses the extent to which modern technology of communication and information compresses time-space relations and sees this as a major feature of the development and character of globalisation. Historically, he sees nation-states as playing a major role in the development of a more global social system – sometimes through the use of military means (points 3 and 4). In contemporary global society, it is the institutionalised military dominance of the United States, usually supported by Britain and to a greater or lesser extent by other Western powers, that significantly underpinned the intervention of the United Nations (e.g. in East Timor) and NATO (e.g. in Kosovo) in various parts of the world. While NATO is a regional not a global organisation, its intervention was presented to the world, including the UN, in terms of the protection of fundamental human rights. It should be said that this claim was received with much scepticism as well as support.

Although Giddens's account of the development of globalisation gives less causal emphasis to the universal ideals that Robertson sees as relevant, he has increasingly turned to issues of value and identity in his more recent work. At the least, he is saying that however globalisation happened, we had better manage it constructively and with humanity or the consequences will be formidably dangerous – the risk side of late modernity. In his tract on political philosophy and policy, *The Third Way* (1998), he advocates that nations develop a 'cosmopolitanism' which embraces their own cultural diversity and which reaches beyond national boundaries to share in meeting the needs of common humanity. He has also given increasing attention to ecological issues. Aware that the causes and effects of potential ecological problems do not stop at national boundaries, he considers that adopting a global perspective is a matter of self-interest as well as humanitarianism. However, Giddens is a realist and has a sharp sense of the risks and dangers brought by late modernity. He counsels care and responsibility at the global as well as the national level:

> Globalizing processes have transferred powers away from nations and into depoliticized global space. Yet like any other social environment, or even more so given its universal importance, this new space needs regulation, the introduction of rights and obligations: 'ubi societas, ibi ius', 'wherever there is society there should be laws'.
>
> (1998:141)

Giddens's description of the character of globalisation resonates strongly with his modernisation theory. He indicates three major characteristics of globalisation: time-space distanciation; disembedding; and reflexivity. The first — in effect, the 'shrinkage' of the problems of time and distance involved in communication is of immense consequences but fairly unproblematic. Disembedding refers to the way local cultures and practices are overturned by wider, national or global mechanisms, such as a national or regional currency or global television network. This point raises two important issues relative to Giddens theorisation of globalisation. First, Giddens both emphasises that globalisation can be resisted or otherwise negotiated at various levels but that globalisation is, nevertheless, an accomplished fact. The two points are not incompatible. Reference back to Figure 7.1 showing the levels of action involved in negotiating globalisation illustrates that these levels are part of the overall globalisation process (the table is not directly derived from Giddens but is consistent with his theory). The second issue relates to Giddens's use of the terms tradition, modern and late modern. He indicates that the traditional can be threatened by the modern/late modern. Is he, then, despite his severe refutation of evolutionary theory sneaking in some evolutionary theory of his own? The answer is 'no'. He is quite clear that the contemporary world mixes the traditional, modern and late-modern in unpredictable ways. The traditional can be reinvented or reasserted — as it has been in certain ways in some Muslim countries. In recognising the variety and difference of late modernity Giddens is in rare agreement with postmodernism. So, although Giddens sees as a matter of historical fact rather than inevitablity, a world being reforged by the forces of (late) modernity, his explanation of how it happened is pluralistic and his description of the outcome is still of a plural world.

The last point brings up the issue of reflexivity which is at the core of all Giddens's social theory. Globalisation is a reflexive process in the sense that human beings consciously review and build upon the past, including its technology. It is also reflexive in the Beck/Giddens sense that globalisation can be 'risky' and strike back with perhaps unforeseen or disregarded dangerous consequences (1994). Finally, it is reflexive because people think about it and — as Giddens constantly suggests — they better had!

Marxist Accounts of Globalisation

Marxists consider that the contemporary world is primarily the product of capitalism and that globalisation is defined by capitalism i.e., it is capitalist globalisation. Immanuel Wallerstein uses the term 'capitalist world system' rather than that of globalisation. The term 'global capitalism' is also widely used by Marxists and some non-Marxists. This indicates that, while the causes of globalisation may be diverse, globalisation takes much of its character from capitalist institutions, values and lifestyles.

From the beginning, Marxist theory described the capitalist search for markets and profits as potentially global in scope. As early as 1848, Marx and Engels comment in *The Communist Manifesto* that the 'discovery of America, the rounding of the Cape ... (t)he East Indian and Chinese markets' opened up fresh ground for the rising bourgeoisie (79). They saw the dominance of capitalism in terms which seem as relevant now as they were then:

The bourgeoisie has through its exploitation of the world market given a cosmopolitan character to production and consumption in every country ... All old-established national industries have been destroyed or are daily being destroyed. They are dislodged by new industries, whose introduction becomes a life and death question for all civilised nations, by industries that no longer work up indigenous raw materials, but raw materials drawn from the remotest zones; industries whose products are consumed, not only at home, but in every quarter of the globe In place of the old wants, satisfied by the products of the country, we find new wants, requiring for their satisfaction the products of distant lands and climes. In place of the old local and national seclusion and self-sufficiency, we have intercourse in every direction, universal interdependence of nations. And as in material, so also in intellectual production ...

The bourgeoisie, by rapid improvement of all instruments of production, by the immensely facilitated means of communication, draws all, even the most barbarian, nations into civilization ... In one word, it creates a world after its own image.

(From *Manifesto of the Communist Party*: 35–6)

So much of what is often thought of as typical of contemporary globalisation is present here that it is tempting to decide that globalisation is not new at all. There is some truth in this proposition. As was discussed above, Roland Robertson traces the development of what has now become globalisation over many centuries and many commentators, not least Marx and Engels, recognise an historically strong global tendency in capitalism. Marx was much more accurate in his analysis of how capitalists behave than he appears to have been about how the working class behave or in his analysis of the likely (inevitable?) breakdown of capitalism. While the working class may, in the longer term, have lacked the militancy Marx had anticipated, capitalists continue to scour the globe for profit. They seem relatively undeterred by the undoubted risks and uncertainties of the system they have created.

Writing in 1991, Wallerstein proposes three elements in 'world systems theory'. These are:

1. that the most appropriate unit of study of social or societal behaviour is a 'world system';
2. that the capitalist world system must be understood in terms of its historical development;
3. that the world system we live in is capitalist and its main characteristics are derived from this (see below).

As far as point one is concerned, it is common ground now for many sociologists of widely differing approaches to accept a world or global level of societal analysis. Similarly, however, sociologists define the causes and character of globalisation, there is virtual consensus that the global societal level has emerged over a considerable period of time – Wallerstein wants to place the beginnings with the spread of commercial capitalism in the sixteenth century. As we have seen, disagreement emerges over the extent to which the 'world system' or 'global system' is capitalist, with Giddens, in particular, arguing that other factors contribute to globalisation. Wallerstein's emphasis is economic and the following are some of the main characteristics of the capitalist world-economy:

the ceaseless accumulation of capital is its driving force;

the view that the capitalist world economy began in one part of the globe (largely Europe) and later expanded to to the entire globe via a process of successive 'incorporations';

the existence in this world system of hegemonic states, each of whose periods of full or uncontested hegemony has, however, been relatively brief;

the fundamental importance of racism and sexism as organising principles of the system.

(266)

I have not included in the above Wallerstein's particular division of capitalism into core–periphery because it has been largely superseded by the fact that capitalism is now so geographically flexible that its centres of power and wealth can shift very quickly and are, in any case, now much less easy to locate in given places. An obvious difference between Giddens and Wallerstein is that the former's account of globalisation is pluralistic and the latter's is monocausal. Otherwise, obvious as it may seem, Giddens and, especially Robertson see substantial positive characteristics in the Western way of life – to the point of wanting to see some retained in a global context – and Wallerstein sees overwhelmingly negative aspects. On the one hand Robertson can celebrate the slow but definitive development of human rights theory and practice emanating from the West whereas Wallerstein can cite the exploitation of women and black people, including slavery, the brutalities of which are among the collective crimes of humanity.

Marxists and some other radicals are highly sceptical about the claim to be defending human rights which the United States and other Western powers have recently used to justify intervention in various part of the world. They argue that 'peace-keeping' forces and 'humanitarian intervention' often masks motives of material self-interest. John Pilger, the campaigning journalist, argued that the United Nations' intervention in East Timor was less about protecting the local population, including their democratic rights, and far more about securing Western interests, including investment (*The Guardian*, 21.9.99). For him this is just one recent episode in the long running story of Western dominance and exploitation of the rest of the world.

Globalisation: Economic, Cultural and Political

Although for the sake of clarity economic, cultural and political globalisation are presented separately, in practice, they greatly overlap and interact. Thus, a world economic boom or recession can affect national politics – perhaps even bringing down a government; exposure to the liberal cultural values expressed in the Western media may challenge the authoritarian norms and structures of some more traditional societies; the pro human rights activities of the United Nations cannot be categorised as exclusively political or cultural and their effects also have potential to transform across all areas of life.

The reason for considering economic, cultural and political globalisation in that order is that the economic and cultural are often considered to have become much more intertwined, almost to the point of being indistinguishable in the late modern period. In my view this observation has some substance and is easier to explore with the economic and cultural sections running consecutively. Political globalisation is considered last because it is at the political level at which decisions are made which seek to regulate and change society. In general, liberals believe that a democratic polity can achieve this effectively and Marxists are much more sceptical. How these views pan out at the global level is discussed in the remainder of this chapter and in particular in the section on political globalisation.

Economic and Financial Globalisation

For economic and financial globalisation to be occurring, a clear and substantial trend to economic and financial interactions occurring at a transglobal level, rather than simply at an inter-national or 'between states' level would be apparent. For instance, there would be an increase in the production and consumption of commodities such as cars (e.g., Ford's 'Mondeo' and 'Focus') or trainers (e.g., brands like 'Nike' and 'Reebok') widely across the world rather than simply in a small number of typically neighbour nation-states.

Although the terms multinational company and transnational company are sometimes used interchangeably, the term multinational will be used here. This is because the term transnational can be used to indicate that a company has become so decentralised in its operation in different markets that it no longer has a single, distinctive national headquarters. The term multinational does not imply such a stage of development but indicates that a company operates significantly across national boundaries. Particular indicators that a company has globalised, are the switching of production around the world to achieve efficiencies, and the production of different parts of a commodity in different countries – often geographically far apart.

Economic globalisation can be examined in terms of production, trade and consumption. However, before demonstrating globalisation in terms of quantitatively more production, trade and consumption of a global kind, it is important to understand in theoretical terms precisely what economic and financial globalisation mean and what is enabling them to occur. Manuel Castells directly and authoritatively addresses these issues.

Castells gives a clear statement of the crucial relationship of information technology to globalisation in *The Rise of the Network Society* – the first volume of his trilogy on the information age. It is control of the means of generating and using information that enables corporations to be, in their own terms, effective and successful and to exercise great power and influence over so many of the globe's inhabitants. In summary, it is the use of information technology in a global context that has produced a 'new economy' and, indeed, a new age – the information age:

> A new economy has emerged in the last two decades on a worldwide scale. I call it informational and global to identify its fundamental distinctive features and to emphasize their intertwining. It is *informational* because the productivity and competitiveness of units or agents in this economy (be it firms, regions, or nations) fundamentally depend on their capacity to generate, process and apply efficiently knowledge-based information. It is *global* because the core activities of production, consumption, and circulation, as well their components (capital, labor, raw materials, management, information, technology, markets) are organised on a global scale, either directly or through a network of linkages between economic agents. It is informational *and* global because, under the new historical conditions, productivity is generated through and competition is played out in a global network of interaction.
>
> (Castells, 1996:66)

The Globalisation of Production and Investment, Global Trade

For Castells, then, it is networks of information that shape globalisation.

The globalisation of production thesis predates Castells' recent work but it is one of the main aspects of the 'new economy' to which he refers. Proponents of this thesis argue that the production of goods and services is increasingly organised on a global basis by transnational companies. An important piece of evidence in support of this thesis is that the amount of Foreign Direct Investment – the money invested by one country in another – has greatly increased in recent years. Gill and Law (1988) state that between 1960 and 1979, it increased six-fold, and a comparable rate of increase was sustained during the 1980s and most of the 1990s. Figures from Eurostat show that in 1997 foreign companies invested a massive 63 billion dollars in Britain. Foreign investment is now behind virtually all of Britains car production and most of its electronics industry, including its computer related industry. It is indicative of the extent to which investment in production now often transcends geographical realities, that in 1997 US inward investment outstripped European investment into Britain by $9.4 to $5.1 billion. It has been well known from the outset of the recent acceleration of globalisation, that 'what the foreign investor gives, the foreign investor can take away'. This happened in 2000 when BMW, the German based owner of Rover withdrew from production of Rover cars at Longbridge, Birmingham. Similarly, when a foreign-owned computer firm was closed in Prime Minister Blair's own constituency, he conceded that there was nothing he could do about it. However the 1998 global financial crisis and economic down-turn did provoke worldwide discussion – as well as some modest action – on the issue of regulating global capitalism.

Britain is just as integrated into the global economy in terms of its Outward Direct Investment. In 1999, Britain invested 212 billion dollars abroad – more than the United States. In 2000, British Telecom was investing in countries as wide apart as Korea, Malaysia and the United States. In the latter case, BT made an alliance with the huge American based corporation AT and T after a similar planned arrangement with another huge American telecommunications company, MCI, had broken down. As well as the more established multinational companies such as BP and Lever Brothers, a number of privatised energy companies such as British Gas and Powergen have begun to invest in regions as far apart as the Middle East and Latin America. Incredibly, given its size, in 1998 the value of international takeovers by British companies exceeded that of any other including, for the first time, the United States. Of course a global capitalist system, requires capitalists and professionals with global expertise and this is contributing to the reshaping the global class system (see below).

Another strong indicator of the globalisation of production is the increase in world trade. Thus, between 1950 and 1997 the export of tradeable goods of OECD (Oganisation of Economic Cooperation and Development) countries rose from 7 to 17 percent of their GDP. Hurst and Thompson have argued that the late Victorian/early Edwardian period was one of comparable globalisation to the present (1996). However, Giddens cites figures which show that in 1911, the export of tradeable goods calculated on the same basis as above was 12 per cent, 5 per cent more than for the still war-ravaged 1950 OECD economy but 5 per cent less than for that of 1997 (1998). Giddens further points out that 'a much greater range of goods, including many forms of services, is tradeable now than was so a century ago. Far more countries are involved in mutual trading arrangements' (1998:30).

The concept of *McDonaldization* is associated with the globalisation of production and culture (Ritzer, 2000). According to Ritzer the McDonaldization of production – and society – involves the application of four basic principles: efficiency; calculability; uniformity/predictability and control through automation. These principles allow for the mass production of standardised products but also for some variation and have been employed by many multinationals as well as McDonald's – notably soft-drink, clothes and car-manufacturers.

A key economic-cultural question is to what extent does McDonaldization promote American/Western global hegemony and global conformity (see pp. 207–8).

Financial Globalisation

The crash of the world's major stock markets of 1998 was partly financial and partly economic in origin. Although seemingly more short-lived in its effects than was first anticipated, it had substantial implications for production, consumption and trade across the globe. Nothing demonstrates more sharply the potential global effects of information technology than the manipulations and gyrations of the global financial markets in the 1990s. What information technology does, is supply instant information and enable instant decision-making. In the context of financial markets that means that companies involved in currency investment/speculation can move in and out of a particular currency. If a company trader 'guesses right' vast amounts of money can be made. If several companies buy or sell a given currency in quantity, the economy of the relevant country may be undermined. As a result of such quasi-collective action, share and currency prices have sometimes swung wildly even within a few minutes and have, in general, become more volatile. It is worth recalling some of the financial crises that increased speculation has helped to precipitate. In 1993, the British pound was forced out of the European Exchange Mechanism as a result of massive selling precipitated by George Soros and other speculators. The government's attempt to defend the value of sterling cost billions of pounds. The Russian currency was devalued in 1998 following speculation and the currencies of several South East Asian and Latin American countries came under similar pressure with varying results. In the case of the Russian and some other currencies there was a genuine argument that the currency was overvalued but there is no doubt that the huge amount of money 'bet' on the fate of currencies contributed to destabilising them.

What has caused this instability in the world financial markets? Three factors can be cited. First, is the new technology which enables decisions to be taken and implemented much more quickly – to the extent of proving crucial to the amount of profit made. In John Urry's terms, financial *flows* can be implemented so rapidly that transactions can be completed virtually in real time across the globe. However, simply because technology makes a particular action possible does not make it inevitable – the rules of global financial trading could be changed to increase regulation of financial investment/speculation. Second, the sheer amount of money flowing in and out of currencies has greatly increased in recent years, with correspondingly greater risks of destabilising the economies of the relevant countries. Literally hundreds of banks and funds are involved in this activity which is regarded as a respectable way of employing clients' deposits. Third, currently (2000), the regulations allowing the flow of money in and out of most countries in the world are generally very liberal. Countries which experience large inflows followed by large and sudden outflows from either currencies, share markets or foreign loans, invariably run into considerable economic difficulty and sometimes hardship for their population, particularly the poor. On the other hand wealthy individual and corporate currency speculators stand to become fabulously rich. These circumstances illustrate why many consider that globalisation should be defined as *capitalist* globalisation.

Liberal/Social Democratic and neo-Marxist Approaches to Economic Globalisation

The classic nineteenth century liberal view of trade is that it should be 'free' i.e., that tariffs and protectionism are in principle a bad thing. The New Right revived the rhetoric of free trade in the 1980s but neither Thatcher's Britain nor Reagan's America did much by way of example to promote it. After the financial convulsions of 1998, most liberal reformist or social democratic opinion is that the world financial system needs closer and more effective regulation. The more radical would restructure the key institutions of world trade and finance with the purpose of achieving greater stability and equity between nations.

David Coate's *Models of Capitalism* (1999) is highly critical of more liberal models and advocates much more control and regulation. He argues for controls on the movement of capital – particularly large-scale, speculative and economically/socially disruptive movement, increased state control of investment decisions and taxation of financial speculation, and guaranteed global labour standards. If such policies of national protection have to be put in at the level of national government so be it. However, Coates does see a potential for international initiatives to achieve fairer conditions of work and trade (see p. 220).

Cultural Globalisation

In analysing cultural globalisation, it is helpful to begin with the established and broadest definition of culture as 'a way of life'. The question then becomes: what cultural experiences are being shared by the world's inhabitants, or at least many of them, that can be said to transcend national and even continental boundaries? The literature on globalisation offers two main responses to this question. One is that a global consciousness is developing based partly on a common sense of humanity and, to that extent, a base of shared cultural values, and the other is that a predatory global capitalist culture is developing. The first position is broadly liberal and the second neo-Marxist/postmodernist. Underlying the differing interpretations of culture of these positions is a disagreement about the nature of capitalism. There are many different views among liberals about how far capitalism should be regulated but all agree that 'the market' is necessary to choice and efficiency. Marxists and many postmodernists are much more critical of capitalism and often opposed to it. There is no need to develop the liberal position much further here as a version of it was presented in the section dealing with Robertson's approach to globalisation. Further, liberal concepts of culture are derived from the liberal concept of political and civil rights and freedom. Robertson's and similar arguments are continued in the section on liberal approaches to political globalisation in which it should become clear that cultural pluralism in the context of tolerance are liberal values and that a common criticism of liberal societies is their failure adequately to achieve them.

Robertson argues that after a long period of historical development certain common values and a common global awareness have recently developed. Humanism is the basic belief underlying these values which find their expression most importantly in a growing articulation of and commitment to universal human rights. Modern media bring immediate awareness of large-scale tragedy and disaster wherever they occur and governmental and public response is often felt and, to some extent, coordinated at an international level. Similarly, ethnic conflict of the kind that has occurred in Eastern Europe and Central Africa is now closely monitored by, among other agencies, the United Nations. The much more narrowly Western and military organisation, North Atlantic Treaty Organisation (NATO) controversially took the initiative in international intervention in Kosovo, with the stated aim of preventing 'ethnic cleansing' of Muslim Kosovans by Serbia. The messy outcome of that war which does not seem to have brought the two ethnic groups closer together indicates just how difficult it is to achieve the diffusion of humanistic values of the kind Robertson supports.

A second approach to understanding cultural globalisation – presented in detail below – is to see it as largely a product of the related information and communications revolutions discussed throughout this book. In this context what is mainly being considered is the global media and its effects – a favoured terrain of postmodernists, many of whom subscribe to the cultural globalisation thesis. An important related issue is the role of consumption in contemporary society. The relevant questions are whether the global media is dominated by a particular interest or ideological tendency or offers enhanced freedom of choice; what values underlie the global media; and what way or ways of life the global media fosters. It may, of course, be that the answers to these questions are complex. As far as other aspects of consumption are concerned, such as shopping, debate similarly focuses on issues of control and manipulation on the one hand and freedom and choice on the other. Considered from this wide vantage point, economic and financial globalisation are just as much part of cultural globalisation as the entertainment and leisure industries which are sometimes considered to be the producers of 'culture' more narrowly defined. This relationship is framed in Marxist terms by the stipulation that the economic base is always fundamental to (if not determinant of) the content of the cultural superstructure. In particular, traditional Marxists argue that the ideology of the dominant class will be strongly expressed through the main cultural institutions which today are the audio-visual media. In contrast, many capitalists themselves, such as Rupert Murdoch, and liberal-capitalist theorists regard the media as relatively open and democratic.

Postmodernist Theory and Cultural Globalisation

Since the collapse of East European communism, Marxist theory has become more diverse and less orthodox. Some theorists still sympathetic to aspects of Marxism have become better known under other labels such as postmodernist or poststructuralist. Thus, Fredric Jameson regards postmodernism as 'the culture of contemporary capitalism' and still works largely within a highly dynamic version of the Marxist paradigm supplemented by postmodern theory. Jean Baudrillard employs poststructuralist theory to deconstruct various texts of contemporary global society but his distrust of big metanarratives makes it difficult to locate him clearly in any political position. At times he seems to be describing a hyper-real global culture virtually resistant to any radical intervention. There are still other radical theorists critical of aspects of capitalist globalisation who would prefer not to think of themselves as Marxist at all but who have contributed to the critical debate on cultural globalisation. Some of these are referred to below.

The following are among the main points that radical critics of the left make of cultural globalisation under capitalism although not all would necessarily subscribe to every one. Each point is discussed in more detail later:

1. *The Profit Motive*

   Global capitalist culture is driven primarily by the desire of capital to make profit rather than the desire to produce something of inherent value (although the two motives are not necessarily incompatible);

2. *The Global Cultural Hegemony of the United States*

   The United States is by far the world's most powerful capitalist country. It is both the major producer, consumer, definer and beneficiary of the global culture of contemporary capitalism;

3. *The Meaninglessness of Style: A Superficial or 'Surface' Global Culture*

   Global capitalist culture is characterised by 'surface style' and image rather than 'substance' (it is a 'surface' culture in Baudrillard's term). This is because its prime concern is to sell commodities (see point 1) but also because it is possible to produce visual images of relatively far greater appeal than most commodities can 'really' deliver. However, the consumption of style fails to supply meaning, to satisfy;

4. *Hyper-reality*

   Some 'post' theorists, notably Baudrillard, go further than the position stated in Point 3. The world has become so saturated with signs and symbols that it is difficult to distinguish what many signals signify. Baudrillard argues that the '*sign-value*' of, for example, status, style and wealth 'means' more than the commodity (material) value. He uses the term *simulacra* to describe entities, including signs, which are detached from any 'real' referent. Thus, people may have 'relationships' with computerised images, characters from 'soaps', or dead pop or film stars. More generally, Baudrillard sees signs in postmodern society as floating free of their original referents and meanings, creating a world of 'hyper-reality'. Signs can be made or taken to mean almost anything. For example, it is quite common for advertisements to adopt and transform the meanings of items from popular culture such as the lyrics of pop-songs.

Further, some critics regard capitalist culture as now so based on profit/consumption which in turn depends on hype through advertising or commercialised popular entertainment (both sometimes using computer generated images) that it has become 'hyper-real' i.e., hyped excessively and absurdly beyond any firm reference to reality;

5. *The Convergence of 'High' and Popular Culture: The Greater Personalisation of Style/Identity*

The relentless search for profit in contemporary capitalist society means that products of so-called 'high culture' as well as popular culture may be *commodified* i.e., marketed and sold for profit. Products of 'high culture' such as the work of 'The Three Tenors' may be processed and performed in a popular mode if the mass market for them is there. In part this is what is meant by the postmodern statement that there has been a loss of distinction between high and popular culture. In so far as globalisation facilitates this trend by opening up mass markets for the products of popularised or 'dumded down' high culture, the two processes can be considered complementary;

6. *The Collapse of the Cultural into the Economic*

The sheer dominance of capitalist values in production and consumption alongside the erosion of traditional values has resulted in a culture in which value is a function of perceived economic worth or stylistic effect. Andy Warhol's reproductions of the Mona Lisa – '30 is better than 1' – can be read as an ironic comment on the 'total commercialisation' of cultural values, especially in the area of high art. Whereas in the 1960s the styles of youth subcultures – embracing music, dress, argot and demeanour – could convincingly be interpreted as originally *resisting* dominant values and lifestyle, by the 1990s style had come to seem all there was – again, the meaninglessness of style. If this seemed an acceptance of impotence it should be remembered that the spectacular subcultures of the 1960s and 1970s had themselves apparently changed little;

7. *Critiqueing Western Constructions of the 'Other' (as 'inferior')*

Edward Said's book, *Orientalism*, describes a wide variety of stereotypes and related fantasies constructed in the West of the peoples of the East or Orient. Image of orientals as evil, mysterious, exotic and even as semi-human abounded. In an interesting framing of Said's text summarised below, Stuart Hall offers a critical poststructuralist influenced account of the West's images of the 'rest' (1992).

It is perhaps worth reiterating that liberal accounts of cultural globalisation are generally less pessimistic than postmodern perspectives. Robertson has a fundamentally humanistic vision of the potential of globalisation and Anthony Giddens sees positive aspects to it. However, for the moment the negative critique of globalised culture will be developed.

Comment on Postmodern Theory of Globalisation

Points 1 and 2: Profit, American Hegemony and Globalisation

To return to the first two points given in the list above, it is not a matter of much disagreement that the driving force behind the production of global culture is the profit motive and that primarily American companies are in the van of this process. Leslie Sklair identifies a basically American ideology of *consumerism* as a new global ideology (1996). The dominance of United States multinational companies is especially marked in the area of popular media, communications and entertainment – areas particularly suited to influencing behaviour through images and ideas. Companies such as Disney and Warner in film production; the Murdoch controlled News Corporation in the production of news, sports programmes and popular entertainment; and

Bloomberg in financial news and analysis reach global audiences with a predominantly American-Western construction of the world. Films such as *Independence Day* and *The Patriot* are shown in major cities throughout the world although local censorship may be exercised, as in the case of mainland China. Of course, it is part of the process of globalisation that these companies have branches in various parts of the world and, to some extent will acknowledge and even accomodate local cultures – especially if they see the prospect of profit in doing so. However, global blockbuster films and television productions are usually set in America and to that extent reflect American norms, values and styles. In Gramsci's terms, American culture is globally hegemonic – a term which indicates cultural ascendancy but not total dominance. American produced advertisements as well as programmes are potent carriers of cultural messages, both overt and hidden. The overt message is usually, 'buy this product' which, if reiterated often enough helps to reinforce a culture of consumerism – but, as will be discussed below, the 'hidden persuaders' in advertisements can also have powerful effects.

Point 3 and 4: From 'Superficiality' to 'Hyper-reality': Hoggart to Baudrillard

The third point raised above concerns the quality of American dominated global culture and in particular that it is superficial and lacks depth. This judgement has recently been presented in postmodernist terms by Fredric Jameson and Baudrillard but reservations about American culture have a long history among British critics. It is worth a detour to illustrate this point. Around the turn of the century Americans who had made their wealth through business and commerce were beginning to be seen as desirable marriage partners by some of the British landed elite, particularly the more impoverished. A little inconsistently, given that the appeal of such marriages was largely money – the view was commonly expressed both in literature and in 'high' society that American culture was 'commercial', materialistic and crude. These judgements were based on the assumed values of Britain's social elite and would be much harder to justify today.

Nevertheless, unease about the quality of American culture has persisted among some British intellectuals. To suggest a similarity in the work of the dry and measured British critic, Richard Hoggart, the extravagant French intellectual, Jean Baudrillard, may seem to stretch a point but, in fact, their target is basically the same, the superficiality of capitalist culture, particularly as confected by America. In *The Uses of Literacy* (1957), Richard Hoggart voiced his concern about the corrupting effects American commercial 'pop' culture might have both on British working class culture and on British youth. The following are brief extracts from Hoggart's reflections on the milk-bar culture of the 1950s:

> ... most of the customers are boys aged between fifteen and twenty with drape-suits, picture ties, and an American slouch ... compared with the pub around the corner, this is all a peculiar thin and palid form of dissipation, a sort of spiritual dry rot amid the odour of boiled milk. Many of the customers – their clothes, their hair-styles, their facial expressions all indicate – are living to a large extent in a myth-world compounded of a few simple elements which they take to be those of American life.

(1957:204–5)

Although Hoggart has more recently conceded that he is 'elitist' if that term means making distinctions between cultural creations on the basis of their quality, here he is comparing American culture unfavourably not to British elite culture but to the way of life of the British working class. Much of his book is a celebration of that culture and a defence of it against the threatening tide of American culture. In the short term, Hoggart was perhaps worrying excessively. The British working class youth demonstrated a muscular, and perhaps too macho, vitality and originality in creating a series of largely indigenous youth subcultures which reverberated across the Atlantic just as the noise of the 1950s American rock-and-rollers had done in reverse direction.

In the longer run Hoggart proved highly perceptive. Modern/postmodern culture does tend to undermine traditional cultures and this has certainly happened in the case of British industrial working class culture. Even the largely symbolic expressions of solidarity and macho toughness of, among others, the skinhead and football 'hoolie', youth subcultures became taken up and transformed by media and sports figures into a commercially saleable and culturally shallow 'new laddishness'. Hoggart's comments on 'milk-bar culture' and the lack of depth and 'showiness' of modern American culture in general may be phrased differently and more nostalgically than those of postmodern thinkers, but the basic judgement seems to be very similar:

> the milk-bars indicate at once, in the nastiness of their modernistic knick-knacks, their glaring showiness, an aesthetic breakdown so complete that in comparison with them, the layout of the living-rooms in some of the poor homes from which the customers come seems to speak of a tradition of balanced and civilized living.
>
> (*Ibid*: 204)

Whereas Hoggart is robust in observation and judgement, postmodern thinkers are often ironic and oblique. Consciously or not, they are perhaps reflecting the erosion of a clear basis on which aesthetic and moral judgements can be made – a situation which they have helped to bring about. Postmodernity destroys or disembeds and rearranges tradition – often according to commercial criteria – but it has nothing that carries the authority of tradition to put in its place. A pub fitted in artificial Tudor or Victorian style – or, just as likely, both – is not quite like 'the real thing' – but if few notice, does it 'really' matter? The perceived absence of anything convincing to put in the place of postmodern society and culture hits ex-Marxists particularly hard, if for no other reason than until recently they regarded communism in some form or other as the only serious and plausible alternative system to capitalism. Long before the collapse of Soviet style communism, many Marxists had begun to face the possibilty that the future might not be as they wished and that capitalism might survive for the foreseeable future, if not indefinitely. As was discussed in an earlier chapter, during the inter-war period, most members of the Frankfurt School became convinced that the revolutionary potential of the working class had been neutralised by consumerism.

The work of the French postmodernist Baudrillard can be used to illustrate the third and fourth point in the above list – the surface quality or depthlessness and hyper-reality of capitalist global culture. Screen images inherently lack depth and Baudrillard extends this into a metaphor for the cultural depthlessness of postmodern culture. Baudrillard is particularly noted for the mix of despair, irony and jokiness which he has exchanged for his earlier more political Marxism. Baudrillard's despair – if one can use such a precise a term of so deliberately elusive man – is apparent in his view that capitalist consumer culture has achieved such a degree of acceptance, not least at a popular level – that there is no real prospect of it being successfully challenged and replaced. Capitalist culture is all the more powerful in that it achieves its hold through the manipulation of image rather than through the delivery of substantial advantages to consumers. The status of brand names becomes more important than price and quality, surface appearance more important than depth of performance.

A reference to Baudrillard's wider social theory helps to explain his emphasis on the media. Baudrillard argues that 'organic' social life has declined to the point of disappearance in postmodernity. By this notion he seems to mean something akin to Habermas's concept of the public sphere. The mass media itself has largely caused this development. Debate, opinion and policy are now 'mediated' at one remove from the people who are reconstituted as 'the mass' of postmodern society. In one of his less obscure remarks he states that 'the masses are ... made up of this useless hyperinformation which claims to enlighten them' (1985:580).

The media enables hype to occur and underlies the construction of 'hyper-reality'. Hyper-reality is the imagined and hyped world initially generated by the media but which has become more real in most people's minds and lives than, let us say, the education of their children or the quality of their water supply – and, certainly, than hunger in the poor world.

In a typically ironic *tour de force*, Baudrillard has asserted that American society has become so saturated by hyper-reality that it is now a 'utopia' and 'less real' than Disneyland. Following the 'logic' of Baudrillard's argument and of some postmodern accounts of globalisation, one might question whether Europe is less real than Euro-Disneyland or Japan less real than Tokyo-Disneyland which attracts the highest number of visitors in the world. It is perhaps not the best approach to Baudrillard to pursue his ideas with rigorous logic. His intention is to discredit postmodern culture as much through mockery as through reason. He fights with calculated absurdity and seeming irrationality a capitalist global culture that manipulates desire through seductive imagery. When he asserts that in late modernity the body has become an extension of network television, we smile – but with uneasy recognition. Whereas Foucault describes techniques of control and surveillance with sobriety, Baudrillard does so with a sense of the absurd. What little hope Baudrillard has of the undermining of postmodern culture is through its *implosion*. This might occur when enough people begin to appreciate its absurdity and empty pretensions.

It is tempting to regard Baudrillard's 'description' of American culture as wildly exaggerated. However, in what would doubtless appeal to him as a hilariously ironic development, Disney Corporation has created an entire town in Florida aimed at providing an idyllic lifestyle for those who can afford to visit or stay there for sometimes extended periods. In this case it does seem possible to argue that the line between what is Disney and what is real has become blurred – or, in Baudrillard's terms, Disney is now the dominant definer of American reality.

John Hannigan describes the 'two key strategies' on which this and many similar sites are based: to create an aura of fantasy, wellbeing and delight and – shades of Foucault – to achieve a largely hidden system of surveillance and control:

> Whereas shopfronts along traditional highstreets are often diverse, and compete with one another visually, the retail establishments in fantasy cities are uniform and harmonious, suggesting consensus and contentment. But reassuring as it may be, Disney-inspired architecture is also blatantly commercial – a fusion of consumerism, entertainment and popular culture ...
>
> Thomas Vonier, an architect who has consulted widely with the US State Department on security matters, cites the Disney theme parks as one of the best contemporary examples of what he terms 'large-scale urban control zones'. At Disney World in Florida, visitors' movements are discreetly but firmly directed by a combination of recorded voices, robots in human form and employees. To ensure that guests are directed away from or towards specific locations, Disney uses a combination of technology ... and physical barriers such as pools, fountains and flower gardens.
>
> (*Observer*: 28.11.98:7)

Are the feelings and experiences generated in such locations any more 'real' than the 'artificial' environments which generate them? Baudrillard and many other critics of contemporary American culture clearly fear that they may not be or, if they are, then, 'the real' has become almost unimaginably superficial. The same concern seems to lie behind John Hannigan's reference to the juxtaposition in Cleveland, Ohio, of the multimillion leisure complex, Playhouse Square, and the adjacent inner city where 40% of the local population continue to live below the poverty line. A society in which far more emotion seems to be spent on, admittedly increasingly cleverly executed cartoon characters than the poor, may seem at once hyper-real and lacking in human imagination.

Point 5: The Convergence of 'High' and 'Popular' Culture

The fifth suggested characteristic of cultural globalisation is a convergence of high and popular culture. Like the third and fourth points, this is an issue raised by postmodernist theory but also has application to globalisation theory. Again, what may be occurring in respect to this suggested convergence may be as much a matter of appearance as reality. Two points are commonly made about how the gap between high and popular culture is being closed or apparently being closed. First, the still relatively few cases where a classical artist performing classical work, such as the violinist Nigel Kennedy, has popular appeal, then, s/he is likely to be given similar commercial and media exposure as a pop artist. In Kennedy's case it was his support of Aston Villa football club that was relentlessly plugged to establish his credentials as a man of the people. However, it is invariably the case that where such conflations of high/pop art occur it is more accessible and more easily 'consumed' items of classical repertoire that are marketed. This is the case with the commercial radio station, 'Classic FM' and some critics fear that Radio 3, the BBC's classical music station will have to 'dumb down' its output in order to compete. Most classical repertoire in its full form is not accessed by most of the public.

A second and related way in which the gap between high and popular culture is apparently being closed is the increasing interest in sport and popular entertainment shown by the middle class generally, as well as by some classical artists. Professional football is an obvious case in point and it has almost become *de rigueur* for leading politicians to sport their popular credentials by attending the finals of major international competitions. Global events such as the World Cup Final are typically preluded by an internationally known opera singer and attended by a clutch of Prime Ministers – some of whom appear to use such occasions to catch a bit of extra sleep!

Postmodernists argue that traditional cultural distinctions are breaking down among ordinary people as well as among celebrities. If so, this would represent a significant shift in culture away from the traditional markers of class towards more personalised or individualised cultural practices which nevertheless are formed in an intensely commercial global environment. Bo Reimer's *Youth Culture and Modern Lifestyles* (1995) studies the extent to which Swedish youth has adopted postmodern attitudes and behaviour, by indulging in both high and popular cultural activities and, relatedly, the extent to which their cultural styles had become more personalised and detached from class and possibly gender. His findings give only partial support for the postmodern position. He found that middle class youth was much more likely to indulge in both high and popular cultural activities, such as going to the theatre and to the cinema. Working class youth was much less likely to do the former. Reimer's findings resonate with what appears to have happened in Britain where middle class 'laddishness' seems to be built on a superficial appropriation of the style of the working class macho lad without any comparable trend occurring in the other direction. Various media figures such as David Gower and even Gary Lineker – once thought to be football's equivalent of Cliff Richard – and many younger comedians have adopted this highly saleable image. However, such attempts to create a mass audience do not mean that there are not significant class based differences in these audiences in terms of their cultural inclinations and pursuits.

A Report title *Crossing the Line* published in Britain in 1999 produced similar findings to those of Reimer on the relationship of the class background of young people, between the ages of 11 and

14, and their tendency to be actively interested in 'high art' such as going to the theatre or art galleries (Gulbenkian Foundation). Significantly, the Report found that white middle or upper class girls were the most likely to develop a taste for high culture whereas these pursuits scarcely occurred to many poorer children. The finding are similar to Reimer's, who found that the two groups most different in their leisure/cultural pursuits were middle class girls and working class boys.

Nevertheless, Reimer found an increasing amount of *differentiation* and *heterogeneity* in youth culture as young people 'picked' and 'mixed' from a wide range of cultural styles and options. The variety of style and the speed at which it changed, notably in clothes and music, made it difficult to link it with deeper structural socio-economic differences. Reimer emphasised that the role of the global media in presenting a vast range of cultural images and options was central to this development. Reimer also found that generally young people found no contradiction between enjoying themselves – hedonism – and taking moral positions on such issues as the environment. The widely held traditional Christian view which has lingered into modernity – that pleasure is somehow wrong – had eroded. Again, in presenting consumption as good – perhaps as the greatest good – the global media had eroded the Puritan ethic which commended work, moral restraint, saving, investment and more work.

What worries many radical critics, not just postmodernists, about the alleged collapse of high culture into popular culture is that it will no longer be possible to use the principles of high culture to criticise commercial culture and the status quo. This is another dimension of postmodernist angst – that capitalism has achieved by consumerism what it could not do by force.

Point 6: The Collapse of the Cultural into the Economic (Jameson)

The sixth point made above about cultural globalisation is implicit in the other five.

Postmodernism is the culture of late capitalism and it is a culture in which everything, or virtually everything is for sale or potentially for sale – the cultural becomes defined in terms of economic value. This argument is widely held among critics of American led globalisation but it is particularly associated with Fredric Jameson. In the following quotation, he makes the point with particular reference to the global reach of American economic power:

> What is indeed the justification for distinguishing these two levels of the economic and the cultural, when in the United States today … the cultural – the entertainment business – is, along with food, one of our most important economic exports, and one the American government is prepared to go to great lengths to defend, as witness the struggles within the Gatt and Nafta negotiations.
>
> … (T)he theory of postmodernity affirms a gradual de-differentiation of these levels, the economic itself gradually becomes cultural, all the while the cultural gradually becomes economic. Image society and advertising can no doubt document the gradual transformation of commodities into libidinal images of themselves, into well-nigh cultural products; whereas the dissolution of high culture and the simultaneous intensification of investment in mass cultural commodities may be enough to suggest that, whatever was the case at earlier stages and moments of capitalism (where the aesthetic was very precisely a sanctuary and a refuge from business and the state), today no enclaves are left in which the commodity form does not reign supreme.
>
> (Jameson in Jameson and Miloshi *ed.*, 1998)

Jameson makes his argument clearly enough but two points merit further elaboration. First, his comment about 'the gradual transformation of commodities into libidinal images of themselves' is a statement to the effect that the use of enticing, often sexual imagery to sell any kind of commodity has developed to such an extent that art is now at the service of commerce. Of course, this statement is open to criticism, but for the moment let us concentrate on illustrating it. This is easy to do: practically everyone has witnessed sexuality being use to sell products from cars to coffee, from icecream to holidays. Other forms of artistically clever and accomplished images than the overtly sexual are frequently used in advertisements and these are also often of a 'libidinal' nature in that they are aimed at enticing emotions that have little directly to do with the product itself. Thus, computers are sometimes advertised as though ownership will enhance status or masculine one-upmanship.

The second point to be raised for comment here relates to Jameson's remarkable and startling statement that 'today no enclaves are left in which the commodity form does not reign supreme'. He is arguing here that whereas in the past, artists often criticised the values and practice of business and government, now they are on the payroll of business along with nearly everybody else. Jameson states his case without qualification and almost invites the criticism of exaggeration. Again, however, let us illustrate his remarks prior to critiqueing them. There are certainly innumerable examples of artists who while seeming radical and rebellious soon get highly involved with and apparently compromised by the monetary rewards of their work. Thus, Bob Dylan, the Beatles and the Rolling Stones all sang some very radical lyrics and became very rich on the sales of them. By the time Oasis came along, rebellion patently seemed to be no more than a fleeting, rather personalised gesture – 'pissing in the wind' as Liam might have put it in a more original moment. The point Jameson is making is not to do with the conservatism of age but the conservatism of money. He argues that overwhelmingly, business controls the marketing and presentation of talent, even angry and radical talent. To adapt the lyrics of a not-very-revolutionary rock group: 'they sing about revolution, they sing about change – at 80,000 dollars a show'! This situation is a product of the system rather than individual 'selling out'. Individuals may choose not to sell out but they are likely to end up singing to themselves as a result.

Despite the uncompromising tone of the quotations given from Jameson, he is a subtle thinker and it would be unfair even to give the impression that he is dogmatic. Elsewhere in the same article he appears to recognise that national and local cultures do not always entirely succumb to the global tide of American popular culture. What is indisputable however is his view that American capitalism is the dominant force in world culture and it is this that accounts for the mood of gloom that pervades much postmodern writing.

The argument that the cultural and economic have become conflated is clearly compatible with the McDonaldization thesis. Both notions raise the spectre of a mindlessly conformist global culture – rationally organised, pleasant to consume, but arguably shallow and controlled. However, both within the West and outside it, criticisms of varying degrees of intensity are made of this cultural hegemony.

Point 7: Critiqueing the West's Construction of the 'Other'

Edward Said's book, *Orientalism*, describes the many negative images constructed within Western culture of 'Orientals' and their cultures. These images were part of a general discourse of Western superiority and legitimised the economic and political domination of the Western power of much of the East. Hall uses Foucault's concept of 'regime of truth' to explain further these images. Regimes of truth contain discourses which 'justify' the behaviour of the powerful. Thus, the exploitation and abuse of labour could be explained by the 'fact' that Orientals were 'stupid' or 'like animals'. Sexual exploitation could be explained in the terms that the behaviour of Oriental women tends to be provocative or sexual anyway.

The reconstruction of positive self/cultural image and identity is crucial for those who have been demeaned and abused. In other writings, Hall has encouraged people who have experienced cultural oppression to do this (see p. 178). Perhaps the issue he has not fully addressed is the extent to which many 'non-Westerners' are attracted by and seek to possess much in Western culture – however much they may reject its negative stereotyping of others. In the end 'the threat of the West' may lie as much in the seductive powers of its own culture as in its behaviour and attitude to others.

Political Globalisation: Power in the Global Context

The main question at issue here is whether the development of problems on a global scale such as economic and financial instability, nuclear proliferation, environmental damage and mass cultural trivialisation and consumer manipulation are generating a political response at the global level. A major aspect of this question is whether power is passing in some degree from the level of the nation-state to some global institution(s) or system(s). In this respect a remark usually attributed to Daniel Bell is apposite: that the nation state is too small to solve the big problems of life and too large to solve the small problems. Not all would agree: A.D. Smith is convinced that the nation-state is a highly effective level of power and action and remains most effective in generating a sense of collective pride and identity (1991). However, there are other levels of power and action than the national and the global, including the regional-bloc such as the European Union, and these also merit consideration if the distribution and use of power in the late modern world is to be understood. It will help to keep in mind the various levels of power described earlier. Although it is possible to indicate strong trends in flows and concentrations of power, change and even instability are characteristics of late modernity.

Although it is easy to reel off some of the issues associated with globalisation which seem to require a political response, the new 'shape' or what Saskia Sassen calls the 'new geography of power' in a globalising world is in many ways still unclear and undoubtedly complex (lecture, LSE, 24.1.2000). One way of coming to grips with the issue is to focus on concrete developments in the area of power rather than make theoretical speculations. Several clear trends can be indicated. First, is an increasing tendency for multinational corporations themselves to settle the disputes that occur between them rather than in national courts (which are time consuming and expensive and may involve legal cases in two or more nations). Thus, there is a shift in power and authority from the state to the multinationals. Of course this does not mean that governments cannot attempt to regulate multinationals within their national jurisdiction and challenge them in the courts. However, as has been pointed out, to do so may risk losing 'the patronage' of multinational economic investment. Second, national governments themselves sometimes choose to pool sovereignty in order to be able to act together more powerfully and effectively. This chapter gives many such examples of which the development of the European Community is closest to hand. This process of *denationalisation* does involve a transfer of power from the nation-state to a relevant transnational (if not necessarily global) body but it may also prompt a redistribution of power within national governments. Thus, ministries dealing with trade and industry and the treasury are likely to experience an increase in power relative to other ministries, as global trade and financial matters become more pressing and pervasive.

A third, and quite crucial area of global power struggle and negotiation is the use and control of cyberspace, including the internet. What tends to be emphasised about cyberspace is its capacity for speedy, cheap and far-reaching communication at a personal and commercial level and its relative openness of access. However, cyberspace is also a contested arena as well as a pleasurable and commercially functional means of communication. This is the case in two ways. Firstly, websites allow for debate and disagreement. For example, the multinational oil companies and various 'green' groups have each used the internet to publicise their views. Another example is the anti-government Mexican radical group, the Zapatistas, which used the internet as a means of conveying its views to a wider audience whose support they gained – 'digital zapatismo'! As is discussed shortly, in late 1999, the internet was used by hundreds of radical groups to (more or less) coordinate their protests against the policies of the World Trade Organisation. Protests occurred around the world but especially in Seattle where the WTO was meeting and where hundreds of diverse radical groups converged. Secondly, is the less well known struggle to control access to cyberspace. Substantial 'amounts' of cyberspace are already privatised – notably by multinational companies. The latter are thus able to run their global businesses with a high level of speed and efficiency and largely without having to be answerable in detail to national or other communities (although, of course, governments may seek to hold them to account in a variety of ways). Hackers with various motives seek to break the privacy and secrecy of corporate and/or government controlled cyberspace. The more politically minded are sometimes referred to as 'Hacktivists'. The potential of hackers to disrupt either government or corporate activity is probably greater than that of activists relying exclusively on military weapons although it appears not yet to have been brought to bear as effectively. However, as neither governments nor multinationals appear keen to advertise their vulnerability to hackers it is difficult to know how effective the latter might so far have been.

Despite the newness of some of the above issues the main lines of debate on political globalisation can still usefully be analysed through broadly liberal/social democratic and Marxist influenced approaches.

So far the former view has been represented by the work of Roland Robertson and to a lesser extent by that of Anthony Giddens both of whom argue that political intervention, including at a global level, is necessary if human rights are to be secured and poverty confronted. In contrast, Marxists see little if any likelihood that any global political system could be effective as long as the world is run on capitalist principles or, in Wallerstein's terms, as long as there is a capitalist world system. In such circumstances, they incline to the view that the economic power of the multinationals is likely to be greater than that of, say, the United Nations, even if the latter were reformed to enable it better to confront the full range of global problems, including the economic. Leslie Sklair suggests that in the absence of a powerful globally organised and effective labour movement, people should begin the process of building for change at the local level – the level at which many NSMs direct much of their effort.

Liberal Accounts of Political Globalisation

Malcolm Waters suggests that David Held has put forward 'the best and most explicit account' of the view that political activity increasingly focuses on cross-societal issues and that the logic of this trend has significant implications for the possible development of a world government. Waters' own summary of the steps in Held's argument is so succinct that I will quote it verbatim only adding examples of the points he makes from the British experience of globalisation. So prevalent are the trends to which Held refers, that examples can be found without difficulty from the period in which this book is being written (1998–2000):

○ Increasing economic and cultural connections reduce the power and effectiveness of governments at the nation-state level – they can no longer control the flow of ideas and economic items at their borders and thus their internal policy instruments become ineffective:

E.g. Increasingly, data and images are stored and transported on discs and tapes and transmitted electronically rather than stored in books and transported physically. This has both intellectual and commercial implications – and in both respects scale and complexity has made the task of government surveillance and control much more difficult. The increasing international trade in illegal drugs is another area in which national governments have found control very difficult and, in fact, international cooperation is routine.

○ State power is further reduced because transnational processes grow in scale as well as number – multinationals for example, are often larger and more powerful than many governments:

E.g. It is not the case that any multinational is remotely as powerful as the British government, but many foreign based multinationals have highly significant economic power in Britain i.e., the power to create wealth and jobs or not. Thus, in 1998, BMW, the German car manufacturer which owns Rover decided to source the supply of certain components from outside Britain – at a cost to the British economy of about £2 billion. In 2000 it insisted on selling Rover.

Small countries such as Belize – where the main source of income is tourism – are in a very weak bargaining position in relation to multinationals.

○ Many traditional areas of responsibility (e.g. defence, communications, economic management) must therefore be coordinated on an international or intergovernmental basis:

E.g. In 1998 Britain and France signed an agreement to cooperate on certain key defence issues – perhaps foreshadowing a common European defence policy in certain areas. In a parallel development there is an increasing tendency for companies involved in military production to merge – because of the cost of research and development, particularly of hightech weapons.

○ States have thus been obliged to surrender sovereignty within larger political units (e.g. EU, ASEAN (Association of South East Asian Nations), multilateral treaties (e.g. NATO, OPEC (Organisation of Petroleum Exporting Countries), or international organisations (e.g. UN, WTO (GATT), IMF):

E.g. Britain, of course as a member of the European Union is subject to its laws and regulations – though not, it has to be said without some nationalistic complaining. It is also a member of all the international organisations listed above, three of which are concerned with the regulation of world trade.

○ A system of 'global governance' is therefore emerging with its own policy development and administrative systems which further curtails state power:

E.g. This and Held's next statement are controversial. However, it is arguable that the United Nations' actions in policing Iraq and Sierra Leone exemplify behaviour that might be termed 'global governance'. One of the controversial aspects of this proposition is that it is doubtful whether this policing would have occurred, especially in the case of Iraq, without the will and military might of a major Western power.

○ This provides the basis for the emergence of a supra-national state with dominant coercive and legislative power:

E.g. Clearly such a world government has not yet emerged and so it cannot be illustrated from fact. Held is suggesting that in total the above developments indicate that such a government would have many useful roles and that a basis for its development exists.

(The text of the above points is from Waters' summary of Held (1995:97) and the examples are mine).

There is a strong element of speculation about the last two points. One of the reasons why the United Nations does not always act effectively is that individual member nations or groups of nations often do not agree with each other. In particular, a great deal of hostility is directed against the United States and, to a lesser extent, Britain. Resentment is expressed across a wide range of economic, cultural, political and military matters. For example, the American-British bombing of Iraq in 1998 was widely opposed not only in most Muslim countries but also in Russia, China and France. It is not inconceivable that far from edging towards some form of world government, either Russia or China or both will revert to more militantly nationalist and anti-American postures.

Although it cannot be assumed that history is marching tidily towards world government, Waters, like Robertson, does accumulate much evidence and argument that there is some sort of trend in that direction even if it is unclear how such a government might finally emerge and what its scope might be. For instance, he finds that there has been a huge increase in the number of international organisations, both governmental and non-governmental in the period since 1945. In 1992 international governmental organisations numbered in excess of 3,000. The increase in international non-governmental organisations (NGOs) has been 'even more remarkable' and includes Friends of the Earth, Greenpeace, International Federation of Red Cross and Red Crescent Societies, and about 15,000 others (113). While Waters is aware that all this international activity does not equate with government, it does mean that increasingly people are addressing problems from a transnational perspective. Waters does not assume that the structure of world government, should one come about, will be highly centralised. It may take the form of a web of organisations differentiated by function but perhaps ultimately responsible to a representative body. Nor should it be naively assumed that NGOs are motivated only out of altruism or that they are always correct in their conflicts with multinationals or governments. Generally, they represent certain causes or interests but are not democratically elected.

If people are increasingly addressing problems transglobally, this is no doubt because the main problems of our epoch are transnational in kind. Indeed, this is the main reason for making such a fuss about globalisation. Waters suggests that chief among such problems are:

○ the planetary environment

○ peace and order

○ human rights

○ development and inequality.

It is no exaggeration to say that the survival of the planet depends on a stable solution being found to the first two, granted that the second one refers to the prevention of the proliferation and use, if not the abolition, of nuclear weapons. Neither the problem of planetary pollution nor that of nuclear weapons can be solved at the national level. Any satisfactory enforcement of regulations covering these matters is likely to require powers of inspection across the globe – which again seems to lead in the direction of a responsible world body of some kind.

The achievement of a world in which human rights are universally accepted, respected and enforced is at the very heart of liberalism. A commitment to human rights was central to Enlightenment thinking and ideals and a part of the inspiration and ideology of both the American and French revolutions. The precise definition and meaning of human rights has varied but there is a perhaps a surprising amount of agreement on what basic human rights are. As Waters remarks there 'have been frequent declarations of universal human rights, normally involving freedom of speech and action, freedom of political association and participation, due process under law, minimum access to health, education and material welfare, and control of one's body especially its reproductive capacities' (102).

Most member countries of the United Nations subscribe to most of these rights even those which appear not to practise them. However, the 'next step', a World Court of Human Rights, seems some way off and, of course, may never occur.

Waters mentions several cases in which one state has interfered in the affairs of another – sometimes with substantial international support – in order to seek to enforce human rights. A more recent celebrated case occurred in Britain in 1998: that of the arrest of General Pinochet, former President of Chile, and the legal ruling that a head of state was not entitled to immunity from arrest or extradition for acts committed when he was head of state. The court of Appeal decided that 'crimes against humanity' fall outside the protection of sovereign immunity and that such crimes can be tried somewhere other than in the country in which they were committed. In other words, in the case of crimes of such magnitude, a former national leader could be tried and, therefore, if found guilty, punished. Although this judgement was later overturned on a technicality, it demonstrates the potential for human rights to be regarded as more important than national sovereignty which, on the basis of any rational and democratically-inspired judgement, they clearly are.

By definition, the concept of universal human rights is based on a notion of common humanity. The principle that all human beings have equal fundamental rights by virtue of their humanity is eminently intellectually defensible. If to defend this principle is 'essentialistic' or 'humanistic', that is not a problem – at least not to this author. Those social theorists – often residual Marxists – who attack human rights as a 'liberal' idea, nevertheless, seldom reject the principles of 'human rights'. What else is there? In fact, there is a lot else. As Beck points out, many cultures and, one may add, many individuals do not observe human rights as they are espoused in the West. As he also points out – therein lies the argument.

Comment on Liberal Approaches to Political Globalisation: The Equality Question

It is in the area of development and inequality that the liberal approach to globalisation, leading perhaps to world government, is most vulnerable to criticism. For all the potential for human rights to provide the basis for a better world, liberals and liberal political philosophy stands accused – from the left – of failing to accept that without much greater material equality and equality of cultural access, human rights will not be very meaningful to much of the world's population, notably the poor. Waters' discussion of development and inequality is largely concerned to note the failure of various approaches to promote dynamic development in most of the poor world or to narrow the inequality gap between the rich and poor world. However, he makes no suggestion of what might be done about it, either now, or by some world government in the future. It is partly the persistence of and, in fact, the increase in global inequality of the last quarter of a century, and the failure of rich capitalist nations to do anything effective about it that gives credibility to Marxist frustration with liberal good intentions and feeble social policies. They argue that it is the capitalist world system itself which produces inequality and that liberal political institutions, whether national or global are unlikely, if not unable, to do much about it.

Another huge problem in establishing global institutions of any kind is to get agreement on what is a fair and equitable basis of doing so, particularly in relation to the representation and power of the world's nations and regional-blocs. Currently, for instance, the Euro-American domination of the UN Security Council is a source of resentment in much of the rest of the world. Yet, it is clear that 'the West' is reluctant to give up this power and the military superiority that supports it. Underlying inequalities of power are deeper problems of principle that make the development of international (or 'global') law based on human rights very difficult. While all the world's nation states apart from two have signed the international convention on human rights, in practice different countries have very different and sometimes conflicting cultures. The treatment of women in different cultures, child labour laws, and issues in relation to media freedom are only some areas of substantial difference. Nevertheless, there is a trend for the UN to assert and defend human rights around the world which, if it continues, may end in establishing common global standards of citizenship.

Marxist Accounts of Political Globalisation

Marxist theory has established itself very strongly in the area of globalisation. Marxist analysis of Western imperialism had already generated a body of work on world capitalism long before the term globalisation became current. Marxist theory generally gives precedence to the economic over the political power i.e., the interests of capital will over-ride others in the political decison-making process. In general terms, therefore, Marxists 'read off' political power from economic power i.e., the former is defined in terms of the realities of the latter. As was described in the two previous sections, Marxists, whatever their theoretical differences, consider that the power of capitalism is dominant in the contemporary world. They observe that the most powerful nations in the world – the North West European, the United States and Japan – are basically capitalist both in terms of predominant ideological conviction and in the practical direction of their domestic and foreign policies. It is part of assumed consensus that governments in these major capitalist societies will pursue the interests of capital and it is part of practical reality that governments themselves are dependent on a capitalist economy. Marxists see the prospect of fundamental conflict between the governments of these countries as extremely remote.

During the period since the second world war, several strands of Marxist theory have developed which allow for a degree of 'relative autonomy' of the superstructure – politics and culture – from the economic base. In other words, there are recent Marxists theories which do not treat political and cultural ideas and actions as simply expressions of the more fundamental realities of economic power and interest but as areas which can themselves meaningfully affect the course of events and history. There is no need to review these theoretical trends here, other than to note the French structuralists, notably Althusser, put forward a relatively weak or qualified version of this approach whereas the Italian Marxist, Antonio Gramsci, put forward a stronger version based on his celebrated concept of hegemony – a concept which embodies the idea that capitalist ideology is often open to strategic challenge at the cultural/political as well as the economic level. However, the emphasis on the potential of cultural and political action for achieving change has not been carried over to the level of global analysis by many contemporary Marxists.

The relative paucity of Marxist thinking on how to grapple with the political dimensions of capitalist globalisation is not surprising. First, no world government or state yet exists, and even if it is established we do not yet know what form it might take. It is reasonable enough therefore for Marxists to concentrate analysis on the overwhelming present reality of the multinationals and the culture they produce. Second, the dynamic political units of global capitalism – other than the defining reality of multinational power – are national governments, overwhelmingly that of the United States, and regional political-military alliances such as NATO. Marxists routinely criticise the national governments of major capitalist countries and the actions of NATO as being supportive of capitalist interests (rather than, say, those of the third world poor, many of whose lives are fundamentally affected by the multinationals). At the same time the traditional Marxist view that the power of governments is not decisive seems vindicated by the obvious fact that national governments are frequently forced to negotiate with multinationals about crucial matters, such as investment and jobs, central to the welfare of the nation's people.

Not all Marxists are defeatist about the prospect of replacing the global capitalist system by a socialist one but they do tend to share the near universal awe at the sheer scale and scope of multinational power and wealth. As one catch-phrase has it, 'capitalism seems to be the only game in town'. For some, including some sympathetic to Marxism, the seemingly unavoidable corollary to the entrenched dominance and widespread popular acceptance of the capitalist system is that radical politics is about reforming capitalism or, at the very best, changing it from within rather than about grandiose notions of revolution, abolishing the system and taking over the state (as was pointed out above – there is no single centre of power or state in the capitalist world system). It is hardly surprising that such perceptions generate a degree of pessimism among Marxists. Nevertheless, many ex or neo-Marxists have continued to critique capitalism and to suggest changes in its operation that might improve the situation of poorer countries and their people. Several Marxists have argued that there needs to be more global regulation of capitalism. In the one-off 1998 edition of *Marxism Today*, both Eric Hobsbawn and Stuart Hall argued that financial speculation was severely disrupting economies in many parts of the world and that there is a need for an increased regulation of global capital flows. In particular, Stuart Hall was scathing of what he saw as the Blair government's acceptance of the inevitability of the power of global capital and of the need, therefore, to placate it rather than regulate it more stringently.

Leslie Sklair, presents a radical and at the same time realistic outline of a strategy for grappling with and changing global capitalism (1995;1998). Sklair retains a sympathetic posture towards Marxism while departing from established Marxist ideas on some issues – it is largely a matter of semantics whether or not one labels him a Marxist. With reference to his own analysis of how global capitalism might be resisted, he states:

> The unmistakable conclusion of this analysis is that Marxism definitely needs to be rethought and the idea of revolution needs to be reinvented.
>
> (1998:293)

Sklair's starting point is that the multinationals have decisive economic power in the world and are highly successful in promulgating an ideology of consumerism. He further recognises that in its current state, the labour movement cannot on its own be regarded as an agency adequate to the task of resisting capitalism. However, he argues that in alliance with certain of the NSMs, the labour movement can continue to play a significant role in bringing about change. Sklair recognises that it is with the NSMs – for instance, feminism, and the environmental movement – that the vitality and dynamism for radical change lies. But how is it possible to establish the extent to which any particular NSM is resisting capitalism or not? On the basis of his own analysis of the core aspects of global capitalism, Sklair offers the following criteria:

> Anticapitalist global system movements ... are those which challenge the TNCs in the economic sphere, oppose the transnational capitalist class and its local affiliates in the political sphere, and promote cultures and ideologies antagonistic to capitalist consumerism.
>
> (1998:297)

Sklair gives several instances of opposition to TNCs including that against Distillers which produced and marketed a drug that caused severe birth defects, and the disaster at the American company, Union Carbide, in the Indian province of Bhopal where a chemical explosion killed hundreds of workers. In both cases outrage was worldwide and a variety of organisations and movements were involved. In both cases, the principles and behaviour of a major multinational came under extensive media and public scrutiny. Sklair does not mention the matter, but the opposition to the way major tobacco manufacturing companies have switched emphasis to selling and advertising in poorer countries as health legislation has begun somewhat to hamper them in the West is a further relevant example. As Sklair points out, popular criticism of rich capitalists is not uncommon even in capitalist countries. He suggests that indignation against particular individuals or incidents – such as, in Britain, the Maxwell scandal, or the 'fat cats' of some of the privatised industries – might be used to make more general points about the greed and inequality of capitalism, including, on an almost surreally inflated scale, global capitalism. On the issue of capitalist consumer ideology, Sklair sees considerable potential for cooperation between those opposed in principle to capitalist consumerism and the environmental movement which is more concerned with health aspects. The controversy over genetically modified food can be suggested here as one which both raises questions about capitalism – the risks capitalists might be prepared to take for profit and convenience/the true extent of consumers knowledge/choice under capitalism – which dove-tail neatly with environmentalist concerns with food quality and health.

In conclusion, Sklair regards opposition to global capitalism as in its early stages. In suggesting an organisational strategy, he in effect advocates the dictum: 'Think globally, Act locally' or as he puts it:

> This will mean disrupting capitalism locally and finding ways of globalizing these disruptions, while seeking the opportunities to transform it that democracy provides
>
> (306–7).

Comment

Marxist thinking in the area of economic and cultural globalisation is more developed than in the political, particularly in respect to describing what the political framework of a world not dominated by the multinationals might be like. For reasons already given, this is understandable. Nevertheless, the severity of Marxists critiques of capitalist economics and culture can obscure the fact that increasingly, Marxists accept that not only must they work within liberal democracy because there is no present alternative but that such a framework has popular legitimacy – at least, in the West. Even Sklair, who is strongly committed to extra-parliamentary politics, argues that those seeking to transform capitalism should use 'the opportunities . . . that democracy provides' (307). The notion that the masses are suffering from false consciousness and require liberation by the 'enlightened' few is no longer sustainable.

It is worth briefly considering whether or not Marxists may be edging towards a more liberal/social democratic political perspective and approach in other respects. In the tradition of Max Weber, liberals do not believe that political power in capitalist society, including the power of the state, is necessarily subordinate to economic power. This is one sense of the term pluralist as applied to liberals – the source of power may be political and economic or cultural (the power of ideas) or some mixture of the three. To the extent that Marxists accept liberal institutions, they seem implicitly to be accepting that the political sphere is, indeed, relatively autonomous from the economic – despite their emphasis on the power of the multinationals. Unlike Marxists, liberals accept capitalism but vary in the extent to which they consider it requires regulation, and in the extent to which its inegaliterian social effects need to be dealt with by social reform. To the extent to which they favour regulation and reform, they may be considered as more socialist or as radicals of the left. Again, it is no longer clear either in the global or local context how Marxists differ in principle from more radical liberal social-democrats.

Globalisation, the New Social Movements and Identity

We cannot yet talk of global social movements on any major scale of significance, although

Greenpeace has shown an ability to intervene effectively in almost any location. However, the internet has enabled radicals with a global awareness to communicate across the globe both with members of their own group and with members of other groups. The convergence of many hundreds of groups to protest at the meeting of the World Trade Organisation (WTO) in 1999 was partly coordinated by communication and planning via the internet.

However, there is no doubt that international capitalism, particularly the multinationals, is far ahead of the radical social movements in the scope and effectiveness of its global strategies. Multinationals such and Microsoft and BPAMOCO have resources far beyond what even the largest NGOs (Non-governmental Organisations) and pressure groups can currently raise. As a result, their global expansion is so far seldom greatly frustrated by radical action. The multinationals' own use of e-commerce occurs on a far greater scale than that of their opponents, although it is potentially vulnerable to disruptive intervention.

As was briefly discussed earlier, Manuel Castells refers to three kinds of identity, as the term refers to social actors: legitimising, resistance, and project identity. These identities have particular application to social movements. Castells describes legitimising identity as 'introduced by the dominant institutions of society'. Thus, membership of a legal political party or church give legitimate social identity. It is such institutions – stretching between family and state but influencing both – that generate civil society. Habermas's hope is that the new social movements will revitalise social life. While his analysis pertained mainly to the nation states of Western capitalism, it is equally applicable in principle to the emerging debate about globalisation.

According to Castells, resistance identity occurs when groups resist a devalued or stigmatised identity imposed by a dominant group. The women's liberation movement, later more generally referred to as feminism, and the black liberation movement have resisted, respectively, the negative definitions and stereotypes of patriarchy and white racism, respectively. In both cases resistance has widely developed into conscious rejection of patriarchal and racist ideology and culture. However, as long as the power relations that underlie oppressive cultures persist, negative definitions and stereotypes re-emerge albeit sometimes in different forms. To the still substantial extent that gender and 'racial' inequality persist, there remains a need for movements that resist and reject them.

Project identity occurs when an alternative, preferred identity is constructed. Such identities have focused, for instance, around gender equality, and/or a non-racist society in which people are treated on merit. Castells reserves the use of the term 'subject' for those who collectively pursue project identity – people who manage to 'reach holistic meaning in their experience' (10). It is worth quoting Castells at greater length here because he is addressing the issue of the construction of meaningful identity which is a key theme in this book. In reading the following it needs to be borne in mind that Castells considers that all three identities are achievable by human beings of any political persuasion. The anti-Federalist American patriots or seemingly mainly right-wing protesters against the high price of petrol in 2000 can be committed to their identities just as much as environmentalists and anti-racists (it is part of the fragmentation of postmodernity that a particular individual may 'mix' these aspects of identity unpredictably):

> (T)he building of identity is the project of a different life, perhaps on the basis of an oppressed identity, but expanding towards the transformation of society as the prolongation of this project of identity, as in the above mentioned example of the post-patriarchal society, liberating women, men, and children through the realization of women's identity. Or, in a very different perspective, the final reconciliation of all human beings as believers, brothers and sisters, under the guidance of God's law, be it Allah or Jesus . . .

> How, and by whom, different types of identities are constructed, and with what out-
> comes, cannot be addressed in general abstract term: it is a matter of social context.
> Identity politics, as Zaretsky writes, 'must be situated historically' (10).

While Zaretsky does emphasise the symbiotic relationship of social movements to social context, like Castells, he does not underplay agency. In his book on new social movements, the first characteristic he attributes to a social movement is that it 'is a group of people who consciously attempt to build a new social order' (1997:4).

The way new social movements seek to bring about a new social order differs from the approach to change of traditional socialism and communism. In the latter case the emphasis was on political means and the gaining of state power. In contrast, as Melucci has illustrated, the new social movements seek to achieve wider social change by first living, as far as possible, the desired 'alternative' lifestyle themselves (1989). Thus, ecological radicals try to live in harmony with the environment, those opposed to genetically modifying and chemically intensive agriculture live 'organically', those who oppose exploitation of the poor world join the 'fair price' movement. The belief and practice that 'the personal is the political' was pursued by some of the cultural radicals of the 1960s and by many feminists. This belief reflects a certain integrity and a commitment to consistency between value and practice. It is also based on the view that seeking change through lifestyle and example ('signalling new ways' to society as Melucci put it) is both more reliable and convincing than the almost inevitably aggressive pursuit of power and the hierarchical and unde-mocratic use of it. The NSMs tend to prefer decentralised organisational forms and networking to top-downward systems of communication and command. Again, the spread of the internet is likely to facilitate these practices.

Melucci goes on to make the related point that NSMs try to make links between their own private and often covert networks and the public world of employment and politics in which they often only appear irregularly or part-time. Such linking is necessary to achieve the social transformation they aspire to. Thus, to provide a recent example, in 1999 there was a broadly based anti-capitalist protest in a key centre of British and now global financial capitalism – the City of London.

'The Battle in Seattle', 1999: The Rebirth of Protest?

In late 1999 the World Trade Organisation met in Seattle to discuss the tarriff and trade regulations of its 135 member countries – a large majority of the world's nation states. Also present were representatives of over 1000 organisations and groups who had come to protest. By and large the protests were peaceful but there was some violence and several hundred arrests. On one of the days of the conference, there was a solidarity protest in London. The intention of mentioning the Seattle conference and protests is to illustrate several points concerning social movements and the complex context they work in. It is also interesting, if highly speculative to raise the question of whether we are on the brink of another period of protest. Disentangling the interests of the various groups at Seattle illustrates just how difficult it is to achieve a clear sense of political direction, let alone achieve significant change.

The United States government wanted to cut agricultural subsidies which overwhelmingly benefit European farmers. In general, reflecting its position as the world's most powerful economy, it wanted to reduce tariffs and move towards greater world free trade. The latter position was extremely popular among American based multinational companies. However, mindful of the influential trade union and environmental lobbies in the United States – and prominent in Seattle – it also favoured tougher trade rules to protect labour standards and the environment. The former position was again fairly popular with US multinationals as the cost of achieving internationally agreed labour standards would be relatively much more difficult for companies indigenous to the developing world than to US based multinationals.

Wary of American economic strength, the (European Union) EU was more protectionist inclined than the United States but relatively willing to see the markets of the richer Northern countries made more open to developing nations. The European nations, partly anxious to steer discussion away from free trade also raised issues concerning consumer health, the environment and cultural diversity. The latter issue reflected a nationalist and regionalist defensive concern of some European nations about American cultural and media global dominance.

The countries of the developing world generally demanded 'special and differential' treatment, firstly because they find it difficult to compete with the rich countries and, secondly, because they are at an historic disadvantage, partly due to having been exploited or 'under-developed' by the West. Several of the major developing countries, including India, Pakistan and Malaysia opposed establishing international labour standards for the reasons given above. There was much effort among the protesters to engage with the arguments and concerns of developing countries and to reconcile positions. Not all developing countries felt they could afford demanding regulation of either the environmental effects of industry or of high labour standards.

Prominent among those present outside the conference hall in Seattle were representatives of the American trade union movement – a core part of the so-called 'Old Left'. They wanted the international labour standards to be established. This was not only or even mainly for humanitarian reasons. The unions believed that cheap labour costs were enabling some developing countries to produce goods more cheaply than in the United States and that they sometimes 'dumped' these goods onto the American markets.

The many environmental or Green groups outside the conference argued that the environment is being harmed by the progressive liberalisation of world trade. One suggestion for reform was that companies significantly involved in world trade should apply for a licence, the terms of which would require them to maintain the environment. Such a suggestion may eventually come about but, in general, the activities of the multinationals are far ahead of any international agreements to control them. However, the environmental groups want the rules of international trade to be redrafted so that nation states can override WTO trade decisions if they turn out to endanger the environment. Overall, they want a rebalancing of the relative importance given to trade and the environment.

A main concern of the many consumer groups at Seattle was to oppose the continued engineering of genetically modified seeds. Others were opposed to the use of hormones and other additives in the development of livestock. Both practices were regarded as not proven to be safe and therefore as potentially dangerous.

Many of the groups involved in the protest had used the internet in their planning and preparation. A group called Mobilisation Against Corporate Globalisation organised accommodation for protesters through a website. Another group calling itself the electro-hippies sought to shut down the Web-Server computers of the WTO by bombarding them with messages. They used a so-called 'pinging programme' which loops back to ask recurrently for access to a site, thereby slowing its operation down. Apparently, this was achieved.

The protests in Seattle are too recent at the time of writing to be able to make a measured analysis of them. However, they provide a fascinating window on globalisation, particularly if similar protests are to become part of the emerging scenario of globalisation itself. First, it may be highly significant that one of the main banners which many of the radicals are prepared to unite under is 'anti-capitalism'. Although the protesters were not by and large 'class ideologists' or socialists, they generally saw the behaviour of the multinationals as 'the problem'. Most of the specific demands of the groups were reformist rather than revolutionary but collectively, and despite some contradictions in their demands, what they sought was radical. A world in which trade is rebalanced in favour of the poorer countries and in which protection of the environment is an established and enforced priority would be a radically different world. A fairer system of world trade as envisaged by many Third World countries and many Western groups would involve a retreat from the 'free trade' goals of the WTO. There would certainly be protectionist tarriffs to allow the fostering of industries in the developing world. It may be that the underlying direction of the new radicalism is to regulate capitalism so that it works for the common good, rather than as it does currently, to increase inequality. Some want to abolish capitalism and if it is very difficult to see how that might happen now it would be foolish to say it could never happen.

A second point raised by the Seattle protests is the issue of whether to pursue protest by non-violent or violent means. The importance of this strategic decision is incalculable for two reasons. One is that if violence is chosen it will certainly provoke a violent response from the state, which has overwhelmingly greater means of violence than the protesters. The turn to violence of some of the 1960s/70s radicals was the signal for the state to use violence to put down the movement. The other reason for the importance of the decision on violent or non-violent means seems to be widely understood by contemporary radicals. It is that the choice of violence or non-violence defines the culture and moral ethos of a movement. People become what they do. Prior to the protests in Seattle, an umbrella organisation called Direct Action Network brought upwards of a dozen groups together provided that they remained non-violent. Ruckus Society, Rainforest Action Network and Global Exchange worked within the DA Network and held seminars and camps to teach members techniques of civil disobedience and more spectacularly how to rappel up and down buildings and otherwise gain maximum publicity for the relevant cause.

Finally, is the comparison between the current emerging radicalism and the radicalism of the 1960s. Both periods spawned a variety of issues and groups. However, Tom Hayden, a prominent radical of the 1960s may be right when he points to a unifying focus of contemporary radicals:

> What we had was maybe one or two issues we were dealing with. You here, you're dealing with everything. That's how big this globalisation thing is.
>
> (Quoted, *Guardian*: 4.12.1999: 16).

Globalisation is a huge issue and what we may or may not be witnessing is the beginning of a popularly based attempt to democratise it and to control it. Since 'the battle in Seattle', there have been other similar protests, including in London and at the Republican and Democratic Party Conventions of 2000 and at the IMF/World Bank meeting in Prague in 2000. How far the new radicals can harness wider public opinion to their cause remains to be seen.

Conclusion: The Dualisms in Global Context

Although David Held and his co-authors (1999) find plenty of evidence of a 'sceptical' view of the globalisation thesis, it is obvious that 'something is happening' on a world scale which has the power to affect all our lives.

Yet despite the rapidity and scale of change, the underlying issues concerning human values and experience have been re-contextualised rather than rendered redundant. This is obvious if the template of the dualisms is held up against recent global developments. The individual/society dualism and the closely related agency/structure dualism are as relevant now as they were 150 years ago. In fact, liberals tend to argue that globalisation has offered individuals more in the way of developing their identities and personal styles than when cultural horizons were more confined. If 'society' is not now just the nation-state but, in part, a region, say Europe, and partly the global 'society' itself, then, that may offer individuals more material on which to re-think and re-shape themselves. Even many commentators who take a pessimistic view of the effects of globalisation on individual autonomy – and these include some postmodernists, neo-Marxists and conservative traditionalists – still adopt a broad individual/society-agency/structure perspective on the issue. However, they incline towards the view that individual agency has been swamped in the cultural maelstrom of global messages. Marxists, in particular, see global capitalist culture as a force towards the creation of superficial conformity and a flattening of alternative cultural forms, whether based on tradition or class. On the specific political-cultural issue of individual rights a similar split between optimists and pessimists occurs, but again much of their thinking is broadly within the terms of the 'old' dualisms. It is arguable that concern with individual rights in relation to the state is more often addressed by contemporary social scientists than it was by those of the nineteenth century.

With the growth of interest in globalisation, the micro-macro dualism also takes on a new, or, at least, somewhat different dimension. Much more than in the past, social scientists are concerned with studying the interaction of the small-scale, particularly the individual and local (micro), with the global (macro). Thus, the micro-macro dualistic focus remains intact but its application is changed by the 'arrival' of the global and the interaction of the global with individuals and localities. The effect of multinationals dis/investment strategies on given localities was discussed above and is, in any case, self-evident (see, pp. 196–8). Economic prosperity or decline has an effect on the culture of a locality but there are many other macro-micro global interactions. For instance, millions daily interact with the global media, including using the worldwide web. So far, social scientists have responded to the theoretical and methodological demands of these 'new' micro-macro dimensions by producing a great deal of new theory and also a growing number of empirical studies of the interaction of the global and the local.

The modern/capitalist society dualism occurs in relation to the global dimension, perhaps as strongly as it did at the societal level, when the latter was generally conceived of in terms of the nation-state or tribe or some other clearly circumscribed social unit. Marxists are right when they argue that globalisation is led by capitalism. Many capitalists agree and have every intention that this should continue to be the case. Giddens takes the view that the modern world is not the product of capitalism alone. Important among the other factors he mentions is the inter-state system. Whether the institutions of that system will prove capable of restraining the more destructive actions of capitalists and effects of capitalism may well become the most pressing concern of the first generation of the new millenium.

SUMMARY

1. DEFINITIONS Globalisation is a 'social process in which the constraints of geography on social and cultural arrangements recede and in which people become increasingly aware that they are receding.' (Giddens). Globality describes how every locality has been or is liable to be affected by globalisation processes. Globalism refers to 'the view that the world market eliminates or supplants political action – that is the ideology of rule by the world market, the ideology of neoliberalism.' (Beck).

   Levels of Globalised Action: Global, bloc, national, regional, local, individual

2. LIBERAL AND MARXISTS ACCOUNTS OF GLOBALISATION
   Liberal Accounts: Robertson describes globalisation as emerging through five stages, the last of which is defined in terms both of practical transnational economic, communications and other links

and a shared consciousness that these exist and of a common humanity. The latter awareness raises the issue of human rights. Giddens explains the development of globalisation in multi-causal terms – contributing factors being capitalism, industrialism, the inter-state system and militarism. Giddens's concept of 'reflexive' awareness of globalisation is similar to Robertson's global 'consciousness'. Both Robertson and Giddens are reformist liberals in that they argue that global capitalism needs regulation and that nation states should be required to observe universal human rights. They should be sharply distinguished from free-market or classical liberals who adhere to what Beck refers to as the ideology of 'globalism' (see above).

Marxist Accounts: From Marx onwards, through Lenin to Wallerstein, Marxists have argued that capitalism was uniting the world into a capitalist market. The radical former Marxist, Castells, argues that the substantial control of the multinationals of the means of global communication and computerised information (especially economic/financial) gives them decisive power (the network society). The liberal/social democratic and Marxist approaches to globalisation 'flow through' the topic. My own view – a radical but non-Marxist one – is that the causes and character of globalisation are various but that the dominant character of globalisation is capitalist. The term capitalist globalisation conveys this. It seems to me that the exploitative and deeply inegalitarian nature of global capitalism mean it needs radical reform but that the choice and flexibility of a much modified market system must be retained.

3. ASPECTS OF GLOBALISATION: ECONOMIC/FINANCIAL, CULTURAL AND POLITICAL
    i)   *Economic/Financial*: A mass of evidence points to the globalisation of much production, investment, trade, financial transactions, and consumption. Nevertheless, 'the globalisation thesis' is contested by 'sceptics' who question the extent and newness of some of these developments.
    ii) *Cultural*: Again there is something of a split between more reformist liberals and, often Marxist influenced, postmodernists. Robertson and Giddens by no means celebrate contemporary culture in the way that free market liberals do but they see real worth and potential in the global human rights agenda and defend the more open and creative aspects of Western culture. In contrast, postmodernists see the pervasive profit motive as corrupting of culture. Baudrillard sees the generation of meaningless signs by the media and their uncritical consumption by 'the masses' as a world of 'hyperreality'. Jameson argues that in the totally commodified world of capitalism, the cultural has collapsed into the economic and no longer provides a source of values alternative to or critical of capitalism.
    ii) *Political*: Although it is possible to exaggerate the decline in power of the nation state, the rise of multinationals and a variety of other transnational organisations and networks means that power is both more diffuse and fluid in the contemporary world. This needs to be qualified by the fact that the United States, the only remaining world superpower, is immensely and disproportionately powerful in all aspects of globalisation. Waters suggests that chief among the increasing number of problems requiring a global response are: the planetary environment; peace and order; human rights; development and equality. Whereas more radical liberals offer suggestions for the reform of the existing framework of the global economy and institutions of global governance which easily become compromised or ignored, Marxists often offer rich criticism of capitalism but now lack a clear strategy of change or idea of what an alternative system might be. The New Social Movements are mainly focused on individual issues but protests involving a myriad of protest groups and Non Governmental Organisations may be the beginning of more co-ordinated and widespread radical protest.

4. THE DUALISMS IN GLOBAL CONTEXT Although globalisation changes the context in which the dualisms are acted out, their relevance is enhanced rather than diminished. In particular, the tension between individual expression and rights and the need for social cohesion and coordination persists.

Chapter 8

The Dualisms: Summary and Further Discussion.

Introduction

In a period of rapid change and apparent fragmentation, it is striking the extent to which the central concerns of sociology, or more precisely of social theory, have remained recognisably the same. Approaching social theory in terms of core dualisms is not new, but it is sufficiently rare to employ them in a sustained way for there to have been doubt about whether they could provide an adequate analytical framework. Using the dualisms in this way has strengthened my view that they generate a substantial and stimulating approach to the sociological theory. It almost seems as if the issues and tensions around the dualisms of individual/society, agency/structure, social integration/system integration, micro/macro and modernity/capitalism socialism are more relevant now than when Marx, Weber and Durkheim wrestled with them. Far from 'solving' the admittedly profound questions of social process and construction raised by the dualisms, postmodernism has brought them right to the fore. Postmodernism and poststructuralism have been rich in the theoretical insight they have provided but they are far from the last word on such matters as the 'death of the subject' or on the relationship of social structure to individual action. Certainly not when thinkers of the stature of Giddens and Habermas are in the other 'camp'! For Giddens in particular, the individual is alive and kicking and has the potential to have a more fulfilling life in late modernity than in any previous epoch.

The Dualisms Revisited

Individual/Society: Human Rights and Citizenship

The rights and potential of the individual has been one of the 'big ideas' of modernity. The individual rights agenda has grown steadily throughout modernity and has been adopted by more and more groups as we approach the present time. It seems sweeping to state it, but since the Reformation/Renaissance many if not most social, political and intellectual movements have reiterated and sought to pursue the value of the individual. Despite the extreme inhumanity of African slavery, and the obscenities of twentieth century totalitarianism, the human rights movement is unbowed, if bloodied. The individual subject, human rights and humanism also seem set to survive the intellectual challenge of the anti-humanist intellectual movements of the latter part of the twentieth century. What has been taken out of these movements by a wider population is their emphasis on difference and diversity. Their tortuous anti-humanism has been largely ignored, Yet, overall, the emphasis of sociology has not been very individualistic. On the contrary, some sociologists have emphasised the social that they have veered towards determinism. More recently, sociologists such as Turner and Giddens have found a place for individual rights theory within sociology. Before returning to the theory of the individual within sociology, it is well worth tracing further the roots of the idea of individuality.

Chapter 1 dealt with the impact of the Enlightenment on early sociology, including the mixed impact of the concept of individualism on its development. Here, I will briefly refer to the earlier period of the Renaissance. Historians are constantly finding examples of individualism and humanism well before the Renaissance but there seems little doubt that these characteristics became more widespread during this period and received fresh impetus during the Enlightenment (see,pp. 4–5).

Martin Luther's break with Catholicism occurred largely on the basis of his belief that, in the final instance, his duty was to follow his own conscience rather than the authority of the Church and Pope. Given the practical need for individuals to conform to authority, this principle is perhaps one of last resort and is often forgotten in contemporary society as individuals submit to the power and command of the institutions that employ them. Nevertheless, the primacy of conscience has constantly been reasserted in the later half of the twentieth century particularly in relation to individual conduct in war. In this context, this principle has become known as the Nuremburg principle – that individuals will be held responsible for the crimes against humanity they commit in war even though they have been commanded to do so by a superior authority.

It is worth briefly dwelling on the Renaissance as the period in which the seeds of the modern enthusiasm for individuality were sewn, and a surge of creative energy let loose which has arguably been sustained to the end of the millennium. One illustration of what was happening is in Renaissance portraiture in which many individual faces and figures come alive with human feeling in a way that was scarcely possible in the paintings of the medieval period when individuals were typically presented as integrated into the all-encompassing divine scheme of things. Literally, humanity was lost in religious 'reality' which also ordained what was taken to be a set and timeless social order. If much Renaissance art possessed a modern psychological insight which broke with more formal and static traditional art, it also tested religious conservatism with its revival of the Greco-Roman celebration of sexuality and human beauty. However, the sharpest clash between the Church and emerging freer thinking and expression was in the area of science or rather science versus theology. This was precipitated by Galileo's celebrated discovery that, in effect, the world could not be the centre of the universe but that, on the contrary, it was a relatively small and, in astronomical terms, unimportant, planet. This contradicted the Church's teaching – illustrated in many 'maps of the universe' in which both God and the earth were prominently presented – that the earth and everything on it had a God-given position in the hierarchy of things. Under the scrutiny of Galileo's telescope, everything looked different and apparently less divinely pre-arranged.

Undoubtedly, the rise of individualism marched hand in hand with secularisation. Humanism became the dominant alternative to religion, at least, among intellectuals (although the term itself was little used until the early nineteenth century). These trends were intensified as a result of the Enlightenment. Voltaire sought to apply the rational, critical methods of enquiry developed by Newton in studying the natural order to the systematic study of human beings and society. Voltaire and Hume developed a secular humanism in part directed against the dogmatic claims of Christian orthodoxy. If reason was the method of humanism, belief in the value and potential of the individual was its ideological core. Given the growing pervasiveness of this belief, it was almost inevitable that movements for both democracy and human rights would develop. As belief in the divinely ordained nature of the feudal hierarchy crumbled, people began to believe more in themselves. If one man (as it still then was) was pretty much as good as another, then, each man should have the same democratic rights. In time this belief was consolidated in the demand for 'one man one vote' and, more recently, 'one person, one vote'. However, the emergence of popular ambition, fuelled by the ideals of radical intellectuals such as Tom Paine and Rousseau, did not envisage the new order simply in terms of democracy. Democratic rights were seen as one of a wider, if often imprecisely defined, range of individual 'human' or 'natural' rights.

The importance of the theory and ideology of human rights in the contemporary world is part of an on-going movement whose origin can be traced back to the early modern period. John Locke is credited with the first clear formulation of natural rights theory and the defence of human rights against the abuse of monarchical and state power was a large part of the justification of the American and French revolutions. In practice, even the universal right to vote was not achieved in either the United States or France as a result of the revolutions, but the idea of the universal suffrage gained ground and was achieved in both these countries well before Britain. Bryan Turner has distinguished between the more *active* citizenship of the United States and France and the more *passive* citizenship of Britain and Germany (206–9). In the former cases, many of the rights of citizenship were achieved by widespread popular pressure from below whereas in Britain and Germany they were largely 'granted' from above. In the case of Germany, he suggests that democratic rights were not as deeply rooted as in France and the United States and that what was granted from above was relatively easily removed from above by Hitler and the Fascists. The British case is more complex and is arguable that the term passive is not so appropriate. The complexity lies partly in the fact that the British system of government and democracy is partly the product of a revolution followed by a compromise which was in turn followed by a long struggle that never quite erupted into revolution. Although the monarchy was abolished in the mid-seventeenth century, it was soon restored with the people as 'subjects' under it. As a result of the restoration settlement, the British people achieved an extension of their civil rights but the monarch remained sovereign (as s/he still does) and voting rights remained restricted to the upper and upper middle classes. Throughout the nineteenth and early twentieth century, men and women of the working and middle classes struggled to gain an extension of the franchise with the universal suffrage as a widely shared eventual aim. What Turner's account usefully does is relate the extent and timing of the implementation of 'human rights' to the political traditions and social contexts of particular societies. Human rights do not automatically flower on the branch of history and in some regimes they scarcely get expressed at all or are actively repressed.

The above account of the development of human/natural rights theory has so far tended to emphasise the achievement of political rights, particularly the right to vote. Other human rights are widely recognised. Certain civil rights were recognised in Britain long before more than a small minority of the adult population had the vote. These included, habeas corpus, i.e. the right not to be imprisoned without trial – a central principle of natural justice. The American Constitution contains a long series of amendments which in effect secure the rights of the individual citizen against the possible tyranny of the state. Famously, these include the fifth amendment, the constitutional right of the accused to silence in a trial, effectively the right not to be legally required to give evidence against oneself. This right also exists in British law but was recently trimmed to allow juries to draw conclusions, perhaps to the detriment of the accused, should the right be exercised, rather than as previously to draw no implications either as to guilt or innocence. T.H. Marshall, the best known British theorist of the rights of citizenship, has argued that following civil and political rights, the achievement of social rights would add a necessary dimension of material security to civil and political freedom.

The political domination and cultural hegemony of the West has meant that the doctrine of human rights has taken on a global dimension. Following the attrocities of the Nazis during and preceding the second world war, the victorious powers and numerous other nations decided to draw up a declaration of human rights, which would state in principle the limits of acceptable human conduct and provide an authority which could be invoked against legal and social oppression. In 1948 the General Assembly of the United Nations adopted a Universal Declaration of Human Rights which included economic and cultural as well as political rights. More specifically, the Declaration included the rights 'to life liberty and security of the person ... recognition everywhere as a person before the law ... freedom of movement ... a nationality ... freedom of thought conscience and religion ... freedom of peaceful assembly and association ... freedom to take part in government' (ODS: 568). The declaration is not legally binding but has been signed up by all but two nations of the world.

Figure 8.1   Human rights have gradually been extended to black people and to women. However, many people in all parts of the world do not enjoy basic human rights.

Even so, it is obvious that these 'human rights' have developed historically and in some cultures more than in others. In practice, the peoples of the world are characterised by a great deal of cultural variety and practice. Various national and cultural norms in relation to, for example, amputation as a form of criminal punishment, child marriages, child care, child labour, female circumcision, restraints on political and civil freedom surely stretch and, many would insist, contravene basic 'human rights'. Some regard the 'human rights agenda' as part of the strategy of Western ideological imperialism and it is certainly in the West that the philosophy of human rights is most energetically proselytised. The Declaration has been followed by a number of international conventions and covenants, including the European Convention for the Protection of Human Rights and Fundamental Freedoms which have been incorporated into or otherwise influenced national legislation. In 1998, the Convention was incorporated into British law and for the first time given a coherent and codified human rights basis to British law. To this considerable extent, Britain now has a constitutional foundation of a similar kind to that of the European Union countries and of the United States for the protection of the individual against abuse by the state or other bodies. The Human Rights Act implementing this change came into force in 2000.

Although the principle of universal human rights by definition seeks to reach beyond differences of political ideology, it is particularly associated with Western liberalism. Weber and Durkheim welcomed the extension of political and social rights and were both liberally inclined in their attitudes to what we would today term human rights. However, in somewhat different ways they were both also concerned with the need for social integration and cohesion as well as with extensions of individual freedoms in the form of various rights. In Durkheim's case, a concern with social solidarity and order was perhaps the dominant theme in his work. He constantly expresses the view – which almost amounts to an anxiety – that the rising tide of modern individualism would loosen the bonds of society and bring social disorder and related social problems. Durkheim emphasised the role of public education as a counterbalance to the forces of social fragmentation and individualism. For his part, Weber was cautious of any substantial extension of the role of the state in order to control and direct individual energies. However, he did see a role for political elites and even the authority of charismatic political leaders in guiding the democratic electorate. Although Weber's commitment to individualism was profound it was far from naive or simplistic. He recognised that the state and other bureaucratic institutions not only establish necessary limits to individual conduct but can also enhance individual freedom by providing opportunity and direction. The interests of the individual and society (including the state) can be complementary as well as opposed. Indeed, the rationale for the modern democratic state is exactly that it is an enabling force for its citizens. However, it often does not work out that way. In the end, Weber's memorable contribution to social science and intellectual thought was his critique of 'the iron cage of bureaucracy', whether state or business, and his passionate commitment to understanding individual meaning and action.

Marx's opposition to capitalist society and his criticisms of it were such that he could not share the view that individual liberty was being generally enhanced in liberal capitalist society. He regarded the limited political and other freedoms in Victorian Britain mainly as 'bourgeois freedom' and as largely exclusive of the working class. He also considered that capitalist society tends to ignore the issue of economic rights. He made the telling point that poor and hungry people need a basis of economic adequacy and security more urgently than they need political and civil rights. Further, sometimes the exercise of political and civil rights depends on having a stable and sufficient material existence. These points still need answering especially in the global context. Globally inequalities of wealth are increasing and in poorer parts of the world thousands of children die or become diseased through lack of an adequate basic diet. As long as this remains the case, the Marxist critique – shared by many non-Marxists – of the lack of serious commitment of liberal capitalism to social justice will remain valid.

Whether Marx would think that the social democratic welfare reforms of the twentieth century adequately deal with social rights we cannot, of course, know, but it seems unlikely. In Britain, or rather England, social democrats have increasingly begun to emphasise responsibilities as well as rights and even make access to certain rights dependent on what government deems 'responsible' conduct. Significantly, Anthony Giddens, who is closely associated with the Blair government presents 'rights/responsibilities' as a couplet in the index of his most political book *The Third Way: The Renewal of Social Democracy* (1998). The principle behind such a coupling is compelling and is seldom contested. However, it is of concern that the intellectual shift to emphasising individual responsibility and enterprise apparent since the Thatcher period may stall further commitment and progress towards establishing social justice and decency. This has hardly been achieved at a national level and at a global level it has scarcely begun to be achieved.

Action/Structure

There is no need to repeat here in any detail the theoretical positions of Marx, Weber and Durkheim on the relationship between action and structure. Their basic views were presented in chapter 1 (pp. 13–30) and have been developed in various other parts of this book. Both Durkheim and Marx showed a strong structural bias in their sociology and even Weber developed a model of action which fully allowed for the influence of social and institutional contexts (e.g., bureaucracy) and cultural traditions (e.g., ethnicity) in shaping individual action. If the story Weber wanted to tell was one of individual action, then, it is arguable that he partially 'lost the plot' and shifted towards the structural emphasis familiar to Marx and Durkheim. Marx's concept of collective social action was crucial in systematically extending theories of action beyond the level of the individual. Marx prioritised class action but in the last thirty years of the twentieth century, many contemporary social theorists have applied the concept of collective action to a range of social movements including those whose identity was predominantly gender, 'race'/ethnic, and sexual. Marx's concept of the dialectic although not currently fashionable is also of use in understanding the relationship between action and structure if stripped of the rigidity Marx's over-scientific conceptualisation gave it. The dialectic can be applied to the relationship between conscious action and social structure. Thus, action is shaped and informed by structure and structure is renewed or changed by action. If we conceive of this process in terms of the modern concept of a continuous feed-back loop between human beings and the environment, then we have a viable if basic model of action/structure.

The story of how social theorists of the second half of the twentieth century have seen the relationship between action and structure is an extraordinary one. It is a story that on the surface looks and, in some of its detail, *is* complex but it is one which has the simplicity of great consistency about it. The story is the steady and cumulative impact of structural and more recently postmodern perspectives on sociology and, of course, on other disciplines. Part of the story, too, is the opposition to these movements and the attempts to use aspects of their theoretical content and to reject others.

The litany of those who have contributed to the growing tide of broadly structuralist theory is long and impressive. The following includes only some of the main characters: Freud, Durkheim, Saussure, Levi-Strauss, Barthes, Althusser, Foucault, Baudrillard, Lyotard and Hall. Merely to put these names in a single sentence is to run the risk of appearing to 'lump together' a number of major and distinctive thinkers and one or two great ones. What they have in common is that, to a greater or lesser extent, they all emphasise or, have often been taken to emphasise, the influence of structure on the individual and to de-emphasise the autonomy of the individual. If we conflate the first two dualisms into individual action/society structure, then, it is the latter they have emphasised.

Freud's lasting contribution was to map the structure of the mind and to demonstrate how the deeper structures of the unconscious and the instincts could subvert and play tricks with the intentions of the conscious mind. After Freud, it was scarcely possible to hold the unqualified view that even the psychologically 'healthy' or 'normal' person was entirely in control of his or her life. Durkheim argued that it is the 'force' of social facts that shape and even 'control' individual and action – and in doing so established a deterministic bias in the French structuralist tradition. Saussure and Barthes theorised that, respectively, the meanings of language and signs/symbols depend on structured relations and that meanings cannot solely be determined by the user (author) but can be read differently by different people. The reader him or herself becomes part of the total context of meaning – thus, different people read the same image, book or object i.e. text, differently. Levi-Strauss argued that different as the main myths and symbols of particular societies might seem on the surface, they conveyed the same fundamental ideas and messages.

Althusser applied structural theory to sociology. Like Durkheim, the structures he referred to were social structures – the economic, political and cultural. With Althusser there emerges what in my view is the crucial and, in intellectual terms at least, tragic over-emphasis and distortion in structuralism – the attempt to kill off 'the Enlightenment' subject. In fairness, Althusser thought that the conscious, autonomous thinking and acting subject of the Enlightenment ideal was already 'dead' because 'he' was never, in any case, more than a myth. Foucault is generally considered to be a poststructuralist but he continued to write within the tradition of French structural determinism. Foucault did reject the approach to structure which conceptualised it as 'something out there'. In Foucault's approach, individuals are caught in and apparently constituted and therefore determined by discourses (see pp. 120–4). Discourses combine power and knowledge in a way that coerces the behaviour of those caught within them. Dominant discourses at the professional or occupational level are those that most people conform to. Belatedly, Foucault came to the view that dominant discourses can be resisted and alternative discourses articulated and although this is clearly a change in his thinking of immense significance, it does not represent the predominant direction of his thought. What he did do was provide a new vocabulary for describing how people can come to be positioned in systems which control and exploit them in ways they may not fully understand.

Baudrillard is usually thought of as a postmodernist partly because of his view that modern culture is a hyper-real construction of the global media – a world of surface experienced superficially. However, the theoretical basis of his thinking draws heavily on the structuralist tradition. In particular he draws on Barthes' analysis of symbolic communication to explain how, in his view, the masses are structured into mindless consumption. He argues that in postmodernity signs are frequently detached from the referents from which they gained rational meaning. Thus, in an advertisement characteristics such as endurance or bravery once associated with particular actions now become associated with or refer to, say, a particular beer. Obviously, the aim is, as Baudrillard sees it, to manipulate the consumer into buying the beer. Rather different associations – often of a romantic kind – might be created for soft-drink advertisements. Baudrillard sees the postmodern world as littered with such hyped and false associations. Signs slip around generating meaningless associations which can become the basis of people's lifestyles which, then, are in danger of becoming no more than patterns of manipulated consumption. Baudrillard takes the deterministic tendency of structuralism one stage further – now it is the signs themselves that dominate, empty of any stable point of reference.

With Baudrillard, the potential for structuralism and postmodernism to arrive at a cul de sac of determinism is achieved. Baudrillard offers no meaningful way out of the hyper-real world. His suggestion that as 'the masses' refuse to join the intellectuals in revolutionary activity the intellectuals should join the masses in the consumption of signs – on the off chance that general realisation will dawn of how silly the system is – is probably a postmodern joke. Ironically, however, there are more than a few signs that this is what some intellectuals have decided to do – witness the emergence of pop-opera and middle-class all-sit-down football 'audiences' (as distinct from stand-up crowds).

With Lyotard's work, postmodernism begins to suggest a way out of the dead-end of determinism. As Ernest Gellner observed postmodernism seems to point in two opposite directions: one in which the individual is constructed as the zombified object of external forces and the other in which groups and perhaps even individuals express their own identities which may be at variance with and different from dominant norms and lifestyles. If Baudrillard represents the first trend, Lyotard represents the second. In *The Postmodern Condition* (1979) Lyotard announces the end of the credibility of all forms of totalistic or totalitarianian creeds be they political or more broadly intellectual. In his later book, *The Difference* (1984), he elaborates on why this is so. In an argument based largely on structural linguistic theory, he states that language always has the potential to sustain a *different* argument than the one being put forward. Given the grim history of totalitarianism, Lyotard has no difficulty in making a case for political and intellectual regimes that allow the expression and development of different points of view. Mutual acceptance of difference has become characteristic of postmodernism both as an intellectual and a practical movement. Once a basis for difference is established and the oppressive imposition of conformity rejected, then, it would seem a short step to embracing individuality as well. Lyotard does not appear to take this short step perhaps wanting to avoid attributing any essential characteristics to human individuality of the kind associated with Enlightenment natural rights theory. In practice, however, it is not easy to embrace differences between people without accepting their 'individuality' as well. However, Lyotard emphasises differences not at the individual level but at the level of 'genres of discourse' i.e., cultural groups that 'speak the same language' or 'see the world in the same way'. There is still the implication that language speaks individuals rather than that individuals use language to construct and communicate meanings – which is the view of Habermas and Giddens and of the liberal Enlightenment. The habit of treating active subjects like dead texts lingers here and there.

Nevertheless, Lyotard's emphasis on difference chimes positively with the emerging postwar social movements of difference although many of their participants surely enjoyed their sense of difference *and* individuality with little if any reference to the complexities of Lyotard's thinking. No doubt gender, sexual, ethnic and other cultural differences and identities would be asserted and celebrated if postmodern thought did not exist but the postmodern movement does provides one intellectual reference point for them.

To a considerable extent, Stuart Hall's personal intellectual history is a mirror image of the structuralist/poststructuralist and postmodern movements – with, it must be said, some other influences thrown in as well, notably that of Gramsci. It is largely through Hall that these influences have been imported into British cultural studies and – much less comprehensively – British sociology. Here, it is the later phase of his thinking, the last fifteen years of the century, and especially the last five, which are to be considered. After having been heavily under the influence of Althusser's structuralism, Hall took something of a postmodern turn around the mid-nineteen eighties as he argued the right of minority ethnic groups to assert and celebrate their own ethnic identities partly as a counterbalance and defence against the oppressive mono-culturalism of Thatcherism (see, pp. 176–7). Part of the motive for this was no doubt political solidarity with minority ethnic groups and to what extent it represented a radical change in Hall's theoretical approach is doubtful. However, by the mid- nineteen nineties, he was ready to acknowledge that the 'erasure' of the subject and traditional notions of identity by 'variants of postmodernism' had left something of a conceptual gap. With reference to such 'essentialist concepts' as identity he states:

> But since they have not been superseded dialectically, and there are no other, entirely different concepts with which to replace them, there is nothing to do but continue to think with them – albeit now in their detotalized forms, and no longer operating within the paradigm in which they were originally generated.
>
> Identity is such a concept – operating 'under erasure' ... an idea which cannot be thought in the old way, but without which certain key questions cannot be thought at all.
>
> (1997:1).

Hall's response to this dilemma is to revive the concept of the subject – but stripped of the fullsome range of characteristics attributed to 'him' by the liberal Enlightenment. In fact, it is the subject in relation to discourse i.e. a poststructuralist version of the subject, that Hall wants to revive. In a crucial quote from and comment on Foucault he sets the terms of this enterprise:

> I agree with Foucault that what we require here is 'not a theory of the knowing subject, but rather a theory of discursive practice . However, I believe that what his decentring requires – as the evolution of Foucault's work clearly shows – is not an abandonment or abolition of 'the subject' but a reconceptualisation – thinking it in its new, displaced or decentred position within the paradigm' (2).

The quotation makes it clear that the one thing that Hall does not intend to do is to re-establish the 'knowing' or consciously aware and intentionally acting individual into social theory. Yet, he is concerned at the absence in Foucault's earlier writing of 'any attention to what might in any way interrupt, prevent or disturb the smooth insertion of individuals into the subject positions constructed by these discourses' (i.e., dominant discourses – my brackets). It is in Foucault's later writings that Hall finds what he (Hall) refers to as the 'interior mechanism' of the subject by which the subject is pulled into dominant discourses and finds his or her identity within them. However, a problem for Hall is that the later Foucault allows too much capacity for intentionality to the 'reconceptualised subject'. Hall prefers an approach developed by Judith Butler which explains 'identification' primarily in terms of unconscious rather than conscious motivation and in terms of being excluded from certain identifications rather than choosing others. Hall cites Butler's explanation of feminism in terms of various responses to manifold exclusions (14–5). Despite the power of patriarchal discourse, the overwhelming extent of women's exclusion pushed many into resistance. Butler also observes that such exclusion does not then lead to the discovery of a shared 'essential' identity between women – something which has been an issue in the women's movement (see p. 170).

As ever, there is insight in Stuart Hall's argument. It is very likely that the psychological processes he refers to would often, and perhaps usually do, play a part in the development of resistant or alternative or simply different identities. Yet as so often in his work, Hall seems to be torturing himself and his prose in his insistence on ignoring the creative and selective capacities of the conscious mind and instead works within a quite deterministic version of the structuralist/poststructuralist approach (which, in any case, is inclined to determinism). The more extreme versions of the structuralist paradigm lead to a writing of history and an account of society with actors left out, and, in the absence of agents, events happen themselves.

One indication of just how depersonalised Hall's approach can be is his use of the term 'mechanism' to describe the linking of the subject with his or her (perhaps we should say 'its') identity within the discursive scheme of things.

The biological analogy of Functionalism was widely considered inadequate to cope with the reality of the social complexity of human beings but this is a return to the even cruder mechanical analogy. It is time to revive the human subject more convincingly as Bauman and Giddens suggest.

The political implications of Hall and Giddens's theoretical disagreements have come into sharper focus as a result of the latter's support for 'The Third Way' and the former's criticisms of it. In what could be the start of one of the 'heavy weight' intellectual confrontations of our time Hall accuses Third Way politics of selfish individualism and calls for a re-emphasis on dealing with market inequalities (1998). Giddens's reply is that Hall is reverting to 'Old Left' politics and that the market must be allowed to produce wealth before it can be redistributed. Echoing Blair he claims to want a community in which individuals can thrive (2000). Watch that space!

The Liberal Enlightenment versus Structuralism:

The following is a list of points for and against each approach broadly in relation to their predominant theoretical position in relation to individuality-agency, on the one hand, and structure/society on the other. Obviously, they are a matter of interpretation and the basis for them is in the rest of this book and particularly the above sections of this chapter.

Strengths of Liberal Theory

1. Has a (relatively) theoretically developed view of Human Consciousness, Agency and Moral Responsibility.
2. Has articulated a set of ideals which – sometimes after reinterpretation – some previously excluded groups have adopted and aspired to achieve.
3. Emphasises pluralism – an acceptance that different groups should freely live together and compete for power – through the theory and practice of democratic compromise.

Weaknesses of Liberal Theory

1. Historically, it has tended to be over-optimistic about 'human nature' (more recently there

has been a greater appreciation of human evil and of the risks to humanity and other species of modern life).

2. Despite the high-minded and universalist ideals of the liberal Enlightenment, many groups were excluded from the benefits of liberal society.

Strengths of Structuralism/Postmodernism

1. Explored the role of the unconscious and of signs and symbols in social life.

2. Rejected the more absolutist, simplistic and essentialist tendencies of Enlightenment idealism, including the notion that science/reason can provide the recipe for 'progress'.

3. Has become pluralistic through a positive acceptance that differently excluded groups have a right to their own identities.

Weaknesses of Poststructuralism/Postmodernism

1. Lacks an adequate theory of the human subject.

2. Is prone to determinism.

It would be quite feasible to integrate elements of the above two approaches into a single theory. To some extent that has been attempted . For instance, Zygmunt Bauman uses much postmodern insight in his work, particularly in relation to the role of symbolism in identity formation, but arguably still maintains a view of the individual subject which owes more to liberalism than to structuralism. Although Anthony Giddens is one of the most notable defenders of the Enlightenment tradition, it is a modified version that he pursues and one informed by some post-modern insight.

It is clear that the theoretical basis of structuralism/postmodernism and liberalism are not of equal status. Despite the achievements of structuralism/postmodernism, there is a human size hole at the centre of the theory. Any theory that fails to engage with individuals as conscious, thinking and choosing beings risks peddling a sociological version of 'the iron cage'. However, a postmodernist approach which integrates individuality, agency and pluralism begins to seem much more com-patible with liberalism. In fairness, the liberalism implicit in postmodernism, particularly in the practice of the new social movements, is a radical liberalism – it is concerned more with the oppressed and excluded than with those who are already more freely celebrating the opportunities and variety of modernity – but it is liberalism nevertheless.

From Parsons to Giddens, this book has discussed several attempts 'to square' the 'agency/struc-ture' dualism. A recent ambitious attempt to do so is John Urry's *Sociology Beyond Societies* (see. pp. 186–8). Certainly, on hearing Urry lecture on this theme I wondered whether he had broken the mould in which these matters are routinely set (York, 2000). It will take some time before Urry's work is fully absorbed and evaluated. On one point he is clear: for him 'social life is presumed to be contingent, unpredictable, patterned and irreducible to human subjects' (16). Nor, however, is it reducible to the networks and flows – the main 'metaphors' with which Urry replaces that of social 'structure'. He includes among the 'mobilities which replace societies ... at the heart of a reconstituted sociology' the creative activity of intellectuals and of the social movements. If the 'flows' constitute the agents, then, the agents also constitute the 'flows' (210).

Social Integration/Systems Integration

The social integration of individuals and groups and the integration of various 'sub-systems' such as the economic and cultural (system integration) are complementary aspects of overall social integration – to the point where it is easier to discuss them relatedly than separately. For instance, when the education system socialises individuals and, many would argue, classes for positions in the economic system the processes of social and systems integration are highly interconnected. This remains the case even when social integration is disruptive to or dysfunctional for the system.

Ian Craib suggests that Durkheim was primarily interested in social integration – that which binds individuals together – and Marx with system integration – that which binds or fails to bind different institutional sectors of society together, such as the economic and political sectors. Examples of more or less integrated social groups are social classes and ethnic and status groups and it is how these link with or fit into or not with 'the system' or parts of the system, such as the economy or polity, that largely determines the overall level of societal integration. Craib's is a fairly accurate assessment of the respective priorities of Durkheim and Marx but the comprehensive models of society each constructed required both of them to address the two aspects of social integration. Durkheim considered that in order for societies to integrate effectively some degree of moral consensus is necessary even though in modern societies mutual self-interest is the main basis of integration. In contrast to Marx, he was more concerned to minimise than to exacerbate class divisions. Marx believed that the social divisions and conflict generated by class could and eventually would break the integration (or 'dis'-integrate) the capitalist system. Weber's approach to sociology was so pluralistic that it is less easy to tease out precise theoretical directions in what is in any case the quite complex area of social integration/system integration. As far as social integration is concerned, he was inclined to the view that caste societies tended to be more harmonious than class societies but he did not consider that the latter would necessarily generate the level of social conflict foreseen by Marx. Weber also understood how modern systems work   particularly in their bureaucratic aspects – but again it was how these impacted on the individual rather than integration itself that he was mainly interested in. In general, he took the view that individuals were over-integrated and too conformist.

Durkheim was concerned that the break-up of traditional moral consensus would lead to anomie – individuals might lack the normative beliefs and internalised moral constraints to achieve an adequate level of social conformity. An inadequate level of social conformity would be one which was dysfunctional for society although he did see a moderate degree of deviance as having certain positive functions for society. He himself pointed to 'abnormally' high rates of crime, alcoholism and suicide as indicators of the scale of the problem of social integration in his own time. These 'social problems' have, if anything, increased in the second half of the twentieth century although alcoholism is now part of a much wider 'drug problem'. One can only guess at what Durkheim would have made of the contemporary statistics behind the so-called 'break-up of the family', the historically very high divorce rate, the declining popularity of marriage and having children, the rising rate of suicide among young men, the high rates of property-related crime … The list of possible indicators of social disintegration is potentially a very long one. It seems quite likely that Durkheim would have been confirmed in his conclusion that modern society is vulnerable to problems of social disintegration as a result of the decline of mechanical solidarity and shared morality and the rise of individualism. He would doubtless also notice the extensive policing, security and surveillance which characterises late modern Britain – in part the price to pay for the coming to fruition of some of the processes he observed in their relatively early stages.

Were he to revisit us today, Marx would no doubt note with the rest of us that so far class conflict has not broken capitalist society apart. He might also be unfavourably impressed by the extent to which nation and ethnic groups have become, if anything, more popular points of identification even than in his own time. Granted that capitalism is still the dominant system, he would not be surprised at the degree to which it has become global. He might well be surprised at the relative lack of class-based opposition to it. It would certainly be interesting to hear his opinions. If only . . .

Perhaps the contemporary theorist closest to Marx in theoretical range and in the declared political and emancipatory purpose of his work is Jurgen Habermas although he has moved some way from Marx's own views. On the issue of social integration/system integration, Habermas sees a growing disconnection between the life world and the system world. In other words, people's experience in their everyday lives is not integrating them meaningfully into the system world of economic organisation and political decision making. Although people may be functionally part of the system world in their jobs, they are largely alienated and apathetic towards it. This is the basis of the crisis of legitimation that Habermas has claimed afflicts Western capitalism. It is a crisis which does show itself in a degree of social disorganisation and disintegration. People who are relatively indifferent to the system world, particularly the political system are less likely to be active, responsible and decent citizens than those who are. What Habermas would like to see is a revival of civil society – a hoped for world of lively debate and action which would bridge the current chasm between the life and system worlds. In so far as Habermas sees this happening it is in the ideas and activities of the new social movements. He applauds their engagement with the media – instead of being flattened into conformity by it, they are using it to launch alternative ideas, images and policies and even an alternative view of how the world might be organised.

Anthony Giddens has a more positive view of capitalism in late modernity than Habermas but also recognises major problems in relation to both social and system integration. Giddens is positive about what he sees as the great possibilities for individual freedom and expression brought about by liberal capitalism. His *The Transformation of Intimacy* can be read as an exploration and even a celebration of these possibilities in personal life and his *The Third Way* can be similarly read in relation to political and social life. Giddens is prepared to live with and work with the system. However, he is also acutely aware of the potential for liberal capitalism to bring about disintegration at the system level and at the everyday level of social life. In a real sense, these tendencies to disintegration are the 'other side' – the social and personal consequences – of unconstrained capitalist individualism. The abuse of individual freedom in personal relations can be highly damaging to others. He argues that among responsible adults relationships should be democratic and based on trust. As he will realise: 'easier said than done' – but it is probably better to pick up the pieces of failed freedom than those of totalitarian control (which in its extreme form is what the patriarchal family was/is).

Giddens is perhaps even more conscious of the risks of capitalism as a global system. With the possible exception of Castells, he has indicated more fully then anyone how various levels of socio-political organisation and identity gyrate and change in response to global capitalism, including global communications (which are mainly owned and operated by capitalists) (see pp. 203–6). Along with Ulrich Beck, he has also emphasised the contribution that capitalism makes to the enormous collective risks faced by those who live in late modernity. One example is global warming. Often, it is in combination with scientific research and experimentation that capitalism produces risks – as, perhaps, in the development of foods containing GM crops.

As perhaps the best known sociologist of globalisation, Giddens has raised in graphic terms the extent to which globalisation creates new issues of social and system integration. The development of a more global perspective has changed the way people perceive other social levels, including the regional bloc, the nation, and localities. Like a number of issues this can be discussed under the heading of more than one dualism and in this case there is some advantage to discussing globalisation in macro/micro terms.

Micro/Macro

In his *Understanding Social Theory* Derek Layder points out that 'there is considerable overlap between' the dualisms of agency-structure and macro-micro (1994:215). He, nevertheless, goes on to point out differences of emphasis and focus:

> Whereas the agency-structure problem tends to focus on the link between human activity and its social contexts, the macro-micro problem is rather more concerned with the level and scale of analysis and research focus (215).

The relationship between macro sociology and comparative/historical methods and quantitative methods, and between micro sociology and qualitative methods has been so frequently presented in textbooks that I have not explored it again in this book other than making an occasional reference. Many sociological works explore a given problem at both levels of analysis – say, the structural factors influencing a person's social class (macro) and the person's experience of social class (micro). As in this case there are always links between the two levels. Layder suggests it is largely how a particular sociologist theorises these links that indicates whether s/he is a macro or a micro sociologist. Marx and Durkheim were mainly macro-sociologists but they were both intensely interested in how structural change and developments in the social system affected individuals and groups. The same could be said of Parsons' earlier work although he notoriously lost touch with the need to account individual experience in his later work. Weber tried to understand society from the individual 'upwards'. His ideal type of social action was the crucial link between the two levels though whether it quite achieved his aim is debatable.

Although he is fully aware that the purpose of sociology is largely to link the micro and macro levels in understanding and explaining human conduct in *Modern Social Theory* (1997), Layder shifts emphasis to exploring the characteristics of the particular levels or domains of social reality. He states that here are four principal domains: psychobiography (a person's mental make-up and the factors that have gone into forming it); situated activity; social setting; and contextual resources. Layder does not fit these precisely into the micro macro schema but it is clear that situated activity is micro-social and contextual resources (i.e.,the institutional resources provided by the system) is macro-social with the social setting being roughly a middle or meso level. Psychobiography is a social-psychological concept which deals with aspects of the person often ignored in sociology. For instance, psychobiography has relevance to how an individual may interact with society in relation to, for instance, agency and intellectual capacity.

Despite its potential, it is not possible to pursue domain theory here. Staying with the terms micro and macro rather than adopting domain terminology, it is relevant to observe how each term can be used to describe how other dualisms relate primarily to one or other level. Thus, if we look at the first three dualisms 'horizontally' as complements rather than vertically as dualisms, we get the following connections:

> individual/action/social integration . . .   micro
> society/structure/system integration. . . .   macro

Layder finds it useful to give distinct conceptualisation to the different social levels or domains. This more easily allows for detailed examination of actions or events that are characteristic of one or other level. Layder particularly admires Goffman's distinction between the interaction order (micro) and institutional order (macro) and argues that such clear designation enables Goffman to examine both the different characteristic of each level and how they link together:

> Goffman concentrates on the dynamics of interpersonal encounters while locating them in a wider institutional context . . .

Goffman's approach is important for domain theory in another sense. His fascination with the details of face-to-face encounters brings our attention firmly back to the realm of everyday life. It is this domain that is often neglected in the approaches (like Parsons' and Marx's) that emphasise the more impersonal, collective and large-scale 'macro features of society.

(1997:12)

Layder saves his sharpest criticism for structuralist and poststructuralist theorists who, as was discussed at some length in Chapter 4, more or less rule out any autonomy at the micro level at all:

Domain theory . . . is quite at odds with those structuralist and post-structuralist theories that have attempted to 'decentre' the human subject. The overall effect of these theories is virtually to abandon any concern with the 'inner' social psychological resources and dispositions of individuals'(12).

One can only agree with Layder and hope that the idea of the death of the human subject will itself die a swift death. It would certainly be to the benefit of sociological theory if it did. It is somewhat more surprising to find Layder firmly disagreeing with Giddens structuration theory. However, given that the premise of structuration theory is to dissolve the distinction between the 'levels' of structure and action he is quite consistent to do so. Layder prefers the term 'duality of social relations' to that of 'duality of structure'. Again, this is because he wants to give due place to the role of action and relationships as well as structure in his theoretical formulations. Which terminology one prefers may well depend on the particular issue under discussion and whether the emphasis is on agency or structure. In any case, the disagreement here is probably more terminological than substantive. Both Layder and Giddens clearly agree that human agents create social structures which also both constrain and enable them.

It was suggested above that the widespread development of a global perspective has shifted the way people see and experience other social levels – micro, macro or whatever. Or, put another way globalisation has affected peoples' sense of identity and what they identify with. Global capitalism has stimulated the formation of a global environmental movement and an embryo 'anti-capitalist' global radicalism (see pp. 216–20). For others, the power of the multinational corporations and the intrusion of largely Americanised global culture has pushed them towards a reassertion of national identity. Others look for support and identity in the wider strength of a regional bloc, such as the European Union. Others still are confused by the flows and shifts of power and imagery characteristic of globalisation and which can scarcely be expressed in the implied stability of the concept of levels at all. However, given that a global level of economics and finance, culture and communication, has been established then more developed global governmental institutions are likely to follow for the purpose of bringing greater order and equity.

Modernity/Capitalism–Socialism

The modernity/capitalism–socialism dualism is a secondary dualism in that it is tied to the particular historical context of the nineteenth and twentieth century. Ian Craib usefully promotes this dualism for consideration in order to highlight the central debate between Marx and Weber on the nature of the contemporary epoch i.e., approximately the last two hundred years. The pros and cons of their two approaches on this matter have been discussed often enough in his book not to require any repetition here. It is more stimulating to consider whether what may be emerging now, in late modernity, is a global social system of a kind which reflects the thinking of both men yet is far from being what either might have precisely anticipated. The 'joker in the pack', the 'thing' that neither could have anticipated is the new technology which is harnessed by human purpose and imagination – destructive as well as positive – and replete with un-anticipated consequences, some of these being the 'risks' referred to by Beck and Giddens. Arguably, the information revolution has changed the way we look at the world to such an extent that the modernity/capitalism-socialism dualism is no longer central to most people's concerns. Questions now focus more on the merits or otherwise of various forms of capitalism than on the 'either/or' of capitalism/socialism.

Marxist theory can take credit for its analysis of the social effects of the unconstrained pursuit of profit and of the willingness of some capitalists to exploit labour and markets with extreme ruthlessness. Further, the instability of capitalist trading and financial markets has been repeatedly demonstrated. For these and other reasons capitalism has needed restraint and reform and in most countries of the world and, to some extent through inter-national and global institutions, it has been reformed. It is widely recognised that the process of the economic and social reform of capitalism needs to continue. However, public/legal restraints on the functioning of capitalism and the amelioration of its more destructive social and environmental effects is not the same as 'the abolition of capitalism'. Reform is not revolution. The question Marx never felt he needed to address was 'what if capitalism is so successful that the vast majority of people 'decide' that it is the system they prefer and that they do not want communism?' For traditional socialists, that outcome turns Marx's vision of the future into a nightmare without awakening – capitalism without the solution of socialist revolution. However, it now seems improbable that there will be a socialist/communist 'happy ending' – although it would be foolish to repeat Marx's mistake of appearing to predict the future. The suspicion that the working class would not prove to be the decisive agency for change has haunted more thoughtful Marxists and socialists since at least the 1920s. Christopher Lasch's book *The Agony of the American Left* referred specifically to the lack of support for socialism in the United States (1970). We can now see that in terms of support for socialist revolution, this is now more or less a global phenomenon. In its extreme formulation, Marx's side of the dualism looks very unlikely to become reality. It looks as though the abolition of poverty, greater equality and social justice will have to be achieved – if it is to be achieved – through the regulation rather than the destruction of capitalism.

However, this does not mean 'total victory' for the modernisation thesis. First, let us take Weber's thesis about the growth of bureaucracy and then the modernisation thesis more generally. Weber's analysis that bureaucracy would prove efficient and productive but would be a blight on human autonomy and creativity has received a receptive audience throughout the twentieth century. As was discussed in Chapter 3, new, less bureaucratic patterns of work and organisation, are now beginning to be established. Power and communication flow less predictably down the tiers of bureaucracy but more laterally and diffusely across the channels of cyberspace. Bureaucracy and its discontents will be with us well into the next millennium but social scientists – and citizens – need a model of power, communication and production that is as informed by Foucault as it is by Max Weber. That is Foucault the analyst of power-knowledge, not the would-be assassin of the human subject.

It is also becoming increasingly clear that the modernisation thesis taken as meaning progress through the application of reason requires a sophisticated revamp. In fact, Giddens and Habermas have, in their different, ways attempted to do this. Both know very well the human, social and environmental cost of capitalist-industrial development and the difficulties of creating a world in which people even begin to achieve their intellectual, creative and communicative potential. But both believe that it is worth continuing to try. Giddens is the more positive of the two about the trends to individualism and self-expression that he sees in late modernity. Habermas is the more radical, retaining a strong belief that a substantial redistribution of wealth is necessary if the majority are to enjoy most of the benefits and pleasures of 'the good society'.

SUMMARY

THE DUALISMS REVISITED

The Individual/Society: Human Rights and Citizenship: The concept of individuality was strengthened and developed during the Reformation/Renaissance, through the Enlightenment, and into late modernity/globalisation. The ideologies that sustained it in each of these periods were respectively – humanism/natural rights, humanism/liberalism, and human rights/global citizenship. Both Weber and Durkheim were personally liberal in their support of an extension of civil and political rights, though Weber's sociology is more liberal in its theoretical foundation (i.e. its emphasis on individual meaning).

Marx developed a different theory of human liberation in which equality is stressed and criticised 'bourgeois liberalism' as a class ideology rather than one genuinely based on human rights.

Action/Structure: The relationship between the individual and collective actions that make society and how existing society constrains and enables action charts a central sociological dualism on which there will never be full agreement. Whereas Weber swayed towards prioritising action, Marx and Durkheim were more structural in emphasis. The mainly French structuralist tradition, transmitted to Britain by Stuart Hall, has clarified how structures of language and signs help to form thought and action but in the interpretation favoured in this book, this tradition is seen as over deterministic. Giddens's structuration theory is more liberal in that it combines action and structure, attempting to integrate the two (Chapter 5).

Social Integration/System Integration: The easiest way to think of social integration is to relate it to socialisation – a term which indicates how individuals and groups are constantly being fitted or refitted into society by others – particularly in the context of families, peer groups, education, the media, and prisons. Systems of integration relates mainly to the macro social level of the 'functional' relationship of, say, the education system, and cultural values. In reality, this predominantly Functionalist separation of people (social integration) and systems (system integration) cannot be sustained. Durkheim most explicitly addressed the issue of integration and Marx was keen to see capitalism 'disintegrate'. Habermas argues that the system world largely fails to engage people. The 'post' theorists tend either to emphasise the extent to which the media has integrated people into the system (Baudrillard) or see them as turning away from it to pursue their own lifestyles.

Micro/Macro: This dualism usefully focuses the methodological implications of the previous three. The first concepts in the three dualisms relate to the small-scale and the second three to the large-scale which, in turn, indicate qualitative or quantitative methods. However, much research employs both approaches. As our perspective on the social changes, so the relationship between the macro and micro can shift. Growing consciousness of the global has recontextualised how other levels of social action are perceived.

Modernity/Capitalism–Socialism: Few sociologists now consider that society is going to progress from capitalism to socialism in the way Marx believed. However, much of recent history has concerned the conflict of the capitalist and socialist systems, and Marx said much that was valid about the way both capitalism and capitalists operate. What is unsustainable is Marx's determinism. The term modernity has the merit of encompassing the instrumental rationalism and bureaucratic character of both large-scale capitalism and communism. Whether we call the contemporary period 'late modernity', 'postmodernity', 'the information age' or a 'second modernity', there seems to be a growing consensus that we are approaching a new historical epoch which neither Marx nor Weber quite foresaw and which will require new and specific theorisation.

Bibliography and References

Abrams M. (1959) *The Teenage Consumer*, London Press Exchange Papers: No 5.

Adorno, T.W. and Horkheimer, M. (1973) *Dialectic of Enlightenment*, London: Routledge, (1947).

Allen, S. (1987) 'Gender, Race and Class in the 1980s' in C. Husband (ed) *Race in Britain*, London: Hutchinson.

Atkinson, J. (1985) 'The Changing Corporation' in D.Clutterbuck (ed) *New Patterns of Work*, Aldershot: Gower.

Back, L. (1996) *New Ethnicities and Urban Culture: Racisms and Multiculture in Young Lives*, UCL Press.

Baert, P. (1998) *Social Theory in the Twentieth Century*, Cambridge: Polity. London: Macmillan.

Ballard, R. and Driver, C. (1982) 'The Ethnic Approach' in *Block 3, E354,* The Open University Press.

Barrett, M. (1998) 'Stuart Hall' in R. Stones (ed) *Key Sociological Thinkers*, London: Macmillan.

Baudrillard, J. (1985) 'The Masses: The Implosion of the Social in the Media' in *New Literary History*, xvi, 3 577–89.

Baudrillard, J. (1995) *The Gulf War Did Not Take Place*, Sydney. Power Publications.

Bauman, Z. (1996) 'From Pilgrim to Tourist: or a Short History of Identity' in S. Hall (ed) *Questions of Cultural Identity*, London: Sage.

Bauman, Z. (1989) *Modernity and the Holocaust*, Cambridge: Polity.

Bauman, Z. (1992) *Intimations of Postmodernity*, London: Routledge.

Bauman, Z. (1998) *Globalization: The Human Consequences*, Cambridge: Polity.

Beck, U. (1992) *Risk Society: Towards a New Modernity*, London Sage.

Beck, U. (2000) *What is Globalisation?*, Cambridge: Polity.

Beck, U., Giddens, A., and Lash, Scott. (1994) *Reflexive Modernisation: Politics, Tradition and Aesthetics in the Modern Social Order*, Cambridge Polity.

Becker, H. S. (1963) *Outsiders: Studies in the Sociology of Deviance*, New York: The Free Press.

Becker, H. S. (1966) *Social Problems: A Modern Approach,* London: John Wiley and Sons.

Bell, D. (1961) *The End of Ideology*, New York: The Free Press.

Bell, D. (1973) *The Coming of Post-Industrial Society: A Venture in Social Forecasting*, New York: Basic Books.

Bennett, A. (1999) 'Subcultures or Neo-Tribes? Rethinking the Relationship between Youth, Style, and Musical Taste' in *Sociology*, Vol. 33, No. 3.

Benton, T. (1999) 'Louis Althusser' in R. Stones (ed) *Key Sociological Thinkers*, London: MacMillan.

Berger, P. and Berger, B. (1979) *Sociology: A Biographical Approach*, Harmondsworth: Penguin.

Blair, T. (1998) *The Third Way: Politics for a New Century*, London: Fabian Society.

Bottomore, T. and Rubel M. (eds) (1956) *Karl Marx: Selected Writings in Social Theory and Social Philosophy*. Harmondsworth: Penguin.

Bourdieu, P. (with Jean-Claude Passeron) (1980) *Reproduction in Education, Culture, and Society*, London: Sage. (1977).

Bourdieu, P. (1984) *Distinction*, London: Routledge. (1979).

Braverman, H. (1974) *Labor and Monopoly Capitalism*, New York: Monthly Review Press.

Bullock, A. and Trombley, S. (eds) (1999) *The New Fontana Dictionary of Modern Thought*, London: Harper Collins.

Burr, V. (1995) *An Introduction to Social Constructionism*, London: Routledge.

Callinicos, A. (1999) *Social Theory: A Historical Introduction*, Cambridge: Polity.

Castells, M. (1996) *The Rise of Network Society*, Oxford: Blackwell.

Castells, M. (1997) *The Power of Identity*, Oxford: Blackwell.

Castells, M. (1998) *End of Millennium*, Oxford: Blackwell.

Cicourel, A. (1976) *The Social Organisation of Juvenile Justice*, London: Heinemann.

Clark, J., Modgil C. and Modgil, S. (1990) *Anthony Giddens: Consensus and Controversy*, London: Falmer Press.

Clarke, J., Cochrane, A., and McLaughlin, E. (eds): (1994) *Managing Social Policy*, London: Sage.

Coates, D. (2000) *Models of Capitalism*, London: Macmillan.

Cohen, S and Taylor, L (1976) *Escape Attempts: The Theory and Practice of Resistance to Everyday Life,* Harmondswort: Penguin.

Cohen, R. and Kennedy, P. (2000) *Global Sociology*, London: Macmillan.

Connell, W.R. (1987) *Gender and Power: Society, the Person and Sexual Politics*, Cambridge: Polity.

Connell, W.R. (1995) *Masculinities*. Cambridge: Polity.

Connolly, M., Roberts, K., Ben-Tovim, G., and Torrington, P. (1991) *Black Youth in Liverpool*, Culemborg; Giordano: Bruno.

Cooke, P. (1989) *Localities*, London: Unwin Hyman.

Craib, I. (1992) *Modern Social Theory from Parsons to Habermas*, London: Harvester Wheatsheaf.

Craib, I. (1997) *Classical Sociological Theory*, Oxford University Publications

Dahrendorf, R. (1959) *Class and Class Conflict in Industrial Society*, London: Routledge and Kegan Paul.

Dahrendorf, R. (1992) 'Footnotes to the Discussion' in D.J. Smith (ed) *Understanding the Underclass*, London: PSI.

Delanty, G. (1999) *Social Theory in a Changing World: Conceptions of Modernity*, Cambridge: Polity.

Devine, F. ' "Affluent Workers" Revisited' in *Sociology Review* Vol 3 (February, 1994).

Djilas, M. (1957) *The New Class*, London: Thames and Hudson.

Docherty, T. (ed) (1993) *Postmodernism: A Reader*, London: Harvester Wheatsheaf.

Durkheim, E. (1960) *The Division of Labour*, New York: Free Press, (1893).

Durkheim, E. (1964) *The Rules of Sociological Method*, New York: The Free Press, (1895).

Durkheim, E. (1970) *Suicide: A Study in Sociology*, London: RKP. (1897).

Durkheim. E. (1961) *The Elementary Forms of Religious Life*, New York: Collier Books, (1912).

Engels, F. (1958) *The Condition of the Working Class in England*, Oxford: Blackwell, (1985).

Engels, F. (1972) *The Origins of the Family, Private Property and the State*, London: Lawrence and Wishart. (1884)

Eysenck, H. (1975) *The Inequality of Man*, United Kingdom: Fontana.

Finn, D. (1987) *Training without Jobs*, London: Macmillan.

Floud, J. (1957) *Social Class and Educational Opportunity*, London: Heinnemann.

Fornas, J. and Bolin, G. (eds) (1995) *Youth Culture in Late Modernity*, London: Sage.

Foucault, M. (1977) *Discipline and Punish: The Birth of the Prison*, London: Allen Lane, (1975).

Foucault, M. (1990) *The History of Sexuality*, Vol 1. Harmondsworth: Penguin. (1976).

Freud, S. (1991) *Introductory Lectures in Psychoanalysis*, Harmondsworth: Penguin.

Fukuyama, F. (1989) *The End of History*, Washington: Irving Kristol.

Gatter, P. (1999) *Identity and Sexuality: Aids in Britain in the 1990s*, London: Cassells.

Gellner, E. (1992) *Postmodernism, Reason and Religion*, London: Routledge.

Giddens, A (1990) *The Consequences of Modernity*, Cambridge: Polity.

Giddens, A. (1981) A *Contemporary Critique of Historical Materialism*, London: MacMillan.

Giddens, A. (1984*) The Constitution of Society: Outline of the Theory of Structuration*, Cambridge: Polity.

Giddens, A. (1991) *Modernity and Self Identity: Self and Identity in the Late Modern Age*, Cambridge: Polity.

Giddens, A. (1992) *The Transformation of Intimacy; Sexuality, Love and Eroticism in Modern Societies*, Cambridge: Polity.

Giddens, A. (1993) *New Rules of Sociological Method*. Cambridge: Polity. (1976).

Giddens, A. (1998) *The Third Way: The Renewal of Social Democracy*, Cambridge: Polity.

Giddens, A. (2000) *The Third Way and Its Critics*, Cambridge: Polity.

Gill, S. and Law, D. (1988) *The Global Political Economy*, Hemel Hempstead: Harvester Wheatsheaf.

Gilroy, P. (1993) *The Black Atlantic: Modernity and Double Consciousness*, London: Verso.

Gleason, D. (ed) (1987) *Youth training and the Search for Work*, London: Routledge and Kegan Paul.

Goffman, E. (1968) *Stigma: Notes on the Management of Spoiled Identity*, Harmondsworth: Penguin.

Goffman, E. (1971) *The Presentation of Self in Everyday Life*, Harmondsworth: Penguin, (1959).

Goffman, E. (1983) *Asylums*, Harmondsworth: Penguin, (1961).

Goldthorpe, J.H., Llewellyn, C. and Payne, C. (1987) 2nd edition: *Social Mobility and Class Structure in Modern Britain*, Oxford, Clarendon.

Gramsci, A. (1971) *Selections from the Prison Notebooks*, London: Lawrence and Wishart.

Greer, G. (1971) *The Female Eunuch*, New York: Bantam Books.

Habermas, J. (1971) *Towards a Rational Society*, London: Heinneman. (1968–9).

Habermas, J. (1972) *Knowledge and Human Interests*, London. Heinneman, (1968).

Habermas, J. (1976) *Legitimation Crisis*, London: Heinneman, (1973).

Habermas, J. (1984) *The Theory of Communicative Action, i. Reason and the Rationalisation of Society*, London: Heinneman, (1981).

Habermas, J. (1987) *The Theory of Communicative Action, ii. The Critique of Functionalist Reason*, London: Heinneman, (1981).

Habermas, J. (1989) *The Structural Transformation of the Public Sphere: An Enquiry into a Category of Bourgeois Society*, Cambridge: Polity, (1962).

Habermas, J. (1990) *Moral Consciousness and Communicative Action,* Cambridge: Polity.

Hall, S. and Jefferson, T. (eds) (1976) *Resistance Through Rituals: Youth Subcultures in Post-war Britain*, London: Hutchinson.

Hall, S., Critcher, C., Jefferson, T., Clarke, J., and Roberts, B. (1979) *Policing the Crisis*, London: Macmillan.

Hall, S. (1992) 'The Question of Cultural Identity' in S. Hall, D. Held, and T. McGrew, (eds): *Modernity and Its Futures*, Cambridge: Polity.

Hall, S. (1992) 'The West and the Rest' in S. Hall and B. Gieben (eds) *Formations of Modernity*, Cambridge: Polity.

Hall, S. (1996) 'Introduction: Who Needs Identity' in S. Hall and P du Gay (eds) *Cultural Identity*, London: Sage.

Hall, S. (1997:)'The Work of Representation' in S. Hall (ed) *Representation: Cultural Representations and Signifying Practices*, London: Sage.

Halsey, A. H., Floud, J., and Anderson, J. (eds) (1961) *Education, Economy and Society*, New York: Free Press.

Halsey, A.H., Heath, A. and Ridge, J.M. (1980) *Origins and Destinations*, Oxford: Clarendon.

Hargreaves, D.H. (1967) *Social relations in a Secondary School*, Routledge and Kegan Paul.

Hebdige, D. (1979) *Subculture: The Meaning Of Style*, London: Methuen.

Held, D. and McGrew, A., Goldblatt D. and Perraton, J. (1999) *Global Transformations: Politics, Economy and Culture*, Cambridge: Polity Press.

Hill, M. (1997) *Understanding Social Policy*, Oxford: Blackwell.

Hoggart, R. (1957) *The Uses of Literacy*, Harmondsworth: Penguin.

Huntington, S. P. (1996) *The Clash of Civilisations and the Remaking of the World Order*, New York: Simon and Schuster.

Hutton, W. (1995) *The State We're In*, London: Vintage.

Jameson, F. (1998) *The Cultural Turn: Selected Writings on the Postmodern, 1983–1998*, London: Verso.

Jameson, F. and Miyoshi, M. (eds.) (1998) *The Cultures of Globalisation*, Duke University Press.

Jenks, C. (1993) *Culture*, London: Routledge.

Jessop, B. (1994) 'The transition to post-Fordism and the Schumpeterian Workfare State' in R. Burrows and B. Loader (eds) *Towards a Post-Fordist Welfare State*, London: Routledge.

Jones, S. (1993) *The Language of the Genes*, London: Flamingo.

Kumar, K. (1995) *From Post-industrial to Post-modern Society: New Theories of the Contemporary World*, Oxford: Blackwell.

Lane, M. (ed.) (1970) *Structuralism: A Reader*, London: Jonathan Cape.

Lasch, C. (1970) *The Agony of the American Left*, London: Andre Deutsch.

Lasch, C. (1980) *The Culture of Narcissus*, London: Abacus.

Lash, S and Urry, J. (1987) *The End of Organised Capitalism*, Cambridge: Polity Press.

Layder, D. (1994) *Understanding Social Theory*, London: Sage.

Layder, D. (1997) *Modern Social theory: Key Debates and New Directions*, UCL Press.

Lea, J. and Young, J. (1984) *What is to be done about law and order?*, Harmondsworth: Penguin.

Lechte, J. (1994) *Fifty Key Contemporary Thinkers: From Structuralism to Postmodernity*, London: Routledge.

Levin, C. (1996) *Jean Baudrillard: A Study in Cultural Metaphysics*, London: Prentice Hall.

Lockwood, D. (1958) *The Blackcoated Worker*, London: Allen and Unwin.

Lynd, S. (1969) *The Intellectual Origins of American Radicalism*, London: Faber and Faber.

Lyotard, J-F. (1983) *The Differend* transl. G. van den Abeele, Manchester University Press.

Lyotard, J-F. (1984) *The Postmodern Condition*, Manchester University Press, (1979).

Lyotard, J-F (1985) 'Note on the Meaning of "Post"' in T. Docherty (ed) *Postmodernism: A Reader*, London: Harvester Wheatsheaf.

Mac an Ghaill, M. (1988) *Young, Gifted and Black*, Buckingham: Open University Press.

MacInnes, J. (1998) *The End of Masculinity*, Buckingham: Open University Press.

Marcuse, H. (1956) *Eros and Civilisation*, London: Routledge and Kegan Paul.

Marcuse, H. (1964) *One Dimensional Man*, London: Routledge and Kegan Paul.

Marcuse, H. (1969) *An Essay in Liberation*, London: Beacon Press.

Marshall, G., Newby, H., Rose, D., and Vogler, C. (1988) *Social Class in Modern Britain*, London: Hutchinson.

Marshall, T.H. (1992) *Citizenship and Social Class*, London: Pluto Press, (1962).

Marx, K. (1959) *Economic and Philosophical Manuscripts*, London: Lawrence and Wishart, (1844).

Marx, K. (1976) *Capital Vol.1*, Harmondsworth: Penguin. (1867).

Marx. K. and Engels F. (1967:70) *Manifesto of the Communist Party*, Peking: Foreign Languages Press (1848).

McRobbie A. and Garber, J. (1976) 'Girls and Subcultures: an exploration' in S. Hall and T. Jefferson (eds), *Resistance Through Rituals: Youth Subcultures in Post-war Britain*, London: Hutchinson.

McRobbie, A. (1978) 'Working Class Girls and the Culture of Femininity' in *Women Take Issue: Aspects of Women's Subordination*, London: Hutchinson.

McRobbie, A. (1994) *Postmodernism and Popular Culture*, London: Routledge.

McRobbie, A. (1996) 'Different Youthful Subjectivities' in I. Chambers and L. Curtis (eds) *The Post-Colonial Question: Common Skies, Divided Horizons*, London: Routledge.

McRobbie, A. (1997) 'Bridging the Gap: Feminism, Fashion and Consumption' in *Feminist Review*, No 55 Spring, 1977.

Mead, G.H. (1934) *Mind, Self and Society from the Standpoint of a Social Behaviourist*, edited with an introduction by C.W. Morris. University of Chicago Press.

Mead, M. (1970*) Containment and Change: A Study of the Generation Gap*, St Albans: Panther Books.

Merton, R. and Nisbet, R. (1976) *Contemporary Social Problems*, New York: Harcourt, Brace, Javonovich

Millett, K. (1970) *Sexual Politics*, London: Abacus.

Mills, C.W.M. (1951) *White Collar: The American Middle Classes*, Oxford University Press.

Mills, C.W.M. (1956) *The Power Elite*, Oxford University Press.

Mills, C.W.M. (1959) *The Sociological Imagination*, Oxford University Press.

Mills, C.W.M. (1961) *Images of Man*, New York: Braziller Press.

Mills, C.W.M. (1967) *The Marxists*, Harmondsworth: Penguin.

Mills, C.W.M. Power Politics and People by Mills C.W.M. (Oxford University Press) 1963.

Mills, C.W.M. and Gerth, H. (eds) (1970) *From Max Weber: Essays in Sociology*, London: Routledge and Kegan Paul.

Modood, T. and Berthoud, R. (eds) (1997) *Ethnic Minorities in Britain: Diversity and Disadvantage*, London: PSI.

Murdock, G. P. (1949) *Social Structure*, New York: Macmillan.

Murray, C. (1990) *The Emerging British Underclass*, London: IEA Health and Welfare Unit.

Murray, C. (1996) *The Bell Curve*, New York: Simon and Schuster.

Murray, R. (1989) 'Fordism and Post-Fordism' in S. Hall and M. Jacques (eds) *New Times and the Changing Face of Politics in the 1990s*, London: Lawrence and Wishart.

Nicholson, L. and Seidman, S. (1995) *Social Postmodernism: Beyond Identity Politics*, Cambridge University Press.

Nisbet, R. (1978) 'Conservatism' in T. Bottomore and R. Nisbet (eds), *A History of Sociological Analysis*, London: Heinnemann.

O'Brien M. and Penna, S. (1998) *Theorising Welfare: Enlightenment and Modern Society*, London: Sage.

O'Donnell, M. (1985) *Age and Generation*, London: Tavistock.

O'Donnell, M. (1991) *Race and Ethnicity*, London: Longman.

O'Donnell, M. (1993) (ed.) *New Introductory Reader in Sociology*, Walton on Thames: Nelson.

O'Donnell, M. (1997) *Introduction to Sociology*, Walton on Thames: Nelson.

O'Donnell, M. and Sharpe, S. (2000) *Uncertain Masculinities: Gender, Youth and Class in Ethnic London*, London: Routledge.

Osgerby, B. (1998) *Youth in Britain since 1945*, Oxford: Blackwell.

Parsons, T. (1937) *The Structure of Social Action*, New York: McGraw-Hill.

Parsons, T. (1951) *The Social System*, New York: The Free Press.

Piore, M. and Sabel, C. (1984) *The Second Industrial Divide*, New York: Basic Books.

Politics, Vol 20, No 3.

Pollert, A. (1988) 'Dismantling Flexibility' in *Capital and Class*, No 33.

Pryce, K. (1986) *Endless Pressure*, Bristol Classic Press.

Redhead, S. (1990) *The End of the Century Party: Youth and Pop towards 2000*, Manchester University Press.

Rex, J. (1986) *Race and Ethnicity*, Buckinghamshire: Open University Press.

Ritzer, G. (2000) *The McDonaldization of Society: An Investigation into the Changing Character of Social Life*, Thousand Oaks, CA: Pine Forge Press.

Robertson, R. (1992) *Globalization*, London: Sage.

Rocher, G (1974) *Talcott Parsons and American Sociology*, London: Nelson.

Said, E. (1985:)*Orientalism: Western Concepts of the Orient*, Harmondsworth: Penguin.

Sassen. S. (1991) *The Global City*, Princeton University Press.

Scott, J. (1994) *Poverty and Wealth: Citizenship, Deprivation and Privilege*, London: Longman.

Seidman, S. (1998) *Contested Knowledge: Social Theory in the Postmodern Era*, Oxford: Blackwell.

Sennett, R. (1999) *The Corrosion of Character: The Personal Consequences of Work in the New Capitalism*, London: W.W. Norton.

Silverstone, R. (1990) 'Television and Everyday Life: towards an Anthropology of the television Audience' in M. Ferguson (ed) *Public Communication: The New Imperatives*, London: Sage.

Simmel, G. (1968) *Sociology*, Berlin: Dunker and Humblot. (1908).

Sklair, L. (1995) *Sociology of the Global System*, London: Prentice Hall.

Sklair, L. (1998) 'Social Movements and Global Capitalism' in F. Jameson and M. Miyoshi (eds), *The Cultures of Globalisation*, Duke University Press.

Sokal A. and Bricmont, J. (1997) *Intellectual Impostures: Postmodern Philosophers' Abuse of Science*, London: Profile Books.

Smith, D.J. (1977) *Racial Disadvantage in Britain*, Harmondsworth: Penguin.

Smith, D.J. (ed.) (1992) *Understanding the Underclass*, London: PSI.

Spelman, E. (1988) *Inessential Woman*, Boston: Beacon Press.

Spybey, T. (ed.) (1997) *Britain in Europe: An Introduction to Sociology*, London: Routledge.

Stevenson, N. (1999) *The Transformation of the Media: Globalisation, Morality and Ethics*, London: Longman.

Stones, R. (ed.) (1998) *Key Sociological Thinkers*, London: MacMillan.

Sturrock, J. (1998) *The Word from Paris: Essays on Modern French Thinkers and Writers*, London: Verso.

Tonnies, F. (1955) *Community and Association*, London: Routledge and Kegan Paul, (1887).

Townsend, P. (1979) *Poverty in the United Kingdom*, Harmondsworth: Penguin.

Turner, B. (1990) 'Outline of a Theory of Citizenship' in *Sociology* Vol 24, No 2.

Urry, J. (2000) *Sociology Beyond Societies: Mobilities for the Twenty-first Century*, London: Routeldge.

Walby, S. (1990) *Theorising Patriarchy*, Oxford: Blackwell.

Walby, S. (1997) *Gender Transformations*, London: Routledge.

Wallerstein, I. (1991) *Unthinking Social Science*: The Limits of Nineteenth Century Paradigms, Cambridge: Polity.

Waters, M. (1995) *Globalisation*, London: Routledge.

Weber, M. (1948) *From Max Weber*, edited by H Gerth and CW Mills. London: Routledge and Kegan Paul.

Weber, M. (1963) *The Sociology of Religion*, Boston, MA.: Beacon, (1920).

Weber, M. (1974) *The Protestant Ethic and the Spirit of Capitalism*, London: Unwin, (1902)

Webster, C. (1998) *The National Health Service: A Political History*, Oxford Paperbacks: OUP.

Webster, F. (1995) *Theories of the Information Society*, London: Routledge.

Weeks, J. (1995) *Invented Moralities: Sexual Values in an Age of Uncertainty*, Cambridge: Polity.

Williams, R. (1999) 'Erving Goffman' in R. Stones (ed) *Key Sociological Thinkers*, London: Macmillan.

Willis, P. (1990) *Common Culture: Symbolic Work at Play in the Everyday Cultures of the Young*, Buckingham: Open University Press.

Wilson, W.J. (1987) *The Truly Disadvantaged*, University of Chicago Press.

Wright, E.O. (1985) *Classes*, London: Verso.

Young, I.M. 1995: 'Gender as Seriality: Thinking about Women as a Social Collective' in L. Nicholson and S. Seidman (eds) *Social Postmodernism: Beyond Identity Politics*, Cambridge University Press.

Zaretsky, E. Z. 1997) *Social Movements in Politics: A Comparative Study*, London: Longman.

GLOSSARY

A

action(agency)/structure this sociological dualism focuses on the relationship between what social actors do and the influence of society on them.

alienation this term occurs in sociology and general speech and refers to a state of disengagement (separation, remoteness) from an activity or group. Marx used it to describe workers' sense of separation from what they produced, from others and from the self in the capitalist mode of production.

amplification is a term used notably by interactionists to refer to 1) the way the media sometimes exaggerates an event or 'story' and 2) the effect this can have on participants who respond by seeking further publicity. Thus, news events become part of a spiral of amplification.

anomie is a term originally used by Durkheim to refer to uncertainty, or breakdown in the bonds of society. Following the decline of traditional values, he sees anomie as 'the modern condition'.

anarchist someone opposed to the state or who, at least, wishes to see its activities greatly limited. Positively, anarchism favours localised democracy and exchange.

B

base/superstructure are terms used mainly by Marxists. Base refers to the economy and structure of stratification and superstructure refers to culture and the political system.

benefits selective benefits are provided only for particular needy groups and are usually means tested whereas universal benefits are provided for all citizens.

C

citizenship refers to the rights – usually civil, political and social – and responsibilities of a member (citizen) of a nation state.

collective conscience as used by Durkheim, refers to the shared norms, values, beliefs and ideas of members of a society.

communicative/instrumental rationality are terms used by Habermas to describe, respectively, the use of reason to achieve truthful communication and the use of reason to achieve self interested goals.

community is based on either shared ideas, beliefs, emotions, symbols or location and more usually some combination of these.

consciousness refers to the human capacity of self-awareness and the resulting ability to think or 'conduct an internal dialogue' with oneself. The term particularly occurs in the context of class consciousness where it means awareness of one's class identity.

conservatism as applied to sociology, indicates approaches that tend to stress the need for social solidarity and order and are wary of radical change. Durkheim is relatively conservative in this respect.

consumerism refers to the modern ideology and practice of seeking satisfaction and even identity through the purchase, enjoyment and display of commodities.

contingent events (and explanations derived from them) refer to unpredictable happenings which can have social consequences such as contributing to change e.g. the Falkland's war helped Mrs Thatcher to win an election.

contradictions this Marxist term is used primarily to describe supposed inconsistencies/weaknesses in the capitalist economic system which, in turn, can weaken capitalist power and may be exploited by the working class.

counter-culture is a way of life or lifestyle opposed to the mainstream or dominant culture: see **culture**.

culture is a term with a wide number of definitions. Here it refers to: 1) 'the way of life' of a given society or group – its values, norms, customs and rituals; 2) 'sign' systems – systems of meaning conveyed by verbal and/or non-verbal signs.

cultural circuit is a concept used by Stuart Hall to indicate the various **sites** in society through which, meaning is produced (and transformed). These include the sites of production, representation (e.g. via the media) and consumption.

D

decentring is a process which removes right of authorship of a given text from a single subject and opens it to other readings. The term is often used to refer to the subject's loss of ownership/control of his or her own identity.

decode/encode refers respectively to the interpretation of language/sign meanings and to the construction of language/sign meanings.

deconstruction refers to the 'reading' or 'taking apart of' a text in order to establish its underlying meaning(s). See **text**.

deskilling refers to a management strategy by which the skills required by workers in production are reduced so that they become disempowered and more easily expendable.

determinism is a view of history and society which sees events or a sequence of events as the inevitable outcome of a causal process rather than as, even in part, the outcome of human action. Marx is often accused of economic determinism and French poststructuralists of cultural determinism. (see **voluntarism**).

deviant career is an interactionist term which refers to how labelling can create an identity for a person, in this case a deviant one, which has significant consequences for their self-image and societal experience/opportunities.

dialectic refers to the interaction of two factors producing a third. In Marxist theory this is described as the thesis and anti-thesis producing a synthesis.

difference has basically the same meaning in sociology as in general usage but indicates particularly the socially constructed nature of (some) differences.

discourse theory was introduced by Foucault and seeks to explain how cultural formations frame the ideas and practices of those subject to them.

discursive/practical consciousness refer, respectively, to a higher form of thought which entails the ability to reflect on practical consciousness which is the taken-for-granted knowledge of actors of how to act.

dominant/subordinate class in Marxist terminology these terms refer respectively to the ruling class and its ideology and the subordinate class which is vulnerable to being misled by the dominant ideology.

dualisms the dualisms are pairs of concepts, usually opposites or near-opposites which indicate central areas of sociological concern. The core dualism is individual/society. The word dualism implies a tension between the two sides of the pair and some approach the dualisms as 'opposites'.

E

encode see decode.

Enlightenment this term refers to the intellectual and political ferment of the eighteenth and early nineteenth century, the influence of which is still felt and debated today. See subject.

essentialism is a philosophy or type of explanation which argues that human beings are endowed with certain innate characteristics such as sex or racial characteristics which explain related social behaviour e.g. men are competitive, women are cooperative because of differences in their biological make-up.

F

flows are what pass through or are transported by networks, e.g. people, information.

Fordism/postFordism Fordism refers to the assembly line process of production and, more generally, to hierarchical and inflexible bureaucracy. Postfordism refers to more flexible and decentralised processes of production and administration.

G

generalisation see scientific law.

globalisation refers to economic, cultural/communications and political developments which are turning the world into a single social system.

H

hegemony(hegemonic) is a term introduced by Gramsci and now in general usage to describe how a class (or, in wider usage, a group) may achieve social ascendancy or dominance through persuasion (ideas) as distinct from merely force. The education system and media are the main means for achieving hegemony which is open to contestation and challenge.

high modernity refers to the current or 'late' Phase of modernity. Giddens uses the term interchangeably with late modernity.

homology refers to the cultural complementarity or fit between various cultural entities such as argot, dress and demeanour. The effect is of a coherent whole.

human rights these are rights considered to be due to people by virtue of their humanity. The concept became very popular in the late eighteenth century and was incorporated in the American Declaration of Independence and the French Declaration of the Rights of Man. More recently the struggle to define and establish universal human rights has become a major feature of political-cultural globalisation.

humanism is a broad theoretical approach which takes the experience and intrinsic value of human beings as its starting point and seeks to contribute to their general needs.

hybridity (cultural) refers to how cultural forms may be constructed from different and possibly widely varying influences. For example, techno-funk.

hyper-reality is a term used by Baudrillard to describe how the postmodern world has become one in which images have become detached from referents and so are superficial and empty.

I

identity is a debated concept, one interpretation refers to the relatively stable core of a person's self and individuality and another to the construction of a person's 'subjectivity' by society. Some definitions draw on both elements.

ideology in general sociology this term refers to the ideas and views of particular groups, usually these reflect group self-interest. Marx used the term ideology to refer to 'false' ideas distorted by class interest which he contrasted with the 'objective' truth of his own 'scientific' method of analysis based on a study of historical 'laws'.

ideological/repressive state apparatus are terms used by Althusser to refer to the means used by the state to dominate and control, respectively, by ideas or coercion/force.

individual/society this dualism refers to the tension or to the opposing claims between the individual and society. The concept of individual human rights has in part emerged out of this tension. (see human rights).

inflection refers to the change or shift in the meaning of a word or other cultural entity.

information age is a term used by Bell and Castells to describe how theoretical information and processed information is axial to the formation of contemporary society.

interaction is communicative and intentional action directed at other actors

inter-subjective refers to a shared, practical agreement by social actors about the meaning of knowledge and actions.

instrumental rationality see communicative rationality.

interpellate is a term used by Althusser to refer to the way advertisements and other signs 'hail'' or summon the reader to take a particular stance, view or attitude.

L

labelling/labelling theory these are interactionist terms which refer to how others may define the identity of another or others and the consequences of such definition.

late modernity refers to the period from the end of the second world war to now. It is preferred by Anthony Giddens and others to postmodernity. Although the term has been periodised here it primarily refers to culture or way of life rather than to a specific time-span. See: modernity, high modernity, post modernity.

legitimise means to establish the authority of an ideology, view or position. In Marxist theory, legitimation of dominant class ideology is considered to be 'false' and against the interests of the subordinate class.

liberalism as applied to sociology, refers to approaches which tend to adopt the Enlightenment view that progress through reason is possible. Politically it refers to a commitment to democratic government, usually representative democracy.

M

macro level research is concerned with large scale research and is usually focused on the influence of or relationships between social structures and institutions.

managerialism (new) is the ideology and practice of running institutions by professional managers (usually in an hierarchical way and on the basis of some version of systems theory).

masculinities refers to the different types or constructions of masculinity or 'being a man'. For example, 'macho man', 'new man'.

McDonaldization refers to the alleged way in which economic/cultural products (such as burgers, soft drinks) are becoming globally standardised.

meaning refers to the capacity of social actors to impart rational intention or/significance to their actions. The way and extent to which actors can do this is fiercely contested.

mechanical solidarity is social integration based on shared values, norms and beliefs embodied in cultural practices and rituals.

metanarrative is a term used by Lyotard to refer to an ideology or belief system which seeks total explanation and/or domination. He considered that intellectually so-called 'objective' science was an example of a metanarrative and, politically, communism.

micro level research is concerned with small scale research and is usually focused on social inter/action. see **macro**.

modernity refers to the period approximately from the Reformation/Renaissance to the second world war: see **high modernity, late-** and **post-modernity.**

moral panic a moral panic is an interactionist term describing how the media may be used to build up public anxiety and concern about a particular issue.

moral entrepreneur a moral entrepreneur is a person or organisation that seeks to use the media to generate a moral panic.

N

negotiation is an interactionist concept now in wider usage which refers to the process by which individuals or groups share in the achievement of an outcome of a particular debate or issue.

network is a set of interconnected nodes (points of communication) through which flows (see above) travel.

New Social Movements (NSMs) these are the non-class based movements of the post second world war period such as feminism, the black liberation movement and the gay movement.

O

objectivity/subjectivity objectivity refers to a widely accepted or consensual 'truth' or meaning which has usually been tested by science or reason. Subjectivity refers to personal response to phenomena.

ontological security is a term used by Giddens and occurs when actors take for granted that they have the knowledge to conduct their daily lives effectively.

organic solidarity is integration of the social system through interdependence caused by a complex division of labour.

other (the) is a poststructuralist derived term which explains identity in terms of binary opposites such as black/white and in this case self/other or us/others. It is a starting point for 'post' identity theory.

P

pluralist is the belief that the political process should be open to more than one group or party and, preferably, to many. In the context of Weber's sociological theory it refers to an approach to society that sees the political, cultural and economic systems as inter-dependent without any necessarily being dominant.

populism refers to political approaches to movements which, respectively, appeal to or reflect the emotions and felt needs of a given 'bloc' of people. Historically, populism has often had a 'mass' emotional appeal.

postFordism see **Fordism**.

postmodernism is a theoretical approach which argues that Western and global society has moved beyond the 'certainties' and 'stability' of modernity to an age of difference and fragmentation. See **post-modernity.**

positivism takes the view that science and social science can only be based on the study of facts, in the latter case social facts. Demonstrated relationships between phenomena provide the basis for developing social laws. Comte and Durkheim and, the more deterministic tradition of Marxism is associated with this approach.

postmodernity is the contemporary period or 'epoch' characterised, according to postmodernist, by postmodern culture, see **late modernity.**

practical consciousness see **discursive consciousness**

pragmatism adopts the view that philosophical and/or political theory and insight should be of practical value to human beings.

public sphere is the area of social life between the political system and family/personal life in which debate about aspects of society may occur.

R

racialise means to explain something with reference to 'race' – e.g. crime or unemployment – for racist rather than rational motives.

radicalism as applied to sociology, this term refers to those approaches which sympathise with the human rights agenda of civil, political and social rights which has stretched from the late eighteenth to the present century. An emphasis on social rights has been characteristic of Marxism and on civil and political rights of radical liberalism.

read in a reference (to texts). See **deconstruction**.

referent is what a sign refers to. See **sign**.

reify is to treat a human being or group of human beings as though they are an object or 'thing'.

reflexivity is used with two related meanings:
1) to refer to the capacity of human beings to reflect upon their social existence (and potentially to change it)
2) the tendency in late modernity for earlier actions, such as the exploitation and use of fossils, to have perhaps unanticipated consequences, such as air pollution.

relative is a term which defines an event or phenomenon as the product of particular circumstances and not of absolute or universal significance.

resistance is a commonly used term in sociology to refer to the attempts by subordinate individuals or groups to disrupt or oppose dominant groups and/or systems.

risk in its current sociological usage refers to the possibly dangerous or socially destructive effects of modern 'progress', particularly the unanticipated effects of technological innovation and change.

romanticism is based on the view that emotions and feelings are most importantly and characteristically human and that too much emphasis on reason and science can smother and destroy them. (see **radicalism**).

S

scapes are networks of machines, technologies, organisations, texts and actors that contribute various interconnected nodes along which flows (see above) can be relayed.

scientific law/generalisation a scientific law stipulates that in constant conditions a causal relationship between two or more objects will always be repeated. Marx and Durkheim thought that social science laws of the same level of certainty as natural laws could be established. Weber disagreed and argued that social science can only establish relationships of probability or generalisations.

Self is made up of the active 'I' and the **me** which is formed mainly by society.

Self-fulfilling prophesy occurs when, because something is stated to be the case, it becomes – at least partly – the case. Thus, an intelligent child labelled as stupid may lose self-esteem and behave stupidly.

Self-referential refers to the human capacity to think and act with one's own priorities and feelings in mind.

semiology is the study of meanings of systems of signs and/or symbols.

sexuality refers to sexual orientation. For example, gay or heterosexual.

sign a sign is an object, image or sound which indicates something else. The 'something else' is termed 'the referent'.

significant/generalised other significant others are those who play a major part in the formation of the self, and the generalised other refers to the moral and normative influence of society as a whole.

signification spiral this term describes how a series of links are made and signified each one of which reinforces the previous one. Thus, drug-taking may be linked with crime which is linked with the decline of 'civilised life'.

signifier/signified/sign are a set of closely related terms. The signifier carries the message, the signified is the message and the two in totality are a sign. Signification may be conscious or unconscious.

social construction is used in two main and conflicting theoretical ways: 1) refers to how society is constructed by the interaction of social actors and social circumstances, and 2) refers to how social forces construct individual or 'subject' identity.

stereotype to stereotype is to attribute to an individual the characteristics of a category on the basis of insufficient evidence.

stigma is a term which describes how a characteristic or apparent characteristic of an individual or group is negatively marked out by others.

structuration theory is an attempt by Anthony Giddens to show that agency and structure are a duality rather than a dualitsm. Structure is seen as the medium of action and as produced and reproduced through it.

subculture refers to a group whose members' lifestyle is distinct from that of the mainstream or dominant culture.

subject is a term favoured by post/structuralists to indicate that, what more voluntarist theorists refer to as social actors or individuals have no inherent or personally constructed characteristics but are, to a greater or lesser extent, constructed or constituted by social forces.

subjective see **objective**.

subordinate class see **dominant class.**

superstructure see **base**.

symbol a symbol is an image or object which, by virtue of its resemblance to something else, can be taken to represent or 'stand for' it.

system (social) refers to the workings or 'functioning' of the total social structure, including the relationship of its various parts.

T

text is a sign or sequence of signs which can be read or deconstructed . See **deconstruct**.

'Third Way' is an attempt by New Labour to produce a new political ideology/practice distinct from socialist collectivism and free-market capitalism.

U

underclass is a controversial term which refers to those who, for various reasons, have limited access to social opportunity.

V

voluntarism is the view that to a greater or lesser extent people's actions can be the product of their own choice. Weber broadly adopted this approach. (see **determinism**).

W

world system world system theory proposed by the Marxist Wallerstein argues that the world has become a single social system dominated by capitalism.

Index